Donald Reid is a senior officer with a national organisation whose functions include curriculum development in human biology for the 14–17 age range. Previously Head of the Science Department at Thomas Bennett School, Crawley, he is also an experienced examiner and is a former member of the AEB Standing Advisory Committee for Human Biology O level. He is the joint author of the widely used twelve book series *Biology for the Individual*.

Angela Reid is a medical social worker with teaching experience. She has extensive experience of social problems related to human biology and health.

Pan Study Aids for GCSE include:

Accounting

Biology

Chemistry

Commerce

Computer Studies

Economics

English Language

French

Geography 1

Geography 2

German

History 1: World History since 1914

History 2: Britain and Europe since 1700

Human Biology

Mathematics

Physics

Sociology

Study Skills

PAN STUDY AIDS

HUMAN BIOLOGY

D. J. Reid and A. E. K. Reid

A Pan Original
Pan Books London, Sydney and Auckland

First published 1987 by Pan Books Ltd,
Cavaye Place, London SW10 9PG

9 8 7 6 5 4 3 2 1

© D. J. Reid and A. E. K. Reid 1987

ISBN 0 330 29940 9

Text design by Peter Ward
Text illustration by M L Design
Photoset by Parker Typesetting Service, Leicester
Printed and bound in Spain by
Mateu Cromo SA, Madrid

This book is sold subject to the condition that it shall not, by way of trade or otherwise, be lent, re-sold, hired out or otherwise circulated without the publisher's prior consent in any form of binding or cover other than that in which it is published and without a similar condition including this condition being imposed on the subsequent purchaser

CONTENTS

Introduction to GCSE and SCE   10

1 ▶	Introduction – how to succeed in your exam	13
2 ▶	Living organisms and their relationships	39
3 ▶	Cells as the basic unit of life	47
4 ▶	The skeleton, muscles and movement	65
5 ▶	Breathing and gas exchange	85
6 ▶	Blood and the circulation system	101
7 ▶	The circulation system and the heart	111
8 ▶	Structure and function of blood vessels and lymph	123
9 ▶	Food and nutrition	135
10 ▶	Energy and food	145
11 ▶	Digestion and teeth	157
12 ▶	Digestion, absorption and assimilation	167

Contents

13 ▶	The skin and temperature regulation	181
14 ▶	Excretion and the kidneys	193
15 ▶	Coordination: the nervous and endocrine systems	203
16 ▶	Response to stimuli: the sense organs	219
17 ▶	Human reproduction	233
18 ▶	Pregnancy, ante-natal care and childbirth	245
19 ▶	The human life cycle: child development, maturity and ageing	257
20 ▶	Variation and genetics	271
21 ▶	Personal health care	293
22 ▶	Causes and prevention of infectious disease	309
23 ▶	Disease, food preservation and experiments with microorganisms	325
24 ▶	Water and waste	339

Contents

25 ▶	Plants and Man	351
26 ▶	Ecology, ecosystems and communities	363
27 ▶	Human populations, conservation and pollution	373
28 ▶	Answers to exam questions	389
29 ▶	Glossary and additional information	415
	Index	423

ACKNOWLEDGEMENTS

The typing of the manuscript was undertaken by Janice Armstrong, Heather Ahearn and Elizabeth Newman. Particular thanks are due to Elizabeth Newman for processing the bulk of the text to a high standard against tight deadlines.

Assistance with artwork was kindly given by Andrew Reid; clerical help provided by Louise Reid and Nicholas Reid.

Permission to reproduce the following diagrams is gratefully acknowledged:

Figs 1.1 and 15.9 are redrawn from *Biology Study Aid* (Pan Books Ltd) by N. P. O. Green, J. M. Potter and G. W. Stout

Figs 5.4, 6.1, 12.1, 16.3, 16.5, 17.1, 17.5, 18.3, 20.2, 20.3 and 22.1 are redrawn after diagrams by D. G. Mackean in *Human and Social Biology* (John Murray, 1975) by D. G. Mackean and B. Jones

Fig 7.6 is adapted from *Prevention and Health – Avoiding Heart Attacks* (HMSO, 1981), and is reproduced by permission of the Controller of Her Majesty's Stationery Office.

Thanks are due to the following Examination Boards for permission to reproduce GCSE specimen and past O Level CSE and SCE questions:

Board	Abbreviations used in the text to identify questions
The Associated Examining Board	AEB
Associated Lancashire Schools Examination Board	ALSEB
Joint Matriculation Board	JMB
London and East Anglian Group	L/EA
Midland Examining Group	MID
Northern Examining Association (including JMB, ALSEB, NRB, North West Regional Examinations Board and Yorkshire and Humberside Regional Examinations Board)	NEA
N. Ireland Schools Examination Council	NI
North Regional Examinations Board	NRB
Scottish Examination Board	APH
Southern Examining Group	SEG
Southern Regional Examinations Board	SREB
The South Western Examinations Board	SW
University of Cambridge Local Examinations Syndicate	C
University of London School Examinations Board	L
University of Oxford Delegacy for Local Examinations	Ox
Welsh Joint Education Committee	W
The West Midlands Examinations Board	WM

Acknowledgements

WARNING: SAFETY

No experiments or practical activities described in this book should be undertaken except under the supervision of a qualified teacher. Even under these circumstances, the authors cannot guarantee the safety of any of the practical work described.

INTRODUCTION TO GCSE

From 1988, there will be a single system of examining at 16 plus in England and Wales and Northern Ireland. The General Certificate of Secondary Education (GCSE) will replace the General Certificate of Education (GCE) and the Certificate of Secondary Education (CSE). In Scotland candidates will be entering for the O grade and Standard Grade examinations leading to the award of the Scottish Certificate of Education (SCE).

The Pan Study Aids GCSE series has been specially written by practising teachers and examiners to enable you to prepare successfully for this new examination.

GCSE introduces several important changes in the way in which you are tested. First, the examinations will be structured so that you can show *what* you know rather than what you do *not* know. Of critical importance here is the work you produce during the course of the examination year, which will be given much greater emphasis than before. Second, courses are set and marked by six examining groups instead of the previous twenty GCE/CSE boards. The groups are:

- Northern Examining Association (NEA)
- Midland Examining Group (MEG)
- London and East Anglian Group (LEAG)
- Southern Examining Group (SEG)
- Welsh Joint Examinations Council (WJEC)
- Northern Ireland Schools Examination Council (NISEC)

One of the most useful changes introduced by GCSE is the single award system of grades A–G. This should permit you and future employers more accurately to assess your qualifications.

GCSE	GCE O Level	CSE
A	A	–
B	B	–
C	C	1
D	D	2
E	E	3
F	F	4
G		5

Remember that, whatever examinations you take, the grades you are awarded will be based on how well you have done.

Introduction to GCSE

Pan Study Aids are geared for use throughout the duration of your courses. The text layout has been carefully designed to provide all the information and skills you need for GCSE and SCE examinations – please feel free to use the margins for additional notes.

CHAPTER ONE

INTRODUCTION – HOW TO SUCCEED IN YOUR EXAM

CONTENTS

- **1.1 The six simple steps to success** — 15

- **1.2 How to obtain syllabuses and past question papers** — 15
  How to order in England, Wales and N. Ireland   15
  How to order in Scotland   16

- **1.3 How to draw up a revision schedule** — 16

- **1.4 How to revise** — 16
  Testing yourself   16
  Timing yourself   16
  Memory aids   17

- **1.5 How to look after yourself while revising** — 18

- **1.6 Maximizing your marks per minute** — 18
  How do examiners mark?   20

- **1.7 How to maximize your marks from diagrams** — 20
  Diagrams for GCSE in Wales   21

Contents

▸ **1.8 Maximizing your marks from experiments**   21
Practical work for GCSE Southern Group candidates   21

▸ **1.9 How your work will be assessed**   22
Assessment for GCSE in England, Wales and N. Ireland   22
Assessment in Scotland: SCE Anatomy, Physiology and Hygiene   26

▸ **1.10 Useful addresses**   26
In England   26
In Wales   27
In N. Ireland   27
In Scotland   27

▸ **1.11 Final preparations**   28

▸ **1.12 Analysis of exam syllabuses**   28

Introduction – how to succeed in your exam

1.1 THE SIX SIMPLE STEPS TO SUCCESS

To make sure of the best possible grade, follow these six simple steps.

1. Send for your board's **syllabus** and **past question papers** – see page 15.
2. Make a **revision schedule** – see page 16.
3. **Work through** your revision schedule, unit by unit – see page 16 for 'How to revise.'
4. **Look after yourself** while revising – see page 18.
5. Find out how to **maximize your marks per minute** – see page 18.
6. For a final rapid recap, buy a set of revision cards on human biology from any bookseller.

1.2 HOW TO OBTAIN SYLLABUSES AND PAST QUESTION PAPERS

Be sure to obtain your syllabus and past question papers from your exam board, unless your school or college can supply them.

HOW TO ORDER IN ENGLAND, WALES AND N. IRELAND

1. **Write** to your exam board at the address given on p26 and ask for details of how to order the syllabus and past questions for GCSE human biology.
2. The Board will send you a list of publications, with prices. When this arrives, order:
   ◊ the **syllabus** for GCSE human biology for the year when you will take the exam;
   ◊ **Specimen question papers** for GCSE.

   These are sample question papers which were produced in 1986 to illustrate the style of the 1988 exam papers, but were never actually used in an exam. They are particularly helpful for the newer parts of the syllabus. After the 1988 GCSE exam you will be able to order the 1988 past questions (after July 1988).

   Don't bother to send for past GCE O-level questions as these can be misleading. There is a good selection of the most relevant questions in this book.

Human Biology

HOW TO ORDER IN SCOTLAND

Write to the Scottish Education Board (see p27) for the syllabus for anatomy, physiology and hygiene (APH). APH, like all Scottish Certificate of Examination subjects, is, of course, entirely different from GCSE. No major changes are planned in the near future, so past papers are a good guide to the exam in future years.

This book covers most of the syllabus for APH on both the Ordinary and Higher Grades. **Chapter 25 and 26** in this book are **not** required for APH; **chapter 27** (except 27.5) is **not** required for APH Ordinary Grade.

1.3 HOW TO DRAW UP A REVISION SCHEDULE

1. **Make a list** of all the topics which you plan to revise. If you're short of time, concentrate on 70% of the chapters in this book and learn these thoroughly. Don't try to skim through every chapter. Avoid any topic which you find very difficult.
2. **Divide the units** by the amount of time available – if there's 10 weeks left and you have 20 units left, aim to cover them at the rate of two per week.

1.4 HOW TO REVISE

TESTING YOURSELF

1. **Using the checklists**. Start your revision by working through the checklist at the end of each unit to find out how much you know already. For example, in the checklist on p59:
   ◊ Do you know the meaning of all the words listed?
   ◊ Can you remember four properties of enzymes?
   ◊ Do you know the difference between aerobic and anaerobic respiration?
2. Now **read the unit** to check your answers. Pay special attention to:
   (a) the diagrams;
   (b) the hints;
   (c) any descriptions of experiments.
   Try constructing your own rhymes and your diagrams as you read (see below).
3. Finally, **work through the exam questions** at the end of each chapter, checking with the answers at the end of the book. **Don't miss out the exam questions**. They are the best revision aid of all!

TIMING YOURSELF

Don't work for long periods without a break. Most people can't concentrate effectively after about 20–40 minutes. This is called the **concentration time**.

Introduction – how to succeed in your exam

Fig 1.1 Take a regular break every 40 minutes or so.

Find out your concentration time and have a 5-minute break when you've reached it. It may vary according to how much sleep you've had, etc.

MEMORY AIDS

HOW TO REMEMBER LISTS OF FACTS

Use rhymes or make up sentences to help you learn lists. For example, the initial letters of the seven characteristics of life (see page 41) can be made into:

Many **N**aughty **R**abbits **E**at **G**reen **R**adish **S**hoots
(Movement) (Nutrition) (Respiration) (Excretion) (Growth) (Reproduction) (Sensitivity)

MAKING FLOW DIAGRAMS

These are useful both for revision and for planning the answers to essay questions.

To make a flow diagram, write down a few key words related to the topic concerned, leaving plenty of space around them. Build up a diagram around these, as shown in Fig. 1.2.

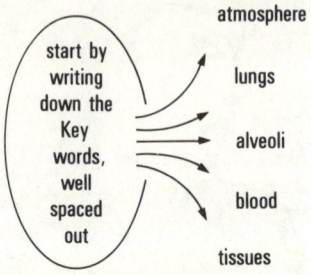

Fig 1.2 Flow diagram for breathing and gas exchange between the atmosphere and the tissues. Use these key words as stimuli to add new ideas.

The advantage of flow diagrams like these is that they are constructed by **you**. By becoming **actively** involved in your revision in this way, you will find that you can remember the key facts much more easily later on.

1.5 HOW TO LOOK AFTER YOURSELF WHILE REVISING

To be at your best when revising and in the exam:
1. Get plenty of fresh air and exercise.
2. Don't work late – you can't think clearly without sleep.
3. Eat light well-balanced meals. Heavy meals slow you down; salads keep you fit and active.
4. Plan something nice for every day; for example, listen to (or watch) a favourite tape when you've finished revising for the evening.
5. If you suffer badly from **hayfever** in summer, see your doctor for advice. Also ask about **periods** or any other medical problems which might affect you during the exam.

1.6 MAXIMIZING YOUR MARKS PER MINUTE

In a typical 2-hour exam paper, up to 100 marks may be available. To obtain maximum marks, you would need to score at the rate of about **one mark per minute**.

1. **Don't spend too much time on short questions.** The marks available per question are usually given on the exam paper. Don't spend 15 minutes trying to work out the answer to a question worth two marks. Leave it and come back to it at the end.
2. **Don't spend too little time on a long question.** If you take two

Introduction – how to succeed in your exam

minutes to answer a question worth 15 marks, you probably haven't given enough detail.

3 Instead **match the length of your answer to the available space.** Most exam papers contain lined spaces for your answers. These are a good guide to the length of answer needed, so try to write answers which just fill the space, but no more (see Fig 1.3).

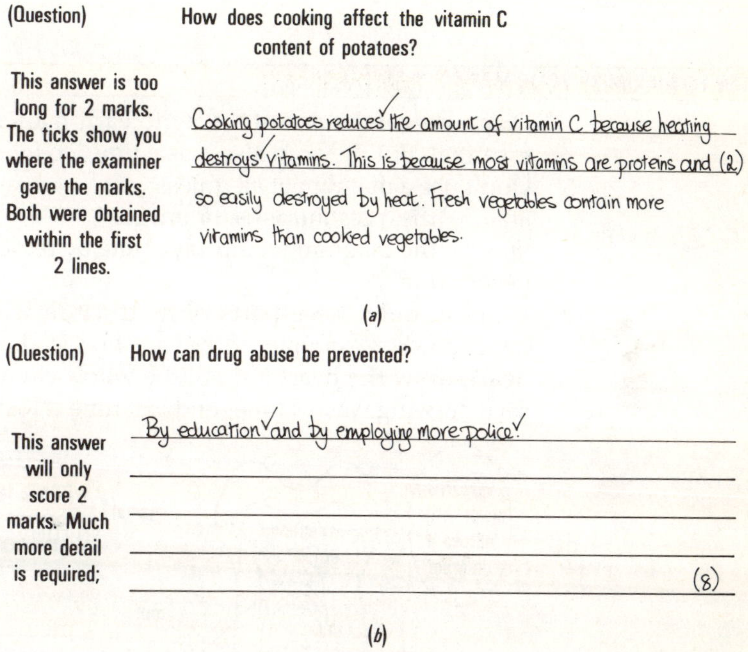

(Question) How does cooking affect the vitamin C content of potatoes?

This answer is too long for 2 marks. The ticks show you where the examiner gave the marks. Both were obtained within the first 2 lines.

> Cooking potatoes reduces the amount of vitamin C because heating destroys vitamins. This is because most vitamins are proteins and (2) so easily destroyed by heat. Fresh vegetables contain more vitamins than cooked vegetables.

(a)

(Question) How can drug abuse be prevented?

This answer will only score 2 marks. Much more detail is required;

> By education and by employing more police. (8)

(b)

Fig 1.3 (a) How to lose time in an exam by writing too much. (b) How to lose marks by writing too little.

4 Make sure you are **answering the question the examiner asked.** Don't try to twist the question round to fit what you know. So don't write down all you know about *breathing* if the question asks about *cell respiration*.

5 **Don't waste time writing out the question** – marks are only given for answers, not for questions.

6 **For essay-type questions** always make out a **plan** first on a piece of rough paper. Use the flow diagram technique in Fig 1.2.

7 **Cross out** any answers which should not be marked. If you leave a wrong answer without crossing it out, the examiner may mark it and then ignore the right answer which follows it.

8 Take **great care over diagrams** – see section 1.7.

Human Biology

HOW DO EXAMINERS MARK?

Check with the answer section (see page 389) for examples of how to obtain maximum marks per minute. We've used marked examples to show exactly where marks are likely to be awarded in the longer answers.

For marks for graphs see the example given on page 409 (Qu 4).

Use **correct biological terms.** You won't lose a mark if you write 'womb' instead of 'uterus', but avoid vague words like 'germs'.

1.7 HOW TO MAXIMIZE YOUR MARKS FROM DIAGRAMS

Diagrams can be a useful way to earn marks quickly – often they're essential. But they can also waste time, so follow these tips:

1. Don't use a diagram at all unless:
   (a)   the question **asks** for one; or
   (b)   the diagram would **save time** by removing the need for a long description.
2. Draw in only those parts of a structure which are **relevant** to the question. For example, if the question is about the circulation in the heart, draw the heart but not the whole circulation system. Unnecessary drawing wastes time, and lost time is lost marks!

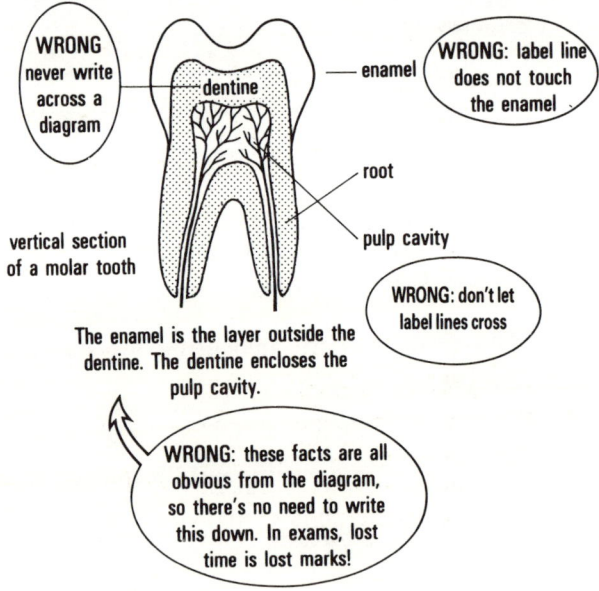

Fig 1.4 How to lose marks on diagrams.

3. Draw outlines **clearly** with a **sharp pencil.** *Never* use red. (And don't write in red either. This annoys the examiners because they mark in red. An angry examiner is a mean marker!)
4. Make sure your **label lines actually touch** the structure to be named. Vague wandering lines earn no marks.

Introduction – how to succeed in your exam

5   **Don't waste time** writing down facts which are already clear from your diagram. For example, if you've already drawn a section through the skin showing the epithelium, there's no need to write down that 'the epithelium is the outer layer of the skin'. You can't earn the same mark twice!

DIAGRAMS FOR GCSE IN WALES

For the Welsh exam, you will only be asked to draw the diagrams listed in the first column of Table 1.1. You may also be asked to label the diagrams listed in the third column, but you will not be required to draw them.

Table 1.1 Diagrams required for GCSE in Wales

Diagram to be drawn and labelled	See page	Diagrams to be labelled only	See page
Leaf and cheek cells	49	Alimentary canal	169
Canine tooth	161	The heart	114
Villus	173	The respiratory system	87
Phagocytes and red cells	104	Nephron	197
The circulatory system	126	Skin in vertical section	183
An alveolus in section	92	Reflex arc	209
The urinary system	196	Endocrine system	212
Kidney (gross structure)	196	Male and female reproductive systems	235–6
Section of the eye	222	Embryo in the uterus	248

1.8 MAXIMIZING YOUR MARKS FROM EXPERIMENTS

When writing up experiments always remember to:
1   state the **aim** of each experiment;
2   state the observed **results**, i.e. what you actually saw;
3   state the **conclusions** – what you thought the results meant.

PRACTICAL WORK FOR GCSE SOUTHERN GROUP CANDIDATES

Questions may be set on the practical work listed in Table 1.2 in Southern Examining Group exam papers.

Table 1.2 Practical work which may be tested in Southern Examining Group exams

Item	See page	Item	See page
Experiments on photosynthesis	355–7	Use of cobalt chloride paper to investigate water loss through the skin	93
Methods for preserving food	332–3		
Examining cells with a microscope	50	Action of salivary amylase on starch and pepsin on coagulated egg white	175–7
Effects of temperature and pH on enzymes	176	Comparisons of inspired and expired air	93
Demonstration of diffusion including dialysis and osmosis, e.g. red blood cells, eggs, dried fruit	57–8	Measurements of lung capacity	90, 91, 97
		Production of tar by cigarettes	304
Use of simple calorimeter	151	Effects of burning and acid on bones	73
Food tests	140–41		

1.9 HOW YOUR WORK WILL BE ASSESSED

ASSESSMENT FOR GCSE IN ENGLAND, WALES AND N. IRELAND

For Scotland, see page 26.

HOW THE MARKS WILL BE AWARDED

Assessment objectives (all boards)

1. Knowledge and understanding – about 50%.
2. Skills, handling of information, analysis of data, interpretation, etc. – about 50%.

Syllabus content

Table 1.3 Syllabus content, as related to the National Criteria for Biology

Theme	Mark allocations for all GCSE boards	Chapters in this book
1 Diversity of living things/Man's place in the living world	About 5%	2
2 The human body: structure and function	About 40%	3–16
3 Life history of man	About 15–20%	17–20
4 Interrelations between man and the environment	About 35% (Northern Board: 20% only, plus 20% for Maintenance of health)	21–27

Introduction – how to succeed in your exam

METHODS OF ASSESSMENT (EXAM PAPERS, ETC.)

Coursework, etc

Your practical work will be assessed by your teacher or college lecturer during the year, unless you are an external candidate.

Types of question

1. **Structured questions** are those where the question is broken down into a number of separate parts, usually worth between one and five marks each. These are the commonest type of question in GCSE and SCE; most of the questions in this book are of this type.
2. **Essay-type questions** are likely to consist of more general questions, requiring longer answers worth 10 marks or more for each part. For example: 'Write an essay on the prevention of pollution.' **Free-response** or **continuous prose** are terms used by some boards, e.g. Welsh, to describe short essay-type questions, worth between 5–10 marks.
3. **Multiple-choice questions** require you to choose the correct answer from a list of four or five options.

Choice of question

On most papers, all questions are compulsory, i.e. you must answer them all (if you can!). Some papers offer a choice of question, especially where essay-type questions are being set.

If you have a choice, try to avoid vague questions like: 'How can cigarette smoking be prevented among the young?' It's easy to write long vague answers to a question like this, which score very few marks.

Instead, try to choose more factual questions such as: 'Describe the damage to the body caused by cigarette smoking.'

Patterns of assessment

Table 1.4 Analysis of patterns of assessment

Paper	Duration in hours	Taken by	Proportion of total marks	Description, types of question, etc.
Southern Examining Group				
1	2	All.	50%	Twenty short answer and two structured questions, all compulsory.
2	Coursework	All.	20%	
3	1½	Those aiming for grades A and B.	30%	Six compulsory structured questions.

Continued

Human Biology

Paper	Duration in hours	Taken by	Proportion of total marks	Description, types of question, etc.
London and East Anglian Group				
1	2	All	50%	Consists of compulsory structured questions. Half of the marks will be for short questions, and half for a few longer questions.
2	1½	Those expecting to achieve grades C–G.	30%	Four or five longer structured question, including some essay-type questions. One question will involve analysis of data or evaluation of an investigation.
3	1½	Those expecting to achieve grades A–E.	30%	Two or three compulsory structured questions, including one involving analysis of data or an evaluation of an investigation. Remaining questions will be essay-type, presented in two pairs. You must choose one question from each pair.
4	Coursework		20%	
Midland Examining Group				
1	40 mins	All.	30%	Multiple choice: 50 items, each asking for the correct answer from five choices.
2	1h 20mins	All.	50%	Section A: 40 mins. Short-answer questions testing knowledge and understanding. Section B: 40 mins. Short-answer questions testing the handling of ideas, interpreting data, etc.
3	1h 15mins	Those expecting to achieve grades A or B.		Section A: 35 mins. Short-answer questions. Section B: 40 mins. Two questions to be chosen from four structured free-response questions.
4	Coursework	All.	20%	
Northern Examining Association				
1	2	All.	35%	Section A: 30 mins. Forty objective questions (multiple choice and matching pairs). Emphasis on knowledge and understanding. Section B: 1½ hours. Structured questions.

Introduction – how to succeed in your exam

Paper	Duration in hours	Taken by	Proportion of total marks	Description, types of question, etc.
2 Level P	1½	Those aiming for grades D–G	35%	Compulsory structured questions.
OR				
2 Level Q	1½	Those aiming for grades A–C	35%	Compulsory structured questions.
Experimental skills (coursework)		All.	30%	

Welsh Joint Education Committee

I	2	Candidates aiming for grades C–G	80%	Both papers contain an easier section A (50%) and a more difficult section B (50%). Section B of Paper I is the same as section A of Paper II.
OR				
II	1½	Candidates aiming for grades A–D	80%	You cannot take both papers. All questions will be structured. Some questions in Paper II will be free-response.
PLUS				
Coursework		All candidates.	20%	

N. Ireland Schools Examinations Council

1	1	All.	20%	Structured questions, all compulsory. Easier than Paper 2.
2	1¼	All candidates.	20%	Section A: 20 compulsory multiple choice questions (25 mins). Section B: compulsory structured questions (50 mins).
3	1¼	Optional for those seeking grades A and B.	40%	Compulsory questions. Structured with some essay-type components.
Coursework		All.	20%	

Human Biology

ASSESSMENT IN SCOTLAND (SCOTTISH EXAMINATION BOARD): SCE ANATOMY, PHYSIOLOGY AND HYGIENE

PAPERS TO BE SET IN 1988 AND THEREAFTER

▷ **Ordinary grade** One 2-hour paper, composed of structured questions.

▷ **Higher grade** Paper 1: 2 hours, worth 120 marks. Structured questions.

Paper 2: 2½ hours, worth 100 marks. Two questions on health topics will contain choices.

▷ There is no assessment of coursework on either grade.

1.10 USEFUL ADDRESSES

Addresses of the examination boards, etc., for syllabuses and specimen question papers.

IN ENGLAND

The GCSE exams are set by four groups of examining boards, made up of the GCE and CSE boards in each region.

Table 1.5 GCSE examining groups in England

Examining group	Examining boards in the group — GCE	Examining boards in the group — CSE	Address for syllabus and papers (or **write to any board in the** group)
Southern	The Associated Examining Board Oxford Delegacy of Local Examinations	The South-East Regional Examinations Board The Southern Regional Examinations Board The South-Western Examinations Board	The Associated Examining Board, Stag Hill House, Guildford, Surrey GU2 5XJ
London and East Anglia	University of London School Examinations Board	East Anglian Examinations Board London Regional Examinations Board	University of London School Examinations Board, Stewart House, 32 Russell Square, London WC1B 5DN
Midland	University of Cambridge Local Examinations Syndicate Oxford and Cambridge Schools Examination Board (no human biology syllabus prior to 1988) Southern Universities Joint Board for School Examinations	The West Midlands Examinations Board East Midland Regional Examinations Board	University of Cambridge Local Examinations Syndicate, Syndicate Buildings, 1 Hills Road, Cambridge CB1 2EU

Introduction – how to succeed in your exam

Examining group	Examining boards in the group		Address for syllabus and papers (or **write to any board in the group**)
	GCE	**CSE**	
Northern Examining Association	Joint Matriculation Board	Associated Lancashire Schools Examining Board	Joint Matriculation Board, Manchester M15 6EU
		North Regional Examinations Board	
		North West Regional Examinations Board	
		Yorkshire and Humberside Regional Examinations Board	

GCSE syllabuses and specimen question papers are available from any of the boards in each group. We have given one address to write to for each group, but you can write to the board used by your own school or college instead, if you prefer.

Whichever board you write to, be sure to ask for the syllabus for the group for which you are entered. Check this carefully with your teacher or college lecturer.

IN WALES

Write to:
> The Welsh Joint Education Committee,
> 245 Western Avenue,
> Cardiff CF5 2YX.

IN N. IRELAND

Write to:
> Northern Ireland Schools Examination Council,
> Examinations Office,
> Beechill House,
> Beechill Road,
> Belfast BT8 4RJ.

IN SCOTLAND

The SCE syllabus for anatomy, physiology and hygiene is obtainable from:
> Scottish Examination Board,
> Ironmills Road,
> Dalkeith,
> Midlothian EH22 1LE

Past question papers are obtainable from the Board's agents:

> Robert Gibson & Sons Ltd,
> 17 Fitzroy Place,
> Glasgow G3 7SF

1.11 FINAL PREPARATIONS

1. **Don't stay up late** on the night before an exam. You'll remember the facts much more easily if you've had plenty of sleep. Even more important, you'll think more clearly as you write.
2. **Don't get up late** on the morning of an exam. And take a little exercise on the way, to wake you up completely before you reach the exam room.
3. Make sure you **take these** into the exam with you:
   - Two sharp HB pencils
   - Pencil sharpener
   - Rubber
   - Ruler
   - Two pens
   - Calculator (check whether this is allowed with your teacher or lecturer)
4. And don't forget to use **yourself**. During the exam, no-one can stop you from counting your own teeth, or checking on the position of your stomach, etc!

1.12 ANALYSIS OF EXAM SYLLABUSES

Table 1.6 gives an analysis of the content of each of the examination syllabuses, with an indication of how they accord with the contents of this book. However, do be sure to **check** your own syllabuses as well.

- •   Topic **included** in syllabus.
- (•)   Topic not definitely mentioned, but **some knowledge** of it may be assumed.
- Blank   Topic **not included**.

Introduction – how to succeed in your exam

Table 1.6 Analysis of examination syllabuses

Chapter or section	S	L/EA	M	N	W	NI	O	H
2 Living organisms								
2.1 Characteristics of living organisms	(●)	●	●	(●)	●	●	●	●
2.2 Plant/animal differences	(●)	●	●	●	●	(●)		
2.3 Varieties of living organisms	●	●	●	●	●	●		
Use of keys	●	●	●	●	●	●		
2.4 Man's place in the animal kingdom	●	●	●	●	●	●		
2.5 Evolution of man from the apes		●						
3 Cells								
3.1 Animal/plant cells	●	●	●	●	●	●		
3.2 Cell structure and function	●	●	●	●	●	●	●	●
3.3 Cells, tissues, organs, systems	(●)	●	●	(●)	●	●	●	●
3.4 Enzymes (in general)	●	●	●	●	●	●	●	●
3.5 Cell respiration	●	●	●	●	●	●	●	●
3.6 Diffusion	●	●	●	●	(●)	●	●	●
Osmosis	●	●	(●)	●	●	●	●	●
Active transport	(●)	●			●	●	●	●
Surface area/volume ratio	(●)	(●)	●	●	(●)	(●)		
4 The skeleton, muscles and movement								
4.1 The skeleton: general functions and structure	●	●			●	●	●	●
4.2 Skull		●				●	●	●
Backbone	●	●				●	●	●
Ribs	●	●				●	●	●
Limb girdles	●	●	●			●	●	●
4.3 Structure of bone and cartilage	●	●	●					●
			●					●
4.4 Joints	●	●	●	●	●	●	●	●
4.5 How muscles work	●	●	●	●	●	●	●	●
Levers							●	●
4.6 Types of muscle	(●)	●			●		●	●

S = Southern L/EA = London & East Anglia M = Midland N = Northern W = Wales NI = N.Ireland O & H = Scotland (APH) Grades

Human Biology

Chapter or section	S	L/EA	M	N	W	NI	O	H
4.7 Muscle tone Posture, lifting and bending	●	●			●			●
4.8 Care of the feet	●							
5 Breathing and gas exchange								
5.1 Breathing and respiration	●	●	●	●	●	●	●	●
5.2 Structure and functions of the respiratory system	●	●	●	●	●	●	●	●
5.3 The mechanism of breathing	●	●	●	●	●	●	●	●
5.4 Measuring lung capacity	●	●	●			(●)	●	●
5.5 Gas exchange in the alveoli	●	●	●	●	●	●	●	●
5.6 Experiments to compare expired and inspired air	●	●					●	●
5.7 Control of the breathing rate	●							●
5.8 Artificial resuscitation	●				●	●		
6 Blood and the circulation system								
6.1 Purpose of the circulation system and the composition of blood	●	●	●	●	●	●	●	●
6.2 Functions of blood	●	●	●	●	●	●	●	●
6.3 Functions of the red cells: role of haemoglobin	●	●	●	●	●	●	●	●
6.4 Clotting	●	●	●	(●)	●	●	●	●
6.5 ABO blood groups Rhesus system	●	● ●	●	●	●	● ●	●	●
7 The circulation system and the heart								
7.1 The double circulation system	●	●	●	●	●	●	●	●
7.2 The structure of the heart	●	●	●	●	●	●	●	●
7.3 Heartbeat	●	●	●	●	●	●	●	●
7.4 Coronary heart disease	(●)	●	●	●	●	●	●	●
7.5 Blood pressure and the pulse	●	●	●	●	●	●	●	●
7.6 Exercise and the circulation system								

S = Southern   L/EA = London & East Anglia   M = Midland   N = Northern   W = Wales   NI = N.Ireland   O & H = Scotland (APH) Grades

Introduction – how to succeed in your exam

Chapter or section	S	L/EA	M	N	W	NI	O	H
8 Structure and function of blood vessels and lymph								
8.1 Comparison of arteries and veins	●	●	●	●	●	●	●	●
8.2 The circulation system	●	●	●	●	●	●	●	●
8.3 Exchange of substances in the tissues	●	●	●	●	●	●	●	●
8.4 The lymphatic system	(●)	(●)	●		●	●	●	●
8.5 Differences between the body fluids	●	●	●	●	●	●	●	●
9 Food and nutrition								
9.1 The need for food	●	●	●	●	●	●	●	●
9.2 Proteins, carbohydrates, fats	●	●	●	●	●	●	●	●
9.3 Vitamins	●	●	●	●	●	●	●	●
9.4 Minerals	●	●	●	●	●	●	●	●
9.5 Water, fibre and milk	●	●	●	●	●	●	●	●
9.6 Food tests	●	●	●	●		●	●	●
9.7 Test for vitamin C					●		●	●
10 Energy and food								
10.1 Balanced diet and daily food requirements	●	●	●	●	●	●	●	●
10.2 Energy requirements and metabolic rate	●	●	●	●	●	●	●	●
10.3 Calculating daily energy requirements	●	●	●	●	●	●	●	●
10.4 Malnutrition				●	●	●		
Starvation					●	●		
Anorexia nervosa			●		●	●		
Obesity		●		●	●	●		
Slimming						●		
10.5 Using a calorimeter to measure the energy in food	●	●	●	●		●	●	●
11 Digestion and teeth								
11.1 The need for digestion	●	●	●	●	●	●	●	●
11.2 Dentition and types of teeth	●		●	●	●	●	●	●

S = Southern   L/EA = London & East Anglia   M = Midland   N = Northern   W = Wales   NI = N.Ireland   O & H = Scotland (APH) Grades

Human Biology

Chapter or section	S	L/EA	M	N	W	NI	O	H
11.3 Structure of a canine tooth	•	•	•	•	•	•	•	•
11.4 Care of the teeth	•	•	•	•	•	•	•	•
12 Digestion, absorption and assimilation								
12.1 The alimentary canal	•	•	•	•	•	•	•	•
12.2 Digestion in the mouth	•	•	•	•	•	•	•	•
12.3 Swallowing and breathing	•	•	•		•			
12.4 Summary of digestion by enzymes and bile	•	•	•	•	•	•	•	•
12.5 Absorption	•	•	•	•	•	•	•	•
12.6 Assimilation and the liver	•	•	•	•	•	•	•	•
12.7 Investigations with salivary amylase	•	•	•	•		•	•	•
Investigating the action of proteases, e.g. pepsin	•		•	•	•	•	•	•
13 The skin and temperature regulation								
13.1 Structure and functions of the skin	•	•	(•)	•	•	•	•	•
13.2 Temperature regulation	•	•		•	•	•	•	•
13.3 Hypothermia		•			•			
13.4 The clinical thermometer					•	•		
13.5 Experiments with temperature control	•	•		•	•			
14 Excretion and the kidneys								
14.1 Excretion	•	•	•	•	•	•		•
14.2 Position and general structure of the kidneys	•	•	•	•	•	•		•
14.3 Functions of the kidneys: the nephron	•	•	•	•	•	•		•
14.4 Effects of climate and diet on the urine	•	•	•	•	•	•		•
14.5 The kidney dialysis machine	•	•	•	•	•	•		

S = Southern   L/EA = London & East Anglia   M = Midland   N = Northern   W = Wales   NI = N.Ireland   O & H = Scotland (APH) Grades

Introduction – how to succeed in your exam

Chapter or section	S	L/EA	M	N	W	NI	O	H
15 Coordination: the nervous and endocrine systems								
15.1 General arrangement of the nervous system	●	●	●	●	●	●	●	●
15.2 The structure and functions of neurones	●	●	●	●	●	●	●	●
15.3 The nervous impulse and the synapse	●	●	●	●	●	●	●	●
15.4 The central nervous system (brain and cord)	●	●	●	●	●	●	●	●
15.5 Reflex and voluntary actions Conditioned reflex	●	●	●●	●	●	●	●	●
15.6 The endocrine system	●	●	●	●	●	●	●	●
15.7 Homeostasis	●	●	●	●	●	●	●	●
15.8 Sensitivity in plants	●				●	●		
16 Response to stimuli: the sense organs								
16.1 How receptors work	●	●	●	●	●	●	●	●
16.2 Structure, functions and protection of the eye	●	●	●	●	●	●	●	●
16.3 Image formation in the eye	●	●	●	●	●	●	●	●
16.4 Focusing and accommodation	●	●	●	●	●	●	●	●
16.5 Adjusting to dim light	●	●	●	●	●	●	●	●
16.6 Fields of vision	●	●	(●)					●
16.7 Common defects of the eye			●			●	●	●
16.8 Receptors in the ear	●	●	●		●		●	●
16.9 Receptors in the skin	●	●	●	●	●	●	●	●
16.10 Receptors in the nose and mouth	●	(●)	●	●			●	●
17 Human reproduction								
17.1 Sexual intercourse and the reproductive organs	●	●	●	●	●	●	●	●
17.2 Ovulation	●	●	●	●	●	●	●	●
17.3 Fertilization	●	●	●	●	●	●	●	●

S = Southern   L/EA = London & East Anglia   M = Midland   N = Northern   W = Wales   NI = N.Ireland   O & H = Scotland (APH) Grades

Human Biology

Chapter or section	S	L/EA	M	N	W	NI	O	H
17.4 Twins	●	●	(●)	●	●	(●)	(●)	(●)
17.5 The menstrual cycle	●	●	●	●	●	●	●	●
17.6 Hormones and pregnancy	●	●	●	●	●	●	●	●
17.7 Promoting fertility				●		●		
17.8 Controlling fertility (birth control and contraception)	●	●	●	●		●		●
18 Pregnancy, ante-natal care and childbirth								
18.1 Development in the uterus	●	●	●	●	●	●	●	●
18.2 Role of the placenta	●	●	●	●	●	●	●	●
18.3 Ante-natal care	●	●	●		●	●		
18.4 Birth	●	●	●	●	●	●	●	●
19 The human life cycle: child development, maturity and ageing								
19.1 Parental care of children	●		●		●			
19.2 Care of the newborn baby	●	●	(●)	●	●			
19.3 Lactation, breast and bottle feeding	●	●		●	●			●
19.4 Growth in height and weight	●	●	●	●		●		
19.5 Growth rates of different organs	●	●	●	●		●		
19.6 Ageing	●	●	●	●		●	●	●
20 Variation and genetics								
20.1 Continuous and discontinuous variation	●	●	●	●	●	●		
20.2 The genetic code	●	●	●	●	●	●		●
20.3 Cell division	●	●	●	●	●	●		●
20.4 Mitosis	●	●	●	●	●	●		●
20.5 Meiosis	●	●	●	●	●	●		●
20.6 The laws of inheritance	●	●	●	●	●	●		●
20.7 How to solve genetics problems	●	●	●	●	●	●		●

S = Southern L/EA = London & East Anglia M = Midland N = Northern W = Wales NI = N.Ireland O & H = Scotland (APH) Grades

Introduction – how to succeed in your exam

Chapter or section	S	L/EA	M	N	W	NI	O	H
20.8 Incomplete dominance	●	●	●	●				●
20.9 Sex determination and sex linkage	●	●	●●	●	●	●		●
20.10 Mutations	●	●	●	●	●	●		●
20.11 Genetic counselling and cousin marriages				●				
20.12 Variation	●	●	●	●	●	●		
Natural selection	●	●	●		●	●		
Evolution	●	●	●		●	●		
21 Personal health care								
21.1 Requirements for health	●	●	●	●	●	●	●	●
21.2 Effects of drugs on the body	○	●	●	●	●	●		●
21.3 Mental health and mental illness		●	●	●				●
21.4 Cancer			●			●		
21.5 Smoking and health	●	●	●	●	●	●		●
22 Causes and prevention of infectious disease								
22.1 Infectious diseases: methods of spread	●	●	●	●	●	●	●	●
22.2 Insect vectors of disease	●	●	●	●	●	●	●	●
22.3 Social conditions and spread of disease	●			●				●
22.4 External defences against infection	●	(●)		●	(●)		(●)	(●)
22.5 Internal defences against infection	●	●	●	●	●	●	●	●
22.6 Immunity and vaccination	●	●	●	●	●	●	●	●
22.7 Prevention of infection in hospitals	●			●				
22.8 Antibiotics	●	●	●	●	●	●	●	●
22.9 Public health	●			(●)				
22.10 Prevention of sexually transmitted diseases	●	●	(●)	●	●	●		●

S = Southern   L/EA = London & East Anglia   M = Midland   N = Northern   W = Wales   NI = N.Ireland   O & H = Scotland (APH) Grades

Human Biology

Chapter or section	S	L/EA	M	N	W	NI	O	H
23 Disease, food preservation and experiments with micro-organisms								
23.1 Infectious diseases – causes and prevention	●	●	●	●	●	●	●	●
23.2 Parasites					●	●		●
23.3 Roles of WHO and FAO						●	●	●
23.4 Food poisoning and the preservation of food	●	●	●	●	●	●	●	●
23.5 Methods for preserving food	●	●	●	●	●	●	●	●
23.6 Experiments with micro-organisms	●	●	●	●	●	●	●	●
24 Water and waste								
24.1 The water cycle	●	●	●	●	●	●		
24.2 Water purification	●	(●)	●	●	●	●	●	●
24.3 Sewage collection and treatment	●	●	●	●	●	●	●	●
24.4 Disposal of solid organic wastes: Dustbins Refuse tips	● ●		● ●	(●) (●)	● ●		● ●	● ●
24.5 Role of environmental health officers			(●)	●			(●)	(●)
25 Plants and man								
25.1 Photosynthesis	●	●	●	●	●	●		
25.2 Experiments on photosynthesis	●	●			●			
25.3 The carbon cycle	●	●	●	●	●	●		
25.4 The nitrogen cycle	●	●	●	●	●	●		
26 Ecology, ecosystems and communities								
26.1 Food chains, energy and feeding relationships	●	●	●	●	●	●		
26.2 Food webs	●	●		●	●			

S = Southern L/EA = London & East Anglia M = Midland N = Northern W = Wales NI = N.Ireland O & H = Scotland (APH) Grades

Introduction – how to succeed in your exam

Chapter or section	S	L/EA	M	N	W	NI	O	H
27 Human populations, conservation and pollution								
27.1 Population and the development of agriculture				•				
27.2 Causes and effects of the population explosion	•	•	•	•	•	•		•
27.3 Preventing future crises	•	•	•	•	•	•		•
27.4 Conservation	•	•	•	•	•	•		
27.5 Pollution of air, land and water	•	•	•	•	•	•	•	•
27.6 Insecticides	•	•	(•)	•	•	•		
27.7 Conservation and land use	•	•	•	•	•	•		

S = Southern   L/EA = London & East Anglia   M = Midland   N = Northern   W = Wales   NI = N.Ireland   O & H = Scotland (APH) Grades

CHAPTER TWO

LIVING ORGANISMS AND THEIR RELATIONSHIPS

CONTENTS

- 2.1 Characteristics of living organisms — 41
- 2.2 Differences between plants and animals — 42
- 2.3 The major varieties of living organisms — 42
- 2.4 Man's place in the animal kingdom — 44
- 2.5 Checklist — 45
- 2.6 Exam questions — 46

Living organisms and their relationships

2.1 CHARACTERISTICS OF LIVING ORGANISMS

The seven characteristics which distinguish living organisms from non-living organisms are as follows.

1. **Respiration** All living organisms obtain energy from the breakdown of complex food substances (see page 52). *Hint: Respiration* is often confused with *breathing* – but they are entirely different. (See page 87).
2. **Nutrition** All living organisms need a supply of complex molecules as a source of energy and for growth. Animals obtain these by eating other organisms, while green plants manufacture complex molecules from simple molecules.
3. **Excretion** All living things excrete wastes produced as a result of chemical processes occurring inside their cells, e.g. exhalation of carbon dioxide and urea in man.
4. **Growth** All living things increase in size at some stage during their life cycle.
5. **Reproduction** All living things are capable of reproducing themselves at some stage during their life cycle.
6. **Sensitivity** and **response** Living things are able to detect and respond to stimuli, i.e. changes in their external or internal environment. For example, animals are sensitive to sound, growing plants are sensitive to light.

    Note: sensitivity and response are sometimes together referred to as **irritability**. Irritability is the ability to respond to a stimulus.
7. **Movement** Living things use energy produced by respiration for movement of the whole organism or its parts (e.g. movement within a cell).

    Hint: movement, nutrition, respiration, excretion, growth, reproduction and sensitivity can be easily remembered as *Many Naughty Rabbits Eat Green Radish Shoots*.

Human Biology

2.2 DIFFERENCES BETWEEN PLANTS AND ANIMALS

Table 2.1 Differences between plants and animals

	Plants	Animals
1 Nutrition	Manufacture their own food by synthesizing (making) complex organic molecules (e.g. starch) from simple substances, using the energy of sunlight (photosynthesis). Obtain energy by respiration of the complex carbohydrate molecules which they have produced in this way.	Feed by eating plants or other animals. Obtain energy by breaking down complex organic substances obtained from plants or other animals.
2 Sensitivity	Relatively **slow** responses due to lack of nervous system. Most responses involve growth, and are controlled by hormones, e.g. tropisms (see page 214).	**Fast** responses to stimuli because impulses from receptors travel rapidly to effectors through the nervous system (see page 206). Most responses involve rapid contraction of muscle fibres.
3 Movement	Rarely capable of independent movement. Usually anchored by roots or free floating.	Usually capable of rapid movement involving muscle contractions to move limbs.
4 Cell structure	Cell wall present. Cytoplasm does not occupy whole cell; vacuole present.	Cell wall absent. Cytoplasm occupies whole cell.

2.3 THE MAJOR VARIETIES OF LIVING ORGANISMS

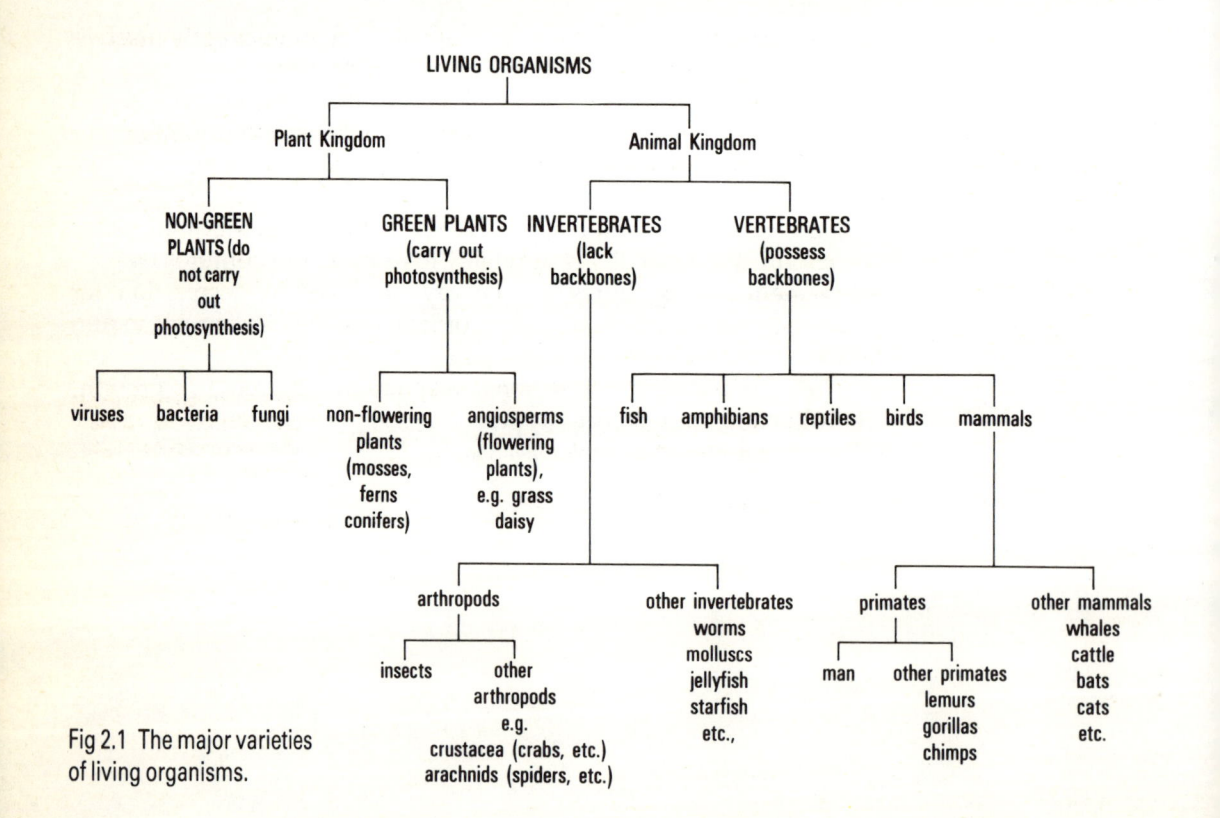

Fig 2.1 The major varieties of living organisms.

Living organisms and their relationships

Fig 2.1 shows the major divisions of the plant and animal kingdoms, while Table 2.2 shows in what way these groups can affect man's life.

Table 2.2 Living things relevant to man

Name	Description	Relationship to man Harmful	Useful
1 Microorganisms (non-green plants)			
Viruses	Very small non-cellular organisms found only as **parasites** inside other living cells. Consist of a protein coat surrounding genetic material. Lack cytoplasm. Live by invading the host cell, taking over its DNA and causing it to produce new viruses. These then invade new cells.	Cause of many infectious diseases including common cold, flu, AIDS, measles.	
Bacteria	Uni-cellular, with cell wall, cytoplasm but no distinct nucleus. Vast majority are free-living, unlike viruses. Most are **decomposers** of organic remains.	Cause many infectious diseases, e.g. pneumonia, tetanus, TB. Spoil human food by causing decay.	Essential for **fertile soils** because they decompose organic remains in the soil releasing: carbon dioxide to the atmosphere, so completing carbon cycle (p. 358); nitrates to the soil, so completing nitrogen cycle (p. 359). Decompose organic remains in sewage. Essential for absorption of vitamin K from large intestine. Used to make yoghurt, cheese, 'single-cell' protein, and the hormone insulin.
Fungi	Typically consist of thread like structures called **hyphae** which form a **mycelium**. Some are single cells, e.g. yeast. Possess cytoplasm, nucleus and a cell wall containing cellulose, but lack chlorophyll. Mostly feed as **decomposers**. Reproduce by spores, sometimes dispersed from cap-like structures, e.g. mushrooms.	Cause skin infections, e.g. athlete's foot, ringworm. Spoil human food by causing decay. Cause serious crop diseases, e.g. potato blight.	Decompose organic remains – same benefits as for bacteria. Used to make **antibiotics**, e.g. penicillin. Yeast is used to **ferment** sugars to alcohol (wine, beer, etc.) and to produce carbon dioxide to make bread rise. A source of food, e.g. mushrooms.

Continued

Human Biology

2 Angiosperms (flowering plants)

Many examples, e.g. grass, all cereals, potato, etc.	Reproduce by producing flowers and seeds. Contain **chlorophyll** and so make food by **photosynthesis**.		The main source of **oxygen** in the world. The ulitmate source of almost all **human food**. Man, and the animals eaten by man, rely on flowering plants for food, chiefly in the form of: storage organs, e.g. potato tubers; seeds, e.g. cereal crops; fruit.

3 Animals

Protozoa	Microscopic one-celled organisms, found mainly in water. Reproduce both asexually (by simple division), and sexually.	Some cause serious illnesses, e.g. *Plasmodium* causes malaria	Some consume pathogens in sewage works (p. 344).
Arthropods	Insects are the main example. These are multicellular, segmented, with an exoskeleton (external skeleton), and six jointed limbs.	Destroyers of crops, e.g. aphids, locusts. Vectors (carriers) of infectious disease, e.g. mosquito carries malaria parasite *Plasmodium*.	Bees produce honey. Insects pollinate flowers – essential for production of many seeds and fruits.

2.4 MAN'S PLACE IN THE ANIMAL KINGDOM

Man belongs to a group of tree-living apes called **primates**, in the class of **mammals**, within the major group of animals with backbones, or **vertebrates** (see Fig 2.1).

Fig 2.2 Evolution of man from the apes (L/EA only). (a) Skull of the human-type ape which lived in Africa 10 million years ago. (b) Human skull.

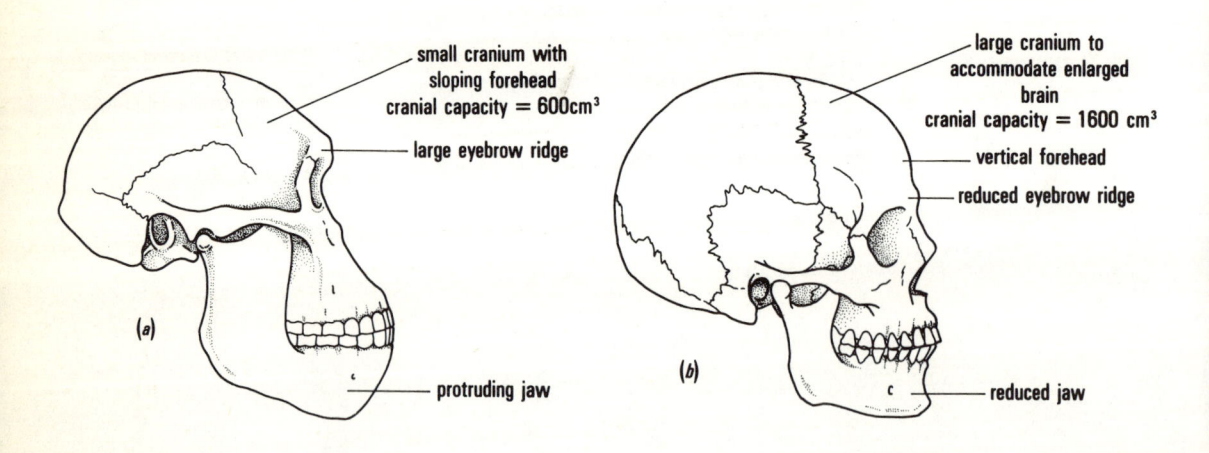

(a) small cranium with sloping forehead
cranial capacity = 600cm³
large eyebrow ridge
protruding jaw

(b) large cranium to accommodate enlarged brain
cranial capacity = 1600 cm³
vertical forehead
reduced eyebrow ridge
reduced jaw

Living organisms and their relationships

Table 2.3 Features of vertebrates, mammals, primates and man

Group	Key Features
1 Vertebrates	Possession of a backbone.
(a) Fish	Possess gills, scales and fins. Aquatic.
(b) Amphibia (frogs, newts)	Moist skin, eggs laid in water.
(c) Reptiles (snakes, crocodiles, turtles)	Dry, scaly skin. Eggs laid, with leathery shell.
(d) Birds	Homiothermic (warm blooded); wings and feathers; eggs have hard shell.
(e) Mammals	See **2** below.
2 Mammals	(a) Presence of **mammary glands**, so that the young are suckled on milk. (b) Most possess a **placenta** during pregnancy so that the young can develop inside the mother. (Exceptions: platypus lays eggs; marsupials possess pouches e.g. kangaroo.) (c) **Homiothermy** – ability to maintain a constant body temperature. (d) Possession of **fur** (hair) and **sweat glands**, both of which contribute to homiothermy. (e) External ears (ear pinnae). (f) Eyelids for protection of the eyes. (g) Whiskers on the face to obtain sensory information. (h) Presence of diaphragm dividing thorax and abdomen. (i) Always possess same number of vertebrae in neck (seven), even in giraffes.
3 Primates Primate features are adapted to a life in trees.	(a) Ability to grasp objects such as tree branches with the hands (**prehensile hands**); presence of fingernails instead of claws. (b) Excellent eyesight, with eyes in the front of the head giving good judgement of distance, e.g. for jumping among branches (p. 226). (c) Presence of a large and complex brain. (d) Production of fewer offspring, which take longer to mature.
4 Man For Binomial system of naming, see page 417 – M only)	(a) Ability to walk upright on two legs only (**bipedalism**) for long periods. (b) Possession of a thumb which can be opposed to the other fingers, allowing for the picking up of small objects and their use as tools. (c) Presence of a **large and complex forebrain**, especially the cerebral hemispheres, compared to other primates. This makes reasoning, learning and language development possible to a much greater extent than in any other animals. (d) Lack of body hair compared to the apes.

2.5 CHECKLIST

- Seven characteristics of living organisms.
- Four major differences between plants and animals.
- Differences between viruses, bacteria, and fungi.
- Viruses:
    - one harmful effect.
- Bacteria:
    - two harmful effects;
    - four useful effects.
- Fungi;
    - three harmful effects;
    - three useful effects.

Human Biology

- The key features of angiosperms, protozoa, arthropods, and vertebrates.
- Angiosperms:
    two useful effects.
- Insects:
    two harmful effects; 2 useful effects.
- Eight features of mammals.
- Four features of primates.
- Four features of man.

2.6 EXAM QUESTIONS

1. In a museum, one of the exhibits consisted of some living bushes with stuffed birds of different sorts arranged on the branches. One bright green bird had a motor hidden inside so that it flapped its wings and opened its beak in a very life-like fashion.
   (a)   State THREE characteristics which a live bird must show to prove it is a living thing. (3)
   (b)   What ONE characteristic of life does the green museum bird appear to show? (1)
   (c)   Man and bird are both vertebrates; state TWO ways in which man differs from a bird, which classify the human species as mammalian. (2)
   (d)   Give TWO differences between the living bushes and the green bird which could prove the bushes are plants. (2)
   [NI]

2. Name FOUR structures found in or on the head of a mammal which distinguishes it from other mammals. (4)   [Ox]

3. (a)   Give TWO features by which man is classified as a primate. (2)
   (b)   In what ways are primates adapted for living in trees? (3)
   (c)   State THREE reasons why you are classified as a member of the human species (known as man or *Homo sapiens*). (3)   [S]

CHAPTER THREE

CELLS AS THE BASIC UNIT OF LIFE

CONTENTS

- **3.1 Structure of animal and plant cells** — 49
- **3.2 Cell structure and function** — 50
- **3.3 Cells, tissues, organs and systems** — 51
- **3.4 Enzymes** — 51
  Properties of enzymes 51
  Names of enzymes 51
  Effects of temperature on enzymes 52
  Two common mistakes 52
- **3.5 Cell respiration** — 52
  Types of respiration 52
  Energy production and transfer during respiration 54
  Aerobic and anaerobic respiration compared 54
- **3.6 Diffusion, osmosis and active transport** — 55
  Diffusion 56
  Osmosis 56
  Active transport 58
- **3.7 Checklist** — 59
- **3.8 Exam questions** — 60

Cells as the basic unit of life

3.1 STRUCTURE OF ANIMAL AND PLANT CELLS

The structure of animal and plant cells is shown in Fig 3.1(a) and (b).

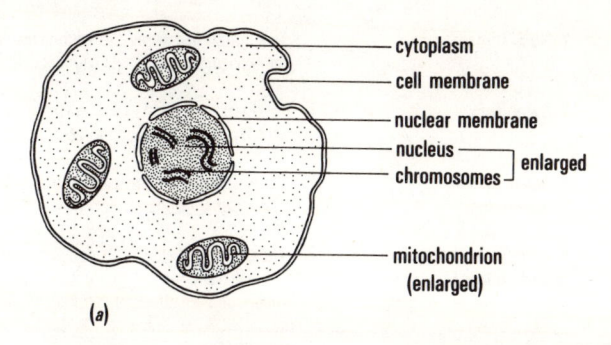

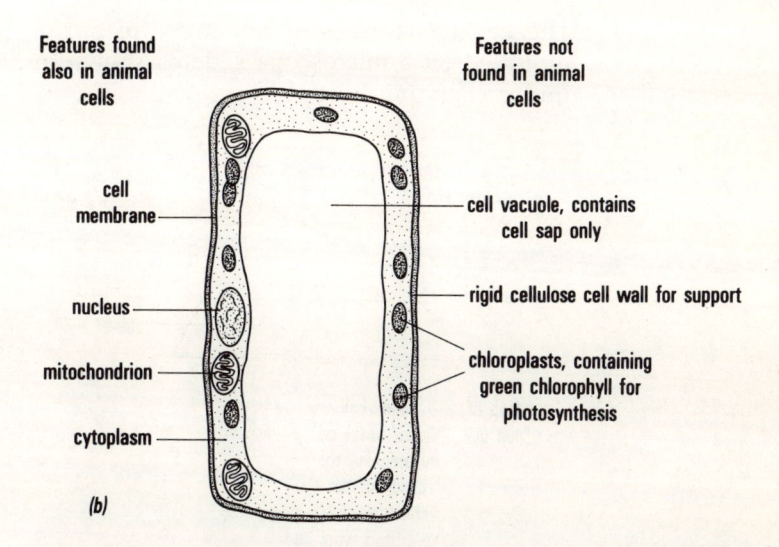

Fig 3.1(a) and (b) Structure of animal and plant cells. (a) Animal cell. (b) Plant cell (palisade cell from a leaf).

All the parts of the animal cell shown in Fig 3.1(a) can be seen under a **light microscope** except for the mitochondria, which can only be seen with an **electron miscroscope**. All of these parts are also found in plant cells.

Human Biology

The plant cell in Fig 3.1(b) is drawn to a smaller scale than the animal cell. Some syllabuses require you to know about **mesophyll** cells, not palisade cells. Mesophyll cells are identical to palisade cells except that they are smaller and rounder.

3.2 CELL STRUCTURE AND FUNCTION

Table 3.1 Cell structure and function

Organelle	Structure and function
1 Nucleus	The control centre of the cell, containing the **chromosomes**.
2 Nuclear membrane	This double membrane surrounds the nucleus. Gaps, called **pores**, allow for exchange of materials with the cytoplasm.
3 Cytoplasm	The basic living material of the cell. Contains 80% water and a mixture of proteins, fats and carbohydrates.
4 Cell or plasma membrane	Outer boundary of the cell. Controls the passage of molecules in and out of the cell. Composed of protein and lipid (fat) molecules.
5 Mitochondria singular: mitochondrion)	The centres for energy production in the cell. Glucose is broken down by cell respiration (p. 52) to produce energy. The enzymes which carry out respiration are attached to folded inner membranes (**cristae**).

The general features of cell structure can be seen in a cheek cell, mounted on a microscope slide as shown in Fig 3.2 and examined under a light microscope.

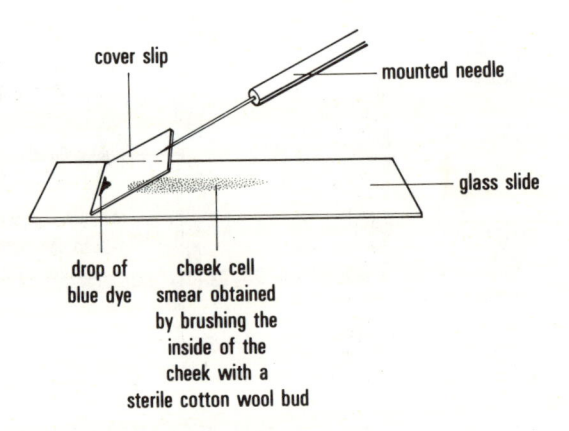

Fig 3.2 Making a cheek cell slide.

Cells as the basic unit of life

3.3 CELLS, TISSUES, ORGANS AND SYSTEMS

Table 3.2 Cells, tissues, organs, systems

Level of organization	Description
1 Cell	The basic unit of life. All cells can produce energy; many are also able to grow and reproduce.
2 Tissue	A collection of cells with similar structure and functions, e.g. nervous tissue.
3 Organ	A collection of different tissues, grouped together in one part of the body to perform the same overall function, e.g. the lungs contain four different tissues, all concerned with exchange of gases.
4 System	A group of organs which work together to perform the same function, e.g. the digestive system, composed of the stomach, intestine, etc.

3.4 ENZYMES

Enzymes are specific, biological catalysts which function best within a narrow range of temperature and pH. Two examples are as follows.
1. **Amylase** in saliva (see page 170) speeds up the breakdown of starch to sugars in the mouth.
2. **Catalase** speeds the release of oxygen from other compounds in most living cells.

PROPERTIES OF ENZYMES

All enzymes are:
1. **proteins** – like all proteins they can be destroyed (**denatured**) by heating;
2. **specific** – each types of enzyme acts on one kind of chemical only, called its **substrate**;
3. **affected by temperature** – enzymes work fastest within a narrow (or optimum) range of temperature, e.g. 35–40°C for human enzymes;
4. **affected by pH** (acidity and alkalinity) – enzymes work best within a narrow pH range, which varies for each enzyme.

NAMES OF ENZYMES

Enzymes are named after their substrates, e.g. **proteases** digest **proteins** only, **carbohydrases** digest **carbohydrates**, etc.

Human Biology

EFFECTS OF TEMPERATURE ON ENZYMES

CHILLING

Below 35°C enzyme activity slows down and it stops completely below −18°C, i.e. the temperature in a three-star deep freezer. But enzymes are not damaged by freezing and can be re-activated even after 3 months at −18°C.

WARMING

Enzymes double their activity for every 10°C rise in temperature to 35°C. Above about 45°C enzyme activity slows down again.

Heating above 60°C permanently changes the shape of an enzyme molecule, so that it is no longer active. The enzyme is then said to be **denatured**.

TWO COMMON MISTAKES

1 '**Enzymes are only found in the digestive system**.' Because the digestive enzymes, e.g. pepsin, are the best known, many people forget that enzymes are necessary for almost every function in the body. Each cell contains hundreds of **intra-cellular** enzymes such as catalase; only the digestive enzymes and a few others are active outside cells (**extra-cellular** enzymes).

2 '**Enzymes are killed by heat**.' Since enzymes are *not* alive, they cannot 'die'. Enzymes are destroyed by heating above 60°C (see above) and become inactive (but not destroyed) if chilled below 0°C.

3.5 CELL RESPIRATION

Cell (or **tissue**) **respiration** is the process whereby cells oxidise sugars such as glucose to produce energy, carbon dioxide and water.

The **purpose of respiration** is to produce energy for the carrying out of work by the cells. Examples of work done by cells include:
- muscle contraction;
- protein synthesis;
- production of heat.

Active tissues respire more rapidly than less active tissues, so high **rates of respiration** occur in liver and muscles, and low rates in bone cells and connective tissue. There is a higher density of mitochondria in active tissues.

TYPES OF RESPIRATION

There are two major kinds of cell respiration:
1 **aerobic** (with oxygen);
2 **anaerobic** (without oxygen).

AEROBIC RESPIRATION

Aerobic respiration is the complete breakdown of glucose to carbon dioxide, water and energy, in the presence of oxygen. It takes place inside the mitochondria in a series of small steps, with release of energy at each stage. Each step is controlled by a separate enzyme. It can be summarized as follows:

$$\text{Glucose} + \text{Oxygen} \xrightarrow[\text{mitochondria}]{\text{Enzymes in}} \text{Water} + \text{Carbon Dioxide} + \text{Energy}$$

The complete oxidation of one gram molecule of glucose (180 g) produces **2830 kilojoules** (kJ) of energy.

Use for bread making

To make bread rise, yeast cells are mixed with flour (which contains sugars) in aerobic conditions. This produces large quantities of carbon dioxide, which forms bubbles in the dough, so creating the light open texture of a typical loaf of bread.

ANAEROBIC RESPIRATION

Anaerobic respiration is the partial breakdown of glucose in the absence of oxygen. It takes place in the cytoplasm, i.e. *not* inside the mitochondria.

$$\text{Glucose} \xrightarrow[\text{cytoplasm}]{\text{Enzymes in}} \text{Lactic acid} + \text{Carbon dioxide} + \text{Energy}$$

The reaction occurs normally as the first stage in aerobic respiration. If oxygen is absent, the lactic acid cannot be broken down further.

Anaerobic respiration produces only **118 kJ** per gram molecule of glucose, because the glucose is only partly oxidized to inorganic compounds. It cannot continue for long periods because of the build-up of poisonous lactic acid.

Occurrence of anaerobic respiration

Anaerobic respiration occurs naturally in the following.

Human tissues Anaerobic respiration occurs in tissues such as muscles during vigorous exercise, e.g. sprinting. Oxygen cannot usually be delivered to the contracting muscle cells quickly enough to oxidize all of the available glucose.

Lactic acid builds up rapidly under these conditions, and eventually causes **muscle fatigue**. This is the inability of muscles to continue contracting, due to an accumulation of lactic acid in the absence of oxygen.

For **recovery after exercise**, deep breathing is necessary to provide sufficient oxygen to break down the lactic acid:

$$\text{Lactic acid} + \text{Oxygen} \xrightarrow[\text{mitochondria}]{\text{Enzymes in}} \text{Carbon Dioxide} + \text{Water} + \text{Energy}$$

The **oxygen debt** is the volume of extra oxygen required to break down the lactic acid which builds up during vigorous exercise.

Plants Anaerobic respiration occurs in plants such as yeast whenever oxygen is lacking. However, the main product is **ethanol**, i.e. the alcohol found in alcoholic drinks. Yeast is therefore used to **ferment** (break down) sugar and plant products (grapes, barley, etc.) under anaerobic conditions to make wine, whisky, beer, etc.:

$$\text{Glucose} \xrightarrow[\text{cytoplasm}]{\text{Enzymes in}} \text{Ethanol} + \text{Carbon dioxide} + \text{Energy}$$

ENERGY PRODUCTION AND TRANSFER DURING RESPIRATION

The energy produced during respiration is used to manufacture a substance called **adenosine triphosphate (ATP)**. ATP consists of an adenosine molecule joined to three phosphate ions.

During respiration, ATP is produced from adenosine diphosphate (ADP):

$$\underset{\text{(ADP)}}{\text{A—P—P}} + \underset{\substack{\text{(phosphate} \\ \text{ion)}}}{\text{P}} + \underset{\substack{\text{(from} \\ \text{respiration)}}}{\text{Energy}} \longrightarrow \underset{\text{(ATP)}}{\text{A—P—P—P}}$$

ATP diffuses out of the mitochondria into all parts of the cell. When energy is required by the cell to carry out work, ATP is immediately broken down again:

$$\text{ATP} \longrightarrow \text{ADP} + \text{P} + \text{Energy}$$

AEROBIC AND ANAEROBIC RESPIRATION COMPARED

Table 3.3 Comparison of aerobic and anaerobic respiration

	Aerobic	Anaerobic
Oxygen required?	Yes	No
Energy produced per gram molecule of glucose	2830 kJ, equivalent to 38 ATP molecules	118 kJ, equivalent to 2 ATP molecules
Chemical products	Inorganic – carbon dioxide and water only	Organic – lactic acid or ethanol
Essential enzymes are situated in the:	Mitochondria	Cytoplasm generally
Importance	Main source of energy for almost all living cells. Used commercially to produce bread, etc.	An inefficient source of energy. Occurs whenever oxygen is lacking, e.g. in muscles during vigorous exercise or fermentation of sugars to produce ethanol.

Cells as the basic unit of life

3.6 DIFFUSION, OSMOSIS AND ACTIVE TRANSPORT

This section explains how molecules move within and between cells.

1. following a meal, glucose molecules arrive in the liver in large quantities
2. the glucose molecules tend to diffuse from a high to to low concentration

A – high concentration
B
C – low concentration

glucose molecules from blood capillaries

typical active cell (eg liver cell)

cell membrane

concentration of glucose molecules in the cell

molecules diffuse down the gradient

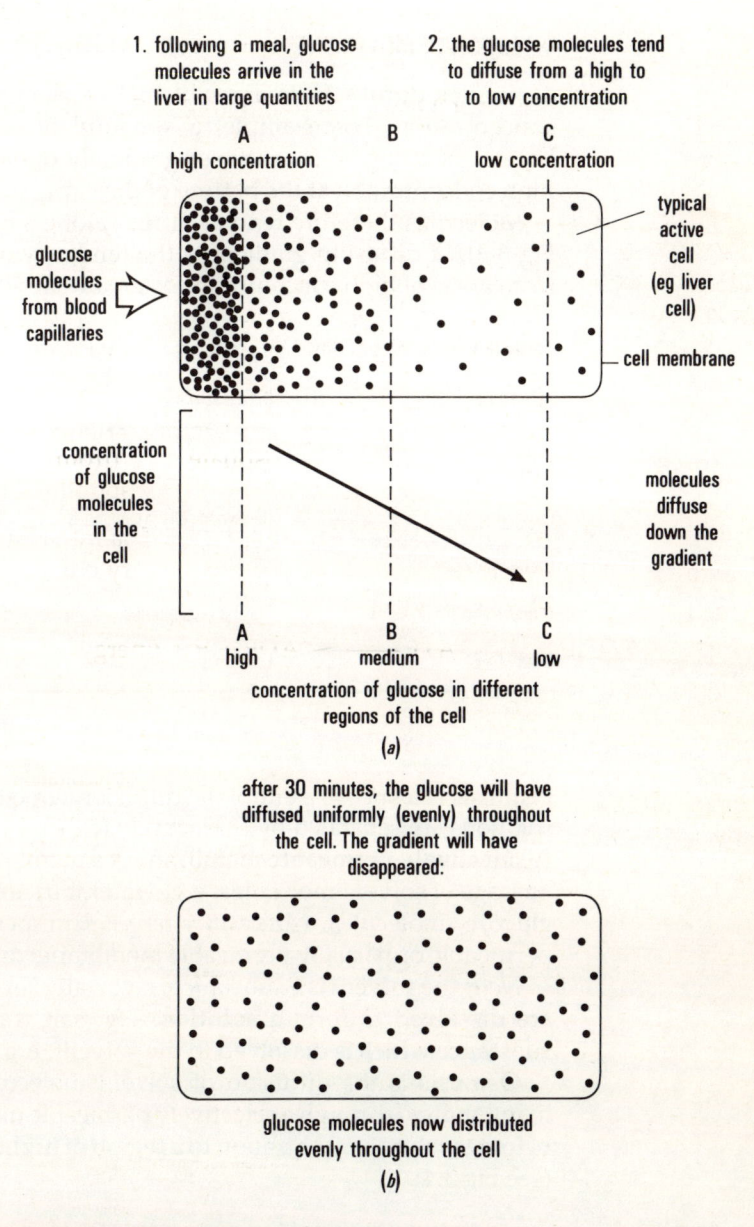

A high | B medium | C low
concentration of glucose in different regions of the cell
(a)

after 30 minutes, the glucose will have diffused uniformly (evenly) throughout the cell. The gradient will have disappeared:

glucose molecules now distributed evenly throughout the cell
(b)

Fig 3.3 Diffusion gradients in cells. (a) How a diffusion gradient is set up. (b) Consequences of a diffusion gradient.

DIFFUSION

Diffusion is the natural tendency of molecules to move randomly through a liquid or gas, e.g. sugar molecules gradually spread out in a cup of tea, even without stirring.

Diffusion occurs in all liquids and is affected by temperature – the higher the temperature, the faster the movement.

DIRECTION OF MOVEMENT

Molecules diffuse from areas of high concentration to areas of low concentration. For example, a spoonful of sugar deposited at the bottom of a cup of tea diffuses gradually outwards from the area of high concentration at the bottom of the cup.

Molecules therefore tend to diffuse along a **diffusion gradient** (see Fig 3.3). A diffusion gradient is the tendency of molecules to diffuse from areas of high concentration to areas of low concentration.

Table 3.4 Examples of diffusion gradients in the body

Substance	Diffuses from	Diffuses to
Oxygen	Alveoli	Red blood cells in the capillaries
Oxygen	Red blood cells in capillaries	Tissues surrounding the capillaries
Carbon dioxide	All cells	Plasma in capillaries
Glucose and amino acids	Plasma in capillaries	Tissues surrounding the capillaries
Urea	Liver cells	Plasma in Capillaries

OSMOSIS

Osmosis is a special example of diffusion which occurs whenever two solutions are separated by a selectively (or semi-) permeable membrane. A **selectively permeable membrane** is a membrane which permits the passage of solvent molecules, e.g. water, but not solute, e.g. dissolved glucose, molecules. (*Alternative terms*: semi-permeable, differentially permeable or partially permeable membrane; dialysis membrane.)

Note: the **solvent** is a substance, e.g. water, in which other molecules are dissolved to form a **solution**, e.g. salt water. The **solute** is the substance which is dissolved in the solvent, e.g. sugar, salt.

Osmosis is the diffusion of solvent molecules only, i.e. water in living things, through a selectively permeable membrane from a region of **lower** solute concentration to a region of **higher** solute concentration (see Fig 3.4).

IMPORTANCE OF OSMOSIS IN LIVING CELLS

Osmosis can occur in almost all living cells because:
1. the cell membrane is selectively permeable;

Cells as the basic unit of life

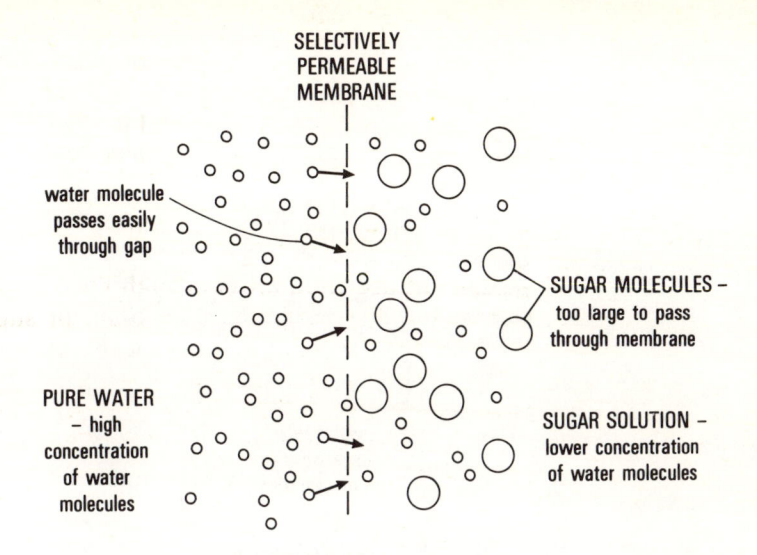

Fig 3.4 Osmosis: diffusion of water into sugar solution through a membrane.

2 the cytoplasm is basically a solution, consisting of glucose and amino acids dissolved in a solvent, i.e. water;
3 most cells are surrounded by tissue fluid, which is basically a weak (3.5%) solution of salts in water; normally, the concentration of tissue fluid is about the same as the cytoplasm.

EFFECTS OF OSMOSIS ON LIVING CELLS

1 If a living cell is placed in pure water, water will enter the cell, e.g. red blood cells placed in water swell until they burst. This explains why human cells can only be kept alive in saline solution (3.5% salt in water – the same salt concentration as occurs naturally in tissue fluid).
2 If a living cell is placed in strong salt or sugar solution, water is lost from the cell, e.g. red blood cells shrink until they collapse inwards. For this reason bacteria cannot live in foods with a high sugar or salt content (see page 333).

This explains why it is essential for body fluids, e.g. plasma, tissue fluids, etc.) to be maintained at the same concentration as the cells. The maintenance of constant concentrations of the body fluids is called osmoregulation (see page 198).

EFFECT ON OSMOSIS OF KILLING THE CELLS

Osmosis cannot occur in cells after they have been killed – the cell membrane is only selectively permeable while it is alive. However, osmosis does occur in artificial (non-living) selective membranes such as Visking tubing (see Fig 3.5).

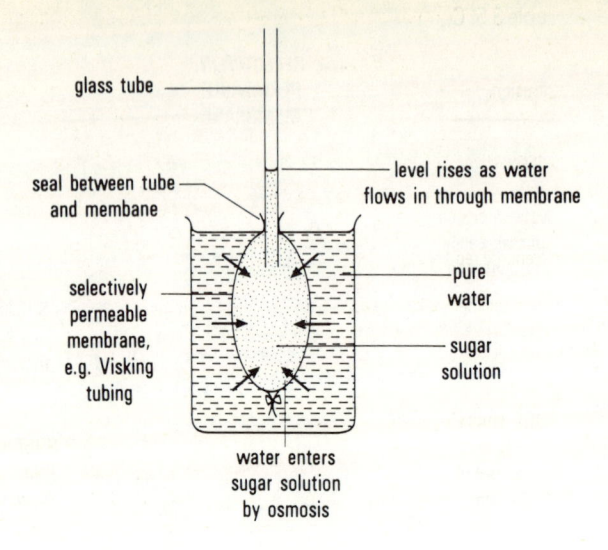

Fig 3.5 Osmosis in a non-living system.

WHEN DOES OSMOSIS STOP?

The flow of water from a weak solution into strong solution normally ceases only when the two solutions have reached the same strengths. However, if the strong solution is surrounded by a rigid wall, e.g. a plant cell wall, increasing pressure inside it may eventually prevent the entry of any further water molecules.

ACTIVE TRANSPORT

In some cases, molecules enter cells *against* a diffusion gradient, or they are taken in at a faster rate than occurs with simple diffuson. This is called active transport.

Active transport means the rapid transport of molecules by cells at rates faster than diffusion, requiring expenditure of energy by the cell. In effect, active transport is a form of cellular 'pumping'.

ADVANTAGES OF ACTIVE TRANSPORT

1 **Faster intake** of substances than can occur by diffusion, e.g. amino acids are absorbed from the small intestine partly by active transport.
2 **Selectivity.** The cell transports only those substances required for its needs at the time, whereas neither diffusion nor osmosis can be controlled by the cell.

Cells as the basic unit of life

Table 3.5 Comparison of passive transport (diffusion and osmosis) and active transport

Passive transport		Active transport
Diffusion	**Osmosis**	
Not selective.	Partially selective; cell membrane cannot prevent entry or exit of solvent molecules, e.g. water.	Selective; cell takes in only the substances needed at the time.
No energy required.	No energy required.	Energy is expended by the cell.
Living cell membrane not essential.	Living cell membrane essential (though can occur in artificial membranes).	Living cell membrane essential.
Any soluble molecule or the solvent itself may be transported.	Applies to solvent molecules only, e.g. water.	Applies to any type of soluble molecule.
Substances move down a concentration gradient.	Solvent moves from a weak solution to a strong solution.	Substances can be transported *against* a concentration gradient.

3.7 CHECKLIST

- Diagrams of animal and plant cells:
    - nucleus;
    - nuclear membrane;
    - cytoplasm;
    - cell wall;
    - mitochondria;
    - chloroplast;
    - cell vacuole.
- How to make a cheek-cell slide.
- Differences between animal and plant cells.
- Cell, tissue, organ, system.
- Enzymes:
    - four properties of enzymes;
    - examples of one extra-cellular and one intra-cellular enzyme.
- Cell (tissue) respiration:
    - aerobic respiration:
        - definition;
        - equation;
        - differences from anaerobic respiration;
    - anaerobic respiration;
        - definition;
        - equation;
        - lactic acid;
        - oxygen debt.
- Uses of respiration in bread and wine making.
- ATP and ADP.
- Diffusion:
    - diffusion gradient.

Human Biology

- Osmosis:
    - selectively (semi-permeable) membrane;
    - solvent;
    - solute;
    - solution.
- Active transport.

3.8 EXAM QUESTIONS

1. Name three structures found in plant cells, but not in animal cells. (3)
2. Explain how a typical animal cell may be modified in different ways to form THREE named tissues. (10) [Ox]
3. To investigate the effect of different temperatures on enzyme activity, an enzyme called catalase was used. This enzyme is found universally in living cells, especially in the liver, kidney and blood. Its action can be demonstrated by adding hydrogen peroxide to liver extract and measuring the volume of oxygen evolved. By keeping the liver extract at different temperatures the graph in Fig 3.6 was produced showing the different volumes of oxygen produced.

Fig 3.6

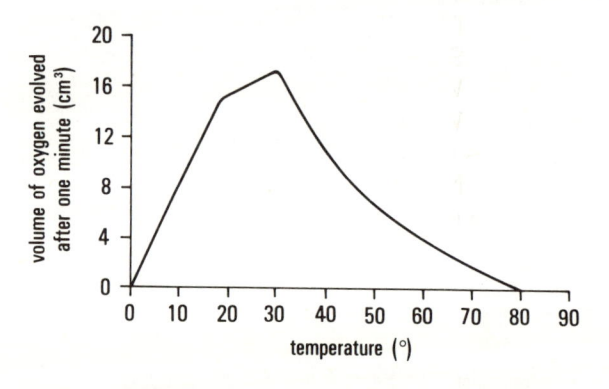

(a) What is the temperature at which this enzyme is most active? (1)
(b) Within the temperature range studied, what are the temperatures at which it is least active? (2)
(c) Between which two temperatures does an increase of 20°C make the least difference in the activity of the enzyme? (2)
(d) A sample of the liver extract kept at 0°C and another sample kept at 80°C were each brought to a temperature of 37°C and then tested with hydrogen peroxide. The results of the two samples were very different.

(i) Which sample would have caused the greater amount of oxygen to be evolved, the sample originally at 0°C or the one originally at 80°C? (2)
(ii) Explain this result. (4)

[SREB]

Cells as the basic unit of life 61

4. The following equation summarizes two chemical reactions.

$$\text{Glucose + Oxygen} \underset{B}{\overset{A}{\rightleftarrows}} \text{Carbon dioxide + Water + Energy}$$

(a) Name the reactions indicated by (i) arrow **A** (ii) arrow **B**. (2)
(b) Name the cell organelles in which (i) reaction **A** (ii) reaction **B** occurs. (2)
(c) (i) Name the energy-rich compound formed directly as a result of the reaction indicated by arrow **A**. (1)
(ii) Name the form of energy in the reaction indicated by arrow **B**. (1) [*JMB*]

5. (a) When glucose is burnt in air it yields energy in the form of heat and light very rapidly. How does this compare with the oxidation of glucose in living cells? (2) [*L*]
(b) How are the chemical substances ADP and ATP involved in gathering up the energy released in the oxidation of glucose in living cells? (3) [*L*]
(c) Why is anaerobic respiration much less efficient than aerobic at producing ATP? (2)

6. In the process of tissue (internal) respiration, ATP and CO_2 are products and oxygen is used up.
(a) Define tissue respiration. (1)
(b) State TWO uses of ATP in the cell. (2)
(c) Where does the carbon (C) in the CO_2 come from? (2)
(d) What change takes place in tissue respiration if the cell receives no oxygen? (2)
(e) Name ONE tissue with a high rate of respiration; and ONE tissue with a low rate of respiration. (2) [*NI*]

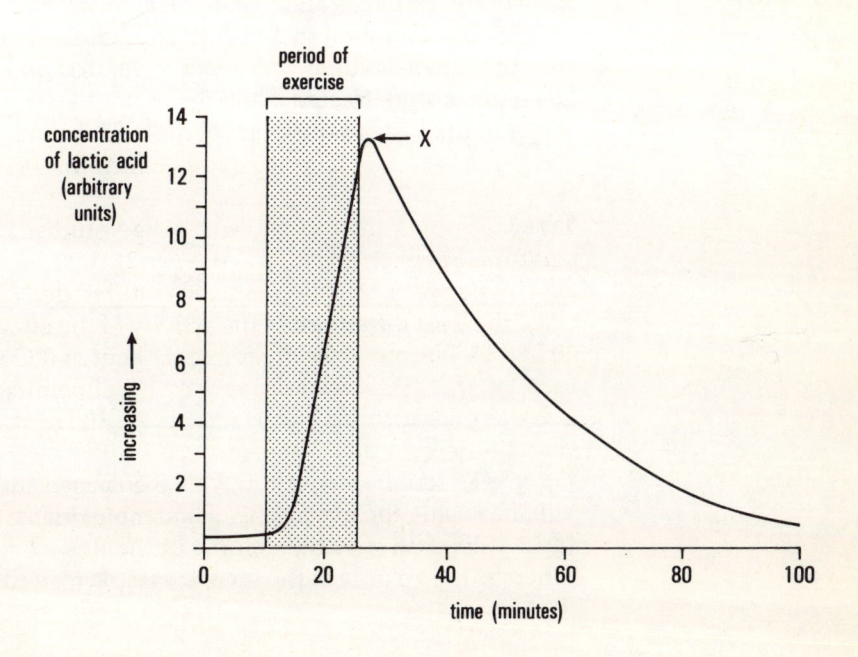

Fig 3.7

7   Fig 3.7 shows the effects of exercise on the concentration of lactic acid in the blood.
    (a)   Suppose the curve for oxygen intake was plotted on the same graph. Describe the appearance of the resulting curve. (2)
    (b)   Why does the lactic acid level continue to rise in the blood after exercise ceases? (2)
    (c)   Explain the reasons for the change in lactic acid concentration from point X onwards. (2)

8   Cell respiration in yeast is used in industry in the manufacture of two entirely different products.
    (a)   Name the two different products. (2)
    (b)   State the useful substance produced by the yeast cells in each case. (2)
    (c)   Explain the differences in the conditions under which respiration occurs, in each case. (2)

9   Examination of fibres from muscles shows the presence of mitochondria. Fibres which can contract for long periods of time have many mitochondria, fibres which tire easily have few.
    (a)   State the function of mitochondria. (1)
    (b)   Name a mineral element connected with this function. (1)
    (c)   Explain why a fibre with few mitochondria may tire long before a fibre with many. (2)   [NI]

10 (a)   Define the term 'diffusion'. Explain the part diffusion plays in osmosis and dialysis. (10)
    (b)   How would you set up an experiment to find out if a membrane was permeable to water but not to glucose? (8)
    (c)   Briefly explain how and where in the body glucose passes through membranes. (11)   [Ox]

11 The volume of 20 sultanas was measured by displacement, using a measuring cylinder and water. The sultanas were then placed in strong sugar solution in a beaker and left for 24 hours. At the end of that time their volume was again measured and recorded. A further 20 sultanas were treated similarly except that they were kept in water for 24 hours instead of sugar solution. The results are shown in Table 3.6.

Table 3.6

	Sultanas in sugar solution	Sultanas in water
Volume at beginning	8.5 cm^3	8.7 cm^3
Volume after 24 hours	8.5 cm^3	12.5 cm^3

   (a)   Describe clearly how you would measure the volume of the sultanas using the measuring cylinder and water. (3)
   (b)   Explain why the volume of the first sample stayed the same, whereas the volume of the second sample rose considerably. (6)

Cells as the basic unit of life

(*c*) What would you expect to happen to the volume of the second sample if, when they had swollen to 12.5 cm^3, they were then transferred to the strong sugar solution for 24 hours? (4)

[*Ox*]

CHAPTER FOUR

THE SKELETON, MUSCLES AND MOVEMENT

CONTENTS

▶ **4.1 The skeleton: general functions and structure** 67
General functions of the skeleton 67
Axial and appendicular skeletons 67

▶ **4.2 Skull, backbone, ribs, limb girdles** 67
Skull 67
The vertebral column 69
The ribs 71
Limb girdles 71

▶ **4.3 Structure of bone and cartilage** 72
Bone 72
Cartilage 73

▶ **4.4 Joints** 74
Arthritis 74

▶ **4.5 How muscles work** 75
Tendons and ligaments 76
Bones as levers 77

▶ **4.6 Types of muscle** 77

Contents

4.7 Muscle tone, posture, lifting and bending — 79
Muscle tone 79
Posture 79
Lifting and bending 80

4.8 Care of the feet — 82
Young children 82
Teenagers and adults 82

4.9 Checklist — 83

4.10 Exam questions — 83

The skeleton, muscles and movement 67

4.1 THE SKELETON: GENERAL FUNCTIONS AND STRUCTURE

GENERAL FUNCTIONS OF THE SKELETON

1. **Support**. The skeleton supports the soft tissues so permitting an upright posture.
2. **Protection**. The skeleton protects the vital organs such as the heart, brain and spinal cord (see Table 4.1).
3. **Movement**. The bones provide a firm surface for the attachment of the muscles, and also act as levers.
4. **Manufacture of blood**. The cells of the red bone marrow produce red and white blood cells.

Hint: when answering the question 'What are the functions of the skeleton?', don't just write 'Support, protection, movement.' *Always* give complete sentences.

Table 4.1 Protective functions of the skeleton

Bone	Organs protected
Skull	Brain, eyes, internal ear
Rib cage	Heart and lungs
Vertebrae	Spinal cord
Pelvic girdle	Uterus, bladder

AXIAL AND APPENDICULAR SKELETONS

The central core of the skeleton (spine, skull, ribs, sternum) is the **axial skeleton**. The remaining bones form the **appendicular skeleton**.

4.2 SKULL, BACKBONE, RIBS AND LIMB GIRDLES

SKULL

The structure of the skull is shown in Fig 4.2.

Human Biology

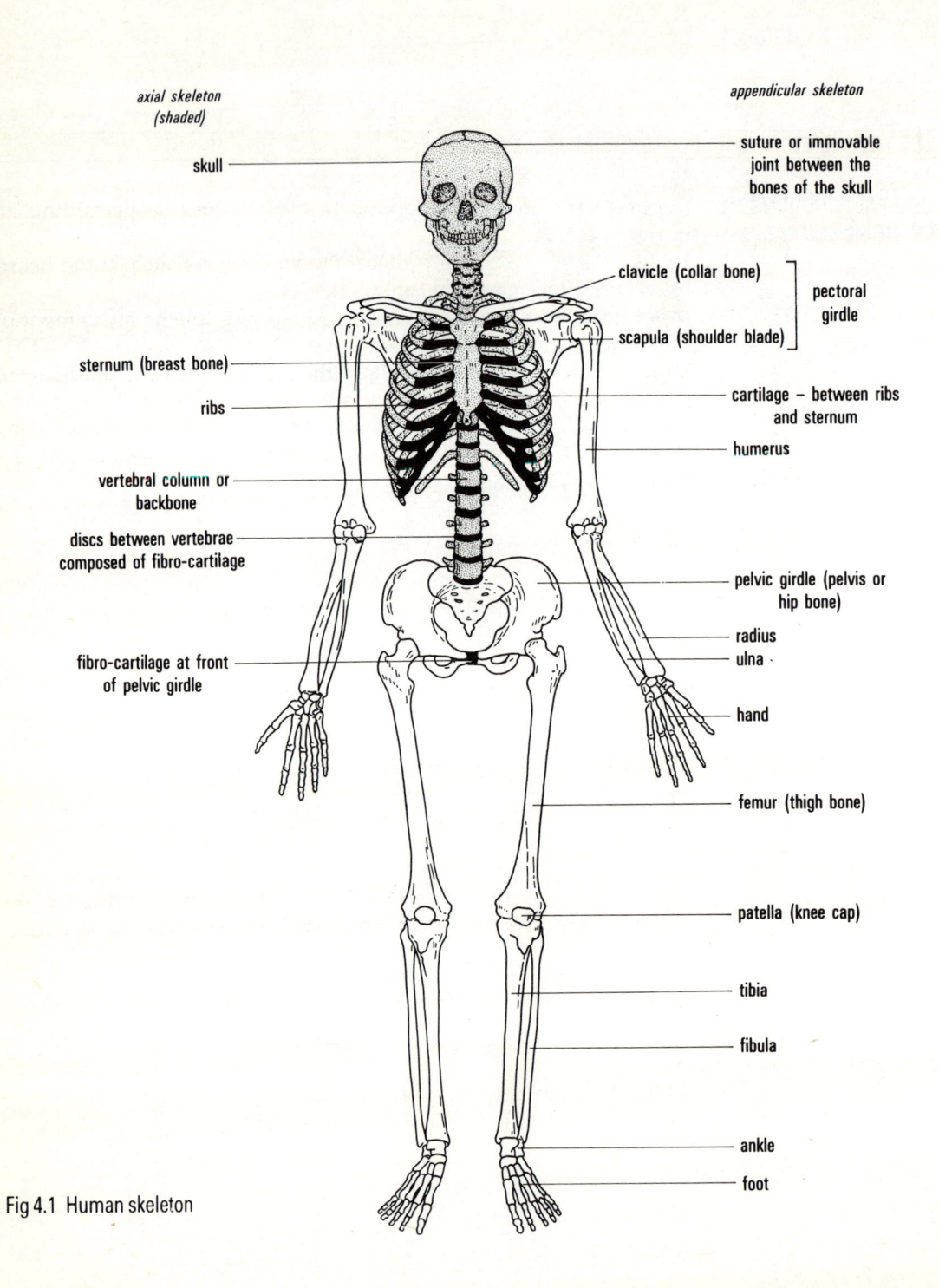

axial skeleton (shaded)   *appendicular skeleton*

- skull — suture or immovable joint between the bones of the skull
- clavicle (collar bone) ⎫
- scapula (shoulder blade) ⎬ pectoral girdle
- sternum (breast bone)
- ribs
- cartilage – between ribs and sternum
- humerus
- vertebral column or backbone
- discs between vertebrae composed of fibro-cartilage
- pelvic girdle (pelvis or hip bone)
- radius
- ulna
- hand
- fibro-cartilage at front of pelvic girdle
- femur (thigh bone)
- patella (knee cap)
- tibia
- fibula
- ankle
- foot

Fig 4.1 Human skeleton

The skeleton, muscles and movement

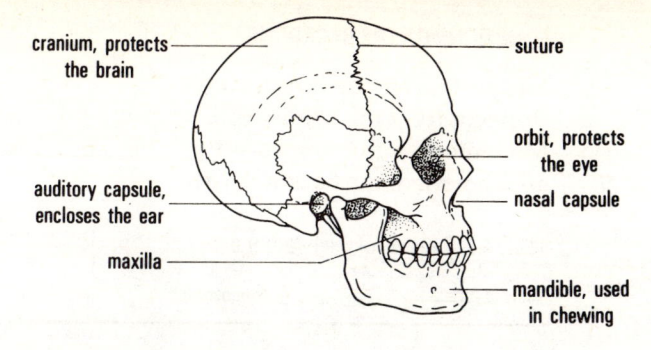

Fig 4.2 The human skull.

| **THE VERTEBRAL COLUMN (BACKBONE)** | This consists of 33 vertebrae, five of which are fused together (See Fig 4.3). The separate bones allow for flexibility when bending. |

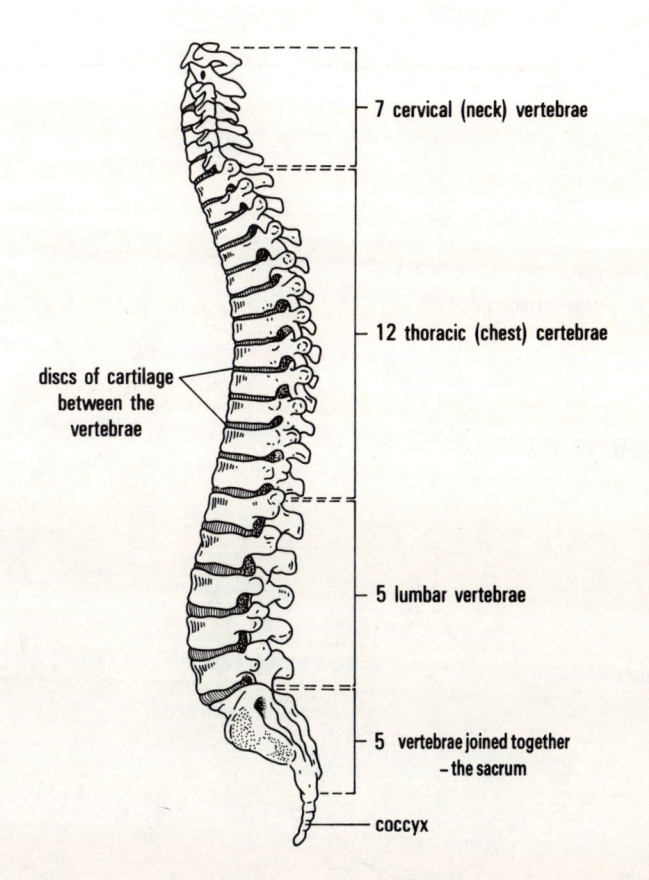

Fig 4.3 The backbone.

Human Biology

FUNCTIONS OF THE BACKBONE

1. **Support** for the body as a whole.
2. **Protection** for the spinal cord.
3. **Movement** – the spines on the vertebrae provide surfaces for the attachment of the back muscles.

Table 4.2 Regions of the backbone

Name of vertebra	Number	Special features
Cervical (neck) (see Fig 4.4)	7	Smallest of all because carry least weight.
Thoracic (chest) (see Fig 4.5)	12	Possess flat surfaces for articulation with the ribs (see Fig 4.7).
Lumbar (see Fig 4.6)	5	Largest because carry most weight.
Sacral (see Fig 4.3)	5 (fused together)	To support the pelvic girdle (see Fig 4.8).

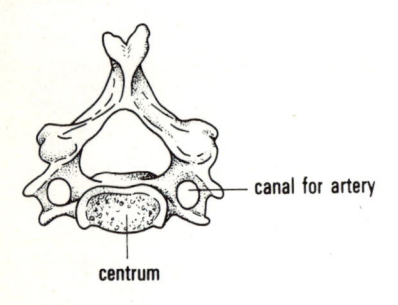

Fig 4.4 Cervical vertebra

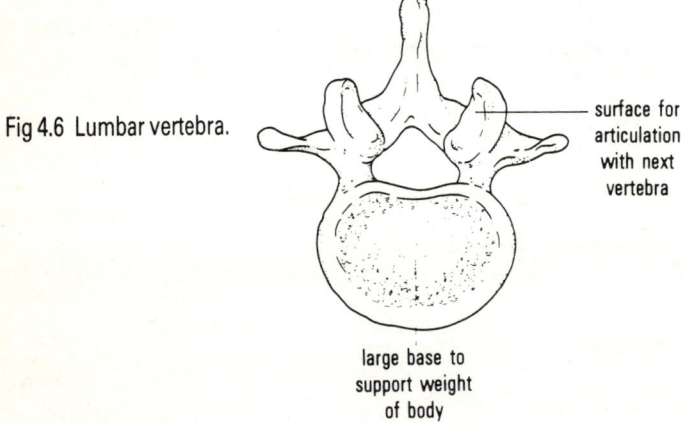

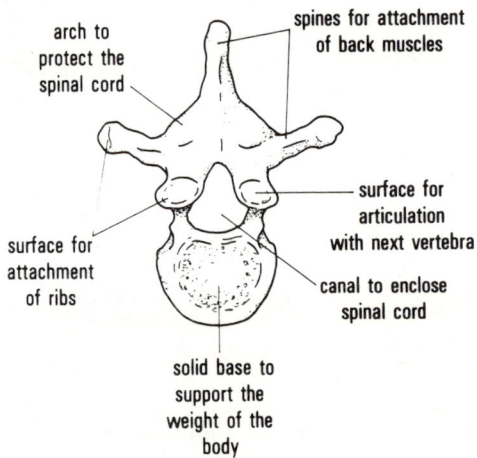

Fig 4.5 Thoracic vertebra – an example of a typical vertebra.

Fig 4.6 Lumbar vertebra.

The skeleton, muscles and movement

THE RIBS

There are 12 pairs of ribs. Ten pairs are joined to the sternum by cartilage, thus allowing free movement during breathing (see Fig 4.7). They also rock to and fro on the thoracic vertebrae (see Fig 4.5).

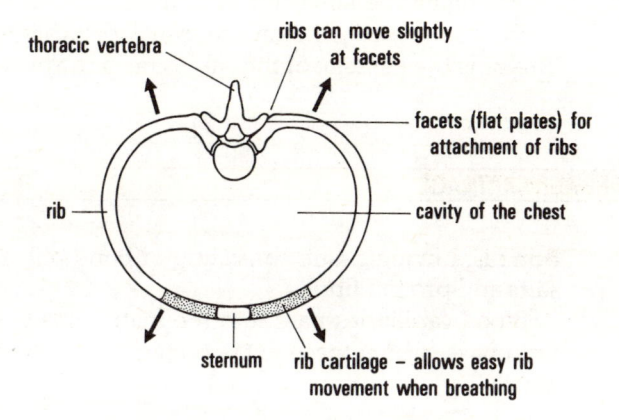

Fig 4.7 How the ribs are attached to the vertebrae.

LIMB GIRDLES

THE PECTORAL GIRDLE

The **pectoral girdle** consists of the clavicles (collar bones) and scapulas (shoulder blades).

The **functions of the scapulas** are to provide a broad flat surface for the attachment of the arm muscles and a socket for the articulation of the humerus.

The **function of the clavicles** is to provide support for the shoulders, so preventing them from collapsing inwards.

THE PELVIC GIRDLE

The **pelvic girdle** (see Fig 4.8) consists of several separate bones fused together in a ring for strength. The functions of the pelvic girdle are:

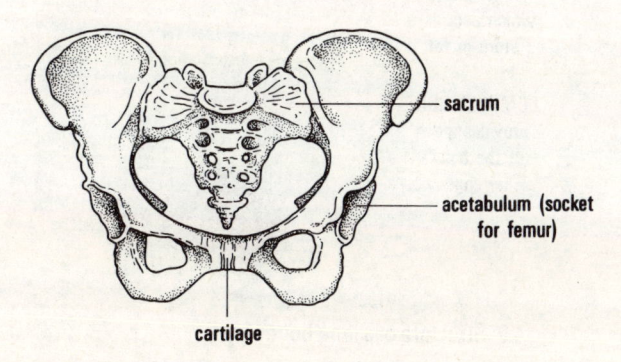

Fig 4.8 The pelvic girdle.

Human Biology

1. to provide a **socket** for articulation with the femur;
2. to **transmit the thrust** from the leg bones to the backbone, and to **transmit the weight** of the body from the backbone to the leg bones;
3. to provide a surface for **muscle attachment**;
4. to **protect** the organs of the lower abdomen.

In women the pelvic girdle is wider than in men, and the cartilage connection (see Fig 4.8) at the front opens slightly during childbirth. This aids the passage of the baby's head during birth.

4.3 STRUCTURE OF BONE AND CARTILAGE

BONE

Bone is a living tissue consisting of bone cells in a matrix of calcium salts and protein fibres.

Blood capillaries pass into the matrix inside special canals. Tissue fluid passes from these to the bone cells through smaller canals in the matrix.

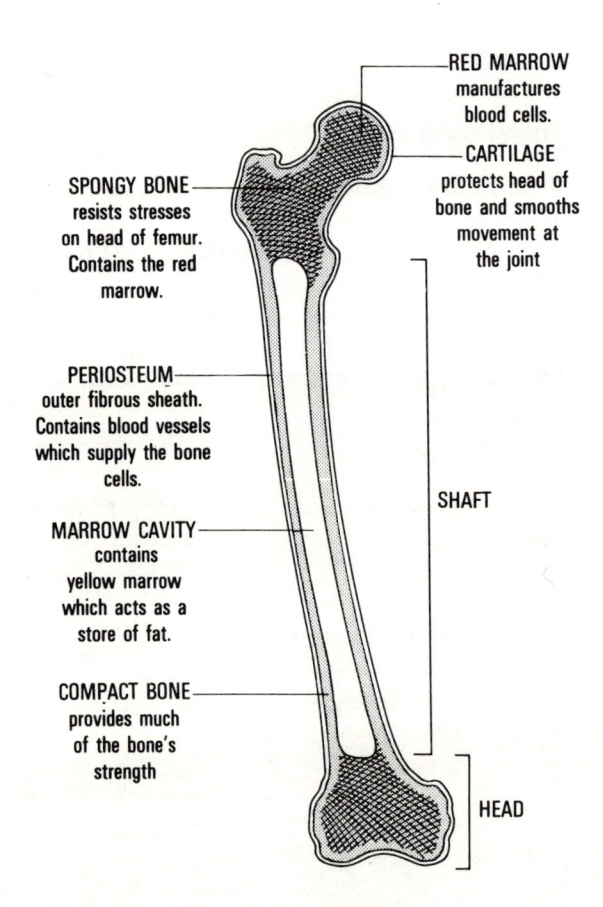

Fig 4.9 Structure of a long bone.

The skeleton, muscles and movement

Bone consists of:
- 50 per cent water
- 50 per cent solids
  - 33 per cent calcium salts (mainly calcium phosphate)
  - 17 per cent protein

The structure of a typical long bone is shown in Fig 4.9.

EXPERIMENTS WITH BONES

To prove that bone contains mineral salts

Leave one piece of bone in dilute hydrochloric acid and a second piece in water (for 2 days).

Result: the bone in the acid becomes soft and rubbery because the salts dissolve in the acid. (Note: wash carefully before handling.)

To prove that bone contains organic material

Burn in a bunsen flame.

Result: the bone turns to ash as the organic material burns off.

CARTILAGE ('GRISTLE')
M, APH (H) only

DIFFERENCES BETWEEN CARTILAGE AND BONE

Cartilage consists of cells in a protein matrix. It is therefore similar to bone but lacks the mineral salts. This makes it weaker than bone but much more **flexible**.

CONVERSION OF CARTILAGE TO BONE (OSSIFICATION)

The skeleton of the foetus consists entirely of cartilage in the early stages. Later, bone cells invade the protein matrix and lay down hard mineral salts to form bone.

POSITION OF CARTILAGE IN THE BODY

In adults, cartilage is found wherever flexibility is important. This includes:
- ear pinnae (outer ear flaps);
- ends of long bones;
- junction between ribs and sternum;
- discs between the vertebra;
- trachea;
- nose (try bending it);
- junction at the front of the pelvic girdle.

Human Biology

4.4 JOINTS

The various categories of joints are shown in Fig 4.10, while Fig 4.11 shows a typical synovial joint – in this case the elbow joint.

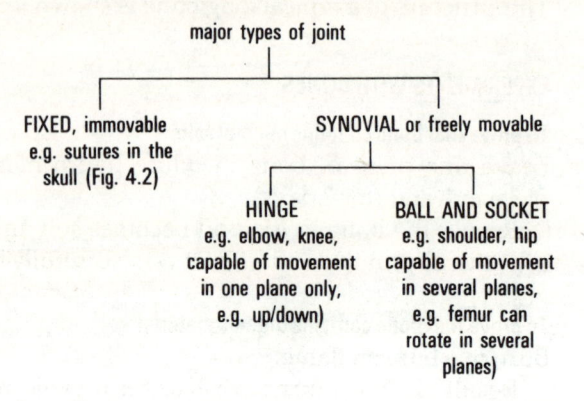

```
              major types of joint
              ┌────────────┴────────────┐
       FIXED, immovable         SYNOVIAL or freely movable
       e.g. sutures in the      ┌────────────┴────────────┐
       skull (Fig. 4.2)       HINGE              BALL AND SOCKET
                          e.g. elbow, knee,      e.g. shoulder, hip
                          capable of movement    capable of movement
                          in one plane only,     in several planes,
                          e.g. up/down)          e.g. femur can
                                                 rotate in several
                                                 planes)
```

Fig 4.10 Different types of joint.

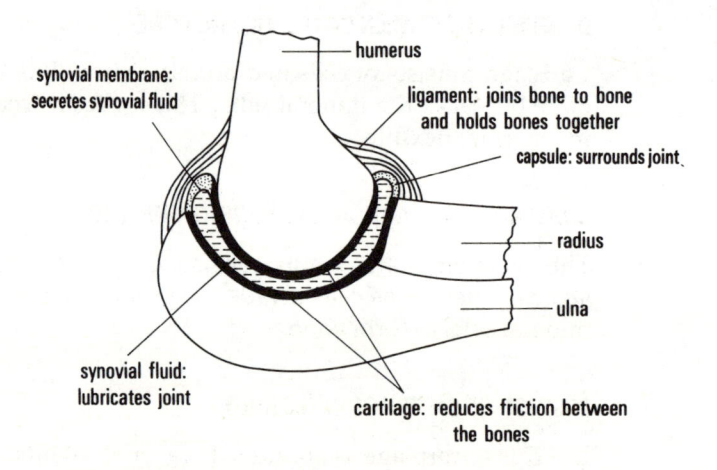

Fig 4.11 Section through a synovial joint – the elbow.

Labels: humerus; synovial membrane: secretes synovial fluid; ligament: joins bone to bone and holds bones together; capsule: surrounds joint; radius; ulna; synovial fluid: lubricates joint; cartilage: reduces friction between the bones.

ARTHRITIS

Arthritis is the name for a group of diseases which affect the joints.

Osteo-arthritis is the wearing away of the cartilage in the joints with increasing age. Almost everyone over 60 suffers from it to some extent. It causes pain, stiffness and immobility, and chiefly affects the hips, knees, fingers and backbone.

The skeleton, muscles and movement

4.5 HOW MUSCLES WORK

Muscles can *only* contract and relax. Muscle fibres contract when stimulated by a nerve impulse. Contraction requires expenditure of energy, produced by cell respiration inside the muscle.

An **antagonistic pair** of muscles oppose each other's actions so that when one contracts, the other relaxes. For example, when the biceps contracts, the triceps relaxes (see Fig 4.12). The **flexor** muscle in an antagonistic pair bends the limb, e.g. biceps; the **extensor** muscle straightens the limb.

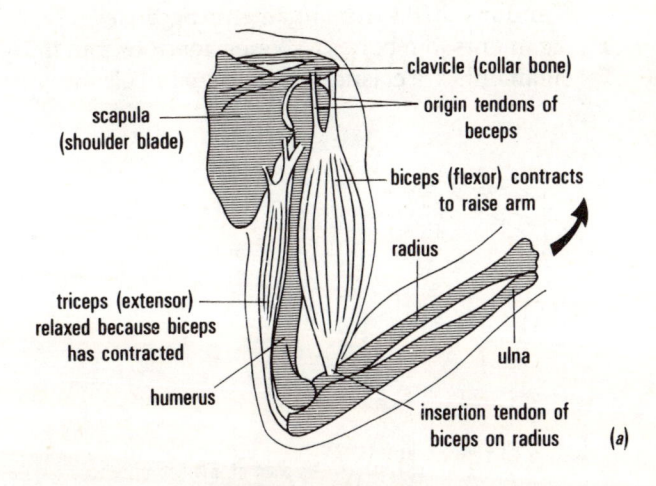

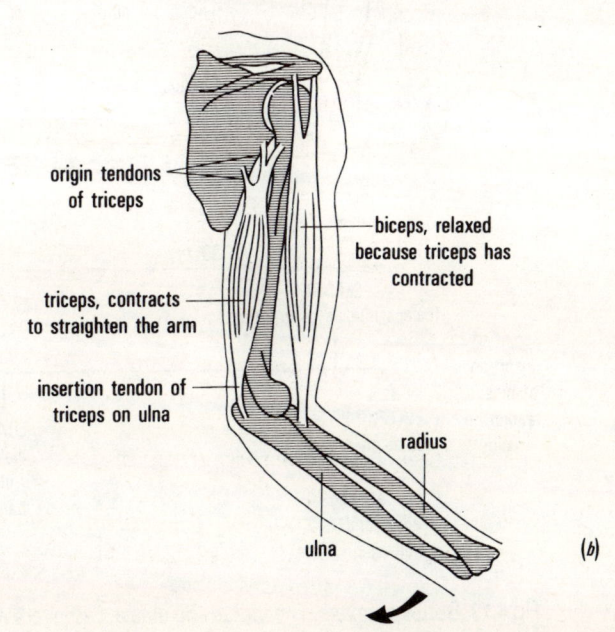

Fig 4.12 Antagonistic muscles of the forearm. (*a*) Biceps contracted, triceps relaxed, arm bends. (*b*) Triceps contracted, biceps relaxed, arm straightens.

Human Biology

The **origin tendon** of a muscle joins the muscle to the bones which are not moved by that muscle, e.g. biceps to scapula. The **insertion tendon** of a muscle joins the muscle to the bones which are moved when the same muscle contracts, e.g. biceps to radius.

Remember: muscles can only bring about movement by contracting. They always pull on bones – and never 'push', 'tighten', 'expand' or 'stretch'. 'Contract' and 'relax' are the only correct words to use when describing the action of muscles.

TENDONS AND LIGAMENTS

Tendons differ from ligaments because:
1. ligaments join bones to bones; tendons join muscles to bones;
2. ligaments are elastic; tendons are not elastic.

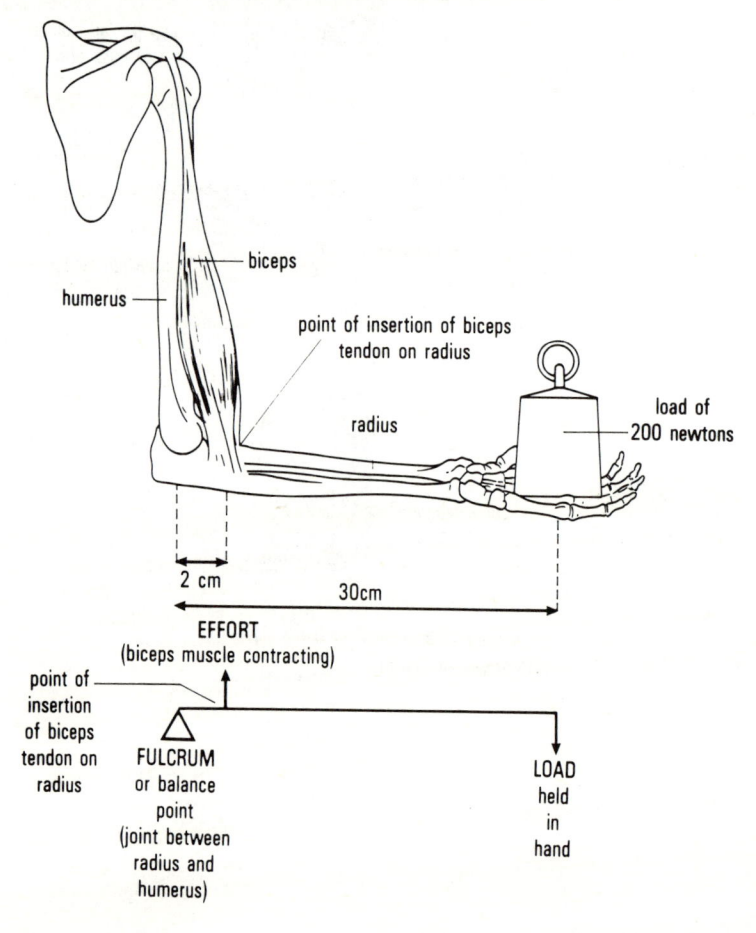

Fig 4.13 Bones as levers. The radius and ulna act as levers with the biceps and triceps muscles. (APH only)

The skeleton, muscles and movement

BONES AS LEVERS
APH only

The radius and ulna act as **levers**, operated by the biceps and triceps muscles (see Fig 4.13). This lever system is designed to give a large movement of a **load** (the arm) for a small movement of the **effort** (biceps). This results in a low **mechanical advantage** (load divided by effort).

To calculate the effort (E), using the figures in Fig. 4.13:

$$E \times \frac{\text{Distance of effort}}{\text{from fulcrum}} = \text{Load } (L) \times \frac{\text{Distance of load}}{\text{from fulcrum}}$$

$$E \times 2 = 200 \times 30 \text{ newtons}$$

$$E = \frac{200 \times 30}{2}$$

$$= 3000 \text{ N}$$

The mechanical advantage is low because the effort required is much larger than the load.

4.6 TYPES OF MUSCLE

Table 4.3 Different kinds of muscle

Type	Alternative names	Function and position in body	Control
Skeletal (see Fig 4.14)	Voluntary Striated Striped	1 Work in antagonistic pairs to move bones. 2 Attached to bones.	Controlled by conscious thought (voluntary action).
Smooth (see Fig. 4.15)	Involuntary	1 Carry out fast automatic contractions. Often essential to regulate the flow of liquids through tubes. 2 Found in the walls of blood vessels, the gut (see Fig 4.16), the iris.	Under unconscious automatic control (involuntary).
Cardiac (see Fig 4.17)	Heart	1 Responsible for the contractions of the heart. 2 Found only in the heart.	Automatic, unconscious. Can beat for a lifetime without becoming fatigued.

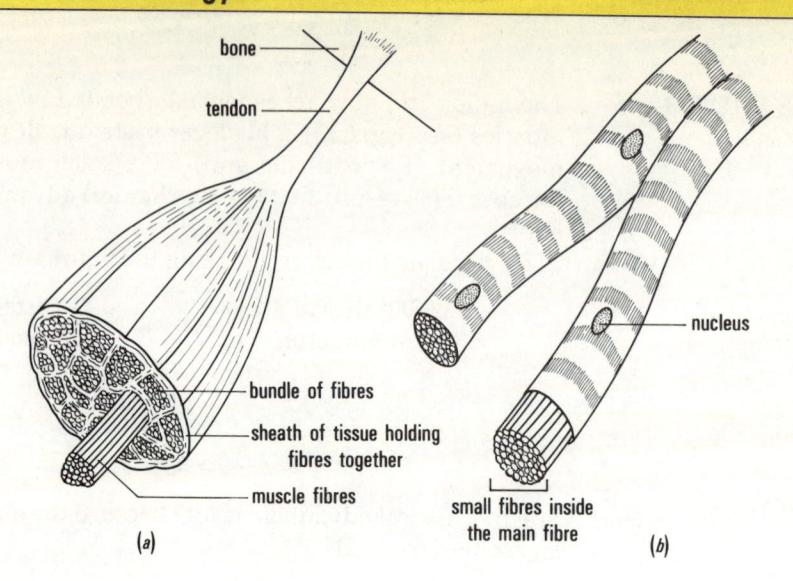

Fig 4.14 Structure of skeletal muscle. (a) Structure of a skeletal muscle. (b) Two fibres from skeletal muscle ×1000.

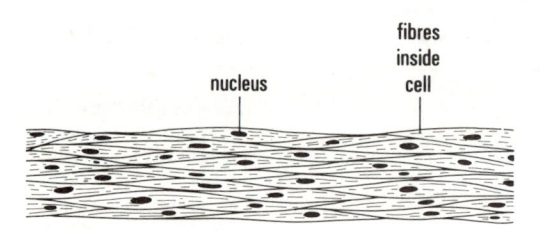

Fig 4.15 Smooth muscle cells ×1000. These cells are found in circular and longitudinal sheets; the circular muscles act as antagonists to the longitudinal muscles, and vice versa (see Fig 4.16).

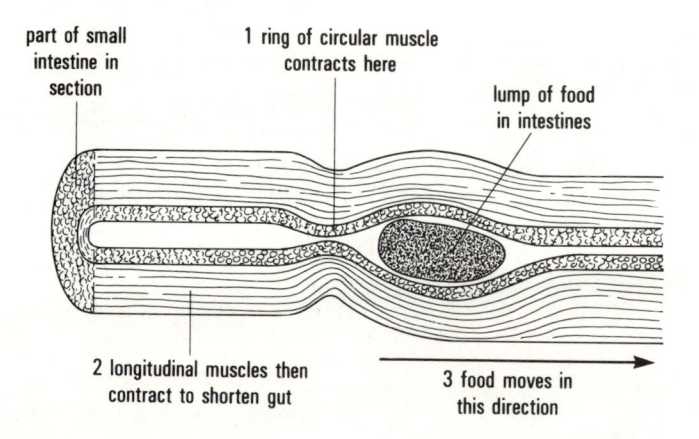

Fig 4.16 How two layers of smooth muscle act as antagonists – peristalsis.

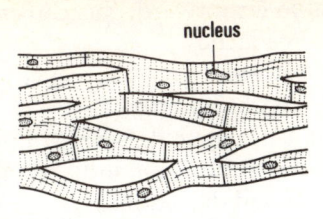

Fig 4.17 Structure of cardiac muscle ×1000.

4.7 MUSCLE TONE, POSTURE, LIFTING AND BENDING

MUSCLE TONE

Muscle tone is the name given to the waves of contraction which create a permanent state of slight tension in all living muscles.

Muscle tone is maintained by the alternate contraction and relaxation of neighbouring muscle fibres. At any moment, a few fibres in every muscle are contracted. This is sufficient to create a state of slight tension in the muscle, but not enough to cause the whole muscle to contract.

The advantages of muscle tone are:
1. the muscles are maintained in a permanently active state and so are capable of rapid contraction when required;
2. muscle tone keeps the body upright and the internal organs in position.

LOSS OF MUSCLE TONE

Muscle tone is lost with increasing age and with lack of exercise, both of which lead to soft 'flabby' muscles.

Muscle tone is also lost as a result of **muscle fatigue** (see page 53). Contraction will only re-start after a brief rest period. Paralysis of a complete muscle due to fatigue is called '**cramp**'.

POSTURE
S. W. L/EA only

Muscle tone in the back and leg muscles keeps the body upright and balanced on two feet. In the best position for good posture (see Fig 4.18) when standing or sitting:
1. the head is held directly above the body's centre of gravity in the pelvic girdle;
2. the spine is slightly curved.

ADVANTAGES OF CORRECT POSTURE

1. Minimum energy is needed to keep the body upright. Bad posture requires extra muscle contractions to maintain balance, leading to fatigue and backache.

2. If the skull is held too far forward, this can cause fatigue in the neck muscles, leading to headaches.
3. Bad posture over several years can cause a deformed backbone, resulting in a permanently bent back.
4. It can also cause flat feet, due to flattening of the arches in the feet.
5. Leaning forward cramps the chest and abdomen, so interfering with breathing movements and digestion.
6. Leaning too far back, so creating a hollow back, results in the stomach being pushed forwards. This causes slack abdominal muscles.

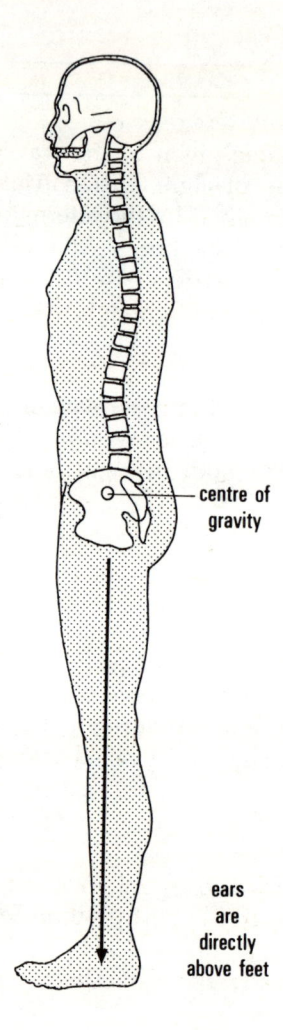

Fig 4.18 Correct curvature of the spine.

LIFTING AND BENDING
S. W. L/EA only

Poor lifting technique can cause fatigued back muscles and even a burst ('slipped') disc.

The skeleton, muscles and movement

The cartilage discs in the backbone are liable to burst because they are designed to resist compression, i.e. being 'squashed', but not tension, i.e. being 'stretched'. To prevent this, the backbone should be kept as straight as possible when lifting (see Fig 4.19). This allows each vertebra to support the bones above it and also reduces the risk of the discs being stretched.

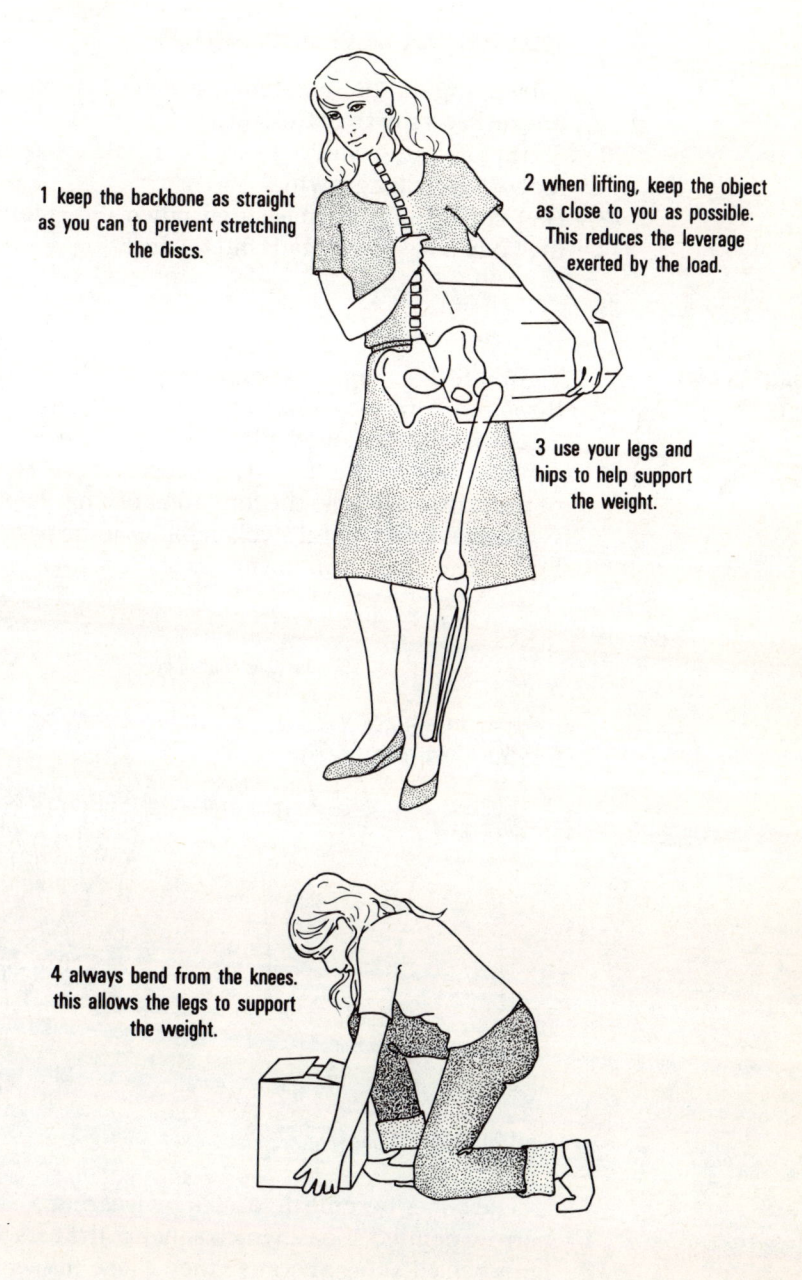

1 keep the backbone as straight as you can to prevent stretching the discs.

2 when lifting, keep the object as close to you as possible. This reduces the leverage exerted by the load.

3 use your legs and hips to help support the weight.

4 always bend from the knees. this allows the legs to support the weight.

Fig 4.19 Safe lifting.

Human Biology

4.8 CARE OF THE FEET

YOUNG CHILDREN
S only

The growing bones of children contain a high proportion of flexible cartilage. This means that tight-fitting shoes can permanently damage children's feet by deforming the cartilage.

RULES FOR THE CARE OF CHILDREN'S FEET

1. Babies should go **barefoot** as much as possible, to allow rapid unchecked growth of the feet.
2. Shoes for young children should be **half a size larger** than the child's foot, to allow for growth.
3. Feet should only be measured when the child is **standing**, because the body's weight spreads out the feet.

TEENAGERS AND ADULTS

Tightly-fitting and wrongly-shaped shoes can cause problems throughout life, especially corns and bunions.

Corns are hardened pieces of skin caused by tight-fitting shoes rubbing against the toes. This causes active growth in the epidermis of the skin, leading to the formation of a hard painful patch of skin.

Bunions are painful swollen joints at the base of the big toe, caused by deformed bones in the toes (see Fig 4.20).

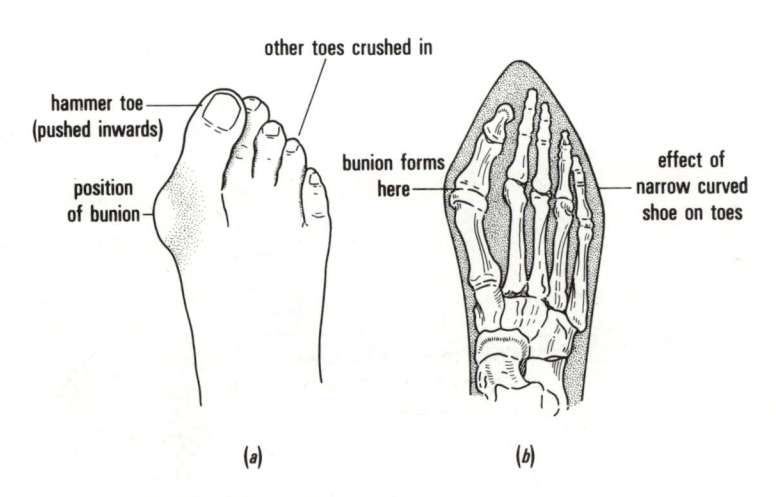

Fig 4.20 How bunions form.

The bones become deformed by wearing:
1. narrow pointed shoes, which squeeze the toes together;
2. high-heeled shoes, because they cause the weight of the body to be forced forward on to the toes.

The skeleton, muscles and movement

4.9 CHECKLIST

- The skeleton:
    - four functions;
    - axial/appendicular (L/EA only);
    - names of bones as in Fig 4.1.
- Skull.
- Vertebral column:
    - three functions;
    - types of vertebra.
- Limb girdles, pelvic/pectoral.
- Structure of a long bone (Fig 4.9).
- Bone and cartilage as tissues.
- Experiments on the composition of bone.
- Joints:
    - synovial;
    - fixed;
    - hinge;
    - ball and socket.
- Arthritis.
- Muscles:
    - antagonistic pairs;
    - flexor/extensor;
    - origin/insertion.
- Ligaments and tendons.
- Types of muscle:
    - skeletal;
    - smooth;
    - cardiac.
- Muscle tone
- Posture
- Lifting and bending.
- Childrens' feet.
- Corns and bunions.

4.10 EXAM QUESTIONS

1 (a) What are the functions of the skeleton? (8)
   (b) List the components of (i) the axial (ii) the appendicular skeleton. (8)
2 (a) State three functions common to all vertebrae. (3)
   (b) Name the main regions of the vertebral column and for each region named give one function which is not carried out by any of the other regions. (8) [WJ]
3 What is the functional importance of the ribs and thoracic vertebra together forming a movable joint? (3) [WJ]
4 (a) State one difference between cartilage and bone. (1)

(b) How could you show by experiments that bone contains
(i) mineral salts
(ii) organic substances? (4)

5   In Fig 4.21:

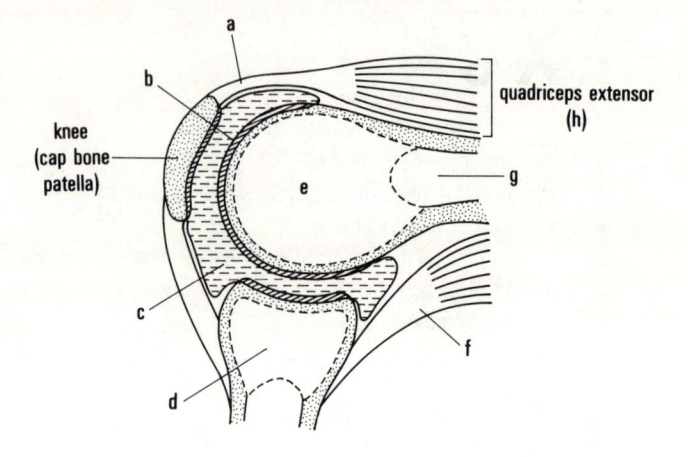

[Figure 4.21: diagram of knee joint with labels a, b, c, d, e, f, g, h; knee (cap bone patella); quadriceps extensor (h)]

(a) Name the structures labelled a, c, e and g. (4)
(b) State the tissues which make up the structures d and b. (2)
(c) What is the main function of g? (1)
(d) A group of muscles known as the quadriceps extensor, is attached as shown.
   (i) What effect will its contraction have on the knee joint? (1)
   (ii) Why is this muscle enlarged in professional cyclists? (2)
(e) What arrangement of structures in the knee joint allows forward and backward movement, but prevents sideways bending? (2)
(f) In osteo-arthritis, the tissue b is often absent so that movement is painful. Explain why this should be. (2) [NI]
(g) Which structure is the antagonist to the quadriceps extensor h? (1)

6   Describe the actions of the musculoskeletal system in raising the right hand to touch the right shoulder and lowering it again. (20)
[L]

7   (a) What are the benefits of good muscle tone? (2)
   (b) What are the advantages of correct posture? (3)
   (c) Why is it desirable to lift heavy objects as close to the body as possible? (2)
   (d) State three other rules for safe lifting. (3)

8   (a) Why are children's feet more easily damaged than adults? (1)
   (b) How can this be prevented? (3)
   (c) How may the frequent wearing of narrow high-heeled shoes damage the feet? (2)

CHAPTER FIVE 85

BREATHING AND GAS EXCHANGE

CONTENTS

▶ **5.1 Breathing and respiration** 87
Definitions   87

▶ **5.2 Structure and functions of the respiratory system** 88
Advantages of breathing through the nose   88
Structure and function of the respiratory organs   88
Common mistakes on breathing   89

▶ **5.3 The mechanism of breathing** 89
Inspiration   89
Expiration   90

▶ **5.4 Measuring lung capacity** 90
Effects of exercise on breathing   91

▶ **5.5 Gas exchange in the alveoli** 91
The alveoli   92
Inspired and expired air   93

▶ **5.6 Experiments to compare expired and inspired air** 93

▶ **5.7 Control of the breathing rate** 94

Contents

▶ **5.8 Artificial resuscitation** 94
Mouth-to-mouth ventilation 94

▶ **5.9 Checklist** 95

▶ **5.10 Exam questions** 95

Breathing and gas exchange

5.1 BREATHING AND RESPIRATION

DEFINITIONS

1. **Breathing** is the act of forcing air in and out of the lungs by the use of the diaphragm and the intercostal muscles. (It is also called external respiration.)
2. **Respiration** is the chemical process occurring in cells by which food molecules are oxidized to produce energy. (It is also called internal, tissue, or cell respiration.)

But *watch out* for the times when the word 'respiration' is used as if it means 'breathing'. For example, 'respiratory system' means 'breathing system', and 'artificial respiration' means 'reviving someone by mouth-to-mouth breathing'.

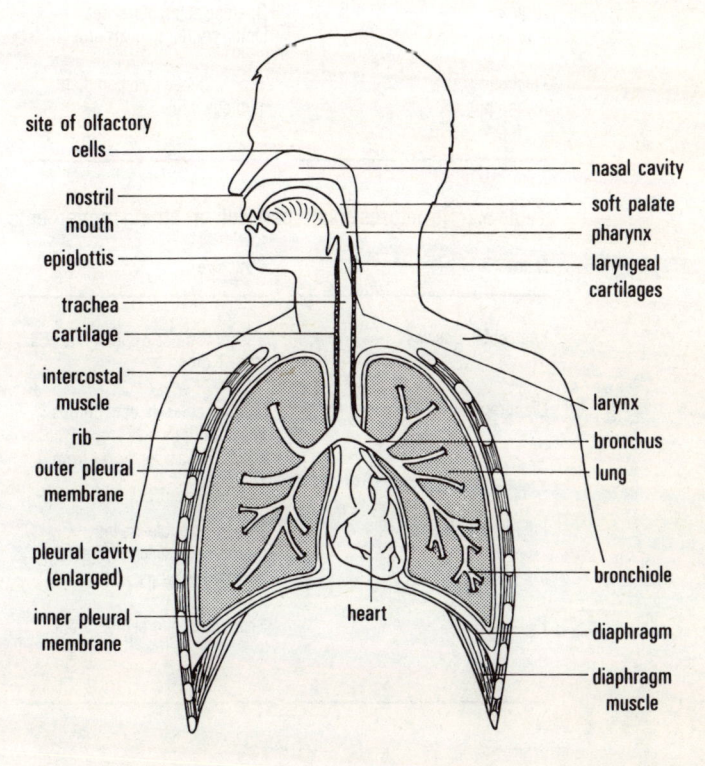

Fig 5.1 Sagittal section of head and thorax.

Human Biology

5.2 STRUCTURE AND FUNCTIONS OF THE RESPIRATORY SYSTEM

The **nose** contains narrow passages supported by cartilage and lined by mucous membrane (mucous membrane is shown in Fig 21.1 on page 302). It also contains olfactory cells, which are sensitive to smell.

ADVANTAGES OF BREATHING THROUGH THE NOSE

1. Because the narrow passages increase the surface area of the epithelium in the nose, incoming air is warmed and moistened.
2. Dust and microorganisms are trapped by the mucus, which is then propelled by the cilia to the throat for swallowing.
3. Chemicals in the air are detected by the olfactory cells.

Hint: No exchange of oxygen and carbon dioxide occurs in the nose.

STRUCTURE AND FUNCTION OF THE RESPIRATORY ORGANS

Fig 5.1 shows the overall structure of the respiratory organs.

Table 5.1 Air passages from throat to chest

Name	Structure	Function
Larynx	Opening at top of trachea. Lining contains vocal cords.	Vocal cords vibrate to produce sounds of voice.
Trachea (windpipe)	Tube stiffened by incomplete cartilage rings.	Carries air from mouth to bronchi. Cartilage rings keep trachea open, even when pressure falls.

Table 5.2 Structures concerned with breathing movements

Name	Structure	Function
Intercostal muscles	Sheets of muscle joining the ribs to each other.	Contract to move ribs up and down during breathing.
Diaphragm	Large circular sheet of fibrous tissue, with muscle around the edges. Separates thorax from abdomen.	Diaphragm muscle contracts to increase volume of thorax during breathing in.
Pleural membranes	Two thin double-walled membranes which completely enclose the lungs.	Maintain airtight seal around the lungs. If punctured, lung cannot expand.
Pleural fluid	Secreted by plural membranes.	Lubricates lung surface to ease lung movements during breathing.

Breathing and gas exchange

COMMON MISTAKES ON BREATHING

1. 'Lung muscles' do *not* exist. There are *no* voluntary muscles inside the lungs. All lung movements are caused by the diaphragm or intercostal muscles.
2. 'Air is sucked into the lungs.' This is *not* true. Air enters the lungs because of **pressure differences**. The pressure of air in the thoracic cavity is lower than atmospheric pressure.
3. 'We breathe in oxygen and breathe out carbon dioxide'. Again this is *not* true. See Table 5.5 for the correct answer.

5.3 THE MECHANISM OF BREATHING

Fig 5.2 illustrates the mechanism of breathing.

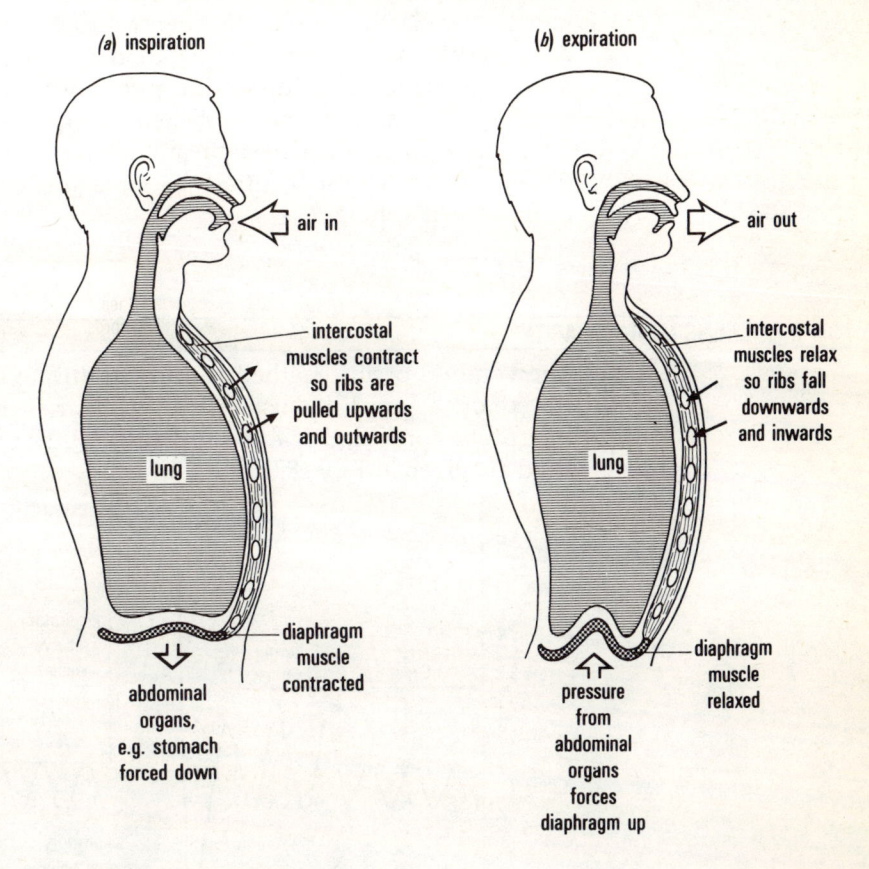

Fig 5.2 (a) Inspiration. (b) Expiration.

INSPIRATION (INHALATION OR BREATHING IN)

1. The volume of the airtight thoracic (chest) cavity is **increased** because:
   (a) the **diaphragm muscle contracts**, pulling the diaphragm downwards until it is flat;

Human Biology

       (b)   the **intercostal muscles contract**, pulling the ribs upwards and outwards.

2 As a result, the pressure of the air inside the lungs *falls* below atmospheric pressure.

3 Air from the outside atmosphere then enters the lungs to fill the partial vacuum so created.

EXPIRATION (EXHALATION OR BREATHING OUT)

1 The volume of the thoracic cavity **falls** because:
    (a)   the **diaphragm muscle relaxes**, allowing the organs in the abdomen to push the central part of the diaphragm upwards into a domed shape;
    (b)   the **intercostal muscles relax**, so that the ribs fall back on to the lungs;
    (c)   the **elastic fibres** in the lungs contract.

2 As a result, air pressure in the thoracic cavity *increases* to above atmospheric pressure, and so air is forced out of the lungs.

    These actions are only sufficient for gentle expiration. During forced expiration, e.g. a deep breath, the muscles lining the body wall of the abdomen also contract to force the abdominal organs up against the diaphragm.

5.4 MEASURING LUNG CAPACITY

The volumes of air breathed in and out during exercise, etc., can be traced on a graph by using a spirometer. You may be asked to interpret figures similar to those in Fig 5.3. Definitions for the terms used are given in Table 5.3.

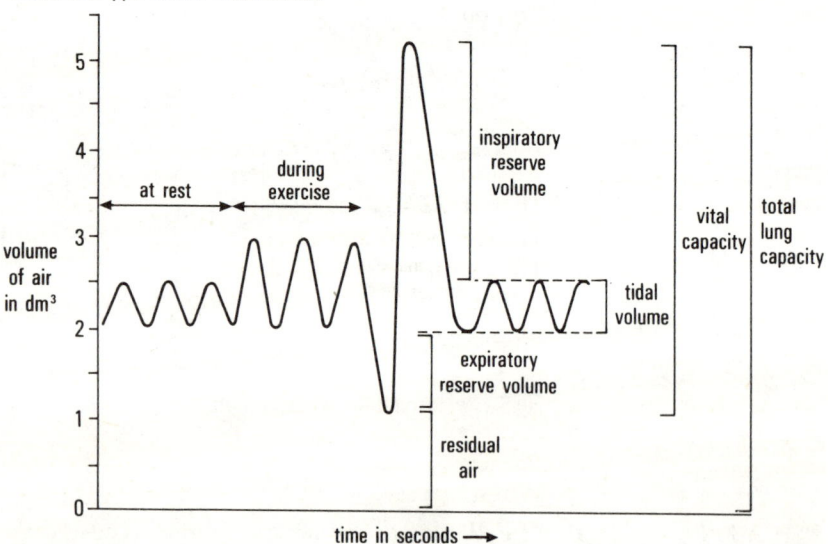

Fig 5.3 Lung volumes derived from spirometer readings.

Breathing and gas exchange

Table 5.3 Lung capacity in an adult

Lung volume	Typical values in dm³	Definition
1 Tidal air	0.5	The volume of air breathed in or out during normal breathing when at rest.
2 Inspiratory reserve volume or complementary air	2.5	The extra volume of air breathed in during a deep breath, in addition to the tidal air.
3 Expiratory reserve volume or supplementary air	1.0	The extra volume of air breathed out during a deep breath, in addition to the tidal air.
4 Dead space	0.2	The volume of air which fills the trachea and bronchi and is expelled without reaching the alveoli.
5 Vital capacity	4.2	The maximum amount of air which can be expelled by forcible expiration following deep inspiration (the sum of **1–4** above).
6 Residual air	1.0	The volume of air which remains in the respiratory system, even after the deepest expiration.
7 Total lung capacity	5.2	The maximum volume of air present in the lungs (the sum of **5** and **6** above).

1. The figures given in Table 5.3 vary greatly from person to person, and can be changed by fitness training, etc.
2. You *don't* need to know the figures – they are given for illustration only.

EFFECTS OF EXERCISE ON BREATHING

A sudden burst of exercise has the following effects:
1. The rate of breathing becomes faster (see Fig 5.3).
2. The depth of breathing increases (see Fig 5.3).
3. The amount of carbon dioxide in expired air increases.

The beneficial long-term effects of regular exercise are summarized on page 119.

5.5 GAS EXCHANGE IN THE ALVEOLI

When inspired air reaches the alveoli, oxygen and carbon dioxide are exchanged by diffusion. Fig 5.4 illustrates this process.

Oxygen diffuses from the air in the alveolus into the blood capillary because there is a diffusion gradient between the alveolar air and

Fig 5.4 Gas exchange in an alveolus

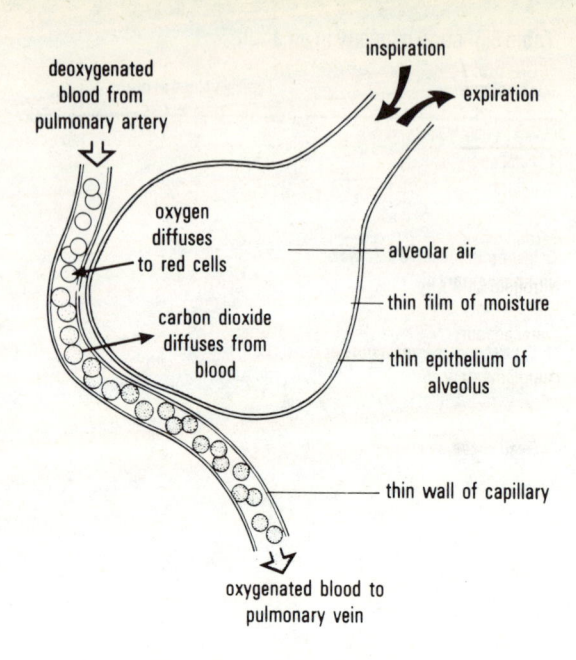

the capillary. This means that there is a higher concentration of oxygen in the alveolar air than in the blood.

Carbon dioxide diffuses from the capillary to the alveolus because there is a diffusion gradient in the opposite direction. During a deep breath, air remains in each alveolus for longer. This increases the time available for gas exchange so that the expired air contains more carbon dioxide.

The air inside the alveoli is not fully exchanged with each breath, so that it contains more carbon dioxide and less oxygen than expired air (see Table 5.4).

Table 5.4 Comparison of alveolar and expired air

	Alveolar	Expired
Carbon dioxide	6%	4%
Oxygen	14%	16%

THE ALVEOLI

The alveoli are **adapted for exchange of gases** by diffusion because they possess:
1. a moist surface in which molecules dissolve;
2. thin walls, so permitting rapid exchange of molecules;
3. a rich blood supply for rapid transport of oxygen and carbon dioxide.

Breathing and gas exchange

INSPIRED AND EXPIRED AIR

Table 5.5 Approximate composition of inspired and expired air

	Inspired, i.e. atmospheric air	Expired air
Oxygen	21%	16%
Carbon dioxide	0.03%	4%
Nitrogen	79%	79%
Water vapour	Varies	Always saturated
Other differences	Cooler; may contain dust	Warmer; most dust particles removed

Note the large amount of oxygen (16 per cent) still present in expired air. This explains why you can revive an unconscious person by breathing into the victim's mouth. (This is a favourite trick question in exams).

5.6 EXPERIMENTS TO COMPARE EXPIRED AND INSPIRED AIR

Table 5.6 Experiments to compare inspired and expired air

To show	Summary of method	Observed results
1 Increase in **carbon dioxide** content of expired air.	Breathe out repeatedly through **limewater** or hydrogencarbonate (bicarbonate) indicator. Compare by repeatedly breathing *in* air through same indicator.	With expired air, limewater turns milky; hydrogencarbonate indicator turns yellow (see Fig 28.1, page 393).
2 Decrease in **oxygen** content of expired air.	Collect sample of expired air in gas jar. Insert lighted **candle**, close lid, and record time taken in identical jar of atmospheric air.	Flame goes out faster in jar of expired air.
3 Increase in **water** content of expired air.	Breathe out on to blue **cobalt chloride** paper. Compare with same paper exposed to atmospheric air. Or breathe out over green anhydrous copper sulphate crystals.	Paper turns pink more quickly with expired air. Crystals turn blue if water vapour present.
4 Increase in **temperature** of expired air.	Breathe out on to **thermometer bulb**, wrapped in moist cloth (to avoid effects of cooling by evaporation). Compare to same thermometer in atmosphere.	Higher temperature recorded with expired air.

5.7 CONTROL OF THE BREATHING RATE

The rate of breathing is controlled by a group of brain cells called the **respiratory centre** in the medulla. The rate can be varied by the following:

1. By **conscious decision**.
2. During a period of steady breathing, by reflex action involving **stretch receptors** in the bronchioles. As the lungs expand, these receptors pass impulses to the respiratory centre which cause inspiration to cease and expiration to begin.
3. During exercise, by **receptors sensitive to carbon dioxide** in the blood, found in the centre itself and also in the walls of the carotid artery. If the carbon dioxide level rises due to increased cell respiration, these receptors stimulate the centre to increase the rate and depth of breathing. This continues until the carbon dioxide level falls to normal again.

The rate of breathing is therefore not affected by lack of oxygen in the blood.

5.8 ARTIFICIAL RESUSCITATION (ARTIFICIAL RESPIRATION)

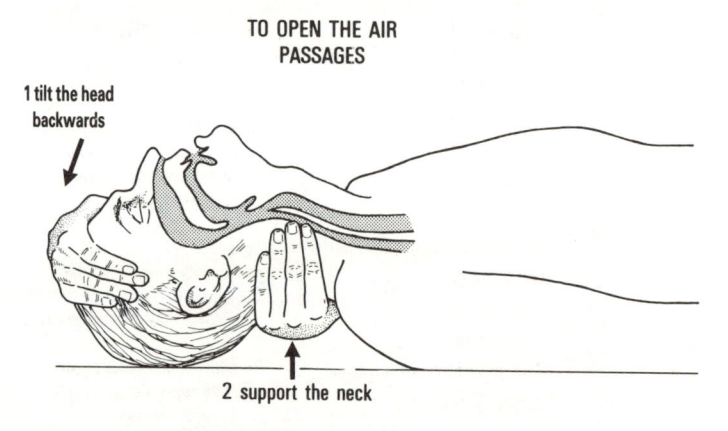

Fig 5.5 Correct position for mouth-to-mouth ventilation.

MOUTH-TO-MOUTH VENTILATION (THE 'KISS OF LIFE')

1. Place the victim on her/his back. Put one hand under the neck, and one on the forehead. Tilt the head backwards to open up the air passage (see Fig 5.5).
2. Push the chin upwards to lift the tongue clear of the air passages. Search for and remove any debris in the mouth.
3. Pinch the victim's nostrils, seal the mouth with your lips and breathe out deeply.
4. Repeat four times quickly.

Breathing and gas exchange

5 Check to see if the chest is rising – if not check for unseen obstructions and tilt the head further back.
6 Continue until the victim resumes normal breathing.

Mouth-to-mouth ventilation is the best method for reviving a person whose breathing has stopped, because:
1 it involves direct inflation of the victim's lungs;
2 the rescuer can check on the movements of the victim's chest while performing the action.

5.9 CHECKLIST

- Breathing v. respiration.
- Breathing through the nose:
    three advantages.
- Structure and function of:
    larynx;
    trachea or windpipe;
    intercostal muscles;
    diaphragm;
    bronchi;
    bronchioles;
    pleural fluid;
    pleural membranes.
- Mechanism of breathing.
- Lung capacity:
    tidal air;
    dead space;
    vital capacity;
    residual air.
- Three effects of exercise on breathing.
- Gas exchange.
- Experiments to compare CO_2, O_2, H_2O and temperature in inspired and expired air.
- Control of breathing rate.
- Artificial resuscitation.

5.10 EXAM QUESTIONS

1 (a) Explain how the volume of the thoracic (chest) cavity is:
  (i) increased during inspiration (2)
  (ii) decreased during expiration (3)
 (b) How does an increase in volume enable air to enter the lungs? (2)
 (c) What is the role of the abdominal muscles during breathing? (3)

2 Fig 5.6 shows a bell jar used to demonstrate relationships of the structures in the thorax.

Fig 5.6

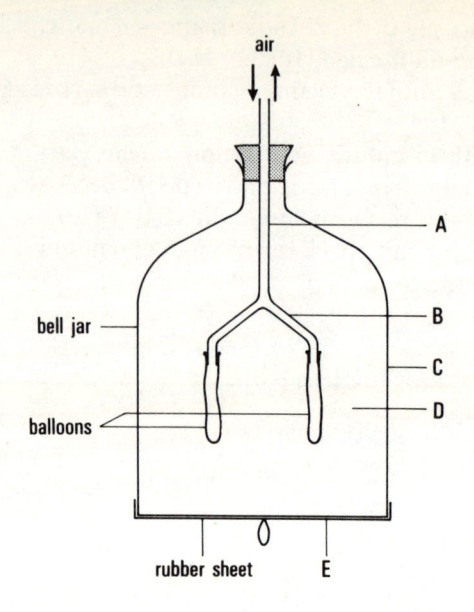

[Diagram of bell jar apparatus with labels: air (at top), A, B, C, D, bell jar, balloons, rubber sheet, E]

(a) When the rubber sheet is pulled down a small amount of air enters the balloons, causing them to inflate slightly. Explain the reason for this. (4)

(b) Name those structures of the thorax which are represented in the apparatus by the letters A to E. (5)

(c) Briefly describe five ways in which the apparatus is a poor representation of the structure of the thorax. (5)

[AEB 1985]

3 (a) Explain the reasons for the differences in composition between expired and alveolar air – see Table 5.7. (2)

Table 5.7 Comparison of alveolar and expired air

	Alveolar	Expired
Carbon dioxide	6%	4%
Oxygen	14%	16%

(b) The apparatus in Fig 5.7 is intended to represent actions concerned with breathing.

(i) Identify the structures represented by the letters A, B, C and D. (4)

(ii) What happens to B and C if D is caused to contract? (2)

Breathing and gas exchange

Fig 5.7

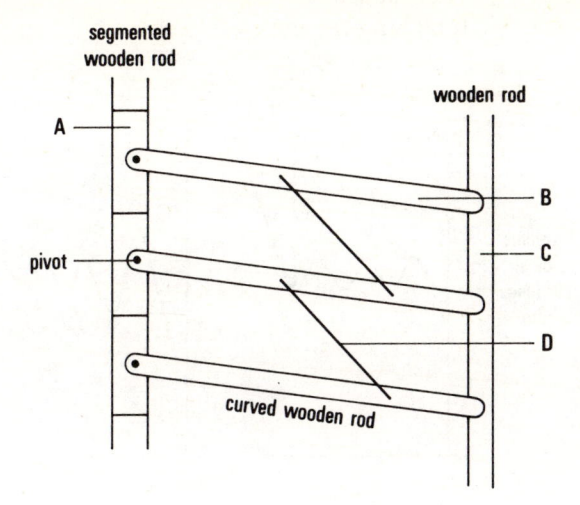

[Diagram showing segmented wooden rod with points A, pivot, and wooden rod with points B, C, D, and curved wooden rod]

4   The apparatus shown in Fig 5.8 is used to measure the working volume of the lungs. The person being tested breathes in deeply and then breathes out through the rubber tube.

Fig 5.8

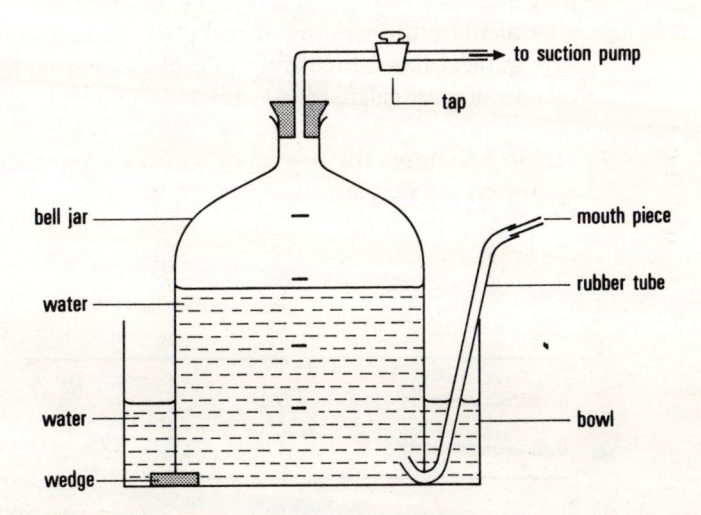

[Diagram of bell jar apparatus with labels: to suction pump, tap, mouth piece, rubber tube, bell jar, water, bowl, wedge]

(a)   What happens to the water in the bell jar as the person breathes out?   (1)
(b)   Why is there a wedge under the bottom rim of the bell jar? (1)
(c)   What things would you need to do to the apparatus before you could measure the lung volume of a second person?   (3)
[ALSEB]

5   In Fig 5.9 identify the letter labelling each of:
(a)   residual volume
(b)   tidal volume

(c) vital capacity
(d) total lung capacity (1 each) [AEB 1985]

Fig 5.9

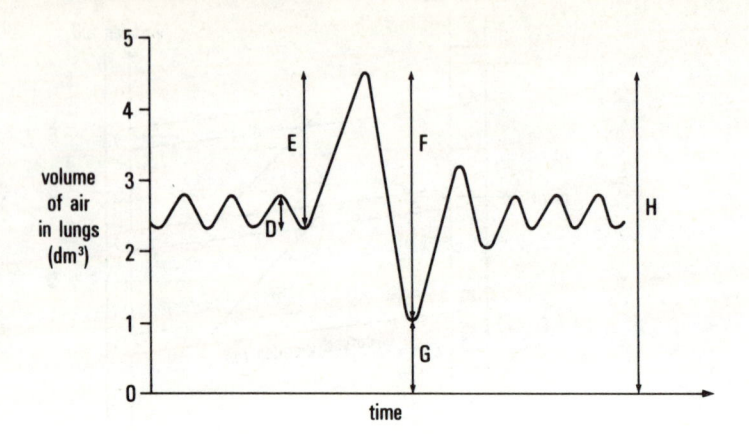

6 An investigation showed that blood carried in the pulmonary artery contained 52 cm³ of carbon dioxide per 100 cm³ of blood, while that in the pulmonary vein contained 48 cm³ of carbon dioxide per 100 cm³ of blood. The volume of blood flowing through the lungs is 5 dm³ per minute.
　　Calculate the volume of carbon dioxide excreted per breath when the subject has a breathing rate of 16 breaths per minute. Show the stages of your calculation. (5) [AEB 1984]

7 Table 5.8 shows the results of observations made on the breathing of a 20 year old woman.

Table 5.8

	Volume of single inspiration cm³ (ml)	Breaths per minute
At rest, before exercise	500	19
During vigorous exercise	1100	36

(a) From the table calculate the total volume of air inspired in each minute at rest and during vigorous exercise. (2)
(b) If the volume of oxygen in atmospheric air is 20 per cent and 16 per cent of exhaled air consists of oxygen, calculate the volume of oxygen entering the blood each minute at rest. Show your working. (3)
(c) Why does the body require oxygen when at rest? (3)
(d) In the example above, the volume of oxygen entering the blood during exercise is 1584 cm³ (ml) per minute. Explain the

Breathing and gas exchange

reasons for this increase compared with your answer to (c) above. (5) [L]

8 Fig 5.10 shows an apparatus which may be used to find if a person breathes out more carbon dioxide than is breathed in.

Fig 5.10

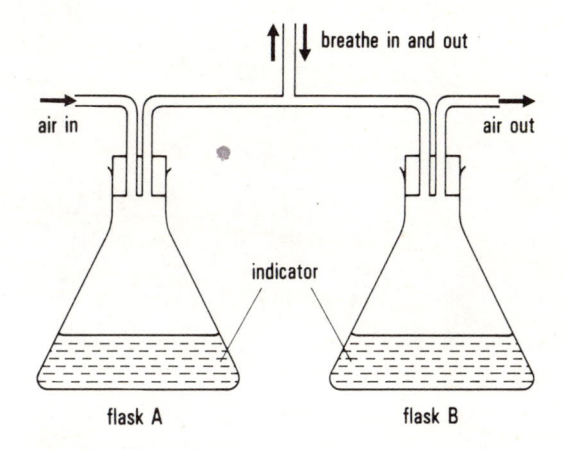

(a) Complete the diagram by drawing in the glass tubes so that the apparatus will work as shown when a person breathes in and out. (4)

(b) Indicate by arrows the direction of flow of air. (1)

(c) Name a suitable indicator for carbon dioxide which could be used in the apparatus. (1)

(d) What changes would you expect in this indicator (in each flask) after someone had breathed in and out gently several times? (2)

(e) If the same person repeated the experiment (using fresh indicator) after vigorous exercise, what difference, if any, would you expect in the results in each flask? (2)

(f) Give a reason for your answers to (v). (1)

[Adapted from *WM*]

9 (a) What is meant by the term 'diffusion gradient'? (2)
(b) Describe the importance of diffusion gradients during the exchange of gases in the lung. (8)

10 (a) Describe the main stages in mouth-to-mouth ventilation. (6)
(b) Why is it possible to restart breathing by breathing out your own expired air? (1)
(c) Why is mouth-to-mouth ventilation recommended as the most effective method for artificial resuscitation? (2)

CHAPTER SIX

BLOOD AND THE CIRCULATION SYSTEM

CONTENTS

- **6.1 Purpose of the circulation system and the composition of blood** — 103
  The need for a circulation system 103
  Composition of blood 103

- **6.2 Functions of blood** — 105

- **6.3 Functions of red cells** — 105
  Role of haemoglobin 105
  Factors affecting oxygen transport by red cells 106

- **6.4 Clotting** — 106

- **6.5 ABO blood groups** — 106
  Importance of blood groups 107

- **6.6 Checklist** — 107

- **6.7 Exam questions** — 108

Blood and the circulation system

Be warned! Blood and circulation is a favourite exam topic. It's virtually certain you'll have a question on some part of this subject.

6.1 PURPOSE OF THE CIRCULATION SYSTEM, AND THE COMPOSITION OF BLOOD

THE NEED FOR A CIRCULATION SYSTEM

The circulation system is needed to transport oxygen, dissolved food substances, hormones, etc., to the cells, and to carry away wastes such as carbon dioxide. Single-celled animals (e.g. *Amoeba*) do not need a circulation system because diffusion is sufficient to carry oxygen and food molecules throughout the cell. However diffusion is too slow to distribute oxygen and food throughout the millions of cells in a large multi-cellular organism.

COMPOSITION OF BLOOD

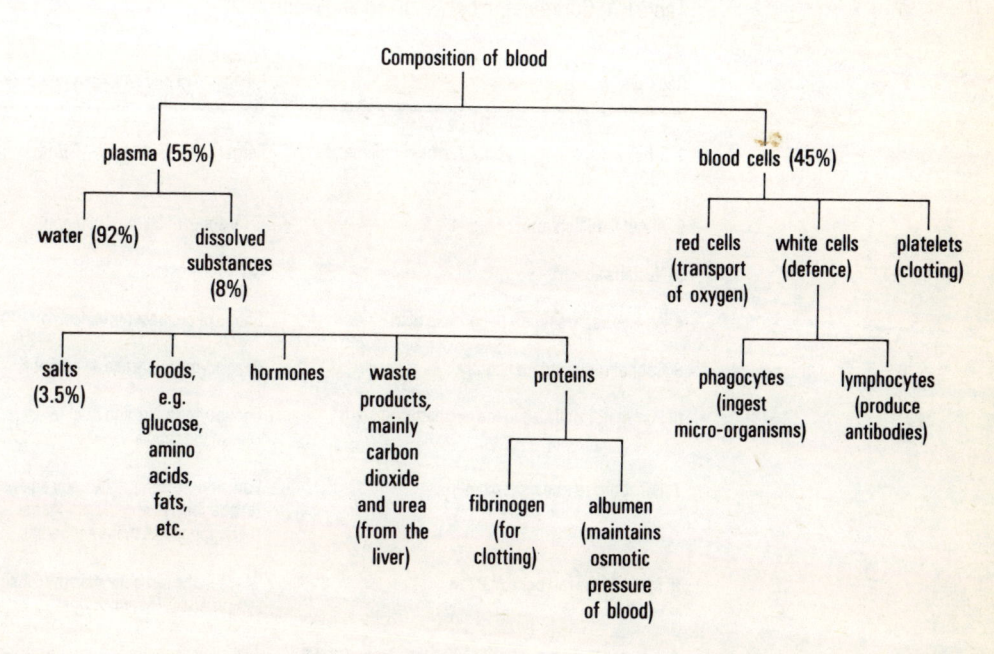

Composition of blood
- plasma (55%)
  - water (92%)
  - dissolved substances (8%)
    - salts (3.5%)
    - foods, e.g. glucose, amino acids, fats, etc.
    - hormones
    - waste products, mainly carbon dioxide and urea (from the liver)
    - proteins
      - fibrinogen (for clotting)
      - albumen (maintains osmotic pressure of blood)
- blood cells (45%)
  - red cells (transport of oxygen)
  - white cells (defence)
    - phagocytes (ingest micro-organisms)
    - lymphocytes (produce antibodies)
  - platelets (clotting)

Fig 6.1 Composition of blood and functions of the major elements.

Fig 6.2 Types of blood cell.

(a) RED CELLS (erythrocytes)

red cells contain haemoglobin, for oxygen transport

red cell shown in section

bi-concave shape increases surface area for oxygen exchange

(b) WHITE CELLS

nucleus

Phagocyte – ingests micro-organisms

Lymphocyte – makes antibodies

(c) PHAGOCYTOSIS: bacteria being ingested by a phagocyte

chain of bacteria, eg streptococci (cause throat infections)

(d) PLATELETS are fragments of cytoplasm, formed in the red bone marrow.

Function: to assist in blood clotting.

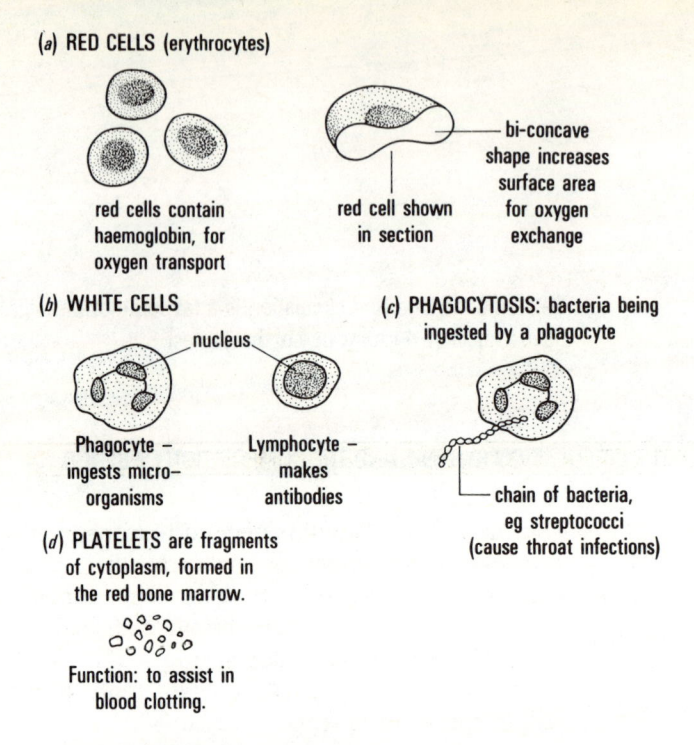

Fig 6.1 shows the composition of blood, while Fig 6.2 illustrates the various types of blood cells. Table 6.1 gives a comparison between red and white blood cells.

Table 6.1 Comparison between red and white cells

Red cells	White cells (phagocytes and lymphocytes)
1 Small cells, diameter about 7.5 micromillimetres (μm).	Larger cells, diameter 8–15 μm.
2 About 5 million/mm³ of blood.	Only about 6000/mm³ of blood.
3 Nucleus absent.	Nucleus present.
4 Always same shape – bi-concave disc.	Shape of phagocytes varies.
5 Cannot move independently.	Phagocytes move like an amoeba.
6 Do not normally leave the circulatory system.	Phagocytes leave and re-enter by passing between cells in the capillary walls.
7 Function: to transport oxygen.	Function: to defend the body against infection: (a) phagocytes engulf pathogens; (b) lymphocytes make antibodies.
8 Made in the red bone marrow.	Made in the red bone marrow (phagocytes) and the lymph nodes (lymphocytes).
9 Life cycle: destroyed after 120 days; broken down and excreted as bile pigments.	Life cycle: survive for varying periods between one week and several years.

Blood and the circulation system

6.2 FUNCTIONS OF BLOOD

1. **Maintenance of a constant internal environment** (homeostasis.)
   - (a)　Distribution of heat throughout the body from actively respiring tissues (liver and muscles).
   - (b)　Distribution of dissolved food substances, water, oxygen and water products evenly throughout the body.
2. **Defence against disease.**
   - (a)　Production of antibodies and antitoxins by lymphocytes.
   - (b)　Ingestion of microorganism by phagocytes
   - (c)　Formation of clots to seal wounds (see below).
   - (d)　Transport of antibodies.
3. **Transport** – see Table 6.2.

Table 6.2 Transport functions of blood

Item	Transported From	Transported To	How transported
Oxygen	Lungs	Tissues	As oxyhaemoglobin in the red cells (see below)
Carbon dioxide	Tissues	Lungs	As dissolved hydrogen carbonate (bicarbonate) ions in the plasma
Urea	Liver	Kidneys	Dissolved in the plasma
Digested foods – glucose, amino acids, fats, etc.	Small intestine	Liver, then all tissues	Dissolved in the plasma
Hormones	Endocrine glands	Target organs, i.e. organs affected by each hormone	Dissolved in the plasma
Heat	Liver, muscles	All tissues	All parts of blood carry heat

6.3 FUNCTIONS OF RED CELLS

The main function of the red cells is to carry *oxygen* from the lungs to the tissues. Red cells are adapted for this function because:

1. they have a bi-concave shape, which provides a larger surface area for absorbing oxygen;
2. they contain **haemoglobin**, a protein with a powerful affinity for oxygen.

ROLE OF HAEMOGLOBIN

Haemoglobin and oxygen unite to form **oxyhaemoglobin** in the lungs because:
1. the oxygen concentration (or partial pressure of oxygen) is high;
2. the pH of the tissues is neutral (due to the absence of carbon dioxide).

Oxyhaemoglobin breaks down to form oxygen and haemoglobin in actively respiring tissues because:
1. oxygen concentration is low;
2. the pH is acid (because of the presence of carbon dioxide).

FACTORS AFFECTING OXYGEN TRANSPORT BY RED CELLS

1. At **high altitudes**, oxygen pressure in the air is reduced so less is taken in by the red cells. People living in high mountains have extra red cells to compensate for this.
2. **Carbon monoxide** from car exhausts, cigarette smoke and badly ventilated gas heaters can replace oxygen by forming **carboxyhaemoglobin.** This can cause drowsiness and even death from lack of oxygen reaching the tissues.
3. Lack of red cells in the blood, known as **anaemia**, can cause tiredness due to shortage of oxygen. Anaemia can be caused by lack of iron in the diet or by heavy loss of blood during monthly periods.

6.4 CLOTTING

When a blood vessel is damaged, a clot is formed to protect the body from invasion by harmful microbes. The stages in clotting are as follows:
1. Platelets form a **platelet plug** around the damaged area.
2. The platelets release enzymes which convert the soluble blood protein **fibrinogen** in the plasma to an insoluble protein called **fibrin**. This happens only if calcium ions are present in the plasma and the damaged area is exposed to the air.
2. A clot forms, consisting of a mesh of fibre containing trapped red cells. This later shrinks to form a fibrous **scab.** The scab protects the tissues underneath, while healing takes place.

6.5 ABO BLOOD GROUPS

Table 6.3 Summary of compatibility of the ABO blood groups

Blood group	Protein carried on red cells (antigen)	Antibody present in plasma	Can donate blood to recipients in these groups	Can receive blood from donors in these groups
A	A	anti B	A and AB	A and O
B	B	anti A	B and AB	B and O
AB	A and B	none	AB only	all groups
O	none	Anti A and anti B	all groups	O only

Blood and the circulation system 107

People in blood group A possess:
1. Red blood cells carrying a protein called A, which acts as an antigen;
2. antibodies in their plasma against blood group B (anti-B).

The other blood groups have comparable combinations of red-blood-cell proteins and plasma antibodies, as shown in Table 6.3.

(For rhesus group see p. 418).

IMPORTANCE OF BLOOD GROUPS

When an injured person needs a blood transfusion, it is essential to know both the donor's and the recipient's blood groups.

If an incompatible (wrong) blood group is given, the recipient's antibodies may attack the donor's red cells, causing them to clump together or agglutinate. If so:
1. the transfusion will be of no value to the recipient;
2. the clumped cells may form small clots in the capillaries, which can cause serious harm in the brain or heart.

6.6 CHECKLIST

- Need for a circulation system in multicellular animals.
- Composition of blood:
    - plasma;
    - red cells;
    - white cells:
        - phagocytes;
        - lymphgocytes;
    - blood proteins:
        - albumen;
        - fibrinogen.
- Comparison of red and white cells:
    - structure (three facts);
    - movement (two facts);
    - functions;
    - manufacture;
    - life cycle.
- Functions of blood:
    - homeostasis (two examples);
    - defence (four examples);
    - transport (six examples).
- Functions of red cells.
- Adaptations of red cells (two).
- Oxyhaemoglobin:
    - formation (two);
    - breakdown (two).
- Effects of altitude, carbon monoxide and anaemia.
- Clotting:
    - platelet plug;

continues on page 108

calcium irons;
scab formation.
- ABO blood groups:
effects of incompatible transfusion (two).

6.7 EXAM QUESTIONS

1. (a) Explain why large multicellular organisms require a circulatory system, unlike small single-celled organisms. (3)
   (b) Briefly summarize the functions of blood in relation to defence against disease. (4)

2. Table 6.6 shows details of the red blood cell count of people living at different altitudes.

   Table 6.6

Altitude above sea level (metres)	Red cell count (per mm^3)
0	5.0×10^6
1560	6.5×10^6
5400	7.4×10^6
5400 (temporary resident)	5.95×10^6

   (a) State one physiological factor which could be the cause of the different red blood cell (erythrocyte) counts. (1)
   (b) Concisely explain the value to mountaineers of spending time at high altitude before undertaking a major climb in the Himalayas. (1)
   (c) Briefly explain one of the effects on the body if this acclimatization is not carried out. (1)   [AEB 1983]

3. (a) Under what conditions in the body is oxyhaemoglobin:
   (i) formed; (2)
   (ii) broken down to oxygen and haemoglobin? (2)
   (b) Why is oxyhaemoglobin in the maternal circulation likely to be converted to oxygen and haemoglobin in the placenta? (2)
   (c) Why is carbon monoxide dangerous to life? (2)

4. (a) What are the advantages of:
   (i) clot formation;
   (ii) scab formation? (2)
   (b) Briefly describe the main events which occur in the skin between the cutting of the finger and the formation of a scab over the wound. (5)

5. In an emergency, a dilute saline solution may be transfused into an accident victim who has suffered a large loss of blood.
   (a) Why is saline used instead of sterile water? (1)
   (b) If blood was available and the victim's blood group was

known to be A, which blood groups could be transfused without fear of a dangerous reaction? (2)

(c) Describe clearly how the recipient would react to blood from an incompatible donor. (2) [NI]

6 (a) Explain why transfusions of blood group O can be given safely to members of both A and B groups, although group O blood contains anti A and anti B antibodies. (2)

(b) Which blood groups are known as:
   (i) 'universal donor';
   (ii) 'universal recipient'?

Give a reason in each case. (4)

CHAPTER SEVEN

THE CIRCULATION SYSTEM AND THE HEART

CONTENTS

▶ **7.1 The double circulation system**   113
Double pump   113

▶ **7.2 Structure of the heart**   114

▶ **7.3 Heartbeat**   114
Diastole   116
Atrial systole   116
Ventricular systole   116
Control of heartbeat   116
The heart valves   116

▶ **7.4 Coronary heart disease**   117
Major causes of coronary heart disease   117

▶ **7.5 Blood pressure and the pulse**   118
Blood pressure   118
Variations in pulse rate   118

7.6 Exercise and the circulation system   **119**
Effects of exercise   118
Effects of long-term exercise on the pulse rate   119

7.7 Checklist   **119**

7.8 Exam questions   **119**

The circulation system and the heart

7.1 THE DOUBLE CIRCULATION SYSTEM

The heart is a muscular pump, whose function is to pump blood around the body through the blood vessels.

DOUBLE PUMP

The heart is described as a double pump because:
1. it consists of two separate pumps (the left and right halves) joined together;
2. blood cannot circulate through the tough barrier (the septum) between the left and right halves.

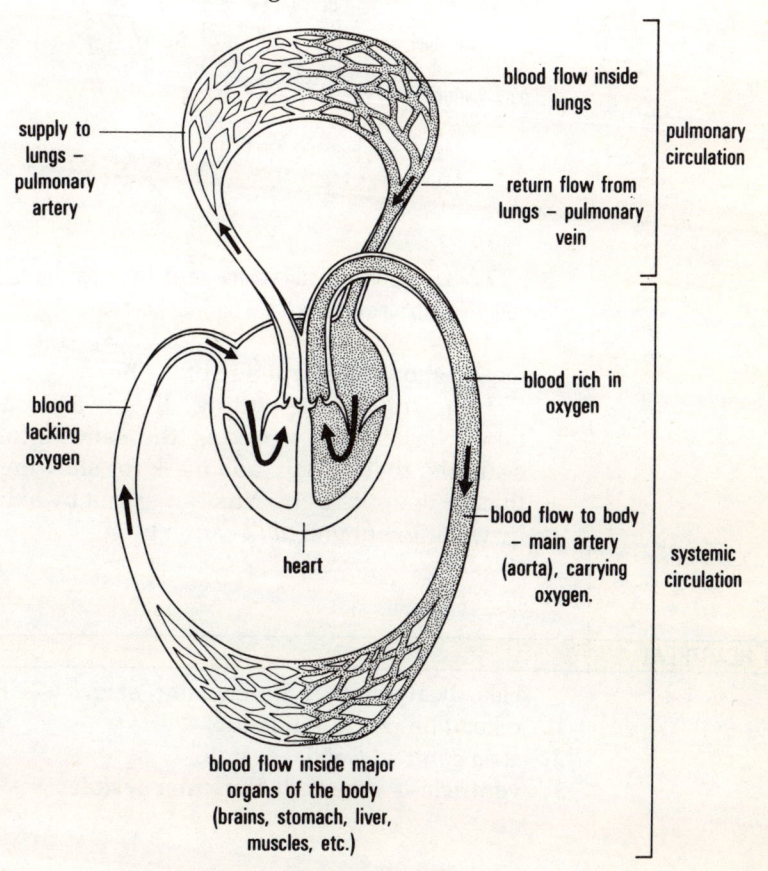

Fig 7.1 Simplified diagram of the double circulation system.

Human Biology

The circulation itself is termed a double circulation because blood must pass through the heart twice during one complete circuit of the body (see Fig 7.1).

7.2 STRUCTURE OF THE HEART

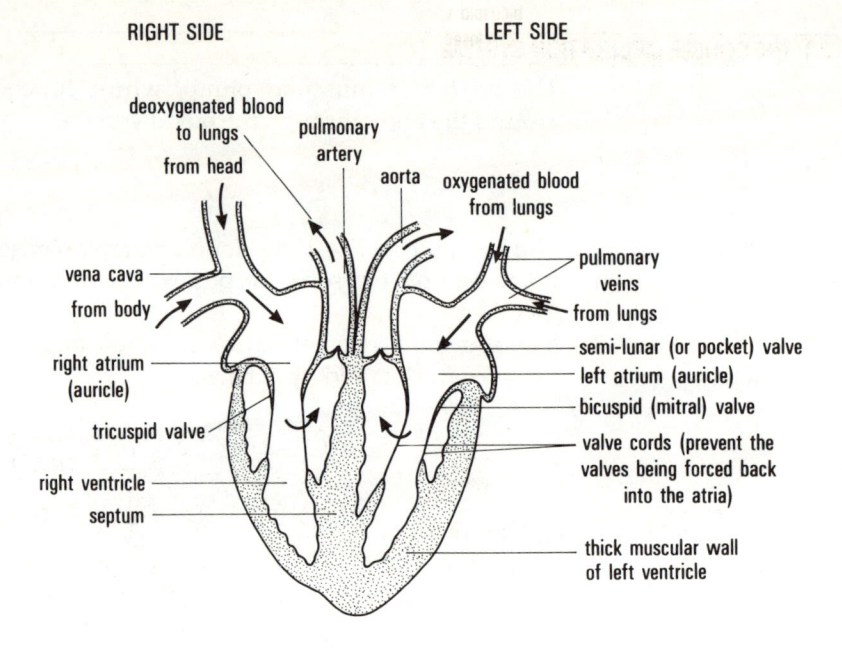

Fig 7.2 Longitudinal section of the heart. Note that the heart is always drawn as if facing you; this explains why its left is on your right.

Fig 7.2 shows the structure of the heart.

Hint: drawing or writing? If you draw a fully labelled diagram, don't waste time repeating the same information in writing. For example, there's only one mark for showing that the left ventricle is thicker than the right. You can earn it by a drawing *or* you can earn it by writing, but you *can't* earn it twice!

7.3 HEARTBEAT

Heartbeat involves three distinct stages (see Fig 7.3):
1. relaxation phase – **diastole**;
2. atria contract – **atrial systole**;
3. ventricles contract – **ventricular systole**.

The circulation system and the heart

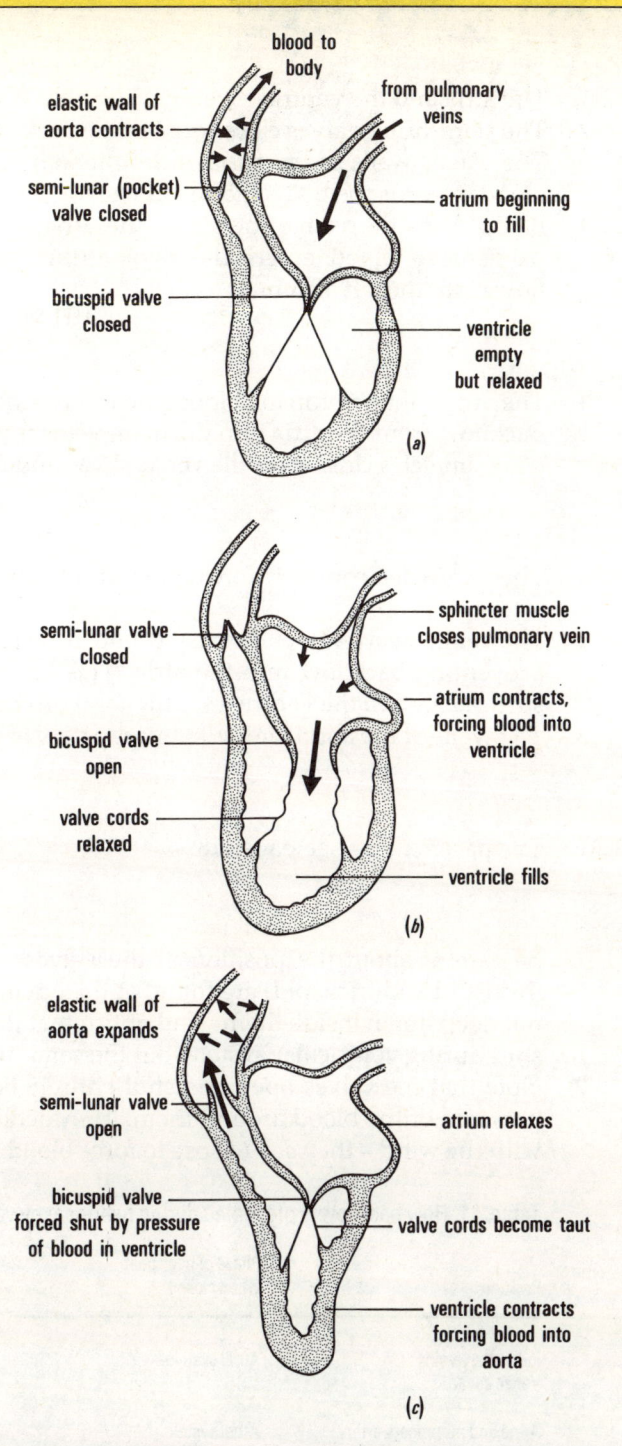

Fig 7.3 Heartbeat. (*a*) Diastole or relaxation phase; heart relaxed, valves closed. (*b*) Atrial systole; atria contract. (*c*) Ventricular systole; ventricles contract.

DIASTOLE	1	The atria and the ventricles relax.
(RELAXATION PHASE)	2	The **semi-lunar valves** close, preventing back flow into the ventricles.
	3	The elastic walls of the aorta and pulmonary artery contract, forcing blood towards the body and the lungs.
	4	Blood from the veins flows into the atria, which begin to fill. De-oxygenated blood enters the right atrium, and oxygenated blood flows into the left atrium.
ATRIAL SYSTOLE	1	The atria contract, forcing blood into the ventricles, which fill.
	2	Backflow from the atria into the main veins is prevented by **sphincter** (ring) **muscles** closing off the venae cavae and the pulmonary veins.
VENTRICULAR SYSTOLE	1	The ventricles contract, forcing blood into the aorta and pulmonary artery.
	2	The **main heart valves** (tricuspid and bicuspid) are forced shut, so preventing backflow into the atria. This happens because the pressure of blood in the ventricles is higher than the pressure in the atria.
	3	The walls of the aorta and pulmonary artery expand.
CONTROL OF HEARTBEAT M,W only		The pacemaker – see page 418.
THE HEART VALVES: *HINTS*	1	Be careful about the position of the valves. The main heart valves (bicuspid and tricuspid) are found at the opening into the ventricles – not deep down inside them. And notice that the main heart valves are shut during ventricular systole, but the semi-lunar valves are open.
	2	Note that the valves open and shut entirely because of the changing pressure of the blood around them. They act like trapdoors swinging with the wind – they *don't* 'close to force blood into the ventricles'.

Table 7.1 How backflow is prevented during heartbeat by valves, etc.

Valve	Position	Phase of heartbeat when closed	Effect
1 Rings of sphincter muscle.	Pulmonary veins. Venae cavae.	Atrial systole.	Prevent backflow from the atria into the main veins.
2 Semi-lunar valves.	Aorta and pulmonary artery.	Atrial systole.	Prevent backflow from the ventricles into the main arteries.
3 Main heart valves – tricuspid and bicuspid.	Between atria and ventricles.	Ventricular system.	Prevent backflow from the ventricles into the atria. Valve cords prevent the valves from being blown back into the atria.

The circulation system and the heart

VALVE SOUNDS

Through a stethoscope, the valves can be heard making a 'lubb-dupp' sound at each heartbeat. The 'lubb' is the sound made by the main heart valves closing, and the 'dupp' is the sound made by the semi-lunar valves closing.

7.4 CORONARY HEART DISEASE

Coronary heart disease is the name given to the gradual blocking up of the coronary arteries, which supply the heart muscle with oxygen.

A **heart attack** or **coronary thrombosis** happens when the blood supply to the heart is reduced as a result of coronary heart disease. A coronary thrombosis may cause part of the heart muscle to stop functioning due to lack of oxygen (see Fig 7.4).

For arteriosclerosis, atherosclerosis and coronary bypass see glossary.

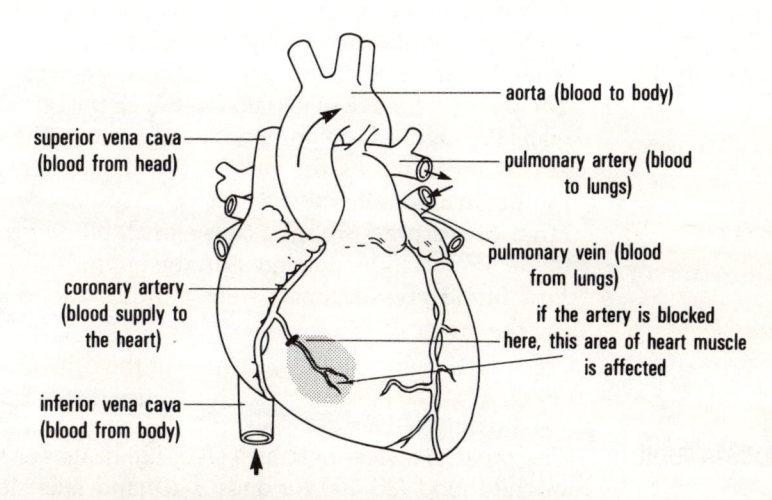

Fig 7.4 Effect of a blocked coronary artery on the heart muscle.

MAJOR CAUSES OF CORONARY HEART DISEASE

1. **Inheritance** – some people inherit an increased risk of heart attack.
2. **Excess fat in the diet** causes blocked coronary arteries due to fatty deposits forming on the artery walls.
3. **Smoking** causes increased deposit of fats inside the arteries. The carbon monoxide in cigarette smoke removes up to 10 per cent of the oxygen in the blood, forcing the heart to work harder.
4. **High blood pressure** also increases the risk of fatty deposits inside the arteries.
5. **Lack of exercise** renders the heart muscle inefficient and so less able to function when deprived of oxygen.

Human Biology

6 **Nervous tension and stress** are also believed to lead to heart attacks.

7.5 BLOOD PRESSURE AND THE PULSE

BLOOD PRESSURE

The pumping action of the heart builds up a high pressure in the circulation system, in order to force the blood through the narrow capillaries.

1. The **ventricles** are the main source of pressure, especially the left ventricle with its powerful muscular walls. The left ventricle is able to generate a pressure equal to 16 kilopascals (kPa) compared to only 2 kPa from the right ventricle.
2. **Blood pressure in the aorta and pulmonary artery** remains relatively steady because their walls (like all arteries) contain elastic fibres. As the ventricles contract, the elastic walls expand (see Fig 7.3(c). When the ventricles relax, the walls contract inwards so forcing blood out through the arteries.
3. As blood travels round the system, **pressure steadily falls**, especially in the smaller branches of the arteries (called arterioles), in the capillaries and the branch veins (or venules) (see Fig 7.7 on page 121).
4. The **pulse** is a wave of expansion which passes along the elastic artery walls throughout the body with each beat of the ventricles. The pulse rate is the same as the rate of heartbeat averaging about 70 beats/minute in an adult when at rest.
5. **High blood pressure** may cause small blood vessels to burst, resulting in strokes if the damage is in the brain.
6. **Low blood pressure** may cause fainting due to lack of oxygen reaching the brain.

VARIATIONS IN PULSE RATE

The pulse is fastest in babies (100–120 beats per minute), slows down in childhood (80–100 for ages 6–10) and falls slowly with age as the metabolic rate gradually declines. It speeds up during stress, illness, exercise or any other event which increases the metabolic rate.

7.6 EXERCISE AND THE CIRCULATION SYSTEM

EFFECTS OF EXERCISE

Anyone who exercises regularly becomes physically 'fit'. The long-term effects of regular exercise include:

1. The muscles become larger and more efficient at using oxygen, because extra mitochondria are produced inside active muscle cells.
2. The circulation becomes more efficient at transporting oxygen. Heart muscle becomes more efficient and pumps more blood per beat.
3. Vital capacity (see page 91) increases so that more air is taken in with every breath.

The circulation system and the heart 119

4   The risks of heart attacks, strokes, and varicose veins decrease because of the improved efficiency of the circulation.

EFFECTS OF LONG-TERM EXERCISE ON THE PULSE RATE

In a fit person, the pulse rapidly returns to the normal resting level after exercise. In an unfit person, exercise makes the pulse rise higher and fall more slowly (see Fig 7.8 on page 122).

7.7 CHECKLIST

- Why the heart is called a double pump (two reasons).
- The double circulation system.
- The heart and associated blood vessels.
- Valves in or around the heart:
  - bicuspid valve;
  - tricuspid valve;
  - cords (function);
  - semi-lunar valves;
  - sphincter muscle in pulmonary vein;
  - valve sounds.
- Heart beat events at each stage:
  - diastole;
  - atrial systole;
  - ventricular systole.
- Coronary heart disease:
  - long term causes (six);
  - effects on coronary arteries;
  - coronary thrombosis.
- Blood pressure:
  - role of left ventricle;
  - role of elastic walls of aorta/pulmonary artery;
  - effects of high and low pressure.
- The pulse:
  - origin;
  - changes in pulse rate.
- Effects of exercise in general:
  - effects on the pulse.

7.8 EXAM QUESTIONS

1   From Fig 7.5:
    (a)   Name the blood vessels labelled **1, 2, 3** and **4**, and for each state whether the blood flowing through it is oxygenated or deoxygenated. (4)
    (b)   Identify the blood vessels labelled **5**. Explain concisely the role they play in the functioning of the heart. (4)

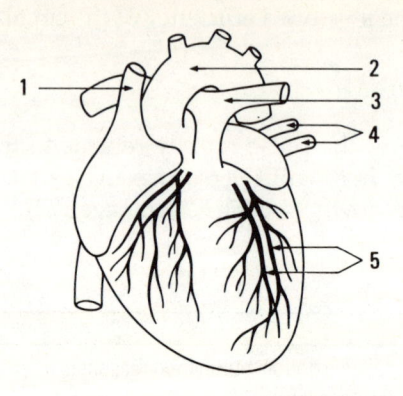

Fig 7.5 Ventral external view of the heart.

(c) Describe the sequence of events occurring in the heart which maintains the movement of blood from its entry into the right atrium (auricle) to its exit from the right ventricle. (11) [AEB 1984]

2 (a) What are the causes of the 'lubb-dupp' sounds from the heart, heard through a stethoscope? (2)
(b) Why would a person with faulty main heart valves be advised not to participate in vigorous activity? (2) [Adapted from NI]
(c) What causes the semi-lunar valves to close at the end of ventricular systole? (2)
(d) What is the function of the valve cords? (2)

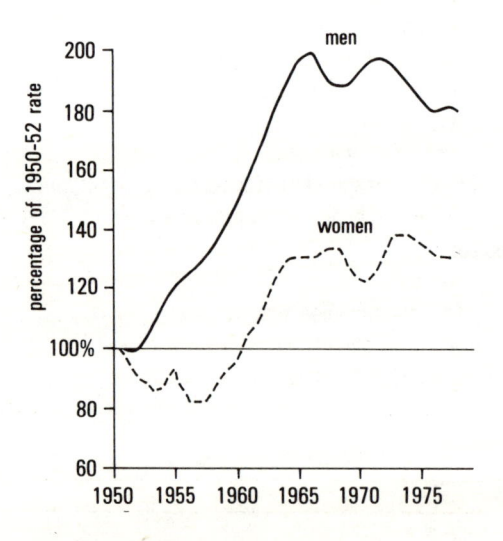

Fig 7.6 Changes in death rates from coronary heart disease in men and women aged 35–44 in England and Wales, 1950–78.

3 Using the information in Fig 7.6:
(a) Compare the main changes in the death rate due to coronary

heart disease among men and women between 1950 and 1978. (6)
(b)   State three reasons for the change in coronary heart disease rates between 1950 and 1965. (3)

Fig 7.7

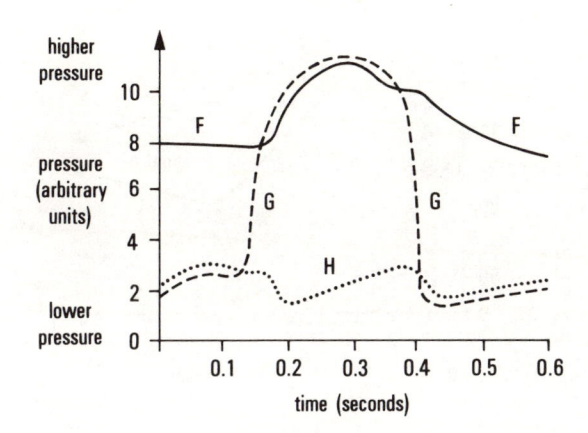

4   Fig 7.7 shows some of the changes in pressure that occur within the left atrium, the left ventricle and the aorta during a single heart cycle.
(a)   State the letter label of the line which shows the pressure changes in each case, and give a reason:
(i) left atrium
(ii) left ventricle
(iii) aorta. (6)
(b)   Mark on the diagram the point at which:
(i) the bicuspid (mitral) valve closes – label it with a letter Y. Give a reason. (2)
(ii) the semi-lunar valve closes – label it with a letter Z. Give a reason. (2)   [AEB 1984]
(c)   State the period of time during which the left ventricle is contracting and give a reason for your answer. (2)
(d)   Explain why blood pressure in the aorta fluctuates less than in the left ventricle. (2)
(e)   In what way would the curve for pressure in the right ventricle differ from that shown above for the left ventricle? (2)

5   Fig 7.8 (p. 122) shows the pulse rates of three teenage girls measured before and after taking the same amount of vigorous exercise.
(a)   What was the pulse rate for girl **A** 6 minutes after she stopped exercising?
(b)   Which of the three is
(i) the least
(ii) the most physically fit?
Give reasons. (4)
(c)   If girls **B** and **C** normally take the same amount of exercise, which is more likely to be a smoker? Give a reason. (2)

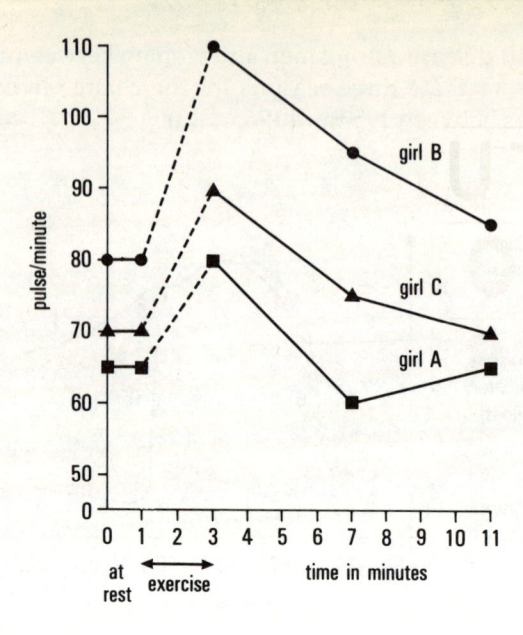

Fig 7.8

CHAPTER EIGHT

STRUCTURE AND FUNCTION OF BLOOD VESSELS AND LYMPH

CONTENTS

▶ 8.1 Comparison of arteries and veins — 125

▶ 8.2 The circulation system — 125
Common blunders 127

▶ 8.3 Exchange of substances in the tissues — 127
Mechanism of exchange 128

▶ 8.4 The lymphatic system — 129
Structure of the lymphatic system 129
Functions of the lymphatic system 129

▶ 8.5 Differences between body fluids — 130

▶ 8.6 Checklist — 131

▶ 8.7 Exam questions — 131

Structure and function of blood vessels and lymph

8.1 COMPARISON OF ARTERIES AND VEINS

Fig 8.1 compares the structure of veins and arteries, while Table 8.1 compares their functions.

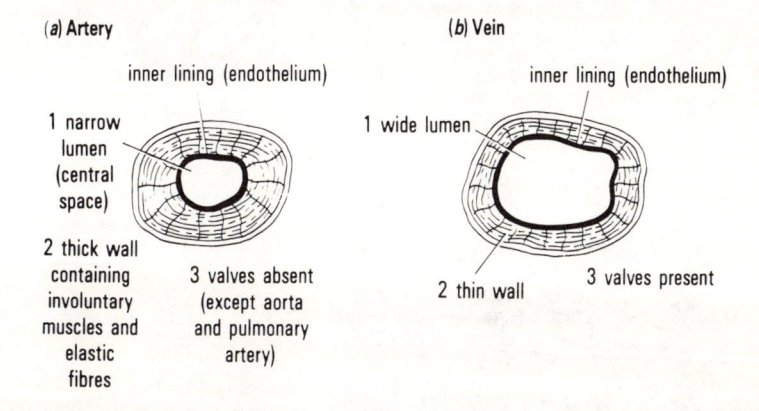

(a) Artery

inner lining (endothelium)

1 narrow lumen (central space)

2 thick wall containing involuntary muscles and elastic fibres

3 valves absent (except aorta and pulmonary artery)

(b) Vein

inner lining (endothelium)

1 wide lumen

2 thin wall

3 valves present

Fig 8.1 Differences in structure between cross sections of arteries and veins (differences are numbered).

Table 8.1 Differences between the functions of arteries and veins

Arteries	Veins
1 Always carry blood away from the heart.	Always carry blood towards the heart.
2 Carry oxygenated blood (except pulmonary artery).	Carry deoxygenated blood (except pulmonary vein).
3 Carry low levels of dissolved carbon dioxide (except pulmonary artery).	Carry high levels of dissolved carbon dioxide (except pulmonary vein).
4 Blood travels under high pressure (see Table 8.2).	Blood travels under low pressure (see Table 8.2).

8.2 THE CIRCULATION SYSTEM

Fig 8.2 gives a diagrammatic representation of the circulation system, while Table 8.2 lists the ways in which blood pressure is maintained in this system. Table 8.3 looks at the detailed blood supply to the liver.

Human Biology

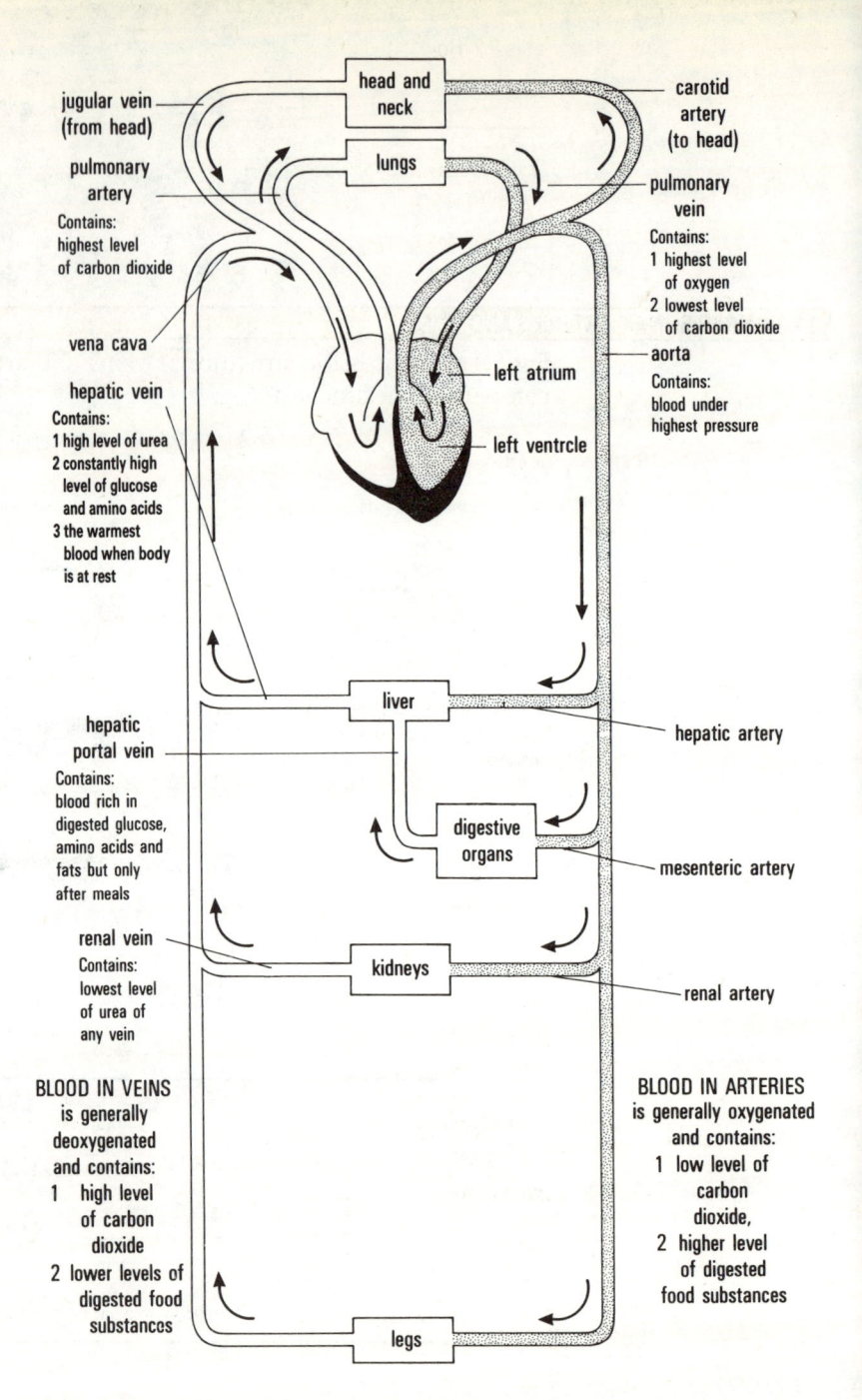

Fig 8.2 The circulation system.

Structure and function of blood vessels and lymph 127

Table 8.2 How blood pressure is maintained in the blood vessels

Arteries	Veins
Blood circulates rapidly under high pressure (12 kPa), created by:	Blood circulates under lower pressure (1 kPa), created by:
1 the contraction of the ventricles;	1 the last traces of the pressure created by the ventricles;
2 the contraction of the elastic fibres in the walls.	2 the negative pressure ('sucking action') created when the atria expand;
	3 the effects of muscles pressing on the veins during exercise, combined with –
	4 the action of the valves in the veins, preventing backflow.

Table 8.3 Functions of the hepatic (liver) blood vessels

Vessel	From	Carries blood To	Levels of concentration of dissolved substances in the blood High	Low
Hepatic artery	Aorta	Liver	Oxygen	Carbon dioxide
Hepatic portal vein	Stomach and small intestine	Liver	Carbon dioxide; after meals, water, glucose, amino acids	Oxygen
Hepatic vein	Liver	Vena cava	Carbon dioxide, urea, glucose (always high, but not as high as hepatic portal vein)	Oxygen

COMMON BLUNDERS

1. 'The blood in arteries is coloured blue.' This isn't true, even for a duke. Arterial blood is **bright red** due to the oxyhaemoglobin; venous blood is **dark red** (less oxyhaemoglobin).
2. 'Capillaries are one cell thick.' No – it's the capillary *wall* which is one cell thick. The capillary itself is wide enough to hold a red cell.
3. 'Arteries have a thick *cell* wall.' It's the wall of the artery itself which is thick.

8.3 EXCHANGE OF SUBSTANCES IN THE TISSUES

Four kinds of small blood vessel are involved in the circulation through any major organ or tissue e.g. the muscles in the leg (see Fig 8.3).

Human Biology

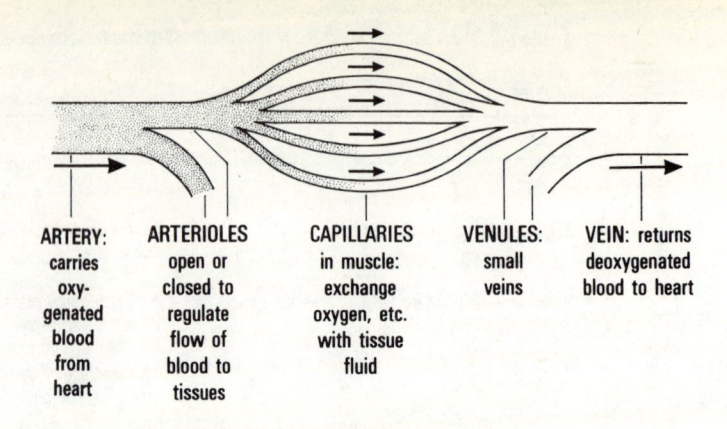

Fig 8.3 Relationship between the smaller blood vessels in the tissues.

ARTERY:	ARTERIOLES	CAPILLARIES	VENULES:	VEIN: returns
carries	open or	in muscle:	small	deoxygenated
oxy-	closed to	exchange	veins	blood to heart
genated	regulate	oxygen, etc.		
blood	flow of	with tissue		
from	blood to	fluid		
heart	tissues			

MECHANISM OF EXCHANGE

As blood flows through the capillaries, there is an extensive exchange of substances with the tissue fluid (see Fig 8.4) because of the following: (see page 129)

Labels on Fig 8.4:
- tissue fluid enters lymph
- white blood cell enters lymph
- lymphatic vessel
- fluid containing oxygen and glucose forced through capillary walls
- cells in the tissues
- tissue fluid containing CO_2 enters blood
- capillary wall
- oxygenated blood from artery under high pressure
- deoxygenated blood to vein at lower pressure

arterial end: blood pressure greater than osmotic pressure
- 4.3 kPa blood pressure
- 3.3 kPa osmotic pressure

venous end: blood pressure is less than osmotic pressure
- 1.6 kPa blood pressure
- 3.3 kPa osmotic pressure

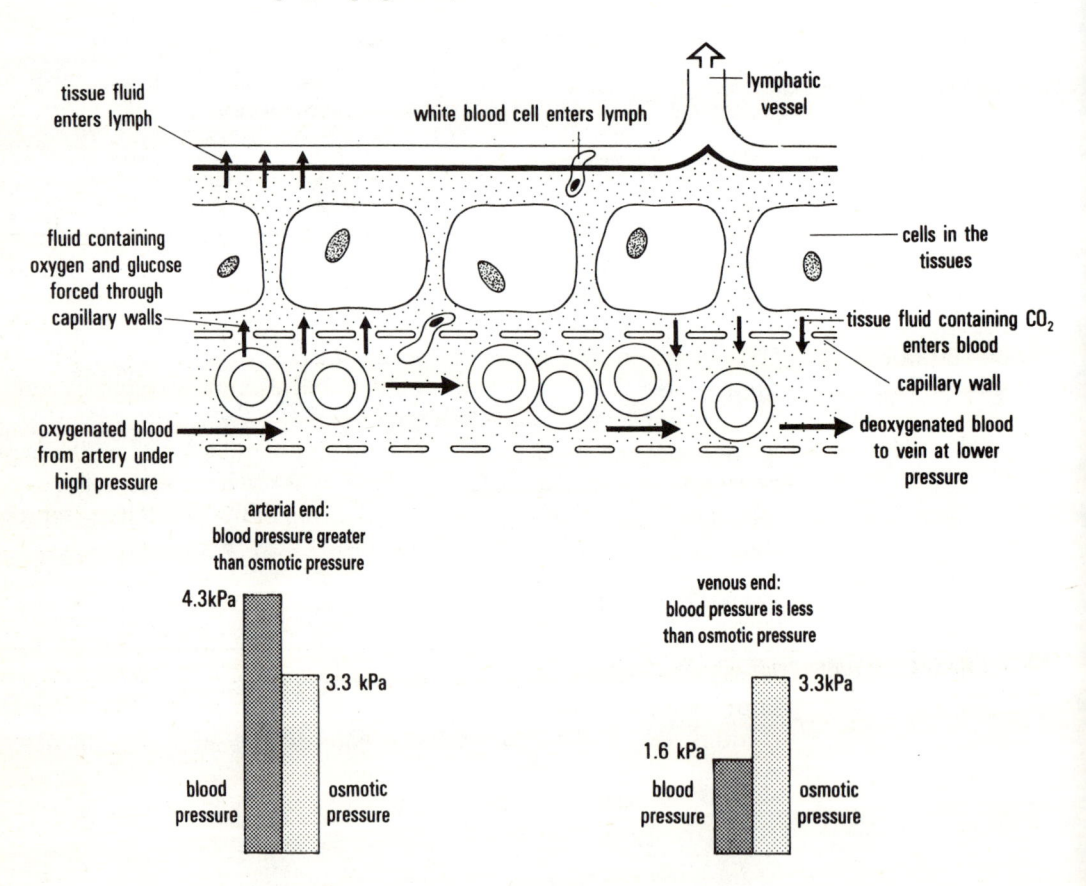

Fig 8.4 How fluid enters and leaves the blood and lymph.

Structure and function of blood vessels and lymph

1. The capillaries are thin-walled and **permeable**.
2. The **high blood pressure** at the arterial end of each capillary forces fluid (mainly water) out through the capillary walls, carrying with it oxygen and digested foods, etc. Proteins and red cells remain within the capillary.
3. Towards the venous end, blood pressure falls but **osmotic pressure** rises owing to the loss of water, until it is higher than the osmotic pressure of the surrounding tissue fluid.
4. This causes fluid containing wastes, such as carbon dioxide, to **diffuse** from the tissue fluid into the capillary.

8.4 THE LYMPHATIC SYSTEM

The lymphatic system consists of a set of vessels similar to the veins. Its two main functions are:

1. to return surplus tissue fluid to the main blood supply;
2. to help defend the body against infection.

Don't be vague about the functions of lymph. *Avoid* answers like 'Drains the body', 'Absorbs food' or 'Fights disease'.

STRUCTURE OF THE LYMPHATIC SYSTEM

1. **Lymph** is a colourless fluid, containing water, waste materials, cell products, such as hormones, and digested fats. Lymph carries lymphocytes which are made in the lymph nodes, and phagocytes which enter by squeezing through the walls of the lymphatic vessels.
2. **Small lymphatic vessels** are found throughout the tissues. These are similar to capillaries, but with closed ends. **Lacteals** are specialized lymph vessels in the small intestine which absorb digested fats (see Fig 8.5).
3. **Lymph nodes** are small swellings found in groups along the lymph vessels, especially in the groin, neck, and armpit (see Fig 8.5). The tonsils and the spleen are examples of large lymph nodes.
4. The main **lymphatic ducts** collect lymph from the small vessels for return to the circulation system. They contain valves and are similar to veins. Lymph is moved through them by the pressure of muscles during exercise, combined with the action of these valves.

FUNCTIONS OF THE LYMPHATIC SYSTEM

Table 8.4 Functions of the lymphatic system

Transport from tissues to main circulation of	Defence against infection by the lymph nodes
1 Surplus tissue fluid.	1 Manufacture lymphocytes which make antibodies.
2 Cell products, e.g. hormones.	2 Trap microorganisms in a fibrous filter which contains phagocytes.
3 Digested fats from small intestine.	

Fig 8.5 The lymphatic system

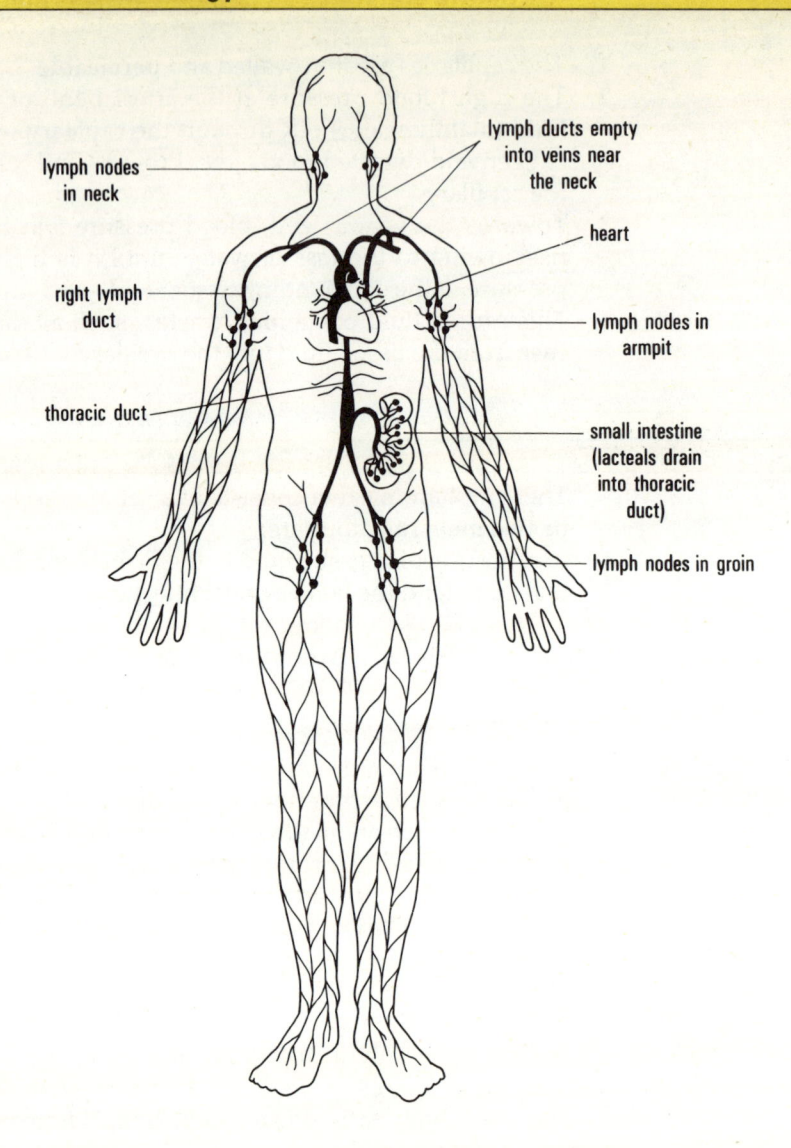

[Diagram labels: lymph nodes in neck; lymph ducts empty into veins near the neck; heart; right lymph duct; lymph nodes in armpit; thoracic duct; small intestine (lacteals drain into thoracic duct); lymph nodes in groin]

8.5 DIFFERENCES BETWEEN BODY FLUIDS

Table 8.5 Comparison between plasma, serum, lymph and tissue fluid

Fluid	Situation	Composition	Cells carried in suspension
Plasma	In the blood vessels; the liquid component of blood.	Contains blood proteins and dissolved food substances.	Red and white cells.
Serum	Made from plasma; carries antibodies (p. 316).	Similar to plasma, but fibrinogen and cells removed.	No cells present.
Tissue fluid	Bathes the cells of the tissues.	No blood proteins present, but contains high level of cell products.	White cells present.

Structure and function of blood vessels and lymph

Fluid	Situation	Composition	Cells carried in suspension
Lymph	In the lymphatic system.	No blood proteins present, but contains high level of cell products, and digested fats (after meals).	High concentration of white cells present.

8.6 CHECKLIST

- Arteries v. veins:
    Four differences in functions;
    three differences in structure.
- Maintenance of blood pressure in arteries and veins.
- Circulation system – Fig 8.2.
- Exchange of substances between capillaries, tissues and lymph.
- Lymphatic system:
    structure;
    functions.
- Differences between plasma, serum, tissue fluid, lymph.

8.7 EXAM QUESTIONS

1 Name the blood vessels (including the chambers of the heart), in correct order, through which a red cell in the toes must pass before it again reaches the toes. (5)

2 (a) Name the blood vessel in which you would expect to find the greatest concentration of the following chemical substances:
    (i) oxygen
    (ii) carbon dioxide
    (iii) glucose
    (iv) urea. (4)
   (b) In which blood vessel would you find
    (i) the warmest blood when the body is at rest
    (ii) blood under the greatest pressure? (2)

3 Fig 8.6 represents part of the circulatory system and the organs linked to it.
   (a) Name each of the blood vessels labelled **A, B, C, D, E** and **F**. (6)
   (b) State the expected differences in concentration of each of the following: *amino acids, glucose* and *urea* in the blood flowing in vessels **A** and **B** following the digestion of a meal (3)   [AEB 1985]
   (c) State **three** ways in which the composition of blood differs in vessels **D** and **E**. (3)

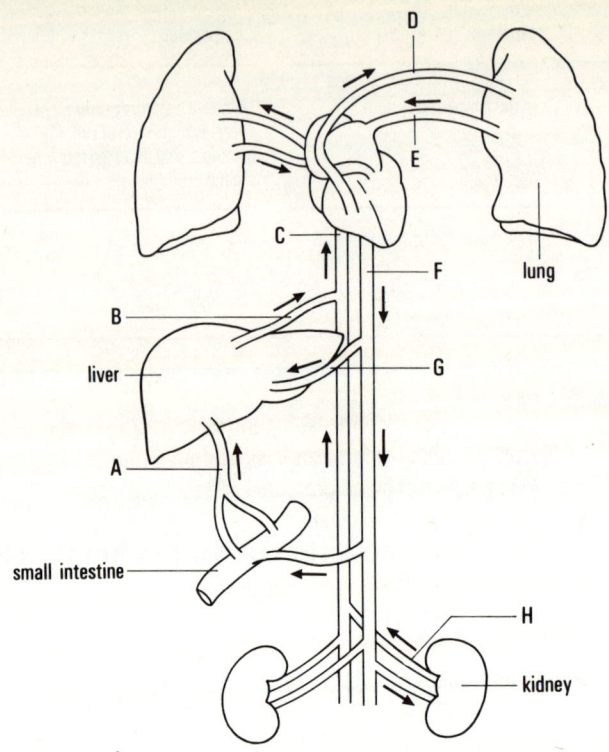

Fig 8.6

4 (a) Fig 8.7 shows the variation in pressure and velocity of blood as it passes through the circulatory system. Study the graph and answer the questions below.

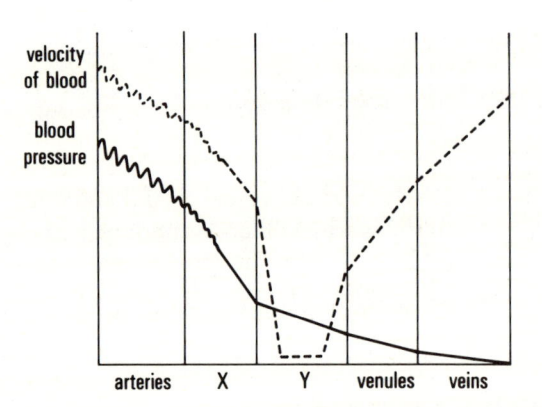

Fig 8.7

(i) What vessels occur at X? (1)
What vessels occur at Y? (1)
(ii) In which vessels is the pressure lowest? (1)

(iii) State the principal cause for the drop in blood pressure as the blood passes around the circulatory system. (2)
(iv) What is the cause of the fluctuations in blood pressure in the arteries? (2)
(v) In which vessels is the velocity of the blood lowest? (1)
(vi) What are the advantages of this slow flow of blood in these vessels? (2)
(vii) State **concisely** how the blood gets back to the heart from the veins in the legs, in spite of the pressure in the veins being so low. (2) [C]

5 Fig 8.8 represents some cells of a tissue and the associated circulatory system.

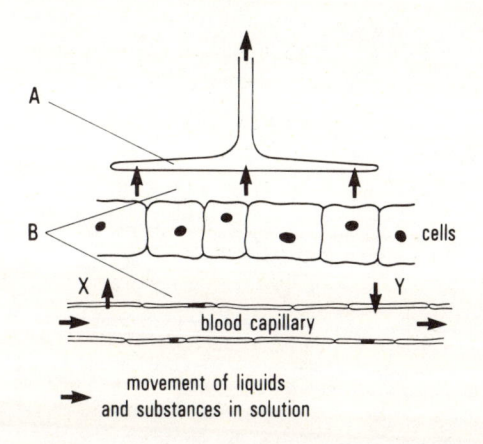

Fig 8.8

(a) Name the fluids which fill the spaces labelled **A** and **B**. (2)
(b) (i) Name two substances needed for the metabolism of the cells which they will acquire from **B**. (2)
(ii) Name one product of their metabolism which will pass from **B** into the capillary. (1)
(c) Name three components of the blood which will not pass into **B** from the capillary. (3) [AEB 1985]
(d) Explain the reasons for the movement of fluids at **X** and **Y**. (2)

6 Describe two major functions of the lymphatic system. (5 each)

7 (a) Give two major differences between blood plasma and lymph. (2)
(b) List, in order, the different structures that extracellular fluid passes through from its point of release at the capillaries to its point of re-entry into the blood stream. (2)
(c) People who are confined to bed or to a wheelchair for a long period of time often find that their legs and ankles swell up yet this seldom happens in active people.
(i) What is the most likely cause of this swelling? (1)

(ii) What two simple practical steps could be taken to combat this problem in a person who was paralysed from the waist down? (2) [*NI*]

CHAPTER NINE

FOOD AND NUTRITION

CONTENTS

▶ **9.1 The need for food** — 137

▶ **9.2 Proteins, carbohydrates and fats** — 137
Different kinds of protein   138

▶ **9.3 Vitamins** — 138

▶ **9.4 Minerals** — 139

▶ **9.5 Water, fibre and milk** — 139
Water   139
Dietary fibre   139
Milk   139

▶ **9.6 Food tests** — 140
Important safety precautions for food tests, etc   140
Carbohydrates – starch   140
Carbohydrates – sugars which act as reducing agents   141
Fats   141
Soluble proteins – Biuret test   141

▶ **9.7 Tests for vitamin C** — 141
DCPIP test for Vitamin C   141
Calculating the concentration of ascorbic acid in food   142
Writing up food tests   142

Contents

▶ **9.8 Checklist** 142

▶ **9.9 Exam questions** 143

Food and nutrition

9.1 THE NEED FOR FOOD

Food is needed to provide the raw materials for growth and the replacement of dead cells, and as a source of energy.

Why do animals need food? All animals, including humans, need a supply of large organic molecules to provide energy and the raw materials for growth. Unlike plants, animals are unable to manufacture these from small inorganic molecules such as water and carbon dioxide (see photosynthesis, page 353).

The **seven main types** of food needed for health are:

1 proteins;
2 carbohydrates;
3 fats (or lipids);
4 vitamins;
5 minerals;
6 fibre (or roughage);
7 water.

9.2 PROTEINS, CARBOHYDRATES AND FATS

Table 9.1 Main food requirements

Food substance and chemical symbols, etc.	Elements present	Required by the body for	Important sources
1 Proteins Made of basic units called amino acids. These are joined together by peptide bonds.	Carbon, hydrogen, oxygen, nitrogen; often phosphorus and sulphur also.	Growth and repair of tissues. 1 g yields 17 kJ of energy.	Lean meat, fish, eggs, milk, cheese, peas, beans, etc.; cereals, e.g. wheat
2 Carbohydrates Basic units are glucose molecules, each consisting of a ring of 6 carbon atoms. Simple carbohydrates like sugars may contain 1 ring only (glucose) or 2 rings (sucrose). Complex carbohydrates, called **polysaccharides**, contain hundreds of basic units. Examples include starch and glycogen.	Carbon, hydrogen and oxygen. Always twice as many hydrogen atoms as oxygen, e.g. $C_6H_{12}O_6$ (glucose).	As a source of energy. 1 g yields 17 kJ of energy.	Cane sugar, sugar beet (sucrose). Fruit and honey (other sugars). Potatoes, rice, corn (starch). Liver (glycogen)
3 Fats and oils (also called **lipids**) Basic units are fatty acids joined to glycerol.	Carbon, hydrogen and oxygen.	As an energy reserve and for insulation. 1 g yields 39 kJ of energy.	Butter, margarine, oils, fatty meat, cheese, fish, milk

Human Biology

DIFFERENT KINDS OF PROTEIN

All proteins are made from combinations of 22 different kinds of amino acid. These belong to two different groups: essential amino acids (8); and non-essential amino acids (14).

1 **Essential amino acids** cannot be made in the body and so must be present in the diet.
2 **Non-essential amino acids** can be made from other amino acids and so do not need to be present in the diet.

SOURCES

Essential amino acids are mainly found in proteins from animal sources, e.g. meat, fish, milk, eggs and cheese.

Proteins from plant sources, e.g. beans, nuts and cereals, contain mainly non-essential amino acids. Soya bean protein is an exception because it is rich in essential amino acids.

COST

Animal protein usually costs more to produce than plant protein (see page 368), especially protein from cattle or sheep. The best value protein foods are therefore those which are both rich in essential amino acids and relatively cheap. These include: soya beans, krill (shrimps from cold water) and proteins from single-celled organisms such as yeast, bacteria, etc.

M only

For vegetarian diets see page 420.

9.3 VITAMINS

Vitamins are organic substances required in small quantities in the diet for certain key metabolic functions. They cannot usually be manufactured in the body.

Vitamins act in a manner similar to enzymes, and are also destroyed by heat.

Table 9.2 Major vitamin requirements

Vitamin	Main sources	Use in the body	Effects of deficiency
A	Milk, butter, liver, fresh green vegetables.	Resistance to infections. Manufacture of eye pigment called rhodopsin.	Skin and respiratory infections. Night blindness
C (ascorbic acid)	Fresh fruit and vegetables, especially oranges, lemons, etc..	Healing of wounds. Resistance to infections.	Scurvy – bleeding gums, poor clotting of blood etc
D	Cod liver oil, cream and egg yolk; also made by the skin in sunlight.	Abosrption of calcium and phosphate from food.	Rickets – weakened bones due to lack of calcium and phosphate
K	Green vegetables, e.g. spinach; produced by bacteria in the large intestine.	Essential for rapid clotting of the blood.	Blood clots slowly

For APH vitamins E and B group are also required.

Food and nutrition

9.4 MINERALS

Table 9.3 Ions of mineral salts required in the diet

Mineral ion	Sources	Use in the body	Effects of deficiency
Iron	Liver, eggs, spinach.	Manufacture of haemoglobin.	Anaemia (shortage of red cells).
Iodine (in the form of iodide)	Tap water in most areas; sea food.	Manufacture of thyroxine.	Sluggish metabolism, cretinism, goitre.
Calcium	Cheese, milk, beans. Tap water in hard water areas.	Clotting of blood, conduction of nerve impulses. Manufacture of bone (with phosphate).	Excess bleeding, nerve disorders. Rickets (weak bones).
Fluoride	Drinking water; fluoridated toothpaste.	Strengthens enamel of teeth.	Dental caries (tooth decay)

9.5 WATER, FIBRE AND MILK

WATER

Water is **essential** for:
1. the transport of dissolved substances around the body;
2. the removal of dissolved waste products;
3. maintaining a constant body temperature, e.g. by sweating;
4. virtually all of the functions of cells, because these involve chemical changes which only take place in solution.

DIETARY FIBRE (ROUGHAGE)

Dietary fibre is mainly indigestible fibrous material found in some fruits and vegetables, especially the husks from grains of cereal (called bran). About 30 g per day is needed in the diet because:
1. it provides bulk to the faeces, so stimulating peristalsis (p. 78) in the gut, and preventing constipation;
2. it also helps to prevent diverticulitis (inflammation of the colon), cancer of the bowel and coronary thrombosis.

Bran is the most effective form of fibre for preventing the above conditions.

MILK

Milk is close to being a complete food because it contains proteins, fats, carbohydrates, vitamins A, B, C and D, together with calcium and other minerals. Since cheese is made from milk, most cheeses also contain protein, fat, calcium and vitamins A, B and D.

9.6 FOOD TESTS

You need to know how to carry out the four food tests plus the test for vitamin C listed below, together with practical details such as safety precautions (see Fig 9.1).

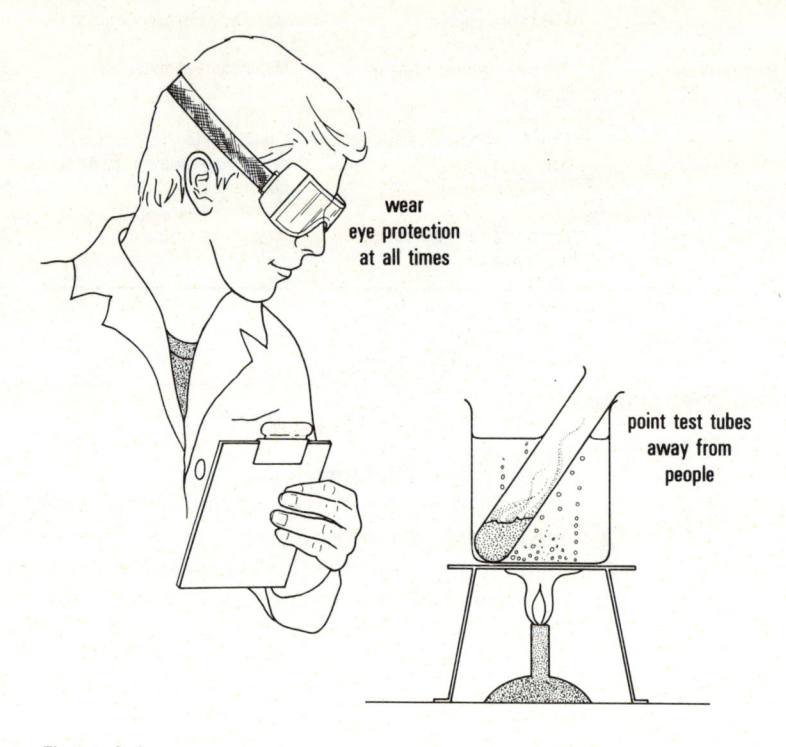

Fig 9.1 Safety precautions.

IMPORTANT SAFETY PRECAUTIONS FOR FOOD TESTS, ETC.

1. **Never taste** any of the chemicals involved – some are poisonous.
2. Wear **eye protectors** (goggles) for all tests involving heat.
3. Always use the **minimum heat** needed.
4. When heating, point the mouth of your tube **away** from other people (including yourself!).
5. **Wipe up** all spills with ample cold water immediately – some of these chemicals can burn skin or clothing.

CARBOHYDRATES – STARCH

Method Add a few drops of iodine dissolved in potassium iodide solution, to a solution or suspension of the food under test.

Expected result The solution turns blue/black.

Conclusion The food contains starch.

Food and nutrition

CARBOHYDRATES – SUGARS WHICH ACT AS REDUCING AGENTS

Method
1. Add 2 cm^3 of Benedict's solution to 2 cm^3 of a solution of the food under test.
2. Boil the mixture for a few seconds.

Expected result The solution turns green/yellow, and an orange precipitate may appear.

Conclusion The food contains a reducing sugar such as glucose.

FATS

Method Rub a sample of the food on a piece of absorbent paper.

Expected result A translucent spot appears on the paper.

Conclusion The food contains fat.

SOLUBLE PROTEINS – BIURET TEST

Method
1. Dissolve a small piece of food in 2 cm^3 of water and add 2 cm^3 of 20 per cent sodium hydroxide.
2. Stir well and add three drops of 1 per cent copper(II) sulphate. Stir again and leave for a few minutes in a warm place.

Expected result A pink, mauve or violet colour.

Conclusion The food contains protein.

9.7 TESTS FOR VITAMIN C

DCPIP TEST FOR VITAMIN C (ASCORBIC ACID)

You can test for ascorbic acid because it decolourizes a blue dye called DCPIP.

Method
1. Use a syringe to place exactly 1 cm^3 of DCPIP in a test tube.
2. Add 1 cm^3 of the food under test, e.g. lemon juice, drop by drop from a second syringe. Be careful not to shake the tube because oxygen from the air restores the blue colour of DCPIP.
3. Record the volume of lemon juice required just to decolourize the blue dye.

Expected result The dye turns pale.

Conclusion Vitamin C is present.

CALCULATING THE CONCENTRATION OF ASCORBIC ACID IN FOOD

Method

1. Repeat the test with a standard solution containing a known concentration of ascorbic acid, e.g. 0.8 mg per cm^3.
2. Write down the volume of the standard solution which just decolourizes the DCPIP.

Calculation Suppose your results were as follows:

1. Volume of lemon juice needed to decolourize 1 cm^3 of DCPIP
$$= 0.4\ cm^3$$
2. Volume of standard solution needed to decolourize 1 cm^3 of DCPIP
$$= 0.5\ cm^3$$
3. Therefore the lemon juice was $\frac{0.5}{0.4}$ times as concentrated as the standard solution

Conclusion If the standard solution contained 0.8 mg ascorbic acid per cm^3 of solution, then the lemon juice contains:

$$\frac{0.5}{0.4} \times 0.8 = 1.0\ \text{mg ascorbic acid per } cm^3 \text{ of solution}$$

WRITING UP FOOD TESTS

1. When describing food tests, *always* use the headings **method, results, conclusions**.
2. Don't write 'The test was positive.' Always describe exactly *what you saw happening*, e.g. 'A yellow colour appeared', etc.

9.8 CHECKLIST

- The need for food.
- Seven main types of food.
- Proteins, fats, carbohydrates – Table 9.1.
- Vitamins – Table 9.2.
- Mineral ions – Table 9.3.
- Types of protein:
  essential/non-essential; animal/plant.
- Definition of a vitamin.
- Four reasons for needing water.
- Value of:
  dietary fibre;
  milk
- Food tests:
  safety precautions;
  tests for starch, reducing sugars, fats, proteins, vitamin C;
  calculating the quantity of vitamin C.

Food and nutrition

9.9 EXAM QUESTIONS

1. Explain why most green plants require only inorganic substances for survival. (4)
2. Explain briefly how fats, proteins and carbohydrate differ from each other in relation to:
   - (a) The elements present in each. (2)
   - (b) The proportions of those elements. (2)
   - (c) Their basic structure. (3)
   - (d) Their function in the body. (3)
3. (a) Why do animals such as cats have no need for vitamin C? (1)
   (b) Which vitamin is likely to be deficient in a diet consisting of bread, butter, chicken pie, boiled eggs and cake, with tea or coffee? (1)
   (c) Table 9.4 shows the results of a study into the effects of additional vitamin C in the diet on respiratory disease in children.

   Table 9.4

Number of children	Amount of additional vitamin C eaten per day (in mg)	Average number of days of respiratory illness per year
123	0	57
98	1000	36
110	2000	34

   (i) From the table what was the effect of added vitamin C? (1)
   (ii) What does the study reveal about the effect of different amounts of vitamin C? (1) [APH]
4. How would you test a sample of urine for
   - (a) albumen (a protein), and
   - (b) glucose? (3 each)
5. (a) If 1 cm^3 of DCPIP solution is just decolourized by 0.9 cm^3 of a sample of fresh lemon juice, and by 0.5 cm^3 of a standard solution containing 2.0 mg of ascorbic acid per cm^3, what is the concentration of ascorbic acid in the lemon juice? Show your working. (3)
   (b) If the same test was repeated with canned lemon juice, how might the result differ? Give a reason. (2)
6. In an experiment, first carried out by Gowland Hopkins, two similar groups of eight young rats were maintained on a basic diet of purified protein, carbohydrate, inorganic salts and water. In addition, Group **A** were given a small amount of milk daily (about 4 per cent of the total food intake). Group **B** received no such addition. After 18 days the milk addition was transferred from Group **A** to Group **B**. Fig 9.2 summarizes the results obtained.

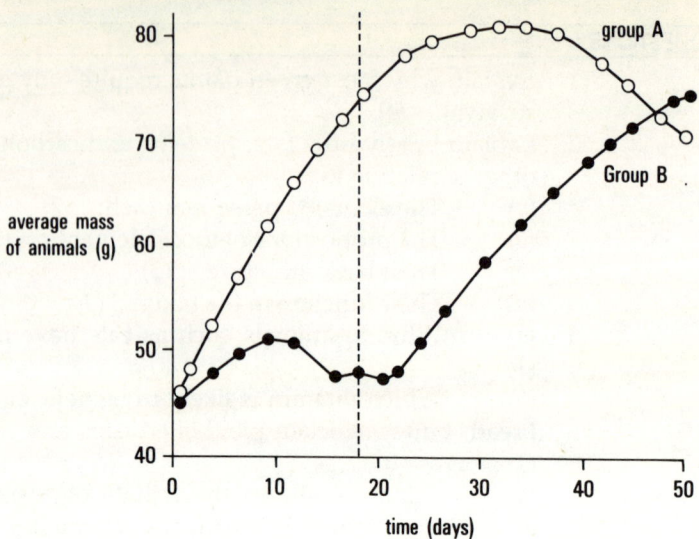

Fig 9.2

(a) Suggest TWO potential sources of experimental error which were eliminated by using two groups of rats rather than two individual rats. (2)

(b) In the first 18 days, what effect did the addition of milk have on the growth of the rats? (1)

(c) Although Group **B** did not receive milk in the first 8 days, they initially showed an increase in mass. Suggest a reason for this. (1)

(d) What was the effect on the growth of both groups of changing the milk addition after day 18? (2)

(e) A possible reason for the results could be that the milk was providing vitamins. State the evidence which supports this view. (2)

[SWEB]

CHAPTER TEN

ENERGY AND FOOD

CONTENTS

- **10.1 The balanced diet and daily food** — 147
  How much food do we need daily? 147

- **10.2 Energy requirements and metabolic rate** — 147
  Measuring energy 147
  Metabolic rate 147
  Variations in metabolic rate 148

- **10.3 Calculating daily energy requirements** — 148
  BMR is given seperately 149
  BMR is included 149

- **10.4 Malnutrition and starvation** — 149
  Anorexia nervosa 150
  Obesity and other problems 150

- **10.5 Measuring the amount of energy in food** — 150
  Simple method 150
  More accurate method 151
  Calculation 152

- **10.6 Checklist** — 152

- **10.7 Exam questions** — 153

Energy and food

10.1 THE BALANCED DIET AND DAILY FOOD

A **balanced diet** contains:
1. sufficient energy for normal daily life;
2. sufficient protein for growth and repair of the tissues;
3. sufficient vitamins, minerals, fibre and water for complete health.

HOW MUCH FOOD DO WE NEED DAILY?

On average, we need each day:
- 30 g of fibre for the optimum health of the digestive system;
- 60 g of protein for growth and repair of the tissues;
- sufficient water to prevent dehydration (see page 200);
- sufficient food (mainly fats and carbohydrates) to provide about 9000–10 000 kilojoules of energy (fat provides 39 kJ/g, proteins and carbohydrates provide 17 kJ/g each).

Very small quantities of vitamins and minerals are also needed to maintain health, but need not necessarily be eaten daily.

10.2 ENERGY REQUIREMENTS AND METABOLIC RATE

Energy is needed:
1. to replace heat lost to the environment;
2. for unconscious activity, e.g. breathing, growth, heartbeat, digestion, etc.;
3. for conscious activity, such as the muscle contractions necessary for movement.

MEASURING ENERGY

Energy is measured in joules (1000 joules = 1 kilojoule (kJ); joules have generally replaced calories (1 kilocalorie = 4.2 kilojoules).

METABOLIC RATE

Metabolic rate means the rate at which energy is used up by the body to produce heat and to carry out unconscious and conscious activities. (Comparison – petrol used by a car on a journey.)

Basal (or basic) metabolic rate means the rate at which energy is used to produce heat and to carry out unconscious activities. (Com-

Human Biology

parison – the petrol used by a stationary car with the engine just ticking over).

So:

$$\text{Metabolic rate} = \text{Basal metabolic rate} + \text{Energy used for movement}$$

VARIATIONS IN METABOLIC RATE

The overall metabolic rate varies with daily activity, especially occupation; for example, it is much lower in a bed-ridden patient than in a manual labourer.

Metabolic rate (Table 10.1) also varies as follows:

1 **by sex** – higher in males; but rises in women during pregnancy and lactation (breast feeding);
2 **by age** – it is highest in new-born babies, then falls slowly with increasing age;
3 **by climate** – Arctic inhabitants use up more energy than people living in the tropics, for the same activities.

Table 10.1 Typical daily energy needs for Europeans

Age in years	Females	kJ	Males	kJ	Age in years
1	Girl	4 500	Boy	5 000	1
5	Girl	7 000	Boy	7 250	5
17	Girl	9 000	Boy	12 000	17
75	Woman	7 000	Man	9 000	75
	Pregnant	10 500	Male office worker	10 500	
	Breast feeding	12 600	Manual labourer	18 000	

A typical 25-year-old European male requires about 7 500 kJ daily to maintain basal metabolism, plus a further 3 000 kJ for an inactive office job *or* an additional 10 000 kJ for heavy manual labour.

Note: you don't need to know these figures by heart, but you do need to know how energy needs vary with age, sex etc.

10.3 CALCULATING DAILY ENERGY REQUIREMENTS

In questions on this topic you may be given figures for energy requirements in which the basic metabolic rate (BMR) is either:

1 shown separately;
2 included.

Energy and food

BMR IS GIVEN SEPARATELY

Suppose a person has a BMR of 240 kJ/hour and spends 8 hours asleep, 8 hours at a desk using an additional 160 kJ/hour, and a further 8 hours engaged in moderate activity (walking, standing, etc.) using an additional 260 kJ/hour. Calculate the total energy requirement for the 24 hours.

Work out the answer like this:

BMR for 24 hours = 24×240	= 5 760 kJ
8 hours asleep: no extra energy used (BMR only) =	0 kJ
8 hours' desk work = 8×160	= 1 280 kJ
8 hours' activity = 8×260	= 2 080 kJ
Total	9 120 kJ

BMR IS INCLUDED

The question above could also be worded like this.

Suppose your basic metabolic rate is 240 kJ/hour. In a typical day, you spend 8 hours asleep, 8 hours at a desk using 400 kJ/hour altogether, and another 8 hours engaged in moderate activity (walking, standing, etc.) using 500 kJ/hour altogether.

Here you don't need to work out BMR separately for the whole 24 hours, so the calculation is as follows.

Asleep, basic metabolic rate only, 8×240	= 1 920 kJ
Desk work, 8×400	= 3 200 kJ
Moderate activity, 8×500	= 4 000 kJ
Total	9 120 kJ

10.4 MALNUTRITION AND STARVATION

Failure to eat a balanced diet may cause malnutrition or starvation (see page 376).

1. If the diet lacks sufficient energy content, e.g. significantly less than 10 000 kJ daily for an active 15-year-old girl, she may gradually lose weight. She will also fail to grow, because the proteins in her diet will be used to provide energy instead of new tissues.
2. If the diet lacks protein, e.g. significantly less than 60 g per adult daily, childrens' growth is stunted, and resistance to infections and healing of wounds will be poorer for all age groups.
3. Absence of particular vitamins or mineral ions leads to specific deficiencies (see Tables 9.3 and 9.4 on pages 138–9).

Human Biology

ANOREXIA NERVOSA

Anorexia nervosa is an illness involving deliberate starvation. It occurs among about 1 per cent of teenage girls and about 0.1 per cent of boys. Symptoms include loss of body fat, shrinking breasts and loss of periods, so that an adolescent girl's body looks like that of a pre-teenage child. The causes are psychological – chiefly an inability to face growing up due to feelings of failure as a teenager.

Sufferers may improve with professional counselling and support from their friends; changes to the diet are not so important as help and advice.

OBESITY AND OTHER PROBLEMS

Obesity means being overweight in relation to bone size, i.e. height and width. It is caused by taking in more kilojoules of energy in the diet than are needed by the metabolism for all daily activities.

The best cure is to **slim sensibly**. This means maintaining a balanced diet while consuming fewer kilojoules than are used up. Exercise also helps but slimming is much more effective. For example, to save 1000 kJ (or 238 kcals) you need either to eat three fewer slices of bread per day, or walk briskly for 45 minutes each day.

Obesity increases the risk of:

1. heart attacks and strokes, because the blood vessels become blocked by deposits of surplus fat;
2. arthritis at the joints, caused by the extra wear and tear of carrying around unnecessary weight.

Too much **sugar** in the diet also contributes to general overweight, increases the risk of diabetes and is an important cause of tooth decay.

Too much **salt** can be a cause of high blood pressure. This increases the risk of heart attacks and strokes in middle-aged and older adults.

10.5 MEASURING THE AMOUNT OF ENERGY IN FOOD

This is carried out by burning food in a calorimeter and measuring the amount of heat given off. Dieticians use the results when selecting menus for hospitals or school meals, etc.

SIMPLE METHOD

Energy values obtained from the simple apparatus shown in Fig 10.1 are always much too low. This is because:

1. heat escapes around the side of the beaker and from the surface of the water, etc.;
2. heat is lost from the burning food before it is placed under the beaker;
3. the food may not be completely burnt;
4. heat may be conducted away through the legs of the tripod.

Energy and food

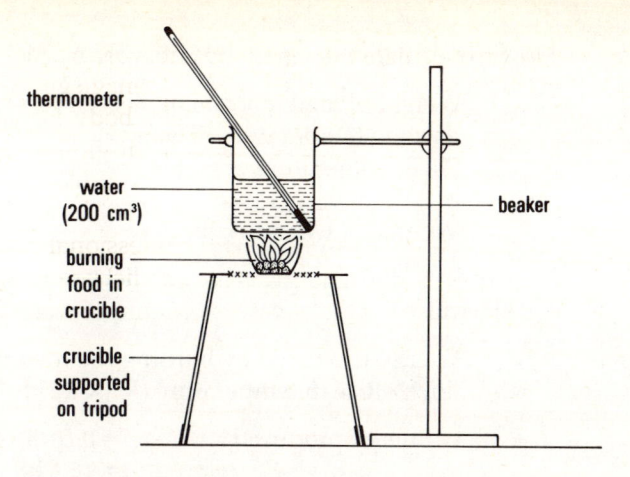

Fig 10.1 Simple calorimeter

MORE ACCURATE METHOD

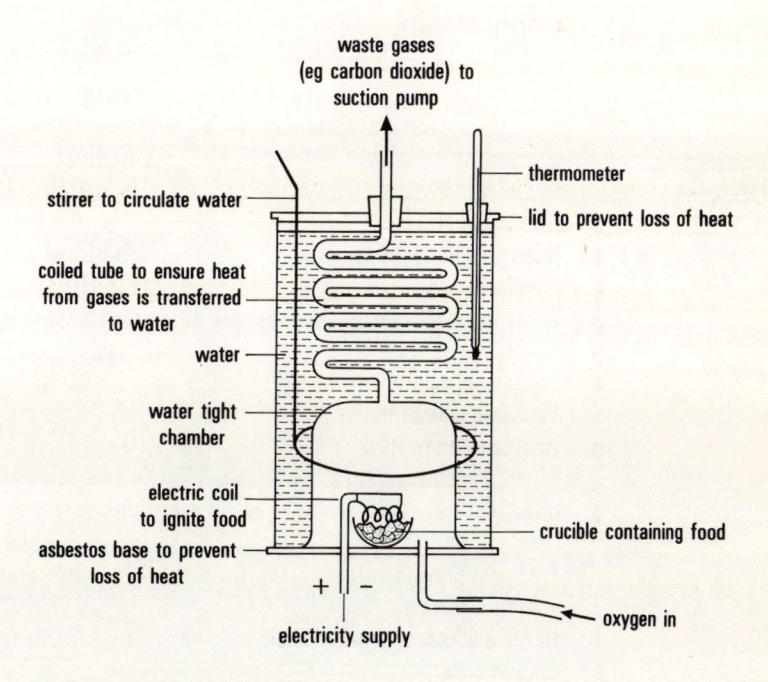

Fig 10.2 Advanced calorimeter.

Fig 10.2 shows an advanced calorimeter which gives more accurate results.

Human Biology

CALCULATION

How to calculate the result (by either method):

Weight of food, e.g. small piece of toast	= 2.5 g
Starting temperature of water	= 18°C
Final temperature of water	= 26°C
∴ Rise in temperature	= 8°C
Volume of water in cylinder	= 500 cm³ (0.5 dm³)

To calculate the energy value of the toast, remember that it takes 4.2 kJ to raise the temperature of 1 dm³ of water by 1°C. So:

Energy produced by burning the food = Volume of water (in dm³) × Rise in temperature (°C) × 4.2 kJ

∴ Energy produced = 0.5 × 8 × 4.2 kJ
= 16.8 kJ

Energy produced per gram = $\frac{16.8}{2.5}$ = 6.72 kJ/gram

Note: the true value for carbohydrates is 17 kJ/gram.

Hint: don't mix up your units! If the volume of water is quoted in cm³, then either convert to dm³ or multiply by 4.2 joules. The answer for the toast will then be 6720 joules/gram, which is the same as 6.72 kJ/gram.

Remember: use joules with cm³ and kilojoules with dm³.

10.6 CHECKLIST

- Balanced diet.
- Need for energy (three).
- Metabolic rate.
- Basal metabolic rate.
- How metabolic rate varies
- Calculating daily energy needs.
- Causes of malnutrition.
- Anorexia nervosa:
    causes.
- obesity:
    causes;
    prevention;
    effects.
- Harmful effects of sugar and salt.
- Calorimeters:
    simple;
    advanced.
- Calculating energy content of food.

Energy and food 153

10.7 EXAM QUESTIONS

1. Give three reasons why the average person needs about 10 000 kJ of energy daily. (3)
2. (a) From Table 10.1 on page 148 estimate the approximate daily energy requirements for
      (i) a boy aged 10
      (ii) a female office worker. (2)
   (b) How would the figures in Table 10.1 differ if compiled for people living in the Arctic? (1) Give a reason for your answer. (1)
3. From the information given in Figure 10.3:

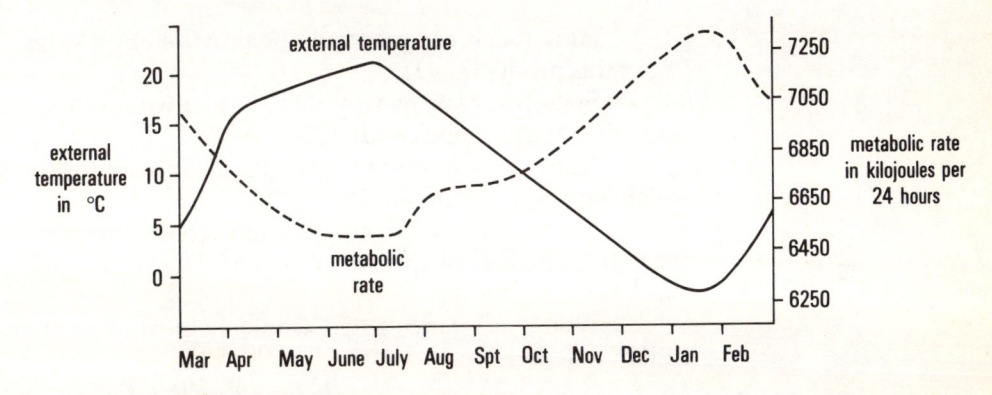

Fig 10.3 How climate effects metabolic rate. The graph shows how the metabolic rate of one person varied with the external temperature during one year (in the northern hemisphere).

   (a) What is the value for the metabolic rate at −1°C? (1)
   (b) Why does the rate rise between September and January? (1)
   (c) Suppose you want to remain the same weight throughout the year, and you take the same amount of daily exercise in every season. Why would you need to eat less in June than in January? (2)
4. A packet of breakfast cereal carries the information shown in Table 10.2.

Table 10.2 Ingredients: rolled oats, sugar, calcium carbonate, malt extract, flavouring, colour (E102, E123, E132), added vitamins.

Nutrient	Quantity per 100 g	Quantity per typical serving (30 g)
Energy	1500 kJ	450 kJ
Protein	10.3 g	3.09 g
Fat	7.2 g	2.16 g
Carbohydrate	77 g	23.1 g

Human Biology

Nutrient	Quantity per 100 g	Quantity per typical serving (30 g)
Dietary fibre	5.8 g	1.74 g
Iron	20 mg	6 mg
Vitamin C	42 mg	12.6 mg
Vitamin D	2.8 int. units	0.84 int. units

An average serving of 30 g of this cereal provides at least half of the recommended daily intake of these vitamins and minerals for a child up to 15 years of age.

(a)   How much energy would be provided by a single helping of 50 g of this product? (1)
(b)   State two reasons why this product would be a valuable part of the diet of a growing child. (2)
(c)   Name two different kinds of substance added to the product which have no nutritional value. (2)
(d)   If a 15-year-old ate no other food containing iron, what is the minimum quantity of this cereal required daily to provide sufficient iron? (1)
(e)   Which substance listed would help to prevent constipation and diverticulitis? (1)

(*In the style of W:GCSE specimen question*)

5   Table 10.3 shows some recommended daily dietary values for certain groups of people:

Table 10.3

	Energy (kJ)	Protein (g)	Ca (g)	Fe (mg)	vit. A (i.u.)	vit. D (i.u.)
Girls – 1–2 years	5040	40	1.0	7	2000	400–800
Girls – 13–15 years	11760	80	1.3	15	5000	400
Women – average activity	9500	60	0.8	12	5000	400
Women – pregnant	10500	85	1.5	15	6000	400–800

(a)   Explain the different values for energy intake shown. (4)
(b)   The energy value for wholemeal bread is 1050 kJ per 100 g. If a non-pregnant woman eats 140 g of bread a day, calculate the percentage of her energy requirement the bread will provide (show your working). (1)
(c)   From the figures given in Table 10.3, say whether these two statements are helpful or not.

Energy and food

    (i) A pregnant woman needs to eat for two. (1)
    (ii) A child should be given half adult portions of everything. (1)   [NI]

6 It has been estimated that if an adult consumes food providing 420 kJ per day more than the energy required by the body then the person can show an increase in body mass of 3.7 kg per year. Briefly explain why eating energy-containing foods which are not needed can result in an increase in body mass. (2)(*SEG:GCSE specimen question*)

7 A shift worker in a slate quarry works for 8 hours a day on heavy manual work. He sleeps for another 8 hours and is active for the other 8 hours. His basic rate of energy use is 300 kJ per hour, for light work it goes up to 500 kJ per hour and for heavy work it rises to 1500 kJ per hour. What are his total energy needs for the day? Show your working. (5)

8 The simple apparatus in Fig 10.1 can be used to measure the energy value of food. The following results were obtained when determining the energy value of 1 g of sugar.

    Starting temperature of water = 18°C
    Final temperature of water   = 30°C

(*a*) How much energy was produced in kJ/g of sugar? Show your working. (3)
(*b*) Is your answer likely to be a higher or lower figure than the result obtained with a specially manufactured calorimeter? (1)
(*c*) State three main reasons for the difference between the results obtained with the two types of equipment. (3)
(*d*) How would the result differ if the same amount of fat was used, instead of sugar? (1)   (*W*)

CHAPTER ELEVEN 157

DIGESTION AND TEETH

CONTENTS

▶ **11.1 The need for digestion**   159
Key terms   159
Digestion in the mouth   159

▶ **11.2 Dentition and types of teeth**   160
Types of dentition   160
Types of teeth   160

▶ **11.3 Structure of a tooth**   161

▶ **11.4 Care of the teeth**   161
Main dental diseases   161
Plaque and dental health   161
Preventing dental caries and periodontal disease   162
Diet and teeth   162

▶ **11.5 Checklist**   163

▶ **11.6 Exam questions**   163

Digestion and teeth

11.1 THE NEED FOR DIGESTION

Digestion is necessary because, until they have been broken down, most food molecules are too large to pass through the walls of the gut. (It is important to understand the use of dialysis tubing to demonstrate this – see question 1 on page 163.)

KEY TERMS

Table 11.1 Key terms in digestion

Term	Meaning
Ingestion	The act of taking food into the alimentary canal through the mouth.
Digestion	The breakdown of large insoluble food molecules into smaller soluble molecules capable of being absorbed into the bloodstream.
Absorption	The process whereby digested food passes from the alimentary canal into the bloodstream.
Assimilation	The incorporation of digested food into the cells of the body, e.g. amino acids are built up into proteins.
Egestion	The expulsion of undigested food from the alimentary canal (also called defaecation).

Hint: don't confuse ingestion with digestion. 'Ingestion' means roughly the same as eating, so if you get a question on ingestion, describe the functions of the teeth, saliva and tongue only. *Don't write pages on the stomach, the small intestine, etc!*

Food is digested in two ways:

1. **Physical digestion** means the mechanical breakdown of food into smaller pieces by the teeth, but without any chemical change in the food molecules.
2. **Chemical digestion** means the breakdown of large molecules to small molecules, by the action of water and enzymes.

DIGESTION IN THE MOUTH

The first stage is digestion in the mouth. This involves:

1. physical digestion by the teeth;

Human Biology

2 chemical digestion by the saliva, which contains water and the enzyme amylase.

11.2 DENTITION AND TYPES OF TEETH

TYPES OF DENTITION

We possess two sets of teeth during our lifetime.
1 **Milk** or **deciduous** teeth in childhood (see page 418 – N only).
2 **Permanent** teeth, which replace the milk teeth from the age of six onwards.

TYPES OF TEETH

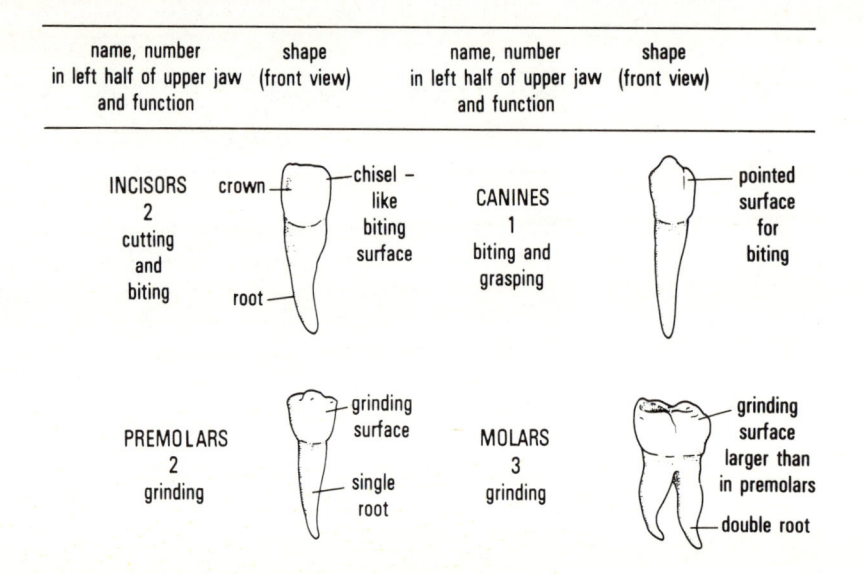

name, number in left half of upper jaw and function	shape (front view)	name, number in left half of upper jaw and function	shape (front view)
INCISORS 2 cutting and biting	crown — chisel-like biting surface — root	CANINES 1 biting and grasping	pointed surface for biting
PREMOLARS 2 grinding	grinding surface — single root	MOLARS 3 grinding	grinding surface larger than in premolars — double root

Fig 11.1 Types of teeth.

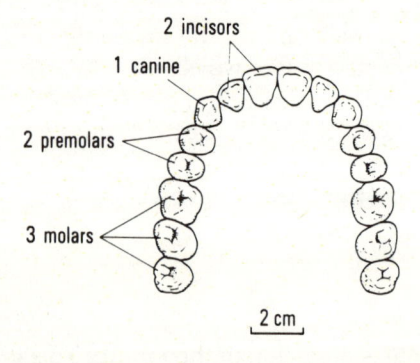

2 incisors
1 canine
2 premolars
3 molars

2 cm

Fig 11.2 Dentition of the upper jaw in an adult. (The dentition of the lower jaw is exactly the same.)

Digestion and teeth

11.3 STRUCTURE OF A TOOTH

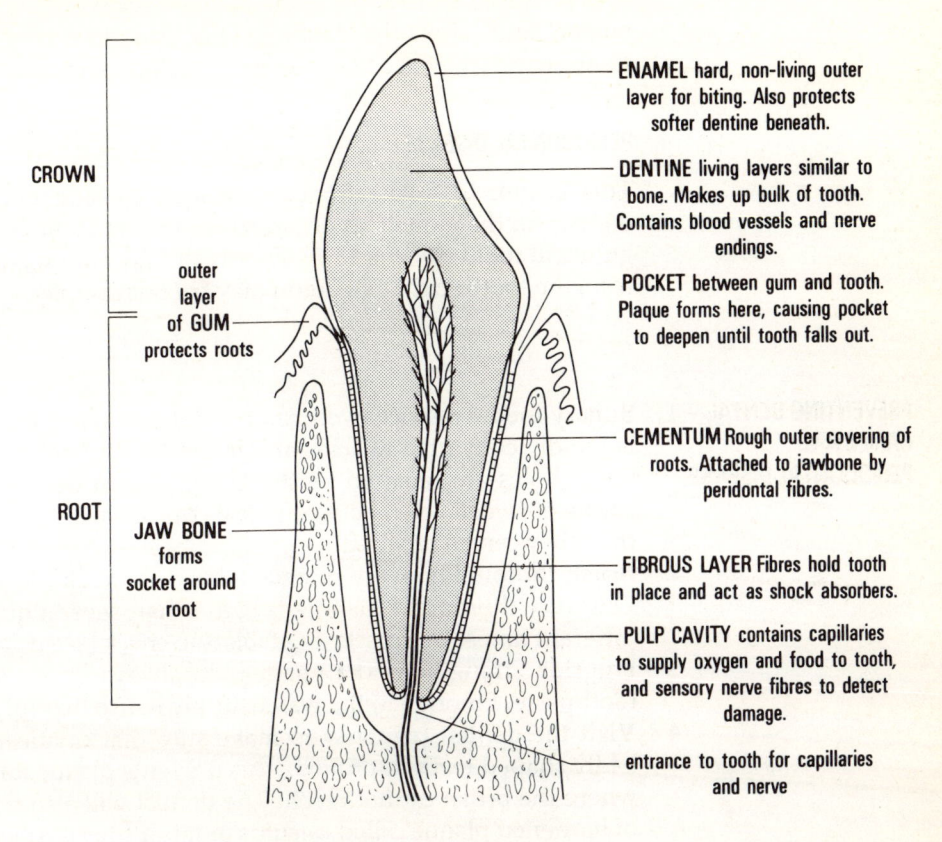

Fig 11.3 Vertical section of a human canine tooth.

Labels on diagram:
- **CROWN**
- **ROOT**
- outer layer of GUM protects roots
- JAW BONE forms socket around root
- **ENAMEL** hard, non-living outer layer for biting. Also protects softer dentine beneath.
- **DENTINE** living layers similar to bone. Makes up bulk of tooth. Contains blood vessels and nerve endings.
- **POCKET** between gum and tooth. Plaque forms here, causing pocket to deepen until tooth falls out.
- **CEMENTUM** Rough outer covering of roots. Attached to jawbone by peridontal fibres.
- **FIBROUS LAYER** Fibres hold tooth in place and act as shock absorbers.
- **PULP CAVITY** contains capillaries to supply oxygen and food to tooth, and sensory nerve fibres to detect damage.
- entrance to tooth for capillaries and nerve

Fig 11.3 shows the structure of a canine tooth.

11.4 CARE OF THE TEETH

MAIN DENTAL DISEASES Teeth are affected by two major diseases:
1. **Dental caries** or tooth decay, which causes holes in the teeth resulting in toothache, and even complete loss of a tooth.
2. **Periodontal** or gum disease which attacks the gums and can eventually cause the teeth to fall out.

PLAQUE AND DENTAL HEALTH Both diseases are caused by **plaque**. Plaque is a mixture of saliva, food and bacteria, which forms naturally on the teeth. The bacteria in the plaque produce acids and also toxins (poisons) from food, especially sugars.

DENTAL CARIES

This is caused by the acid in the plaque dissolving the minerals in the enamel and, later, the dentine. This leads to a cavity (hole) in the tooth, which may become infected, causing toothache.

PERIODONTAL DISEASE

This is due to toxins from the plaque causing inflammation and damage to the gum. This occurs in the pocket at the junction between gum and tooth (see Fig 11.3). Eventually the gum recedes (pulls back) from the tooth so that the tooth may fall out completely in later life.

PREVENTING DENTAL CARIES AND PERIODONTAL DISEASE

1. **Sugary food** – restrict sweet food and drink to mealtimes only. Sugar is rapidly converted to acids and toxins by the bacteria in the plaque. Small holes are repaired by the living cells in dentine, but frequent eating of sweets, etc., between meals causes fresh holes to form faster than they can be repaired.
2. **Brush** thoroughly every day to remove as much plaque as possible. One very thorough brushing is better than several quick attempts at different times. Use disclosing tablets to check (see below).
3. **Fluoride** strengthens the enamel, so always brush with a fluoride toothpaste. Fluoride in the water supply is also helpful.
4. **Visit the dentist regularly** to make sure that cavities are filled, and badly shaped teeth improved. This prevents plaque forming in places where the brush cannot reach. The dentist will also remove deposits of hardened plaque called calculus or tartar (this is called **scaling**).

USE OF DISCLOSING TABLETS

Pink disclosing tablets can be used to stain plaque on the teeth and so check on the effectiveness of tooth brushing. The method of use is:

1. clean teeth thoroughly;
2. chew a disclosing tablet and then rinse off with water;
3. use a mirror to examine your teeth thoroughly;
4. any plaque remaining on the teeth will be stained pink – brush again to remove all traces.

DIET AND TEETH

Calcium, phosphate and vitamin D are required for the manufacture of enamel and dentine (in addition to fluoride).

Digestion and teeth

11.5 CHECKLIST

- Ingestion.
- Digestion.
- Absorption.
- Assimilation.
- Egestion.
- The need for digestion.
- Use of dialysis tubing as a 'model gut' – see Q.1.
- Physical *v.* chemical digestion.
- Milk *v.* permanent teeth.
- Structure, functions and position of:
   - incisors;
   - canines;
   - premolars;
   - molars.
- Structure of a tooth:
   - enamel;
   - dentine;
   - cementum;
   - fibrous layer;
   - pulp cavity.
- Symptoms and causes of:
   - dental caries;
   - periodontal disease.
- Origin of plaque.
- Prevention of caries and periodontal disease:
   - four precautions.
- Use of disclosing tablets.
- Value of calcium, vitamin D and fluoride (see Q.4) for healthy teeth.

11.6 EXAM QUESTIONS

1. Fig 11.4 shows the apparatus used in an experiment. The experiment was set up as follows.

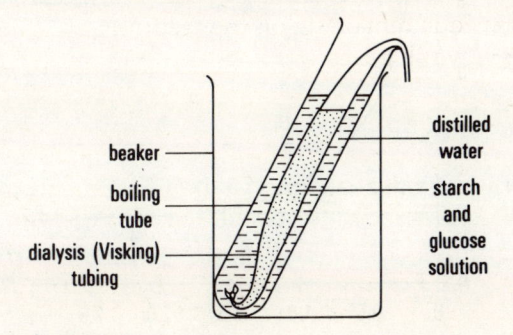

Fig 11.4

(1) Dialysis tubing, knotted at one end, was filled with a mixture of starch and glucose solution.
(2) The outside of the tubing was washed under a running tap.
(3) The tubing and contents were put into the distilled water in the boiling tube, which was supported in a beaker.
(4) Immediately, a small sample of the distilled water was taken and tested for starch and glucose.
(5) The dialysis tubing and contents were left in the distilled water.
(6) After 15 minutes, another sample of the water surrounding the dialysis tubing was taken, and tested again for starch and glucose.
(a) What was the purpose of step (2)? (1)
(b) How would you take a sample of the distilled water from the boiling tube in step (4)? (1)
(c) If, in step (4), both starch and glucose were found to be present, what TWO possible deductions could be made? (2)
(d) (i) In step (6), what results would you expect? (2)
(ii) How would you account for this? (2)
(e) This apparatus is sometimes described as a 'model gut'. What do the following parts of the apparatus represent:
(i) dialysis tubing;
(ii) distilled water? (2)

[L/EA: GCSE specimen question]

2 Explain the following facts.
(a) Holes in the enamel layer of a tooth cannot be repaired by the body but are not usually painful. (1)
(b) Holes in the dentine can cause painful sensations when eating, but are self-repairing to some extent. (1)

3 Why are the following habits liable to cause dental disease?
(a) Giving a young child a feeder containing a sugary drink to suck for long periods. (2)
(b) Drinking fizzy (carbonated) drinks containing acid frequently between meals. (2)

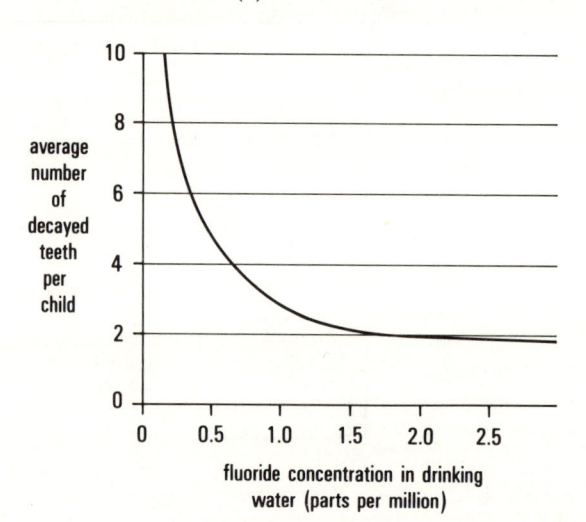

Fig 11.5

Digestion and teeth

4   Fig 11.5 shows the number of decayed teeth in children in relation to fluoride found naturally occurring in drinking water.
   (a)   What is the effect, as shown by the graph, of fluoride in drinking water?   (1)
   (b)   Fluoride may be added to drinking water artificially. This is done to produce a concentration no greater than 1.0 parts per million of the fluoride. Using information from the graph suggest why higher concentrations of fluoride are not used.   (2)
   (c)   What is the average number of decayed teeth when the fluoride concentration is 0.4 ppm?   (1)
   [SEG GCSE specimen question]
   (d)   How much additional fluoride is needed to reduce the average number of decayed (etc.) teeth from about 8 to about 3?   (1)

5   In an experiment, food debris from the teeth, glucose and a yellow indicator are placed in test tubes as shown in Table 11.2. The test tubes are kept at body temperature. The indicator changes to a red colour in acid conditions. The colour of the indicator was recorded after 45 minutes.

Table 11.2

	Tube contents	Colour of indicator after 45 minutes
A	Glucose+Indicator	Yellow
B	Food debris+Indicator	Yellow
C	Glucose+Food debris+Indicator	Red
D	Glucose+Boiled food debris+Indicator	Yellow

   (a)   Concisely explain the conclusion that 'both glucose and food debris must be present for the formation of acid in the mouth'.   (2)
   (b)   Briefly explain the effect of boiling the food debris in test tube D.   (1)
   (c)   Explain why food debris should be cleaned from the teeth regularly.   (2)   [AEB 1983]

CHAPTER TWELVE 167

DIGESTION, ABSORPTION AND ASSIMILATION

CONTENTS

- 12.1 The alimentary canal — 169
- 12.2 Digestion in the mouth — 170
- 12.3 Swallowing and breathing — 171
- 12.4 Summary of digestion by enzymes and bile — 171
- 12.5 Absorption — 172
  The small intestine   172
- 12.6 Assimilation and the liver — 173
- 12.7 Investigations with enzymes — 174
  Salivary amylase   174
  A protease enzyme – pepsin   176
- 12.8 Checklist — 177
- 12.9 Exam questions — 178

Digestion, absorption and assimilation

12.1 THE ALIMENTARY CANAL

Fig 12.1 shows the overall features of the alimentary canal.

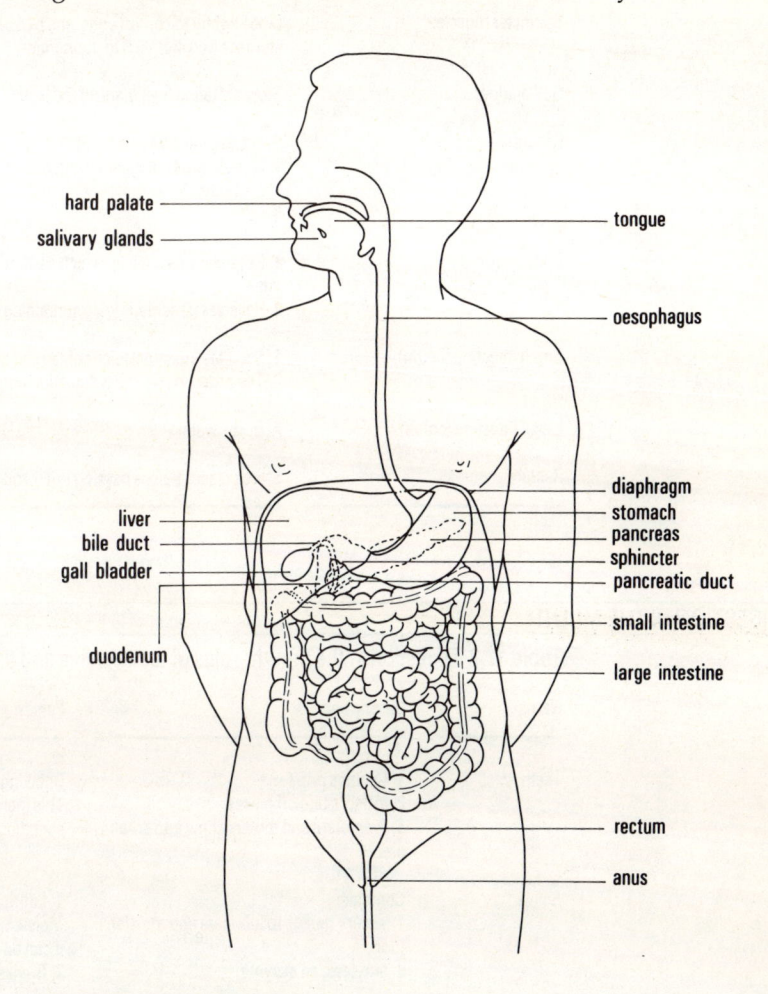

Fig 12.1 The alimentary canal

Human Biology

Table 12.1 General functions of the alimentary canal

Part	Function
Oesophagus	Transports food to stomach by peristalsis.

Stomach	1 Churns food until semi-liquid.
	2 Secretes (manufactures and produces) gastric juice containing:
	   water to dissolve food;
	   hydrochloric acid to kill microorganisms;
	   digestive enzymes, (proteases).
	3 Absorbs alcohol and glucose.
	4 Stores food, releasing small quantities at a time to the duodenum

Sphincter muscles	Close tightly to control entry and exit of food from oesophagus to stomach and stomach to duodenum.
Gall bladder	Stores alkaline bile, made in the liver.
Pancreas	Secretes digestive enzymes: 1 carbohydrase (pancreatic amylase); 2 protease; 3 lipase.
Duodenum	1 Receives alkaline bile, which neutralizes stomach acid and emulsifies fats. 2 Receives pancreatic juice containing enzymes.
Small intestine (ileum)	1 Secretes intestinal juice containing enzymes. 2 The organ where most digestion and absorption take place.
Large intestine (colon)	Absorbs water.
Rectum	Stores faeces before passing out through anus (egestion or defaecation).

12.2 DIGESTION IN THE MOUTH

Table 12.2 Digestion in the mouth: roles of teeth, saliva and tongue.

Name	Description	Functions
Teeth	1 Canines grip food. 2 Incisors bite off pieces. 3 Premolars and molars chew into small pieces.	Chewing breaks food into smaller pieces. This increases its surface area, so speeding up digestion by enzymes.
Saliva	Contains: 1 watery mucus to lubricate and moisten food; 2 amylase, an enzyme.	1 Lubrication aids swallowing. Moistening dissolves food slightly so that it can be tasted by the tongue. 2 Breaks down starch to maltose.
Tongue	Contains: 1 taste buds; 2 rolls food into a ball or bolus by muscular action.	1 To detect different tastes in food. 2 To assist in swallowing.

Digestion, absorption and assimilation 171

12.3 SWALLOWING AND BREATHING

Fig 12.2 shows how the parts of the mouth and throat act together during swallowing and breathing.

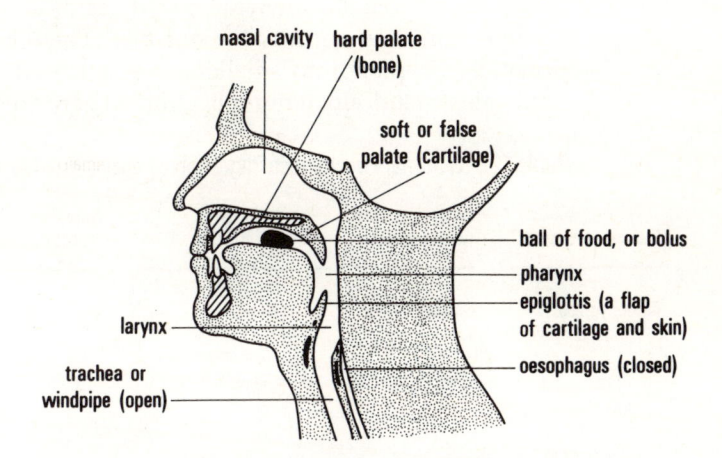

(a) Breathing; windpipe open, oesophagus closed.

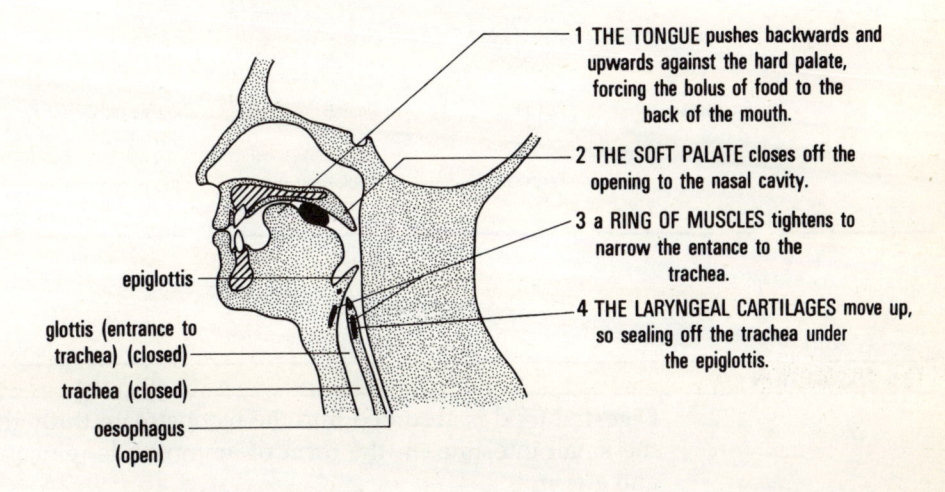

1 THE TONGUE pushes backwards and upwards against the hard palate, forcing the bolus of food to the back of the mouth.

2 THE SOFT PALATE closes off the opening to the nasal cavity.

3 a RING OF MUSCLES tightens to narrow the entance to the trachea.

4 THE LARYNGEAL CARTILAGES move up, so sealing off the trachea under the epiglottis.

(b) Swallowing; windpipe closed, oesophagus open.

Fig 12.2 Sections through the head to show swallowing and breathing. The purpose of the swallowing action is to prevent food entering the windpipe when passing from the mouth into the oesophagus. This action is entirely automatic.

12.4 SUMMARY OF DIGESTION BY ENZYMES AND BILE

1 **Proteins** are broken down to amino acids by **protease** enzymes. This process begins in the stomach but is mainly carried on in the small intestine.

Human Biology

2 **Carbohydrates** are broken down to simple sugars such as glucose, by **carbohydrase** enzymes, e.g. amylase and maltase, mainly in the small intestine.

3 **Fats** are first broken down into small droplets by the alkaline salts in bile. This increases the surface area for later digestion by the enzyme **lipase**. Lipase breaks down fats to fatty acids and glycerol.

Hint: don't get confused about bile. The alkaline bile salts break down fat droplets into smaller sizes, but without changing the fat molecules chemically (**emulsification**). There are *no* enzymes in bile.

Table 12.3 Summary of chemical digestion by enzymes

Region	Enzymes present	Source (where made)	Optimum pH	Substrate (substance acted on)		Product
Mouth	Carbohydrase: salivary amylase	Salivary glands	Neutral	Starch	→	Maltose
Stomach	Protease: pepsin	Lining of stomach	Acid pH 2–3	Proteins	→	Peptides
Duodenum and small intestine	Carbohydrases: pancreatic amylase	Pancreas	Neutral	Starch	→	Maltose
	maltase	Wall of small intestine	Neutral	Maltose	→	Glucose
	Proteases	Pancreas	Neutral	Proteins and peptides	→	Peptides and amino acids
	Lipases	Pancreas	Neutral	Fats	→	Fatty acids and glycerol

12.5 ABSORPTION

Digested food is absorbed into the bloodstream through the walls of the small intestine, in the form of amino acids, glucose, fatty acids and glycerol.

THE SMALL INTESTINE

The small intestine is adapted for absorption because of the following:
1 It has a very large **surface area** due to:
   (a) its length – up to 6 metres long;
   (b) its richly-folded epithelium, which forms millions of projecting villi (see Fig 12.3).
2 The epithelium is very **thin**, so allowing rapid passage of dissolved molecules.
3 Each villus has a **rich blood supply** and a lacteal containing lymph for rapid transport of absorbed molecules.

Digestion, absorption and assimilation 173

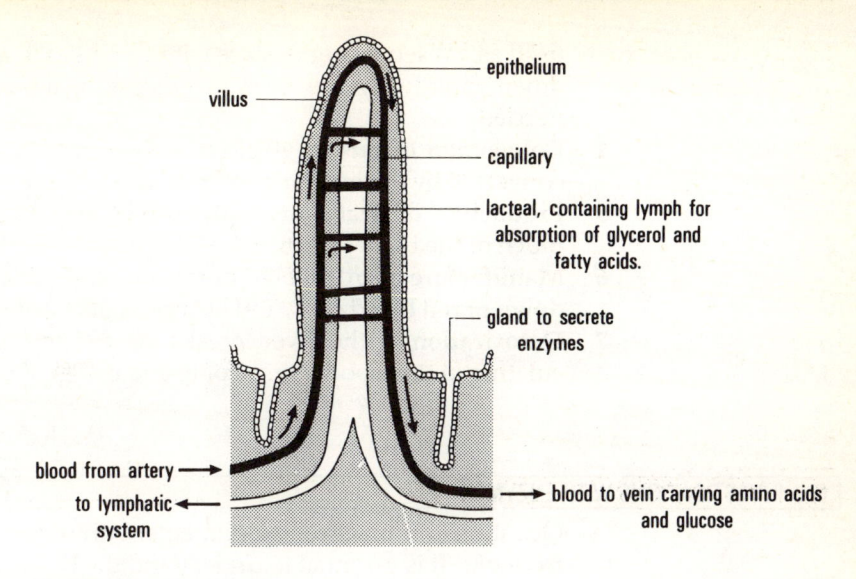

Fig 12.3 Structure of a villus.

12.6 ASSIMILATION AND THE LIVER

Table 12.4 Fate of absorbed food

End product of digestion	Destination	Uses in the body
Amino acids	Travel from villi to liver along hepatic portal vein.	1 Converted to protein for growth and repair of cells, etc. 2 Excess amino acids are deaminated by the liver to produce urea and glucose.
Glucose	Travels from villi to liver along hepatic portal vein.	1 To cells generally for use in respiration. 2 Surplus glucose stored as glycogen in the liver.
Fatty acids and glycerol	Travel from lacteal in lymph system into bloodstream.	1 Reformed into fats. 2 Used for insulation and as a store of energy.

All absorbed food is first processed by the liver, whose functions include the following:

1 **Manufacture of proteins from amino acids** – the liver manufactures a number of proteins, including fibrinogen, which is important in clotting (see page 106), and albumen.

2 **Breakdown of unwanted amino acids by deamination** to glucose and urea. The urea is excreted by the kidneys, and the glucose used for energy.

3 **Manufacture of glycogen from glucose** – glycogen is a carbohydrate

Human Biology

used as a reserve energy store (similar to starch in plants). It is broken down rapidly by the liver to glucose again when extra energy is needed.
4 **Conversion of fats to glycogen** – fats are a long-term energy store, converted by the liver to glycogen when required.
5 **Production of heat** – the high level of activity in the liver produces much of the body's heat.
6 **Manufacture of bile** – bile contains wastes produced from the breakdown of red blood cells, and also bile salts used to emulsify fats.
7 **Detoxication** – the liver breaks down poisonous substances circulating in the blood, e.g. alcohol and drugs.

12.7 INVESTIGATIONS WITH ENZYMES

Questions on practical experiments with digestive enzymes are very frequent. It is essential to understand the basic principles thoroughly. Fig 12.4 and Table 12.5 shows a typical experiment with salivary amylase, while protein digestion is discussed in Tables 12.6 and 12.7 and Fig 12.5.

SALIVARY AMYLASE

Fig 12.4 shows the sequence of events in the experiment.

Table 12.5 Action of salivary amylase on starch – results

Time in minutes after adding starch to tubes A and B	Colour of iodine with one drop from tube A	Colour of iodine with one drop from tube B
0	Dark blue	Dark blue
2	Dark blue	Dark blue
4	Pale blue	Dark blue
6	Dark brown	Dark blue
8	Dark brown	Dark blue
10	Dark brown	Dark blue

Conclusion: salivary amylase at 37°C breaks down starch solution within 6 minutes.

Hint: these results prove only that the starch in A had *disappeared* after 6 minutes. You *can't* say that the starch had changed to glucose – you need to test with Benedict's solution (see page 141) to find out if glucose is present.

Digestion, absorption and assimilation 175

1 collect a sample of saliva by chewing and spitting into a tube. Make this up to 2 cm³ with distilled water.

2 cm³ saliva and distilled water

2 stir and divide the sample into two separate tubes, labelled A and B. Place in a water bath at about 37 °C.

1 cm³ of saliva and distilled water

3 boil tube B. Allow to cool and replace in the water bath.

4 add 1 cm³ of 0.5 cm³ starch solution to A and B.

0.5 cm³ starch solution

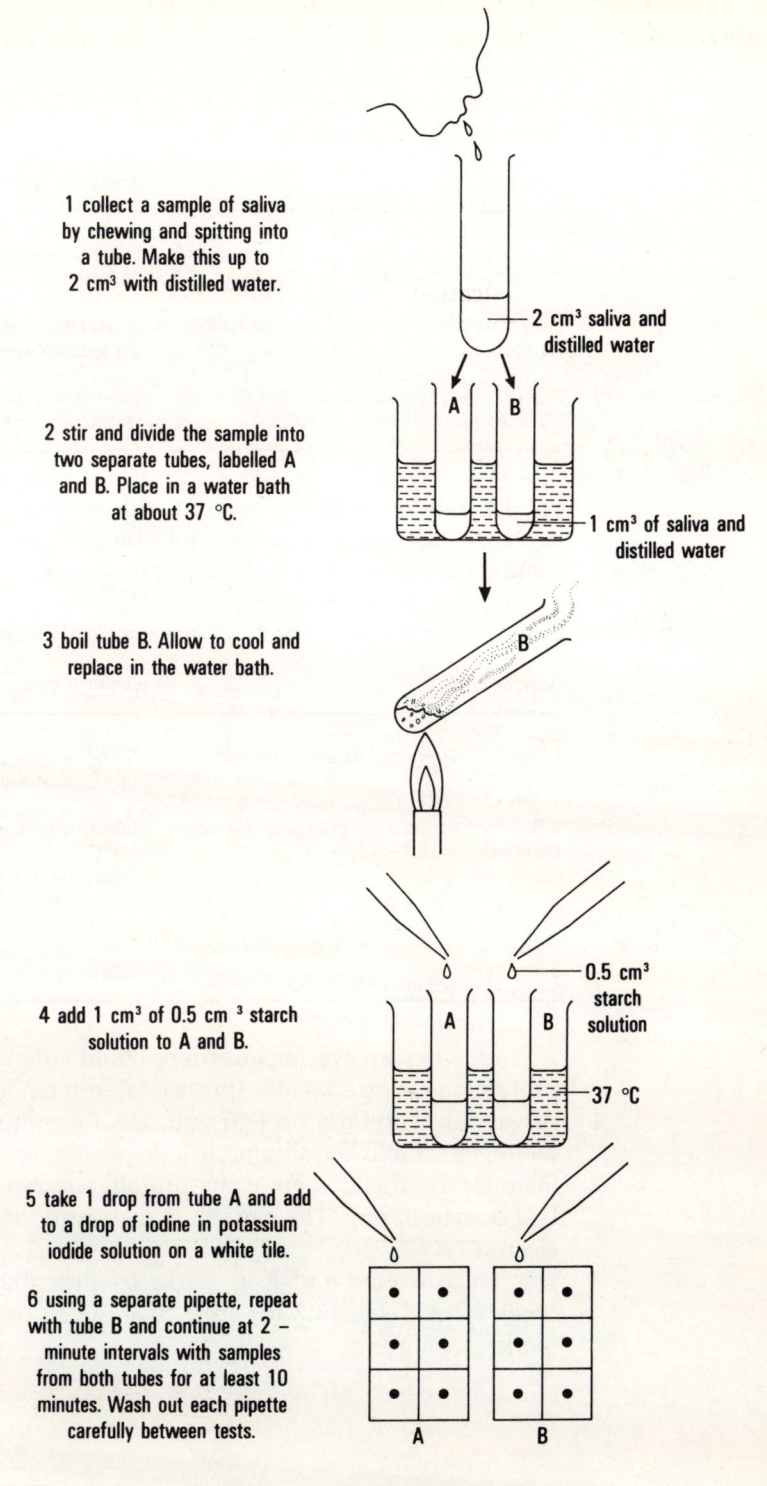

37 °C

5 take 1 drop from tube A and add to a drop of iodine in potassium iodide solution on a white tile.

6 using a separate pipette, repeat with tube B and continue at 2 – minute intervals with samples from both tubes for at least 10 minutes. Wash out each pipette carefully between tests.

Fig 12.4 To investigate the action of salivary amylase on starch.

A PROTEASE ENZYME – PEPSIN

Proteases can be tested on any substance containing protein (see Table 12.6).

Table 12.6 Effects of proteases

Substance	Effect of protease
Lumps of meat. Pieces of solid egg white.	Solid proteins slowly shrink as they are dissolved by the protease.
Suspension of liquid egg white (contains the protein albumen).	Cloudy suspension gradually clears as the protein is dissolved by the protease.
Exposed photographic film (contains dark silver salts in a base made from the protein gelatin).	The protease dissolves the gelatin, causing the silver salts to fall out. The film then turns clear.

Fig 12.5 shows a typical experiment, to investigate the action of a protease (pepsin) on gelatin, while Table 12.7 lists some other experiments that can be designed around proteases.

Table 12.7 Designing experiments with proteases, e.g. pepsin

Question	Content of tubes
1 Describe how pH affects the action of pepsin.	Tube A – enzyme, protein, acid at 37°C. Tube B – enzyme, protein, water at 37°C.
2 How does temperature affect the action of a named protease?	Tube A – enzyme, protein, acid (only if using pepsin) at 35°C. Tubes B, C, D, E, F, G, H – as A, but kept at 0°C, 10°C, 20°C, 30°C, 50°C, 60°C and 100°C.
3 Describe an experiment to investigate the action of a named protease.	Tube A – enzyme, protein, acid at 37°C. Tube B – boiled enzyme, protein, acid at 37°C.

Hint: when answering questions about your own experiments with protein digesting enzymes (proteases), remember the following.

1. Always describe the protein you used: was it solid like cooked egg white, or soluble like albumen?
2. State clearly the change in the protein which showed that digestion had occurred, e.g. 'The egg white dissolved' or a 'cloudy suspension cleared'.
3. Don't waste time and lose marks by describing unnecessary extra tubes – see Table 12.7 for style to adopt in order to maximise your marks per minute.

Digestion, absorption and assimilation 177

Fig 12.5 To investigate the action of protease (pepsin) on gelatin.

1 Set up six tubes each containing a 2 cm strip of dark (exposed) photographic film as shown:

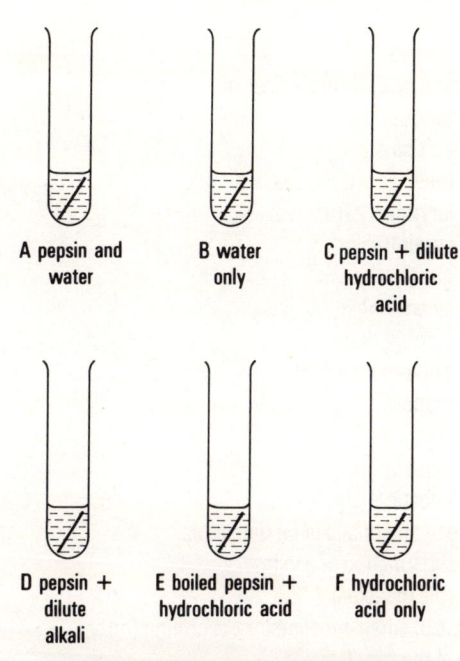

A pepsin and water

B water only

C pepsin + dilute hydrochloric acid

D pepsin + dilute alkali

E boiled pepsin + hydrochloric acid

F hydrochloric acid only

2 Place all six tubes in a water bath at 37°C

3 After 30 minutes examine the appearance of the film in each tube

Results
In tube C, the film turns clear. There is no change in any of the other tubes.

Conclusion
The enzyme pepsin dissolves the protein gelatine at 37 °C, only in the presence of dilute hydrochloric acid.

12.8 CHECKLIST

▶ Structure and functions of alimentary canal and associated organs:
- oesophagus;
- stomach;
- sphincter muscles;
- gall bladder;
- pancreas;
- duodenum;

178 Human Biology

- small intestine;
- large intestine;
- rectum.
- Digestion in the mouth – roles of:
    - teeth;
    - saliva;
    - tongue.
- Breathing and swallowing – roles of:
    - tongue;
    - soft palate;
    - muscles around trachea;
    - laryngeal cartilages;
    - epiglottis;
    - glottis.
- Digestion by enzymes:
    - carbohydrates;
    - salivary amylase;
    - maltase.
- Proteases:
    - pepsin;
    - intestinal proteases.
- Role of lipase and of bile in fat digestion.
- Structure and function of a villus:
    - role of lacteal
- Adaptations of small intestine for absorption (three).
- Functions of the liver (seven).
- Fate of absorbed foods (assimilation).
- Experiments with salivary amylase and pepsin.

12.9 EXAM QUESTIONS

1. Explain with a diagram how it is possible for food to pass from the mouth to the stomach while a person is upside down. (*Warning: Don't try it yourself.*) (4)

2. Meat, egg and fish products are rich sources of protein in our diet, but the proteins they contain are of little use to the body in the form eaten. They must undergo a process of digestion and absorption before being assimilated into the body structure.
   (a) Why is it necessary for food materials to be digested? (2)
   (b) How can the body tissues be composed of proteins which were not the same as those present in our diet? (2)
   (c) Carbohydrates in our food can be converted into fats for storage; give one chemical reason why proteins cannot be made from carbohydrates. (1) [*NI*]

3. (a) Describe the stages in the digestion of a piece of cheese. (10)
   (b) What use is made by the body of the products of its digestion? (4)

4. (a) What is the role of the liver in nitrogen metabolism? (5)

Digestion, absorption and assimilation 179

(b)   How does the liver maintain the composition and concentration of the blood? (15)

5   In the experiment on salivary amylase (see Fig 12.4 on page 175):
    (a)   Why were the tubes kept in a water bath at 37°C? (1)
    (b)   Explain why samples from both tubes turned the iodine dark blue after 2 minutes. (1)
    (c)   Explain the reason for the difference between the results in A and B. (2)

6   Fig 12.6 shows an experiment carried out to represent a model gut. The apparatus was set up and left incubated at 35°C for 30 minutes. At the start and at the end of this time the contents of the tubing and beaker were tested for starch and reducing sugar. The results are given in Table 12.8

Fig 12.6

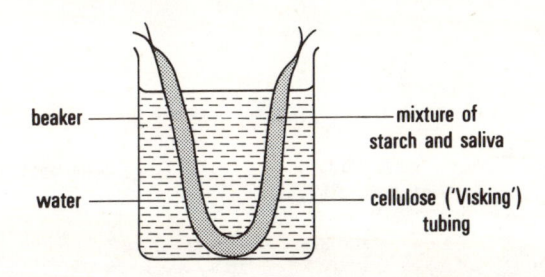

[Diagram: beaker containing water with Visking tubing holding mixture of starch and saliva]

Table 12.8

	At time 0 minutes In tubing	At time 0 minutes In beaker	At time 30 minutes In tubing	At time 30 minutes In beaker
Starch	✓	✗	✓	✗
Reducing sugar	✗	✗	✓	✓

✓ = present   ✗ = absent

Explain these results. (8)   [AEB 1984]

7   (a)   Some tissue from a living organism was ground in a pestle and mortar with water, together with a little sand to break open the cells. The material was then filtered to obtain an aqueous extract of the cells. Some of this extract was then used to set up the experiment shown in Table 12.9 on page 180.
        (i) What conclusions can you make about the substance present in the cellular extract? (4)
        (ii) Describe and explain further experiments which you could do to test the accuracy of your conclusions. (6)
    (b)   Saliva can cause the digestion of starch. Saliva present in the mouth before a meal does not digest starch as fast as saliva produced during a meal.
        (i) Suggest a reason for this. (1)
        (ii) Outline an experiment you could do to find if your suggestion is true. (4)   [SEG: GCSE specimen question]

Human Biology

Table 12.9

Tubes	A	B	C	D
Contents of tubes at start of experiment	Cell extract plus starch	Cell extract plus starch plus hydrochloric acid	Cell extract plus insoluble protein plus hydrochloric acid	Cell extract plus insoluble protein
Appearance at start	Cloudy	Cloudy	Cloudy	Cloudy
Appearance after several hours	Clear	Cloudy	Cloudy	Clear

8 Fig 12.7 shows two starch agar plates, after flooding with iodine in potassium iodide solution.

Fig 12.7

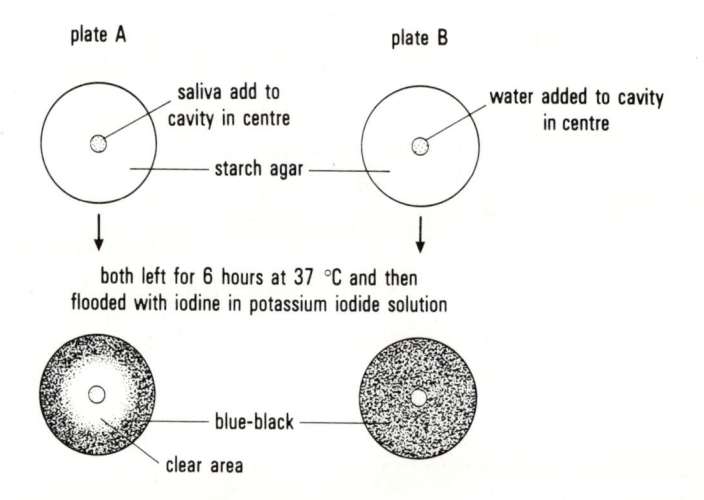

plate A — saliva add to cavity in centre
plate B — water added to cavity in centre
— starch agar —

both left for 6 hours at 37 °C and then flooded with iodine in potassium iodide solution

— blue-black
— clear area

(a) Explain the difference in appearance between plates A and B. (2)

(b) What new substance will be present in the clear area in plate A? (1)

CHAPTER THIRTEEN

THE SKIN AND TEMPERATURE REGULATION

CONTENTS

13.1 Structure and functions of the skin — 183
Structure and function 183
Hints on drawing the skin 184
How the skin works 184

13.2 Temperature regulation — 185
The skin's role in temperature regulation 185
Clothing and temperature regulation 186

13.3 Hypothermia — 187
Occurrence 188
Prevention of hypothermia 188
Treatment for hypothermia 188

13.4 The clinical thermometer — 188
Using the clinical thermometer 189

13.5 Experiments with temperature control — 189
Explanation 190

13.6 Checklist — 190

13.7 Exam questions — 191

The skin and temperature regulation

13.1 STRUCTURE AND FUNCTIONS OF THE SKIN

STRUCTURE AND FUNCTION

Fig 13.1 shows the structure of the skin, while Table 13.1 links up the structure with its functions

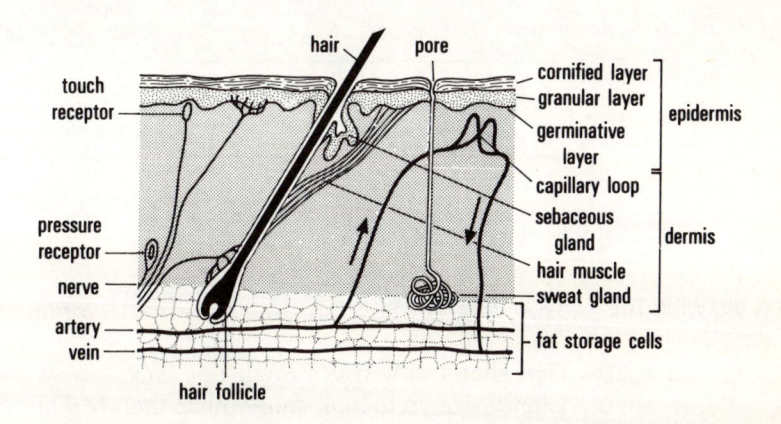

Fig 13.1 Section through the skin

Table 13.1 Structure and functions of the skin

Structure	Description and function
1 Epidermis	
(a) Cornified layer	Consists of flat, dead cells containing the protein **keratin**. Tough, waterproof layer for protection against dehydration, infection and mechanical damage. Constantly replaced by new cells from the layers below.
(b) Granular layer	Contains cells produced by the Malpighian layer below. These fill with keratin to become the new cornified layer.
(c) Malpighian (germinative) layer	Contains actively dividing cells which move up to form the cornified layer. Also contains black **melanin** pigment for protection against ultra-violet rays.

continues on page 184

Human Biology

Structure	Description and function
2 Dermis	
(a) Hair follicles	Deep pits lined by Malpighian layer cells. These cells become filled with keratin, and form a cylinder of dead cells. Hairs prevent loss of heat, chiefly from the head, and assist in temperature regulation.
(b) Hair erector muscle	Raises hair during cold conditions.
(c) Sebaceous glands	Produce oily **sebum** which helps to waterproof the skin and also prevents microorganisms from multiplying on the skin.
(d) Sweat gland	Produces **sweat** for cooling and excretion. Sweat is 99% water, 0.3% sodium chloride (salt), with urea and lactic acid.
(e) Arterioles and capillaries in the dermis	Assist in temperature regulation by dilating and constricting.
(f) Nerve endings (receptors)	Detect pain, pressure touch, temperature, etc.
3 Fat (or adipose) layer (also called subcutaneous layer = 'under the skin')	Acts as a reserve energy store and as an insulating layer, to conserve heat.

HINTS ON DRAWING THE SKIN

This diagram is often drawn badly. Common mistakes include the following.
- Hair shafts shown as a single line only.
- Glands drawn to look quite unlike their real life appearance.
- Capillaries drawn as a series of meaningless squiggles.
- Label lines failing to reach the correct part.
- Too much use of colour.

HOW THE SKIN WORKS

Table 13.2 How the skin performs its functions

Function	Method
1 Prevention of dehydration (loss of water from the tissues)	(a) The sebum forms a waterproof layer on the skin. (b) The cornified layer of the epidermis prevents water loss from the cells below.
2 Prevention of infection	(a) Sebum prevents certain types of microorganisms from multiplying on the surface of the skin. (b) The cornified layer of the epidermis contains dry dead cells which cannot be penetrated by microorganisms, as long as it is intact.
3 Prevention of mechanical damage	The tough cornified layer resists penetration by sharp objects
4 Prevention of damage by ultra-violet rays (sunburn)	Melanin pigments in the Malpighian layer absorb ultra-violet radiation, so protecting the delicate cells below.

The skin and temperature regulation

Function	Method
5 Acting as a sense organ	Receptors in the dermis detect pressure, pain, heat, cold and other stimuli.
6 Acting as an excretory organ	Small amounts of urea and lactic acid are excreted in sweat.
7 Temperature regulation	See Table 13.3.

13.2 TEMPERATURE REGULATION

The temperature of the human body is normally maintained at about 37°C. This is an example of **homeostasis** (see page 213).

Body temperature is controlled by the temperature regulating centre in the hypothalamus. This receives impulses from:
1. receptors in the **skin** when the skin temperature changes;
2. receptors in the **hypothalamus** itself when the temperature of the blood changes.

The hypothalamus then transmits impulses to the skin and other organs as listed in Table 13.3.

Table 13.3 Temperature regulation

Organ or function	Action to lose heat if temperature rises	Action to conserve heat if temperature falls
Arterioles in the skin	Expand (vasodilation) so that more blood flows through the skin capillaries and heat is lost faster.	Contract (vasoconstriction) so that blood flow through the skin is reduced and heat is lost more slowly.
Sweat glands	Actively produce sweat. As drops of sweat evaporate from the skin, heat is taken from the body, so cooling the skin. This is called the 'latent heat of evaporation'.	Cease to produce sweat so that no cooling effect occurs.
Hairs on skin	Hair erector muscles relax so hair lies flat.	Hair erector muscles contract to pull hairs erect. This traps a deeper layer of warm air next to the skin, acting as an insulator. Effective mainly on the head.
Shivering	Does not occur.	Voluntary muscles undergo spasmodic reflex contractions, so producing heat.
Metabolic rate	Falls due to lowered thyroxine production. Less heat energy produced.	Increases because hypothalamus stimulates production of hormone thyroxine to raise metabolic rate. This increases energy production.

Human Biology

The **advantage of a constant body temperature** is that it permits normal activity in most weather. This allows humans to live anywhere from the tropics to the Arctic. (Compare to reptiles, which become sluggish in cold weather and can also be killed by sudden exposure to the sun.)

Note:
1. heat is **produced** during cell respiration in all cells, but especially by the liver and muscles;
2. heat is **conserved** by the adipose (fat) layer under the skin;
3. heat is **lost** from the body to the atmosphere by radiation, conduction and convection.

Hint: don't confuse heat production and heat loss with temperature regulation. Heat production and loss are normally in balance, resulting in a steady body temperature. Temperature regulating mechanisms *only* become active when the body's temperature begins to rise or fall.

THE SKIN'S ROLE IN TEMPERATURE REGULATION

Fig 13.2 shows how the skin helps in temperature regulation.

SWEATING

The production of sweat does not by itself cool the skin. The cooling effect only happens when the sweat evaporates.

In hot damp weather, sweat evaporates slowly so that it is much more difficult to keep cool.

VASOCONSTRICTION AND VASODILATION

The arterioles in the skin constrict (close down) or dilate (open up) in cold or warm conditions. They do *not* move up or down in the skin.

CLOTHING AND TEMPERATURE REGULATION

In **cold** climates, wear many layers of clothes. These should have the maximum space between them in order to trap a layer of warm still air next to the body. Still air is an excellent insulator. Fur linings are especially valuable because the fur traps air in the same way as body hairs.

In **warm** climates, wear:
1. cotton clothes in preference to synthetic fibres – cotton and other natural fibres allow water from perspiration to pass through them but synthetics do not;
2. light-coloured clothes because they reflect heat – dark colours absorb heat;
3. loose-fitting clothes, which allow circulation of air around the body and so speed up loss of heat by evaporation of sweat.

The skin and temperature regulation

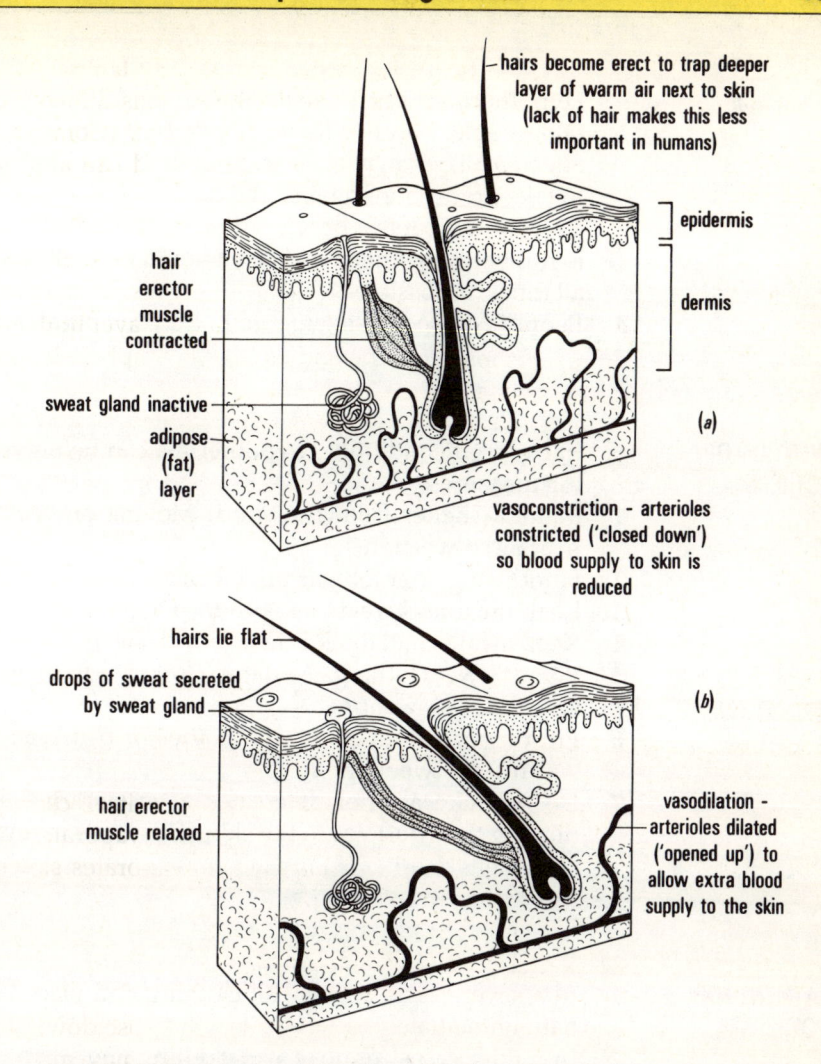

Fig 13.2 The skin's role in temperature regulation, shown (a) in cold conditions and (b) in hot conditions. Note that the fat layer helps prevent heat loss but is not involved in temperature regulation because it does not change with changing temperatures.

13.3 HYPOTHERMIA

W, L/EA only

Hypothermia is the medical name for a marked drop in body temperature, due to exposure to cold.

The **symptoms include:**

1. a fall in body temperature to 33°C or lower;
2. feelings of drowsiness;
3. a slow pulse.

If the victim falls asleep, the circulation slows down, blood pressure falls, and the temperature drops still further until death occurs at about 26°C.

Human Biology

OCCURRENCE

Hypothermia occurs chiefly among the following groups of people:
1. Old people, because their temperature regulating mechanism is less effective. They may also lack money for fuel, or may be too confused to take precautions against the cold.
2. Very young babies, because their temperature-regulating mechanism is not yet fully effective. They should be kept in rooms at 15–20°C at all times, if possible.
3. People exposed to severe cold in exposed places such as mountains.

PREVENTION OF HYPOTHERMIA

In exposed conditions, hypothermia can be prevented by the following measures.
1. Make a shelter from the wind. Moving air removes removes body heat by convection.
2. Huddle together for warmth if in a group.
3. Keep the muscles active to produce body heat.
4. Keep awake; metabolic rate falls with sleep.
5. Remove wet clothing. As damp clothes dry, they cool the body in the same way as sweating.
6. Put on several layers of dry clothes or blankets; these trap layers of warm air between them.
7. Do *not* take alcohol. It creates a temporary feeling of warmth by dilating the arterioles in the skin. This leads to further loss of heat and so hastens death.

TREATMENT FOR HYPOTHERMIA

1. In a severe case, remove all clothing and place the victim in a warm bath immediately.
2. In milder cases, remove wet clothing and wrap the victim in several layers of dry clothes or blankets (or even newspapers).
3. Give hot drinks (*not* alcohol!) and keep in warm surroundings until body temperature returns to normal.

13.4 THE CLINICAL THERMOMETER

W, NI only

The **clinical thermometer** (Fig 13.3) is used to measure human temperatures in the mouth. Its special features include:
1. coverage of a **restricted range** of temperatures (35–42°C);
2. inclusion of a narrow bend or **kink** in the tube to prevent the mercury falling back after removal from the mouth. This keeps the mercury steady while it is being read.

The skin and temperature regulation

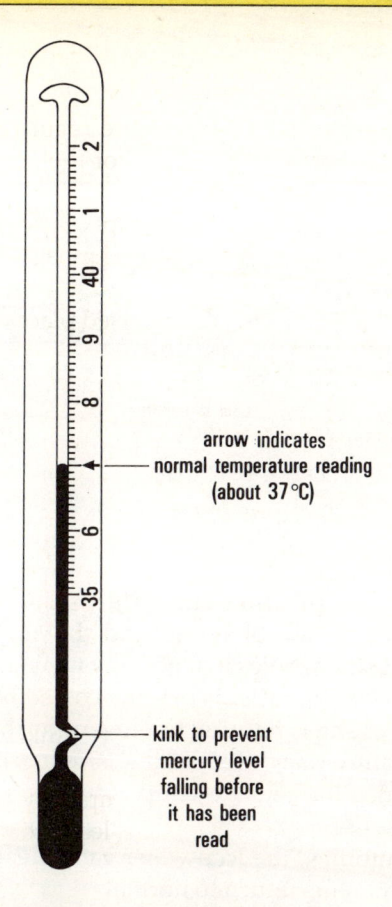

Fig 13.3 The clinical thermometer.

- arrow indicates normal temperature reading (about 37°C)
- kink to prevent mercury level falling before it has been read

USING THE CLINICAL THERMOMETER

1. Temperatures should *not* be taken immediately after taking hot food, drink, or exercise.
2. The thermometer *must* be sterilized in disinfectant between patients. If boiling water is used, the thermometer may shatter.
3. It *must* be shaken between readings to restore the mercury to its normal level.

13.5 EXPERIMENTS WITH TEMPERATURE CONTROL

The body's main 'thermostat' is situated in the hypothalamus and is sensitive to changes in blood temperature but not to changes in the outside air temperature. If a person is placed in a hot room at 45°C and then drinks a large quantity of iced water, this has surprising effects on the body, as shown in Fig 13.4.

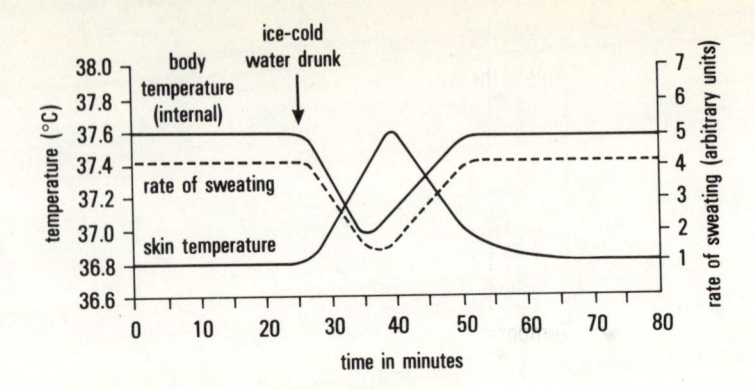

Fig 13.4 The effects of drinking ice-cold water.

EXPLANATION

1. **Internal body temperature falls.** This is due to the cooling effect of the cold water on the blood around the stomach. As a result, the temperature of the whole circulation system falls slightly.
2. **The rate of sweating falls.** When the cooled blood reaches the hypothalamus, sweating is reduced to prevent further cooling.
3. **Skin temperature rises.** If sweating is reduced, the skin is no longer kept cool. Since the outside temperature is so hot (45°C), skin temperature must rise.
4. After a few minutes, the iced water gains heat from the body and all three measurements return to normal.

    Note: questions on the experiment shown in Fig. 13.4 are set almost every year by at least one exam board.

    Alternatively, you might be asked similar questions about experiments which involve cooling the blood supply to the brain, e.g. the blood in the carotid artery. This causes the hypothalamus to increase the metabolic rate, etc., to prevent heat loss.

13.6 CHECKLIST

- Structure and functions of the skin:
    epidermis;
    cornified, granular and Malpighighian layers;
    keratin;
    melanin;
    dermis;
    hair follicles;
    hair erector muscle;
    sebaceous glands, sebum;
    sweat glands, sweat;
    arterioles;

The skin and temperature regulation 191

- nerve endings;
- fat layer.
- ♦ Role of the skin in preventing:
    - dehydration;
    - infection;
    - mechanical damage;
    - ultra-violet rays.
- ♦ Role of skin as:
    - a sense organ;
    - an excretory organ.
- ♦ Temperature regulation:
    - role of hypothalamus;
    - advantages of a constant body temperature;
    - role of shivering;
    - changes in metabolic rate.
- ♦ Heat production and loss.
- ♦ Role of skin in temperature regulation:
    - vasodilation and constriction;
    - hair erector muscles;
    - effects of evaporation of sweat.
- ♦ Clothing for warm and cold climates.
- ♦ Hypothermia:
    - causes;
    - prevention;
    - treatment.
- ♦ Clinical thermometer:
    - functions;
    - method of use.
- ♦ Interpreting experiments on temperature regulation.

13.7 EXAM QUESTIONS

1 (a) Explain how the structure of the skin enables it to carry out the following functions:
  (i) to act as a sense organ;
  (ii) to act as an organ of excretion;
  (iii) to give mechanical protection;
  (iv) to reduce water loss from the body. (10)
  (b) Why does the skin show little sign of wear although it is constantly being rubbed away? (2)

2 Describe and explain the part played by the skin in maintaining a constant body temperature (14).   [Ox]

3 (a) Explain why: (i) evaporation of sweat cools the surface of the skin (2) (ii) temperature control is more difficult in a hot, humid climate. (2)
  (b) Why is it difficult for the body to control its temperature in climates which are both hot and humid? (2)   [L]

(c) Why is it necessary to take salt tablets when undertaking manual work in a hot climate? (2)

4 (a) Explain briefly the value to the body of maintaining a constant body temperature. (2) [W]

(b) Describe the importance of the hypothalamus of the brain in the maintenance of a constant body temperature. (3) [W]

5 After a person has swum the length of a pool and climbed out of the water, their skin temperature is likely to be very low but their deep body temperature would be normal.

(a) Name TWO different body structures which are producing heat in large quantities to keep the person warm. (2)

(b) Why is the skin surface likely to be cold for some time after leaving the water? (1)

(c) What change in the body explains the paler colour of cold skin? (1)

(d) Why is it an advantage for long-distance swimmers to have a higher body fat content? (1) [NI]

6 From the information given in Fig 13.4 (see page 190) state:

(a) Why did drinking ice cold water cause:
(i) body temperature to fall? (1)
(ii) skin temperature to rise? (1)

(b) Identify the major source of heat which caused the rise in the skin temperature. (1) [in the style of Ox and L]

(c) State, with reasons, the effect on body temperature of cooling the blood passing through the arteries to the head for 40 minutes. (3)

CHAPTER FOURTEEN

EXCRETION AND THE KIDNEYS

CONTENTS

- 14.1 Excretion — 195
- 14.2 The kidneys — 195
- 14.3 How the kidneys work — 196
  Functions of the nephrons   197
- 14.4 Effects of diet and climate on the composition of urine — 199
- 14.5 Kidney dialysis machine — 200
  Transplant or dialysis?   201
- 14.6 Checklist — 201
- 14.7 Exam questions — 202

Excretion and the kidneys

14.1 EXCRETION

Excretion is the removal from the body of the waste products of metabolism.

Table 14.1 Excretion of metabolic wastes

Waste product	How produced	How excreted
Carbon dioxide	From cell respiration.	In expired air, from the lungs.
Urea	From deaminated amino acids in the liver.	In urine, from the kidneys. Small amount present in sweat.
Water	From cell respiration and from the diet.	In urine.
Salts	From the diet.	In urine and in sweat.
Red pigments	From breakdown of red blood cells.	In the bile, as bile pigments.

Excretion is mainly carried out by the kidneys. The kidneys have several other functions, all concerned with maintaining the constant composition of the body fluids. These are examples of homeostasis (see page 213).

Hint: don't confuse **defaecation** with **excretion**. Defaecation is the passing out of undigested food in the faeces, from the anus. Undigested food never enters the circulation and so does not form part of the metabolism.

There are small quantities of excreted material in the faeces, but 95% of the faeces consists of bacteria, dead cells from the intestines and undigested food.

14.2 THE KIDNEYS

Fig 14.1 shows the position of the kidneys and related organs in the body, while Fig 14.2 shows the overall structure of the kidney.

The general functions of the kidneys are:
1. removal of urea from the bloodstream;
2. Regulation of the body fluids by controlling the water and mineral ion concentration of the blood.

Human Biology

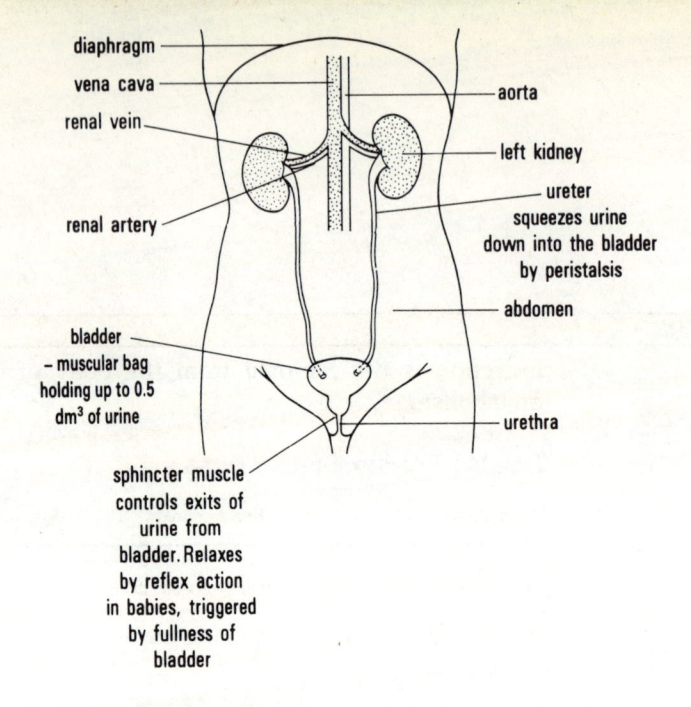

Fig 14.1 The position of the kidneys in the body.

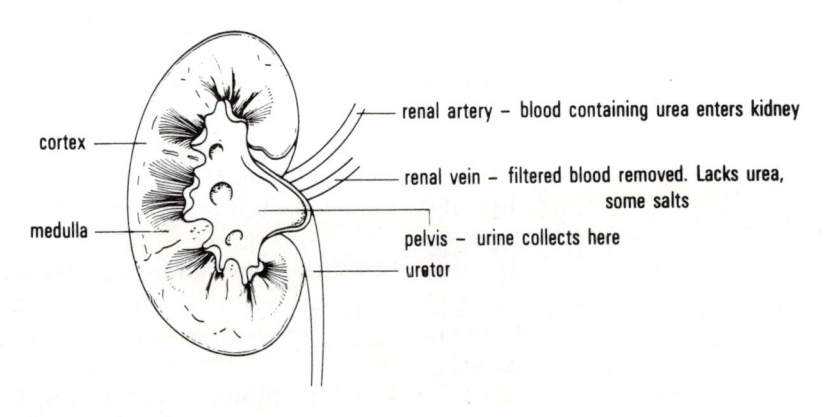

Fig 14.2 Structure of a kidney, as seen with a hand lens.

14.3 HOW THE KIDNEYS WORK

Each kidney consists of thousands of minute tubes called **kidney tubules** or **nephrons**. Each nephron consists of a cup-shaped **Bowman's capsule**, connected to a long tube. A knotted mass of coiled capillaries, called a **glomerulus** (plural glomeruli), lies inside each capsule (see Fig 14.3).

Excretion and the kidneys

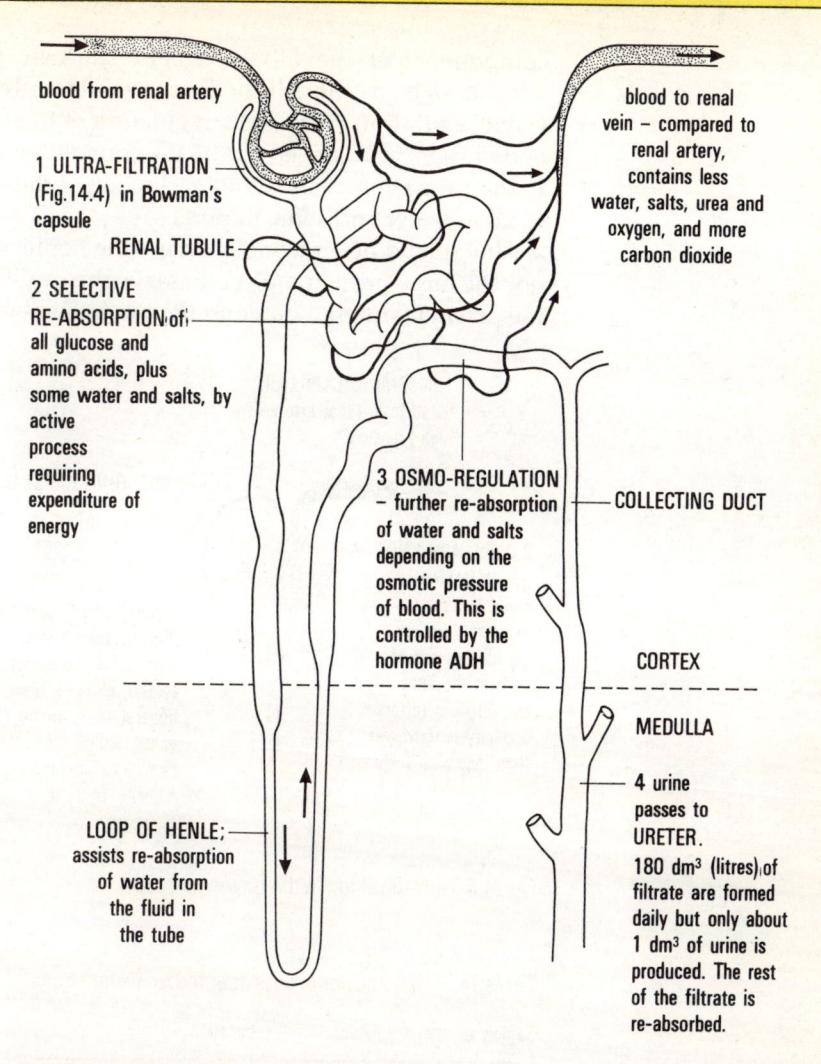

Fig 14.3 Re-absorption, osmoregulation and urine formation in the nephron. Note that the nephron consists of the capsule, glomerulus and tubule.

FUNCTIONS OF THE NEPHRONS

The nephrons are designed to:
1. filter out the smaller molecules from the blood plasma, under pressure;
2. re-absorb useful substances;
3. allow waste materials to pass to the bladder as urine.
   This is achieved by the following processes.
1. **Ultrafiltration.** This is the filtering out of the urea, water, salt and glucose from the blood as it passes through the glomeruli (see Fig 14.4).
2. **Selective reabsorption.** This is the active reabsorption of the useful

components of the filtrate, chiefly glucose, plus some water and mineral salts, by the cells of the convoluted tubules.
3. **Osmoregulation.** This is the regulation of the osmotic pressure of the body fluids, also carried out by the convoluted tubules.
4. **Urine formation.** This is the production of the liquid urine, composed of urea, water and some mineral salts.

Hint: blood never actually enters the nephron. Neither the red cells nor the large protein molecules leave the capillaries, but about 20% of the plasma *is* filtered out (and then mostly re-absorbed) every hour.

1 INCOMING CAPILLARY: blood from renal artery at high pressure

OUTGOING CAPILLARY

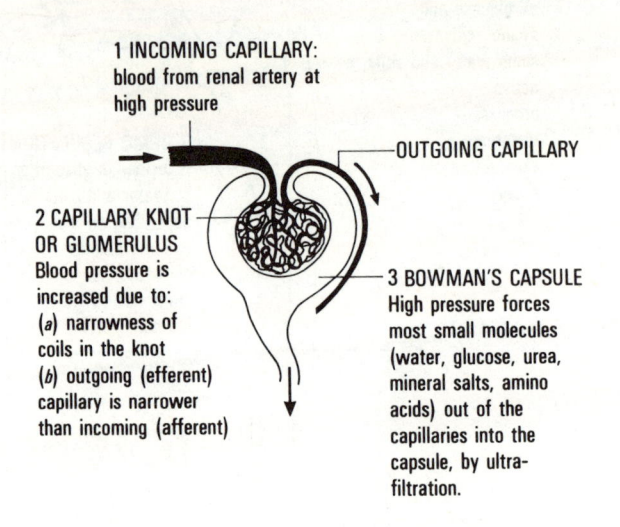

2 CAPILLARY KNOT OR GLOMERULUS
Blood pressure is increased due to:
(*a*) narrowness of coils in the knot
(*b*) outgoing (efferent) capillary is narrower than incoming (afferent)

3 BOWMAN'S CAPSULE
High pressure forces most small molecules (water, glucose, urea, mineral salts, amino acids) out of the capillaries into the capsule, by ultra-filtration.

Fig 14.4 Ultra-filtration in the Bowman's capsule.

Table 14.2 How the nephron is adapted for its functions

Region	Function	Adaptation
1 Glomerulus	Ultra-filtration	(a) Outgoing capillaries are narrower than incoming, so increasing the blood pressure. (b) Network of capillaries in the knot increases the surface area through which fluid is forced out.
2 Tubule main part	Selective re-absorption	(a) Length, number (1 million) and coiling of tubules increases surface area for absorption. (b) Epithelium cells of tubule possess micro-villi to increase surface area. (c) Tubule cells contain numerous mitochondria for active pumping.

continues

Excretion and the kidneys

Region	Function	Adaptation
3 Tubule (region next to collecting duct)	Osmo-regulation	The epithelium of this part of the tubule is sensitive to anti-diuretic hormone (ADH). ADH is produced by the hypothalamus of the pituitary gland when blood osmotic pressure rises. It causes additional absorption of water, so preventing water loss in the urine.

Table 14.3 Comparison of plasma and urine

Constituent	Plasma	Contents in grams per 100 cm^3 Filtrate in tubule	Urine	Notes
Water	91.0	91.0	96.0	Varies according to state of body fluids.
Urea	0.02	0.02	2.0	
Various salts	0.42	0.42	1.18	
Proteins	6.5	0.0	0.0	
Glucose	0.10	0.10	0.0	Glucose appears in the urine if there is excess glucose in the plasma. This is a symptom of diabetes.

14.4 EFFECTS OF DIET AND CLIMATE ON THE COMPOSITION OF URINE

1. A high protein diet increases the urea content (from the breakdown of the additional amino acids).
2. Cold weather increases water content and therefore total urine volume. This is because less water is lost by sweating. The urine is pale and dilute.
3. Hot dry weather decreases water content and urine volume. This is because more water is lost by sweating. The urine is yellow-brown and concentrated.

Human Biology

Table 14.4 The body's water balance for a typical cool day

Water intake	Volume	Water losses	Volume
1 Liquids drunk, e.g. water, coffee, tea, etc.	2.0 dm^3	1 Urine	1.5 dm^3
2 Water content of food, e.g. vegetables, fruit	0.5 dm^3	2 With the faeces	0.2 dm^3
3 Water produced by cell respiration	0.5 dm^3	3 In expired air	0.4 dm^3
		4 Through the skin; sweat, plus some water lost directly through the epidermis	0.9 dm^3
Total	3.0 dm^3	Total	3.0 dm^3

14.5 KIDNEY DIALYSIS MACHINE

A person suffering from kidney failure can be kept alive by being connected from time to time to a **kidney dialysis machine** (see Fig 14.5). This carries out the same functions as the kidney:

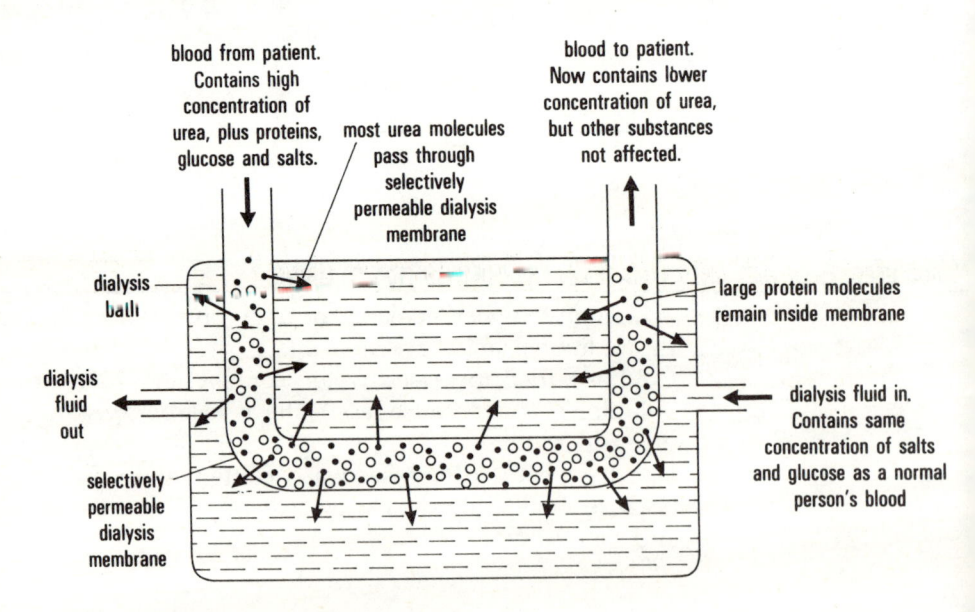

Fig 14.5 The kidney dialysis machine.

1 **The kidney machine** contains a selectively permeable dialysis membrane (see page 56). This allows small molecules to pass through it, but is impermeable to large molecules.

Excretion and the kidneys

2. **Urea molecules** in the patient's blood are small enough to diffuse through the dialysis membrane into the dialysis fluid.
3. **Other small molecules** such as glucose and water do not leave the blood because there is usually an equal concentration inside and outside the membrane. This means that there is no diffusion gradient for glucose between the blood and the dialysis fluid.
4. **Osmoregulation** is carried out automatically by the dialysis machine because water enters or leaves the blood according to the osmotic concentration of the patient's blood. If the blood has a high salt content, water enters from the dialysis fluid; if the blood is too dilute, water leaves the blood. Salts, such as sodium ions, may also diffuse in or out along the diffusion gradients.
5. **Protein molecules** are too large to pass through the membrane and so remain in the blood.

TRANSPLANT OR DIALYSIS?

Transplants of complete kidneys are preferable to dialysis because the machines are expensive to operate and inconvenient to use. Patients need to spend several hours per week attached to them, so that normal life can be seriously disrupted. By comparison, a person with a single transplanted kidney can lead an entirely normal life.

14.6 CHECKLIST

- Excretion: definition.
- General functions of the kidney (two).
- Excreted products (five).
- Excretion v. defaecation.
- Kidney structure and functions:
    - cortex;
    - medulla;
    - pelvis;
    - ureter;
    - renal artery;
    - renal vein.
- General functions of the nephron (three).
- Ultra-filtration.
- Selective absorption.
- Osmo-regulation.
- Urine formation.
- Detailed functions of the nephron – roles of:
    - Bowman's capsule;
    - glomerulus;
    - incoming/outgoing capillaries;
    - loop of Henlé;
    - collecting duct;
    - ADH.
- Adaptations of the nephron for its functions (six).

- Effects on the composition and concentration of the urine of:
  - a high protein diet;
  - cold weather;
  - hot, dry weather.
- Comparison of plasma and urine.
- The body's water balance.
- How the kidney dialysis machine works.

14.7 EXAM QUESTIONS

1. State the main difference between the processes of defaecation and excretion. (2)
2. (a) Explain why the loop of Henlé is relatively much longer in desert rats than in humans. (2)
   (b) How would you expect the urine of a desert rat to differ in composition from human urine? Give reasons. (2)
3. (a) State three differences in composition between blood leaving the kidneys compared to blood entering the kidneys. (3)
   (b) Explain the reasons for the differences. (3)
4. Explain how the composition of the urine might be affected by:
   (a) a high protein diet;
   (b) hot, dry weather;
   (c) cold weather;
   (d) lack of insulin in the bloodstream. (2 each)
5. (a) From Fig 14.5, as blood passes through the tube, explain why there is a reduction in urea concentration but no change in protein concentration. (2)
   (b) How is the function of osmoregulation performed by a dialysis machine? (2)
   (c) Under what circumstances might glucose diffuse from the patient's blood into the dialysis fluid? (1)
6. On a typical cool day, a teenage girl loses 3.0 dm^3 of water. 1.5 dm^3 is lost with the faeces, or from the lungs and skin.
   What is the other major source of lost water and what volume is lost in this way? (2)

CHAPTER FIFTEEN

COORDINATION: THE NERVOUS AND ENDOCRINE SYSTEMS

CONTENTS

- **15.1 General arrangement of the nervous system** — 205
  Definitions 206

- **15.2 The structure and function of neurones** — 206
  Types of neurone 207

- **15.3 The nervous impulse and the synapse** — 208
  The nervous impulse 208
  Synapses 208

- **15.4 The central nervous system** — 208
  The brain 209

- **15.5 Reflex and voluntary actions** — 209
  Events in a typical voluntary action 210

- **15.6 The endocrine system** — 211
  Hormones 211
  The endocrine glands 211

Contents

▶ **15.7 Homeostasis** 213
Negative feedback 213

▶ **15.8 Sensitivity in plants** 214

▶ **15.9 Checklist** 215

▶ **15.10 Exam questions** 216

Coordination: the nervous and endocrine systems

15.1 GENERAL ARRANGEMENT OF THE NERVOUS SYSTEM

The function of the nervous system is to coordinate the activities of the body, as shown in Fig 15.1.

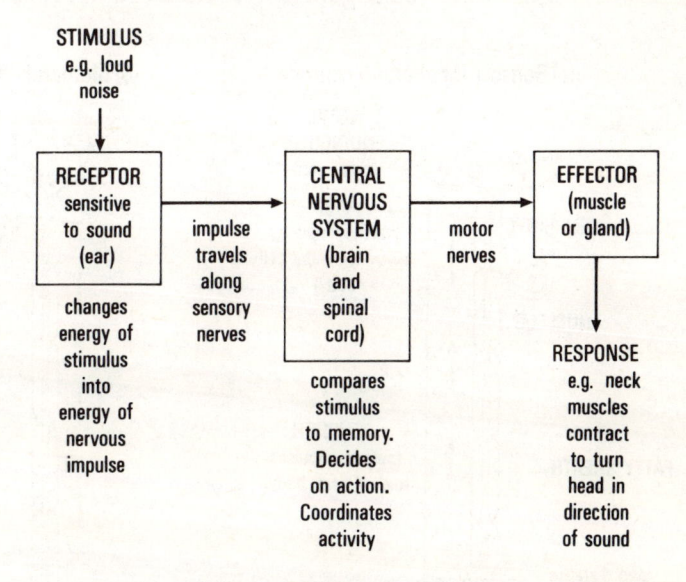

```
STIMULUS
e.g. loud
noise
   ↓
┌──────────┐            ┌──────────┐            ┌──────────┐
│ RECEPTOR │            │ CENTRAL  │            │ EFFECTOR │
│ sensitive│            │ NERVOUS  │            │ (muscle  │
│ to sound │  impulse   │ SYSTEM   │  motor     │ or gland)│
│  (ear)   │  travels   │ (brain   │  nerves    │          │
└──────────┘  along     │ and      │            └──────────┘
              sensory   │ spinal   │                 ↓
 changes      nerves    │ cord)    │
 energy of              └──────────┘              RESPONSE
 stimulus                                         e.g. neck
 into                   compares                  muscles
 energy of              stimulus                  contract
 nervous                to memory.                to turn
 impulse                Decides                   head in
                        on action.                direction
                        Coordinates               of sound
                        activity
```

Fig 15.1 General arrangement of the nervous system.

The nervous system is divided into two parts, as shown in Fig 15.2:

```
              THE NERVOUS SYSTEM
                     │
         ┌───────────┴───────────┐
CENTRAL NERVOUS            PERIPHERAL
SYSTEMS (CNS):             NERVOUS SYSTEM:
brain and spinal            the nerves
    cord                   joining the CNS
                           to all parts of
                              the body
```

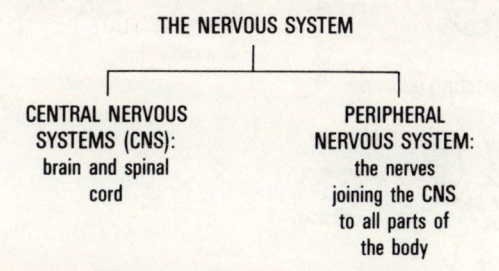

Fig 15.2 The divisions of the nervous system.

1. **central nervous system** (CNS);
2. **peripheral nervous system**.

Human Biology

DEFINITIONS

1. **A stimulus** is any change inside an organism or in its environment which leads to a response.
2. **A response** is any action carried out by an organism on receipt of a stimulus. It usually involves either muscles or glands.
3. **A receptor** is a cell which is sensitive to a particular stimulus, e.g. light.
4. **An effector** is an organ which carries out the response to a stimulus.

15.2 THE STRUCTURE AND FUNCTION OF NEURONES

Fig 15.3 shows the general structure of a neurone.

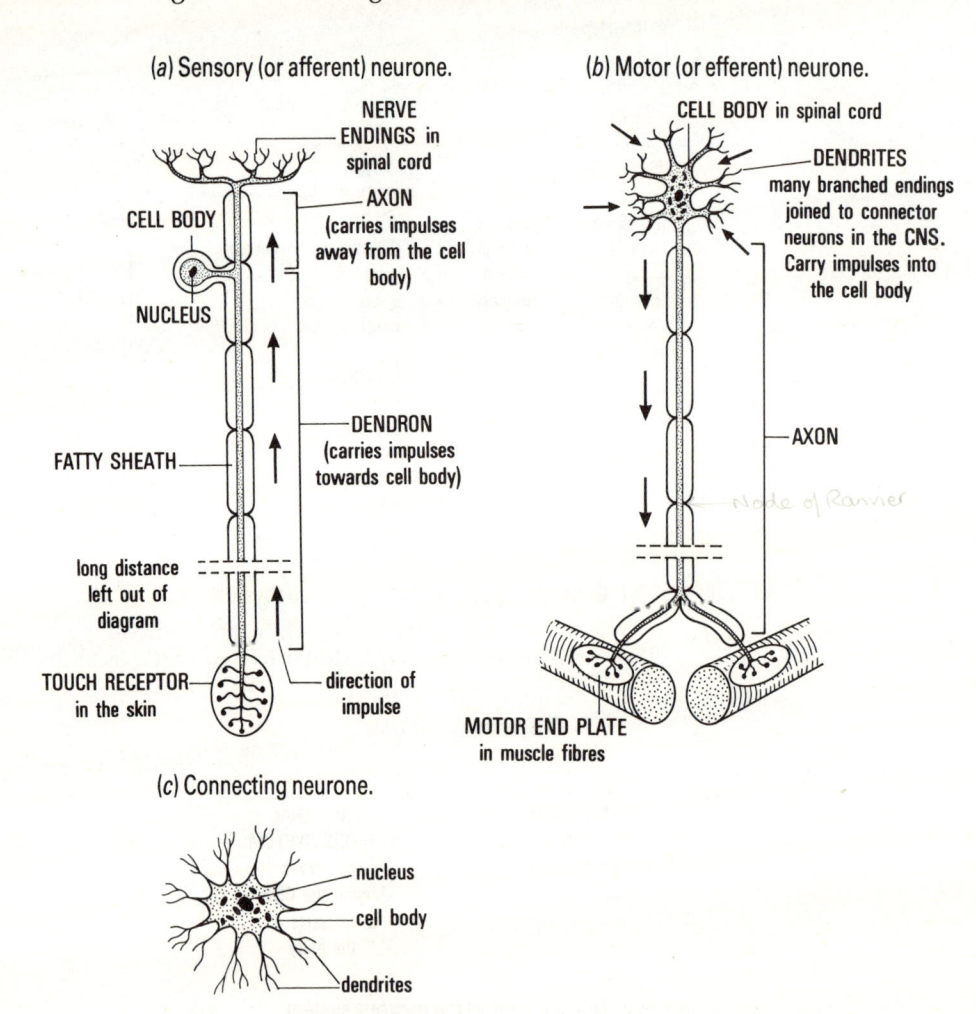

(a) Sensory (or afferent) neurone.

NERVE ENDINGS in spinal cord
AXON (carries impulses away from the cell body)
CELL BODY
NUCLEUS
DENDRON (carries impulses towards cell body)
FATTY SHEATH
long distance left out of diagram
TOUCH RECEPTOR in the skin
direction of impulse

(b) Motor (or efferent) neurone.

CELL BODY in spinal cord
DENDRITES many branched endings joined to connector neurons in the CNS. Carry impulses into the cell body
AXON
Node of Ranvier
MOTOR END PLATE in muscle fibres

(c) Connecting neurone.

nucleus
cell body
dendrites

Fig 15.3 The structure of neurones.

Coordination: the nervous and endocrine systems

Table 15.1 Structure and functions of the parts of a neurone

Structure	Function
Cell body	Contains the nucleus.
Dendron	Thin fibre which carries impulses towards the cell body.
Axon	Thin fibre which carries impulses away from the cell body.
Fatty (myelin) sheath	Layer of fatty cells wrapped around the axon and dendron. Provides insulation to prevent loss of electrical energy.
Dendrites	Finely branched endings, connecting the neurones to other cells.
Sensory nerve ending	Usually receptive to stimuli, and therefore acts as a receptor.
Motor nerve ending	Transmits impulses to an effector, e.g. a muscle.
Synapse	Junction between two neurones.
Nerve fibre	Name used for any long length of a neurone, axon or dendron.

TYPES OF NEURONE   The different types of neurone are also illustrated in Fig 15.3.

Table 15.2 Types of neurone (nerve cells)

Name (with alternatives)	Function	Special features
Sensory (afferent)	To carry impulses from the receptors to the CNS.	Cell body is located in a ganglion (swelling) close to the spinal cord. Dendron is longest part.
Motor (efferent)	To carry impulses from the CNS to the effectors.	Cell body is inside spinal cord. Axon is longest part.
Connecting (connector, relay, intermediate)	To carry impulses from sensory to motor neurones within the CNS.	Short axon with many branching dendrites. Found only within the CNS.

15.3 THE NERVOUS IMPULSE AND THE SYNAPSE

A **nervous impulse** travels along the nerve fibre as shown in Fig 15.4.

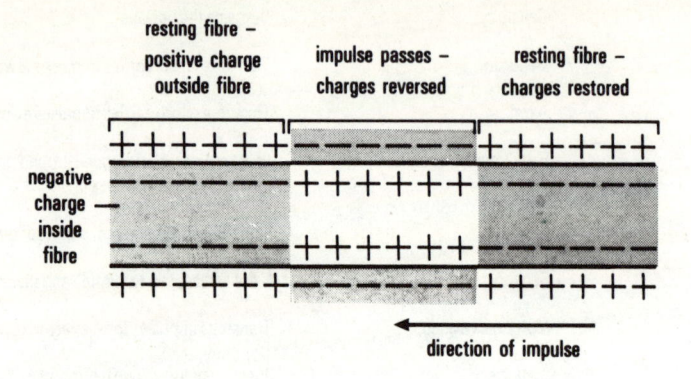

Fig 15.4 How the nervous impulse travels along a nerve fibre.

THE NERVOUS IMPULSE This is a wave of electrical activity which passes along a nerve fibre. In a resting nerve, there is a negative charge inside the fibre and a positive charge outside it. The charges are reversed when an impulse passes, and then quickly restored again.

SYNAPSES The electrical wave cannot cross a synapse. When an impulse reaches a synapse, a chemical called **acetylcholine** is produced at the end of the fibre. This diffuses rapidly across the gap between two neighbouring fibres and triggers off a fresh impulse in the cell on the other side.

Hints: Don't use phrases like: 'nerves carry messages or signals,' 'The brain tells the leg what to do.'
    Always mention impulses, e.g. 'Nerves carry impulses,' 'Impulses pass from the brain to the leg.'

15.4 THE CENTRAL NERVOUS SYSTEM

The central nervous system (CNS) consists of the brain and spinal cord. Both contain:
1. **grey matter**, consisting mainly of the cell bodies of neurones;
2. **white matter**, consisting mainly of nerve fibres (so called because the fatty sheaths appear white);
3. **cerebrospinal fluid**, which circulates around the outside of the CNS

Coordination: the nervous and endocrine systems

within tough membranes, and also inside a central canal. The membranes provide protection and the fluid acts as a shock absorber.

Hint: don't confuse 'spinal column' with 'spinal cord'. The spinal **column** is the backbone; the spinal **cord** is the main nerve running through the backbone.

THE BRAIN

Fig 15.5 shows the structure and function of the brain.

CEREBRAL HEMISPHERE, showing deeply folded outer cortex. The cerebral cortex controls all conscious thought, together with memory and learning.

FOLDS in cerebral cortex increase surface area of cortex. This increases intelligence because more cells are present.

CEREBELLUM. Coordinates muscular activity, so is essential for balance.

HYPOTHALAMUS
PITUITARY GLAND

SPINAL CORD

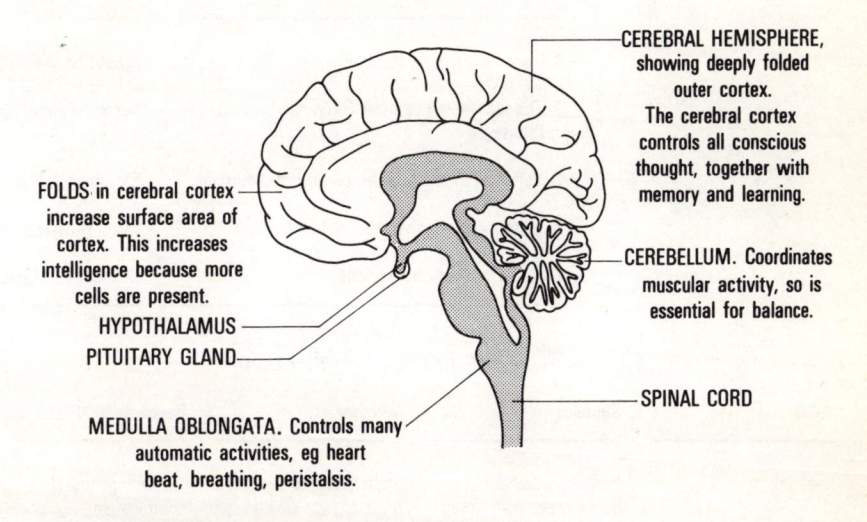

MEDULLA OBLONGATA. Controls many automatic activities, eg heart beat, breathing, peristalsis.

Fig 15.5 Functions of the brain; section through the brain.

15.5 REFLEX AND VOLUNTARY ACTIONS

thorn pricks finger

swelling or ganglion containing cell bodies of sensory neurones

sensory neurone

connecting neurone

dorsal root of spinal nerve ('dorsal' means 'back')

pain receptor in skin

spinal nerve

direction of impulse

motor neurone

motor end plates in biceps muscle (effector): hand withdrawn rapidly

gray matter

central canal

white matter

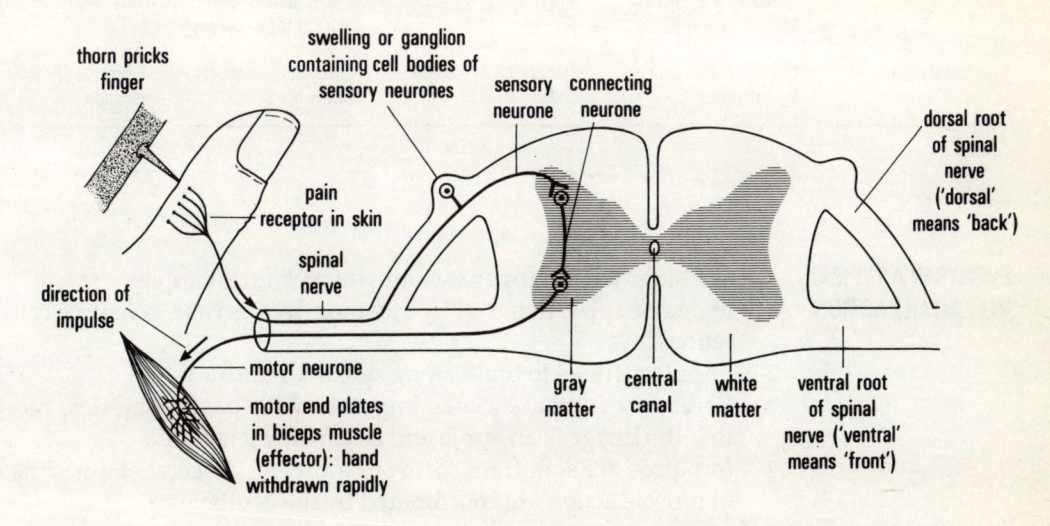

ventral root of spinal nerve ('ventral' means 'front')

Fig 15.6 Reflex action – the reflex arc.

1. **A reflex action** is a rapid automatic response to a stimulus. Many such actions are protective, e.g. blinking (protects the eye), sudden withdrawal of the hand when a finger is pricked (see Fig 15.6).

(For conditioned and voluntary reflexes see page 417, M only).

2. **A voluntary action** is a conscious action, always controlled by the cerebral hemispheres in the brain.

Table 15.3 Comparison of reflex and voluntary actions

Reflex action	Voluntary action
1 Involves the spinal cord only.	Always controlled by the brain.
2 The same stimulus always produces the same response.	Response varies according to circumstances.
3 Very fast; may involve as few as three neurones.	Slower; may involve thousands of neurones.
4 Memory not involved.	Memory essential in deciding nature of response.
5 Automatic and unconscious.	Deliberate and always requires conscious thought.

Table 15.4 Examples of reflex actions

Reflex	Stimulus	Receptor	Response by effector	Purpose
Knee jerk	Pressure on tendon below kneecap stretches thigh muscle.	Stretch receptor in muscle.	Upper thigh muscle contracts, so straightening knee.	Helps keep the balance when walking.
Blinking	Object approaching eye.	Retina.	Eyelid muscles contract.	Protects eye.
Salivation (production of saliva)	Sight or smell of food.	Retina or olfactory cells in nose.	Salivary glands produce saliva.	Preparation for digestion.
Pupil	Increased brightness of light.	Retina.	Circular muscle in iris contracts to narrow pupil.	Improves vision and protects eye.
Withdrawal of hand	Damage to skin of finger, e.g. when burnt.	Pain and heat receptors in skin.	Arm muscles contract to remove hand.	Protects against further damage.

EVENTS IN A TYPICAL VOLUNTARY ACTION

Consider what happens when you pick up an apple:
1. Image of apple detected by receptor (in this case, sensitive cells in the retina).
2. Impulses travel to brain along sensory neurones.
3. Cerebral cortex associates impulses with past memories; recognizes that the image is an apple and so can be picked up.
4. Impulses are sent from cortex to muscles, via cerebellum. Fine details of muscle action are coordinated by the cerebellum.

Coordination: the nervous and endocrine systems

5 Impulses pass via motor neurones to muscles of arm. Muscles contract so that arm moves, and fingers flex to pick up apple.

5.6 THE ENDOCRINE SYSTEM

Endocrine glands are glands which secrete chemicals called hormones directly into the bloodstream. They differ from **exocrine glands**, e.g. salivary glands, which secrete their products through ducts (tubes) leading to the outside of the body or into the gut.

Hint: the pancreas is both an exocrine *and* an endocrine gland. It acts as an exocrine gland when secreting digestive enzymes into the duodenum through the pancreatic duct; and as an endocrine gland when secreting the hormone insulin directly into the bloodstream.

HORMONES

These are chemicals which circulate in the bloodstream and cause metabolic changes in specific target organs.

Compared to the nervous system, endocrine glands coordinate long-term slower bodily activities such as growth and reproduction.

Table 15.5 Comparison of nervous and hormonal coordination

	Nervous coordination	Hormonal coordination
Form of transmission	By means of electrical impulses.	By means of chemicals, called hormones.
Route of transmission	Along nerve fibres.	In the bloodstream.
Relative speed of transmission	Very fast.	Slow.
Termination (end) of transmission	When impulse reaches effector.	When hormone molecules are destroyed by the liver.

THE ENDOCRINE GLANDS

There are a number of endocrine glands around the body (see Fig 15.7). Many of these glands are themselves controlled by the pituitary gland, which is known as the 'master gland'.

Fig 15.7 Position of the main endocrine glands.

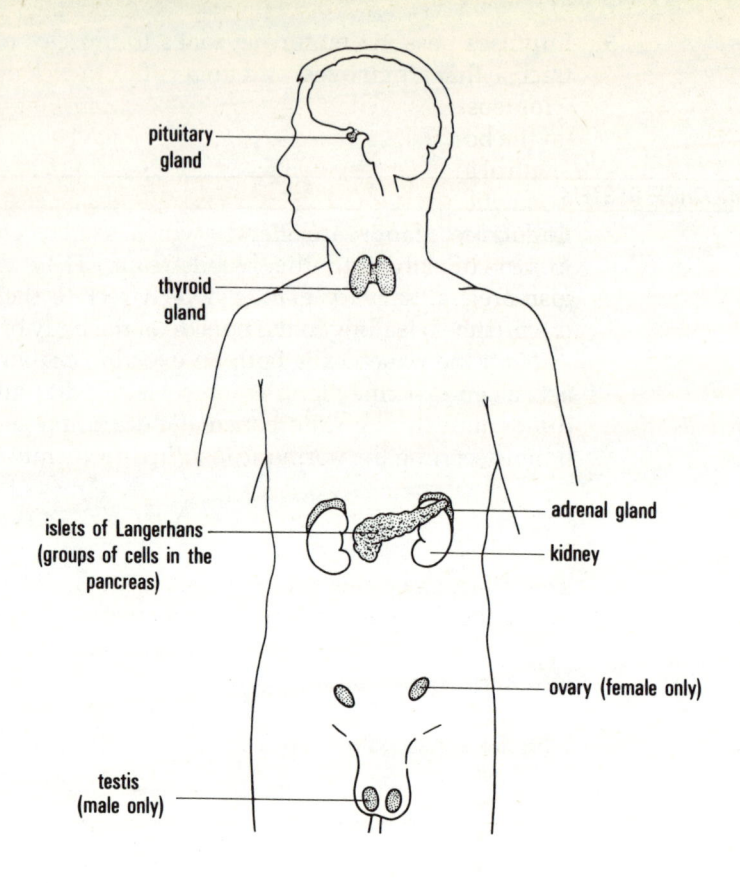

Table 15.6 Secretions of the main endocrine glands

Gland	Hormone	Function
Pituitary	1 Growth hormone (pituitrin)	Stimulates growth of the long bones.
	2 Thyroid-stimulating hormone	Stimulates thyroid gland.
	3 Prolactin	Stimulates milk production by the mammary glands.
Thyroid	Thyroxine	Stimulates metabolic rate. Essential for normal growth and brain function in childhood.
Islets of Langerhans in the pancreas	1 Insulin	Reduces the level of glucose in the blood by stimulating conversion to glycogen.
	2 Glucagon	Stimulates conversion of glycogen to glucose.
Adrenal	Adrenaline	Causes rapid increase in rate of heartbeat, pulse, breathing, cell respiration; directs blood from digestive system to muscles. Secreted at times of stress, or before sudden exercise.
Ovaries and testes (see pages 235–6).		

Coordination: the nervous and endocrine systems

15.7 HOMEOSTASIS

Homeostasis is the maintenance of a constant internal environment in the body, e.g.:
- control of blood sugar level;
- regulation of body temperature;
- regulation of blood urea level;
- control of blood carbon dioxide level;
- osmoregulation of body fluids.

Homeostasis involves **negative feedback**.

NEGATIVE FEEDBACK

This is a control system in which an increase in the level of the factor under control triggers off a response which causes the level of that factor to decrease. Let us take the control of blood sugar level as an example (see Fig 15.8).

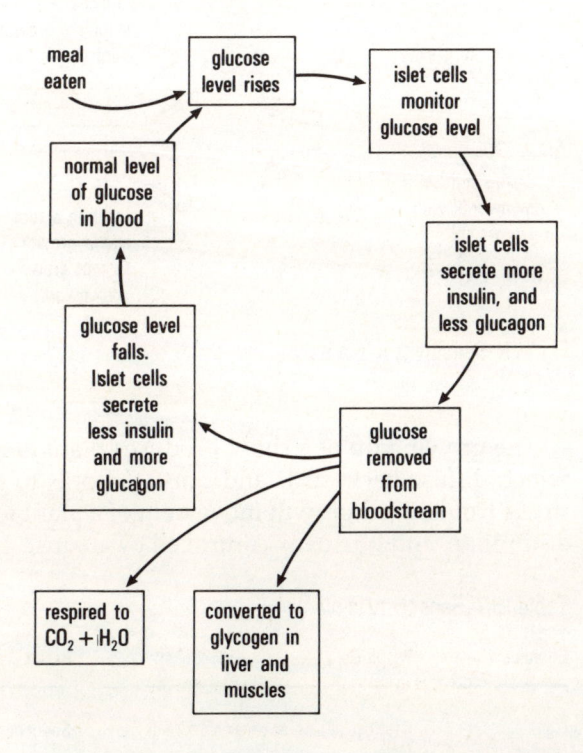

```
meal          glucose
eaten    →    level rises    →    islet cells
                                  monitor
                                  glucose level
    ↑
normal level
of glucose
in blood
    ↑                              islet cells
                                   secrete more
                                   insulin, and
                                   less glucagon
glucose level
falls.
Islet cells
secrete
less insulin                       glucose
and more                           removed
glucagon                           from
                                   bloodstream

respired to        converted to
CO₂ + H₂O          glycogen in
                   liver and
                   muscles
```

Fig 15.8 Control of blood glucose by negative feedback. *Note*: the blood glucose level is also reduced by thyroxine and adrenaline, but neither is involved in the negative-feedback loop shown above.

1 The islet cells of the pancreas act as receptors, constantly monitoring the level of glucose in the blood.
2 In the glucose level rises above normal, the islet cells respond by secreting insulin. This **reduces** the level of glucose in the blood.

Human Biology

3 If the glucose level falls, the islet cells cease secreting insulin and secrete glucagon instead. This **raises** the level of glucose in the blood.

15.8 SENSITIVITY IN PLANTS

S, W, NI only

Plants are sensitive to stimuli such as light, gravity and water (see Fig 15.9).

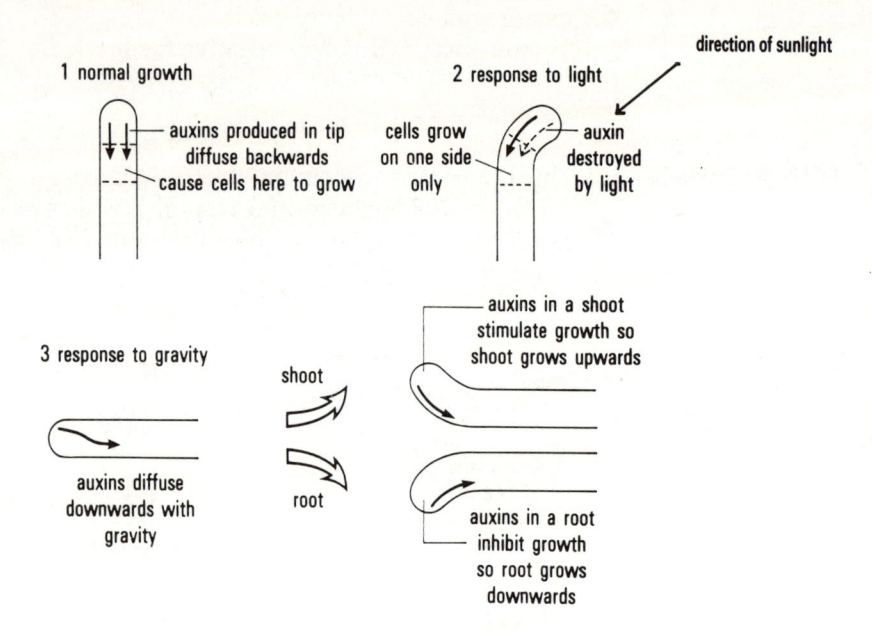

Fig 15.9 Sensitivity in plants.

The growing tip of a shoot produces plant hormones called **auxins** which diffuse backwards and cause the cells to grow just behind the tip. A **tropism** is a growth movement of a plant towards or away from a stimulus, and is usually controlled by auxins.

Table 15.7 Sensitivity in plants

Stimulus	Response	Result
Light	Destroys auxins, so cells on dark side grow faster.	Shoot bends towards light.
Gravity	Auxins move downwards, causing cells on lower side to grow in shoots.	Shoots grow upwards.
	In roots, auxin inhibits growth on lower side.	Roots grow downwards.
Water		Roots grow towards water.

Coordination: the nervous and endocrine systems

15.9 CHECKLIST

- Stimulus, response.
- Receptor, effector.
- Central nervous system.
- Peripheral nervous system.
- Motor sensory nerves.
- Neurones; differences between:
    - motor;
    - sensory;
    - connecting.
- Axon, dendron, dendrite, cell body, fatty sheath.
- Motor end-plate.
- Synapse.
- Grey matter/white matter.
- Cerebrospinal fluid.
- Cerebral hemispheres.
- Functions of (Fig 15.5):
    - cerebral cortex;
    - hypothalamus;
    - pituitary gland;
    - cerebellum;
    - medulla oblongata.
- Reflex and voluntary action:
    - definitions;
    - comparisons (five);
    - examples.
- Reflex arc.
- Endocrine/exocrine glands.
- Hormones.
- Target organs.
- Functions of endocrine glands:
    - pituitary;
    - thyroid;
    - islets of langerhans;
    - adrenal;
    - ovary/testis.
- Nervous v. hormonal coordination (four comparisons).
- Homeostasis and examples.
- Negative feedback.
- Control of blood sugar level.
- Sensitivity in plants; responses to:
    - light;
    - gravity;
    - water.
- Auxins.
- Tropisms.

15.10 EXAM QUESTIONS

1 (a) In Fig 15.10, name the type of neurone shown and give a reason for your choice. (2)

Fig 15.10

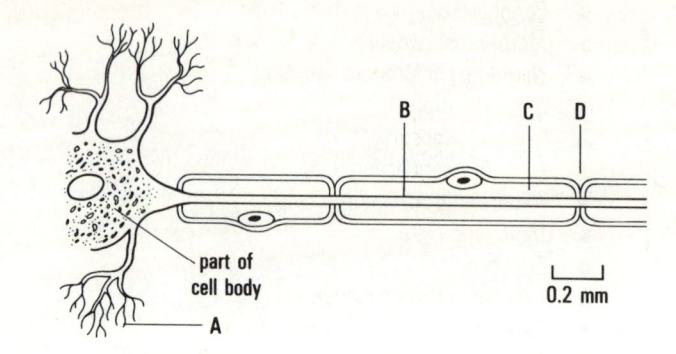

(b) What are the functions of **A**, **B**, and **C** in relation to the transmission of nerve impulses? (3)
(c) What is the real distance from the middle of the cell nucleus to point **D**? Show your working. (1)

2 Which parts of the brain are responsible for the following:
(a) Higher mental faculties of thought, memory and intelligence? (1)
(b) Coordination and posture? (1)
(c) Control of breathing and heartbeat? (1) [Ox]

3 (a) Describe, with a diagram, the main events in a named reflex action. (10)
(b) Describe an experiment to test the speed of your own reaction time. (3)
(c) Suppose the nerve fibre running from the cord to the arm in Fig 15.6 (see page 209) was cut. How would this affect:
(i) movement
(ii) sensation in the arm?
Give reasons. (4)

4 (a) Name the hormone produced by the thyroid gland. (1)
(b) State the importance of this hormone in a growing child. (2)
(c) Describe the function of this hormone in adults, mentioning the effect of over- and under-secretion. (6)
(d) In a table give four differences between coordination by the nervous and endocrine systems. (4) [W]

5 Fig 15.11 (page 217) shows the changes in blood glucose level in a person over a period of 90 minutes.
(a) Vigorous exercise was taken 10 minutes after the start. Explain why this caused the change in level between A^1 and A^2, naming the hormone involved. (2)
(b) What event at **B** might explain the change between **B** and **C**? (1)

Coordination: the nervous and endocrine systems

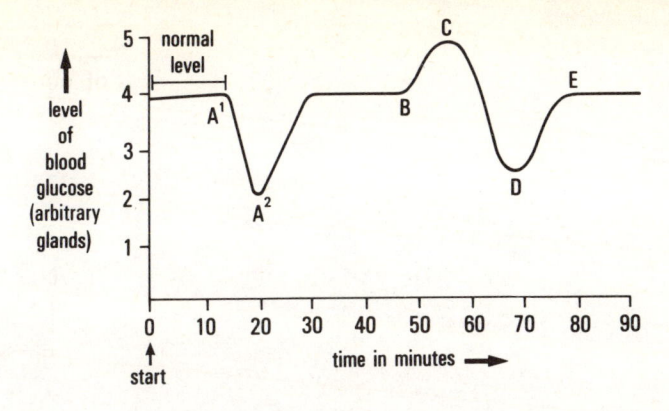

Fig 15.11 Changes in blood glucose level.

(c) What changes in level occurred between:
(i) C and D and
(ii) D and E? (2)
(d) Give reasons for the changes described in (c) naming any hormones involved. (4)
(e) How might the shape of the graph between C and D differ from Fig 15.11 in a diabetic? Give reasons. (2)

S, W, NI only

6 Briefly explain the responses of plants to light, gravity and water. (5)

CHAPTER SIXTEEN

RESPONSE TO STIMULI: THE SENSE ORGANS

CONTENTS

- **16.1 How receptors work** — 221

- **16.2 The eye** — 222
  Protection of the eye 222

- **16.3 Image formation in the eye** — 223

- **16.4 Focusing and accommodation** — 224
  The stages in accommodation 224

- **16.5 Adjusting to dim light** — 224

- **16.6 Fields of vision** — 225
  Advantages of all-round vision 226
  Advantages of an overlapping field of vision 226

- **16.7 Common defects of the eye** — 226
  Long sight 226
  Short sight 227

Contents

▶ **16.8 Receptors in the ear** 227
Hearing 227
Balance 228
Gravity 228

▶ **16.9 Receptors in the skin** 228
Experiment to investigate density of touch receptors 228

▶ **16.10 Receptors in the nose and mouth** 229
Smell 229
Taste 229

▶ **16.11 Checklist** 230

▶ **16.12 Exam questions** 231

Response to stimuli: the sense organs

16.1 HOW RECEPTORS WORK

The purpose of the sense organs is to detect stimuli, i.e. changes in the external or internal environment. All sense organs contain specialized cells sensitive to stimuli, called **receptors** (definition on page 206). Each different stimulus reaches the body as a form of energy, e.g. light energy, heat energy, sound energy, etc.

The **function of a receptor** is to convert the energy of the stimulus into the energy of the nerve impulse (see page 208). The impulse then travels along a nerve fibre to the brain.

Table 16.1 Stimuli detected by receptors in the body

Stimulus causing response	Receptor	Location
1 External stimuli		
Light energy	Light-sensitive cells (rods and cones)	In the retina of the eye.
Sound waves	Sound-sensitive cells	In the cochlea of the inner ear.
Smell	Chemoreceptors (olfactory cells)	In the mucous membrane of the nose.
Taste (separate receptors for sweet, sour, bitter and salt)	Chemoreceptors	In the taste buds on the tongue.
Temperature – heat and cold	Heat-sensitive and cold-sensitive receptors	In the dermis of the skin, especially lips, back of hands, elbows.
Pressure	Pressure receptors	In the dermis of non-hairy skin.
Touch	Touch receptors	
Pain	Pain receptors	
Gravity	Gravity receptors	In the inner ear.
2 Internal stimuli		
Muscle tension	Stretch receptors	Inside voluntary muscles (see page 77).
Blood temperature (see page 185)	Temperature receptors	Hypothalamus of brain.
Osmotic pressure of blood (see page 199)	Osmoreceptors	
Level of carbon dioxide in the blood (see page 94)	Receptors sensitive to acidity level of blood	Hypothalamus and walls of carotid artery.

16.2 THE EYE

PROTECTION OF THE EYE The eye is protected in the following ways.
1. Each eye is situated in a deep bony **socket** called the orbit.
2. The **eyelids** close suddenly when there is a sudden movement towards the eye (blinking reflex).
3. The **eyelashes** prevent dust entering the eye.
4. **Tears** are secreted by tear glands in the corners of the eye. These keep the cornea moist, and destroy bacteria.
5. The cornea is protected by a thin epithelium called the **conjunctiva**.
6. The iris closes in bright light to protect the retina. Very bright light can damage the retina cells permanently.

Fig 16.1 shows the structure of the eye.

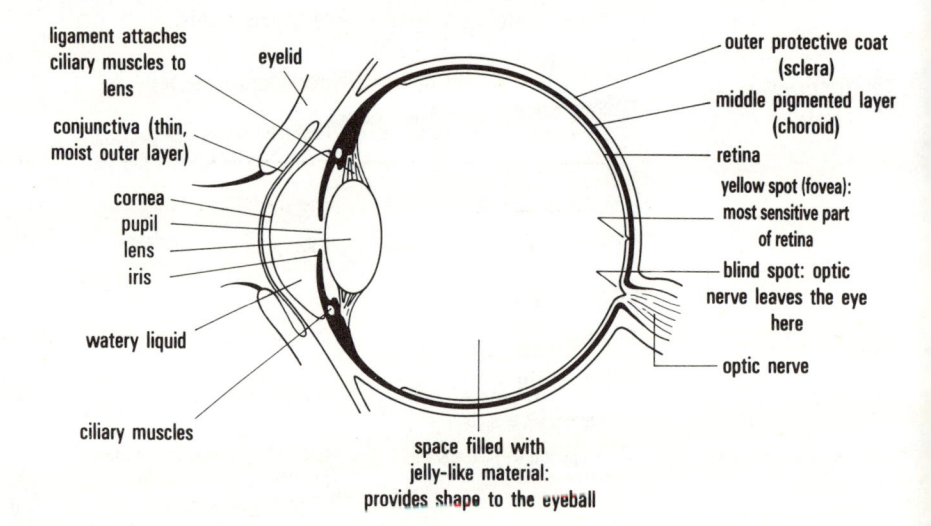

Fig 16.1 Section through the eye.

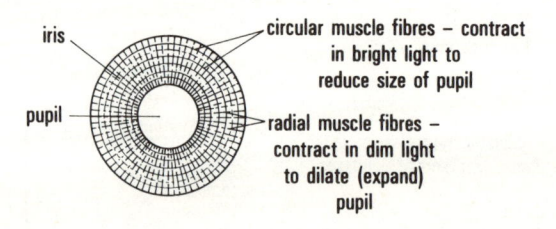

Fig 16.2 Iris of the eye in front view.

Response to stimuli: the sense organs

Table 16.2 Structure and functions of the parts of the eye

Part	Description	Functions
Cornea	Outer, transparent front part of the eye.	1 Protects the eye. 2 Refracts light entering eye to form an image on the retina.
Middle pigmented layer (choroid)	Dark layer of pigment cells behind the retina.	1 Prevents internal reflection of light within the eye. 2 Contains blood vessels which supply the retina.
Retina	Layer of light-sensitive cells.	Sensitive to light. Converts energy of light waves into nervous impulses.
Iris	Contains antagonistic circular and radial muscles (see Fig 16.2)	Controls amount of light entering eye.
Lens	Flexible, transparent structure.	1 Refracts light on to retina. 2 Changes shape to focus light from different distances.
Ciliary muscles	Ring of muscles in front of lens.	Alters the shape of the lens.
Optic nerve	Sensory nerve from retina to brain.	Carries nervous impulses from the retina.

16.3 IMAGE FORMATION IN THE EYE

When light rays from an object enter the eye, they are refracted (bent inwards – see Fig 16.3) by the cornea and the lens.

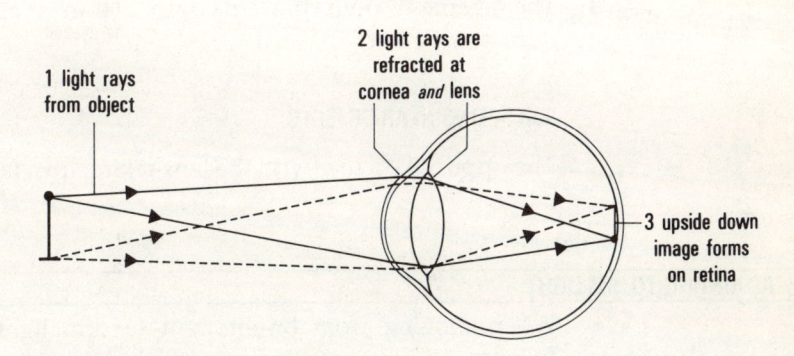

Fig 16.3 Image formation in the eye.

This produces an upside-down image on the retina, which is automatically corrected by the brain.

16.4 FOCUSING AND ACCOMMODATION

Accommodation is the adjustment made to the shape of the lens in order to focus objects at different distances (see Fig 16.4). This changes the refractive power (focal length) of the lens.

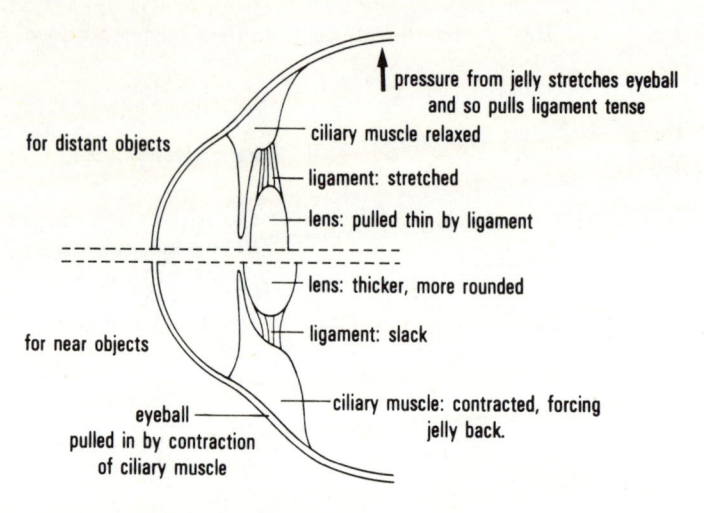

Fig 16.4 Focusing and accommodation.

THE STAGES IN ACCOMMODATION

FOR SEEING DISTANT OBJECTS

1. The ciliary muscles relax.
2. As a result, pressure from the jelly stretches the ligament.
3. The ligament pulls the lens into a thin shape, so **decreasing** its refractive power.

FOR SEEING NEAR OBJECTS

The opposite occurs, with the lens taking up a fat shape.

16.5 ADJUSTING TO DIM LIGHT

When moving from bright light to dim light, the eye adapts as follows.

1. The pupil **dilates** (expands), because the radial muscles of the iris immediately contract (see Fig 16.2). This allows more light to fall on to the retina.
2. Adaptation of the retina. Rods (see Table 16.3) are only sensitive if they contain a purple pigment called **rhodopsin**. This is destroyed by

light, but gradually builds up in semi-dark conditions, over about 30 minutes. Vitamin A is needed to manufacture rhodopsin.

Hint: *never* say that rods help you to 'see in the dark'. No one can see anything in *total* darkness, but the rods do help you to see in very dim light.

Table 16.3 Types of cell found in the retina

Type of cell (receptor)	Position on the retina	Sensitivity
Cones	Mainly in the centre	Sensitive to colours, i.e. light of different wavelengths. Not sensitive to dim light.
Rods	Towards the sides	Not sensitive to colour. Sensitive to very dim light.

16.6 FIELDS OF VISION

S, L/EA, M, APH only

See Fig 16.5.

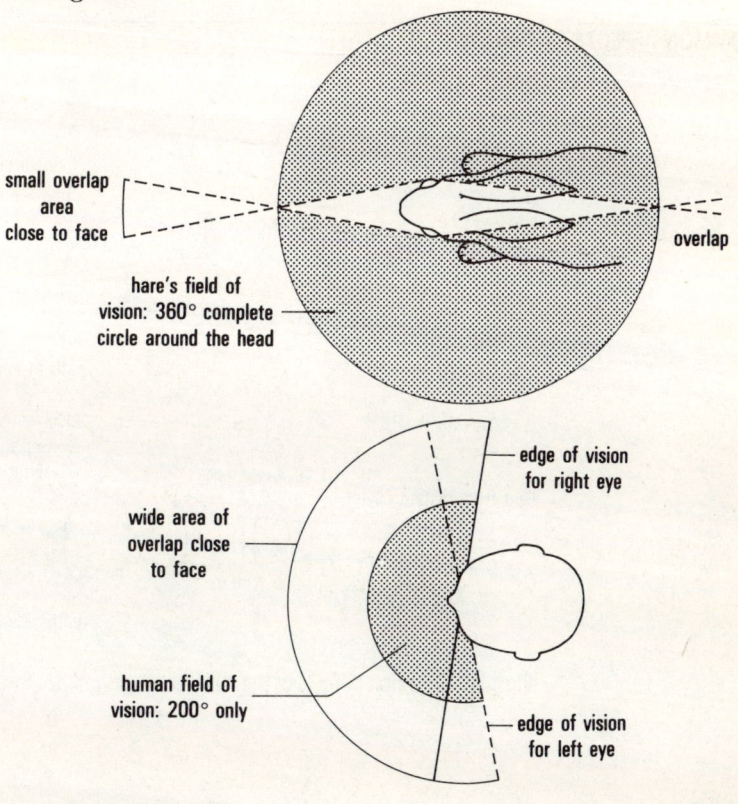

Fig 16.5 Fields of vision.

Human Biology

ADVANTAGES OF ALL-ROUND VISION

Animals with eyes in the side of the head, e.g. herbivores such as hares, have a field of vision of up to 360°, i.e. a complete circle around the head. This allows them to detect the movement of predators behind them when they are feeding.

ADVANTAGES OF AN OVERLAPPING FIELD OF VISION

Humans have a field of vision of only about 200°, but the fields of vision of two eyes overlap. This means that slightly different images of the same object are sent to the brain, which combines the two images to give three-dimensional or stereoscopic vision.

The advantages of this are as follows.
1 **Stereoscopic vision** helps judgement of distance – the greater the difference in the two images of an object, the closer it is to the face. Accurate judgement of distance is useful for animals which jump or spring, e.g. predators pouncing on prey or tree-dwellers leaping among branches, e.g. apes.
2 **Overlapping vision** eliminates the effect of the blind spot.

16.7 COMMON DEFECTS OF THE EYE

M, NI, APH only

See Fig 16.6.

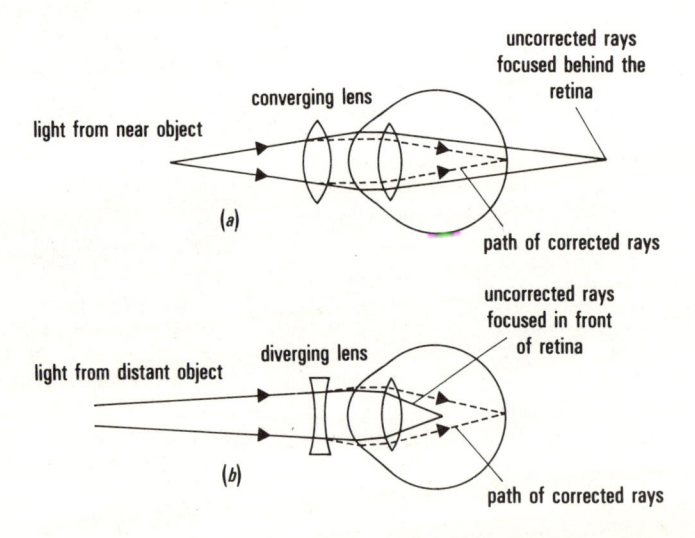

Fig 16.6 Common defects of the eye. (a) Long sight. (b) Short sight (myopia).

LONG SIGHT

1 **Symptoms** – near objects, e.g. a book, cannot be focused.
2 **Causes**:
 (a) eyeball too small;

Response to stimuli: the sense organs

    (b) lens loses elasticity (especially with age).
 3 **Remedy** – wear spectacles with converging lenses to decrease focal length of lens when reading.

SHORT SIGHT
 1 **Symptoms** – distant objects cannot be focused.
 2 **Causes**:
  (a) eyeball too large;
  (b) lens too powerful.
 3 **Remedy** – wear spectacles with diverging lenses to increase focal length, e.g. when driving a car.

16.8 RECEPTORS IN THE EAR

The ear contains receptors sensitive to sound and also to the direction of movement of the head, etc. (See Fig 16.7).

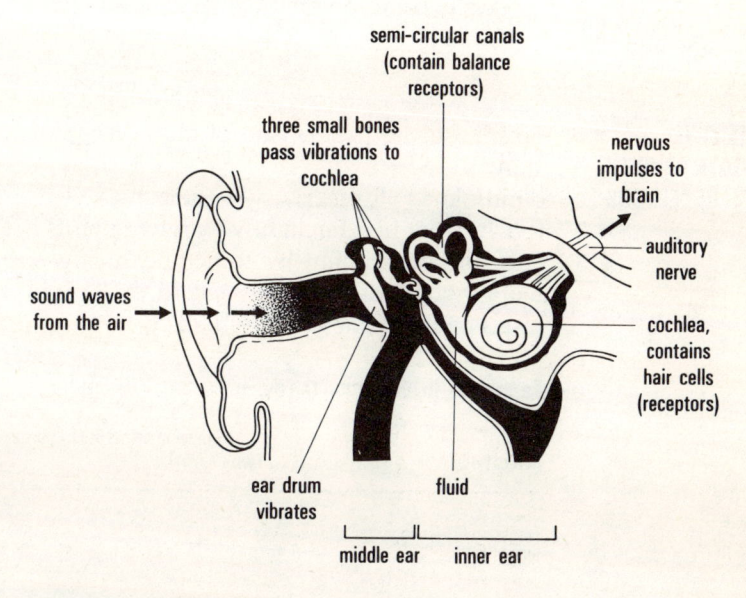

Fig 16.7 Simplified diagram of the ear.

HEARING
Sound waves reaching the ear are changed into mechanical vibrations and then into nervous impulses, as follows.
1. Sound waves strike the ear drum, causing it to vibrate mechanically.
2. These vibrations cause the three small bones in the middle ear to vibrate.
3. In turn, their vibrations set off movements in the lymph-like fluid in the inner ear (cochlea).

4   These movements are detected by receptor cells containing hairs, which pass impulses on to the brain.

BALANCE

Movement of the head is also detected by hair cells in canals above the cochlea. Impulses from these cells provide information to the brain which is used to help maintain balance.

GRAVITY

The position of the head in relation to gravity is detected by hair cells in structures close to the canals in the inner ear.

16.9 RECEPTORS IN THE SKIN

The dermis of non-hairy skin contains specialized nerve endings sensitive to touch, pressure, pain and temperature. These are especially common on the fingertips and lips.

EXPERIMENT TO INVESTIGATE DENSITY OF TOUCH RECEPTORS

To investigate the density of touch receptors in various parts of the skin:
1   blindfold a volunteer;
2   touch her or his skin lightly with two points held about **5 cm apart**;
3   vary the experiment by sometimes using one point and sometimes using two points, but only record the results when using two points. Use a table similar to Table 16.4.

Table 16.4 Investigating the density of touch receptors

Part of body	Number of points felt by partner when touched with two points	
	Two	One
Finger tip of first finger on left hand	✓✓✓✓	✓
Back of neck	✓✓	✓✓✓✓

EXPECTED RESULT

The two points can usually be felt as separate points in sensitive areas such as the lips and fingertips. In other parts e.g. the neck or the back of the hand, they feel like one point.

Response to stimuli: the sense organs 229

CONCLUSION

Touch receptors are denser on the fingertips than on the back of the neck.

16.10 RECEPTORS IN THE NOSE AND MOUTH

SMELL

Receptors sensitive to smell, called olfactory receptors, are found in the roof of the nasal cavity (see Fig 16.8). These detect chemicals from the air which dissolve in the mucous membrane of the nasal cavity.

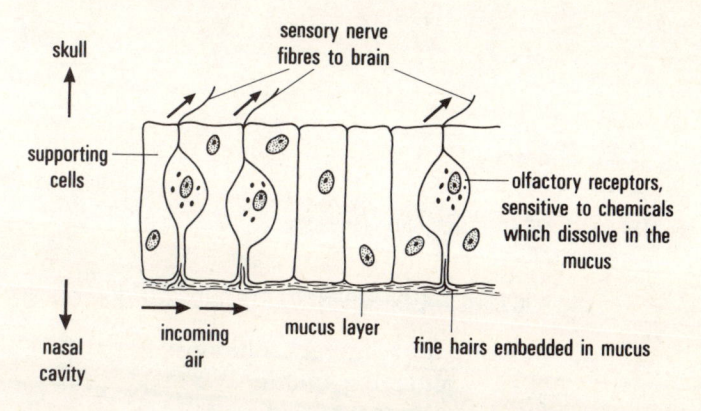

Fig 16.8 Olfactory receptors in the roof of the nasal cavity.

TASTE

Taste receptors, found in **taste buds** on the tongue (see Fig 16.9), are sensitive to chemicals which dissolve in the mucous layer on the tongue.

(a) Taste buds on a papilla of the tongue

(b) Enlarged diagram of a taste bud

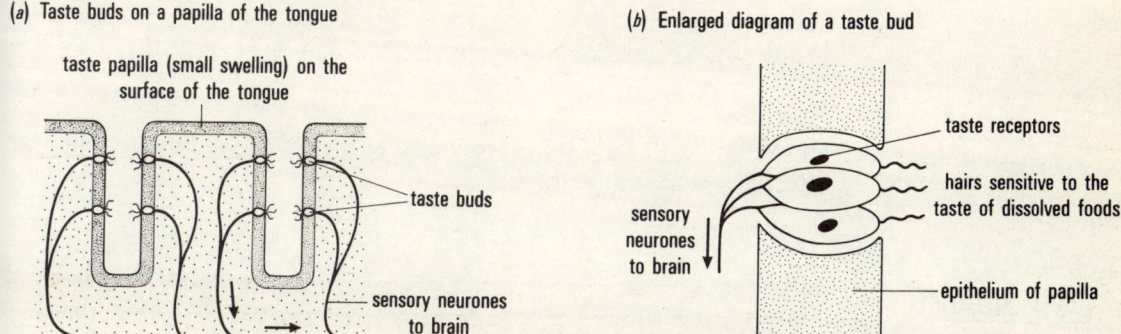

Fig 16.9 (a) Taste buds on a papilla of the tongue. (b) Enlarged diagram of a taste bud.

Human Biology

Each taste bud detects **one** of only four sensations:
1. sweet;
2. sour;
3. salt;
4. bitter.

The different taste buds are found on different parts of the tongue (see Fig 16.10). All other information about taste comes from the sense of smell.

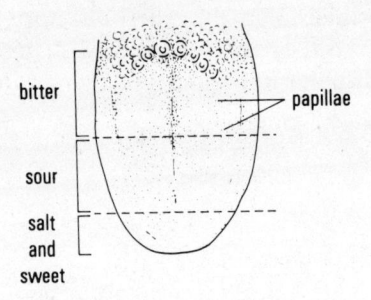

Fig 16.10 Regions of the tongue.

MAPPING THE DIFFERENT TASTE BUDS ON THE TONGUE

1. Make up four different solutions:
   - (a) bitter, e.g. quinine;
   - (b) salt;
   - (c) sweet;
   - (d) sour, e.g. vinegar.
2. Find a volunteer and place drops of each solution on to different parts of the tongue, using a pipette or glass rod. Wash out the mouth and the pipette between trials.
3. Draw four outlines of the tongue and record the positions where each solution can be tasted.

Expected result
Four outlines, marked for each different taste as in Fig 16.10.

Conclusion
Sweet and salt taste buds are found at the tip of the tongue, bitter at the back, and sour at the sides.

16.11 CHECKLIST

- Function of a receptor.
- Responses to 14 stimuli (see Table 16.1).
- Protection of the eye (five).
- Structure and functions of:
    - cornea;

Response to stimuli: the sense organs

        pigmented layer;
        retina;
        rods;
        cones;
        iris;
        lens;
        blind spot;
        yellow spot.
- Image formation.
- Accommodation – roles of:
        ciliary muscles;
        ligament;
        lens.
  Adjustment to dim/bright light.
- Fields of vision:
        overlapping;
        all round.
- Common eye defects (*M, NI, APH* only).
- Hearing – conversion of sound waves to nervous impulses.
- Role of sense organs in balance.
- Gravity receptors.
- Receptors in the skin.
- Investigation into the sensitivity of touch receptors.
- Olfactory receptors.
- Taste receptors.
- Mapping the location of taste buds on the tongue.

16.12 EXAM QUESTIONS

1. How is the eye protected from damage and external infection? (4)
2. (a) Describe the changes in the eye when moving from bright sunlight into a dimly-lit room. (4)
   (b) Describe the changes which occur in the eye to bring about clear focusing of a page in a book when a person stops watching birds in flight and starts to look at the book. (8)   [*AEB* 1985]
3. (a) Explain why a person should not try to select coloured clothing under very dim light conditions. (3)   [*AEB* 1985]
   (b) (i) How might the retina of an entirely nocturnal mammal differ from the human retina? (1)
   (ii) How would the nocturnal mammal benefit as a result? (1)
4. (a) Explain why very faint stars can sometimes be seen only out of the sides of the eye. (2)
   (b) Which vitamin deficiency affects vision in poor light?
5. (a) What is the advantage of overlapping fields of vision? (5)
   (b) If you hold this book about 60 cm away, close the left eye and stare at the cross in Fig 16.11 with the right eye, the dot will slowly disappear as you bring it nearer. Explain why. (2)

Fig 16.11   +   •

(c)   To demonstrate the presence of the blind spot in the left eye, you would close the right eye. Would you then look at the cross or the spot (in Fig 16.11)? (1)   [SREB]

6 (a)   Fig 16.12 shows an eye suffering from short sight. Add to the diagram a suitable correcting lens and show what this does to the two rays of light **A** and **B**. (5)   [SREB]

Fig 16.12

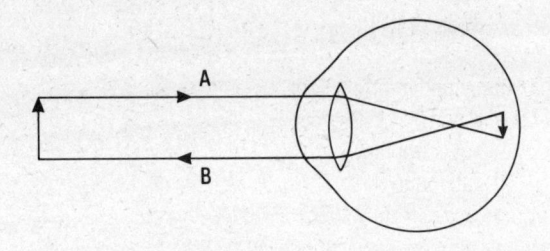

(b)   Redraw Fig 16.12 to show an eye suffering from long sight. Add a suitable correcting lens and indicate the effect on rays **A** and **B**. (5)   [SREB]

7   Which structures in the eye
 (a)   convert light energy to nerve impulses?
 (b)   convey nerve impulses from the eye to the brain? (1 each)

8   Which structures in the ear convert
 (a)   sound waves to mechanical vibrations
 (b)   mechanical vibrations to nerve impulses? (1 each)

9 (a)   Describe an experiment in which you could use two pins to find out which of the following parts, the palm of the hand, the forehead and the back of the hand, is most sensitive to touch.
 (b)   What result would you expect? (2)
 (c)   Why are two pins used instead of one? (2)   [WM]

10   Explain why:
 (a)   Dry food cannot be tasted. (1)
 (b)   Cold in the nose causes loss of taste. (1)   [NI]

CHAPTER SEVENTEEN 233

HUMAN REPRODUCTION

CONTENTS

- **17.1 Sexual intercourse and the reproductive organs** — 235
  Sexual intercourse and fertilization 235
  Stages in sexual intercourse 235

- **17.2 Ovulation** — 237
  Stages in ovulation 237

- **17.3 Main stages in fertilization** — 237

- **17.4 Twins** — 238

- **17.5 The menstrual cycle** — 238
  Stages in the menstrual cycle 239

- **17.6 Hormones and pregnancy** — 240
  Testing for pregnancy 240

- **17.7 Promoting fertility** — 240
  Methods for promoting fertility 240

- **17.8 Controlling fertility** — 241
  Birth control 241
  Sterilization 241
  Contraception 241

- **17.9 Checklist** — 242

- **17.10 Exam questions** — 243

Human reproduction

17.1 SEXUAL INTERCOURSE AND THE REPRODUCTIVE ORGANS

SEXUAL INTERCOURSE AND FERTILIZATION

1. **Sexual intercourse** (also called **copulation**) means the passing of sperm from the penis of the male to the vagina of the female.
2. **Ejaculation** is the sudden expulsion of **semen** (a mixture of sperm, nutrients and enzymes) from the penis into the vagina by muscular contractions.
3. **Fertilization** is the fusion of the nuclei of the gametes, i.e. one sperm with one ovum, to form a zygote. It usually takes place in an oviduct.

   Hint: if you're asked to describe fertilization, *don't* write down all the details of sexual intercourse. Just describe the main stages of fertilization (see page 237).

   And it's *wrong* to say 'The gametes fuse' or 'The sperm and egg join together.' Instead, you should write 'The nuclei of the sperm and ovum join together.'

STAGES IN SEXUAL INTERCOURSE

1. Mutual stimulation by the partners causes the male's penis (see Fig 17.1) to fill with blood and become **erect**.

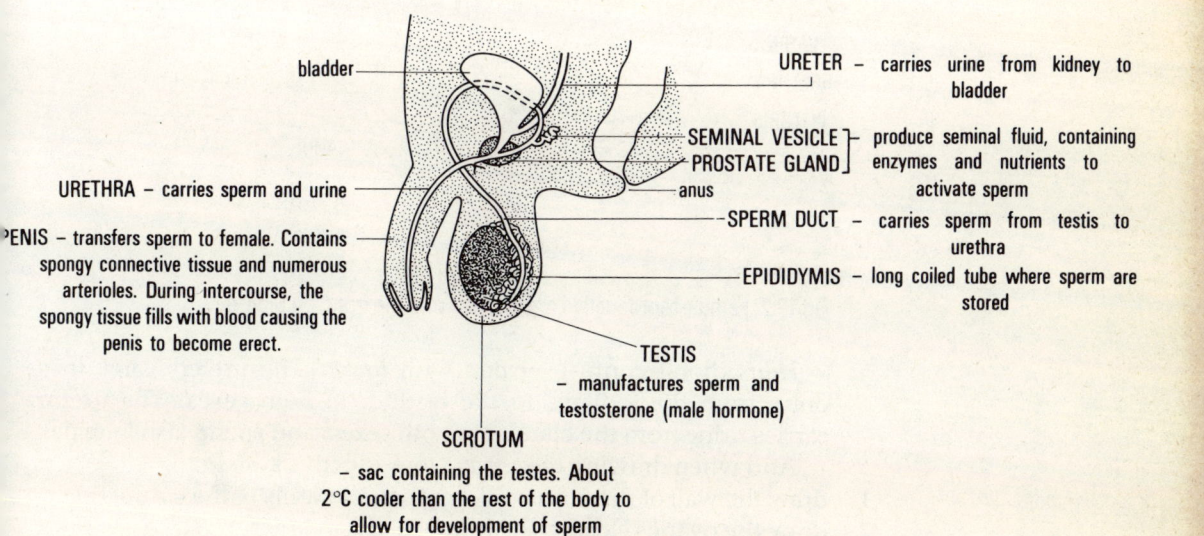

Labels on diagram:
- bladder
- URETER – carries urine from kidney to bladder
- SEMINAL VESICLE ⎫ produce seminal fluid, containing
- PROSTATE GLAND ⎭ enzymes and nutrients to activate sperm
- anus
- SPERM DUCT – carries sperm from testis to urethra
- EPIDIDYMIS – long coiled tube where sperm are stored
- URETHRA – carries sperm and urine
- PENIS – transfers sperm to female. Contains spongy connective tissue and numerous arterioles. During intercourse, the spongy tissue fills with blood causing the penis to become erect.
- TESTIS – manufactures sperm and testosterone (male hormone)
- SCROTUM – sac containing the testes. About 2°C cooler than the rest of the body to allow for development of sperm

Fig 17.1 Male reproductive organs (side view, in section).

Human Biology

2 **Muscular contractions** of the sperm ducts force sperm out of the epididymis into the urethra.
3 The **prostate gland** and the **seminal vesicle** add seminal fluid to the sperm as it passes. This contains nutrients and enzymes which stimulate the sperm to commence active swimming.
4 The seminal fluid is **ejaculated** into the vagina (see Fig 17.2) by muscular contraction. Several million sperm are released at each ejaculation.
5 The sperm then swim through the uterus and into the oviducts.

OVIDUCT – carry ova from ovaries to uterus; fertilization occurs here
FUNNEL OF OVIDUCT
CERVIX – ring muscle which closes neck of womb
VULVA – area surrounding vagina

OVARY – manufactures oestrogens (female hormones) and ova (egg cells)
UTERUS – the foetus develops here during pregnancy
VAGINA – receives sperm from the penis during intercourse

(a)

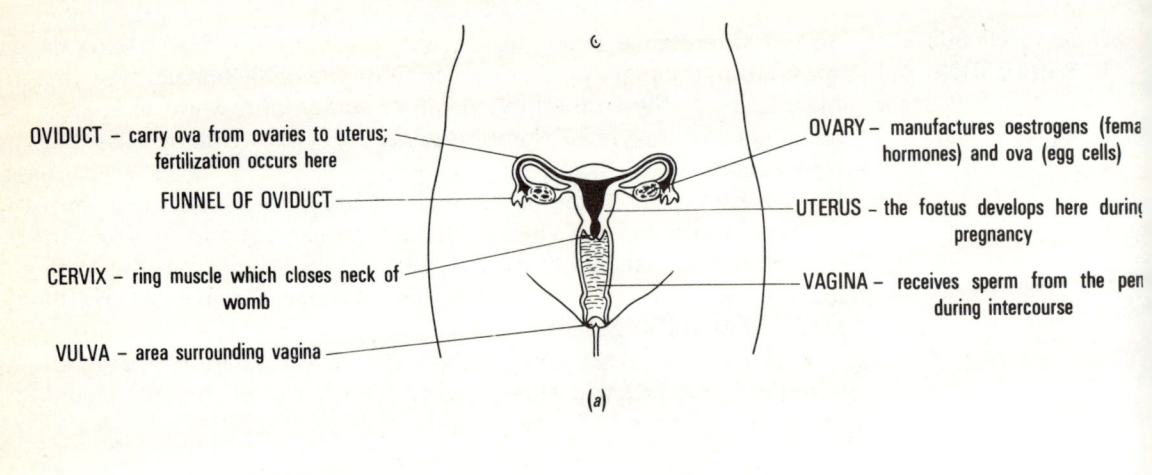

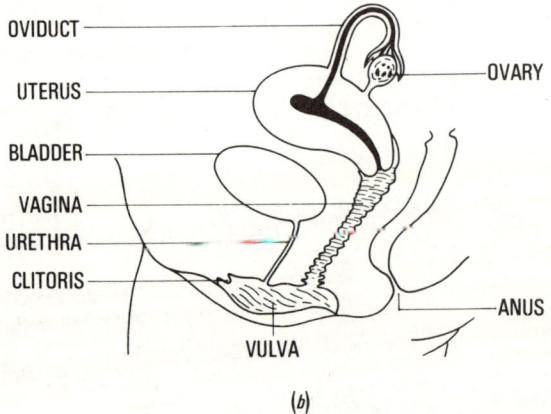

OVIDUCT
UTERUS
BLADDER
VAGINA
URETHRA
CLITORIS
OVARY
ANUS
VULVA

(b)

Fig 17.2 Female reproductive organs. (a) From the front. (b) Side view.

Hints: don't confuse *urethra* with *ureter*. The ureters carry urine only, from the kidneys to the bladder in both sexes. The urethra carries urine from the bladder in both sexes, and sperm also in males.
 And when drawing the female reproductive system:
1 draw the wall of the uterus thicker than the walls of the oviduct;
2 draw the ovaries close to the funnel of the oviduct.

Human reproduction

17.2 OVULATION

From the age of puberty (about 12, on average) one ovum is released every month by each ovary alternately. This continues until about the age of 45–50 (the '**menopause**').

STAGES IN OVULATION See Fig 17.3.

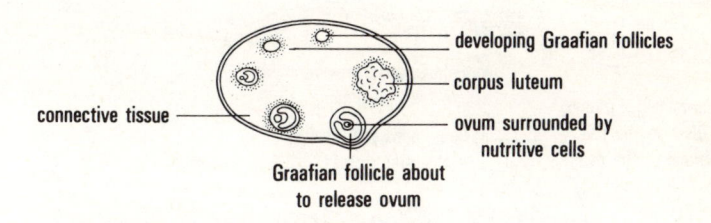

Fig 17.3 Section through ovary to show the stages in ovulation.

1. When an ovum starts to mature, the cells around it divide rapidly and form a fluid-filled **Graafian follicle**.
2. The functions of the cells in the Graafian follicle are:
   (a) to nourish the developing ovum;
   (b) to produce oestrogens (female hormones).
3. The follicle grows until it projects from the surface of the ovary, bursts and releases the ovum into the funnel of the oviduct. This is called **ovulation**.
4. Meanwhile, the follicle cells continue to grow, and form a mass of tissue called the **corpus luteum**. If the ovum is fertilized, the corpus luteum produces the hormone **progesterone** during the first three months of the pregnancy.

17.3 MAIN STAGES IN FERTILIZATION

See Fig 17.4.

1. When a **sperm** reaches an **ovum** in the oviduct, enzymes carried by the sperm cause the follicle cells to disperse. This must happen within 24 hours of intercourse, because the ova die 24 hours after ovulation.
2. The first sperm to reach the ovum produces enzymes to dissolve the ovum's cell membrane.
3. The head of this sperm enters the ovum and its nucleus fuses with the nucleus of the ovum to form a **zygote**. Meanwhile, a new impermeable membrane forms around the ovum to prevent other sperm from entering.
4. The zygote then begins to divide, first into two cells and then into four, etc., while travelling down the oviduct to the womb.

Human Biology

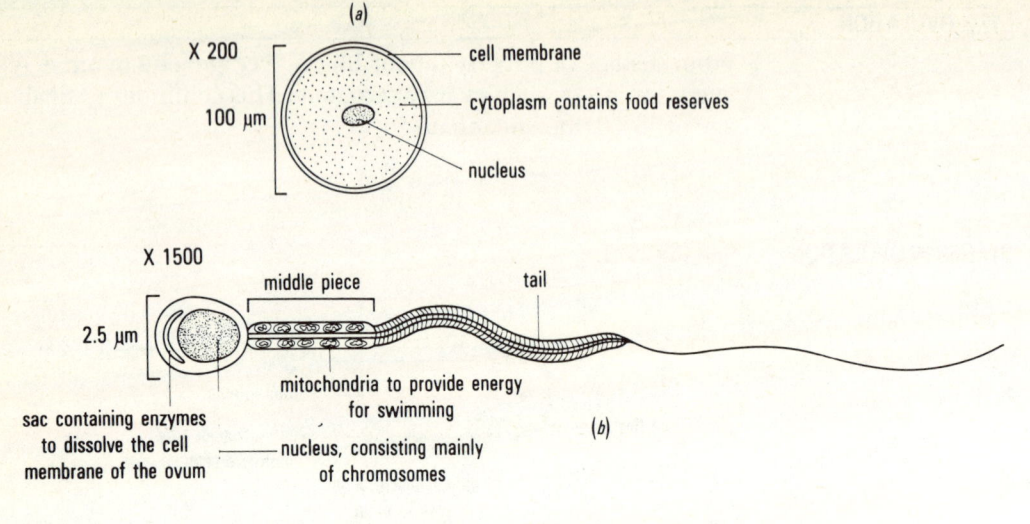

Fig 17.4 Structure of the gametes. (a) Ovum (egg cell). (b) Spermatozoon (sperm).

17.4 TWINS

Table 17.1 Different kinds of twin

	Fraternal (non-identical) twins	Identical twins
Gametes involved	Two ova and two sperm.	One ovum and one sperm.
Origins	Both ovaries release an ovum at the same time.	The fertilized ovum divides completely into two after fertilization.
Appearance	No more alike than any other two children of the same parents.	Identical in appearance.
Sex	Can be of different sex.	Always same sex.
Genetics	Genes not identical.	Genes identical.
Placenta	Each has its own placenta.	Often share the same placenta.

17.5 THE MENSTRUAL CYCLE

The **menstrual cycle** is a regular cycle of events, including the regular build up and shedding of the lining of the uterus and the release of an ovum from an ovary. **Menstruation** is the word used to describe the monthly flow of blood from the uterus, also called a period.

The menstrual cycle occurs in women on average every 28 days from puberty to age 45–55. The purpose of the menstrual cycle is to prepare the lining of the uterus to receive the fertilized ovum. If the ovum is not fertilized, the lining is shed.

Human reproduction

STAGES IN THE MENSTRUAL CYCLE

The cycle (see Fig 17.5) has three main phases, all controlled by the hormones oestrogen and progesterone.

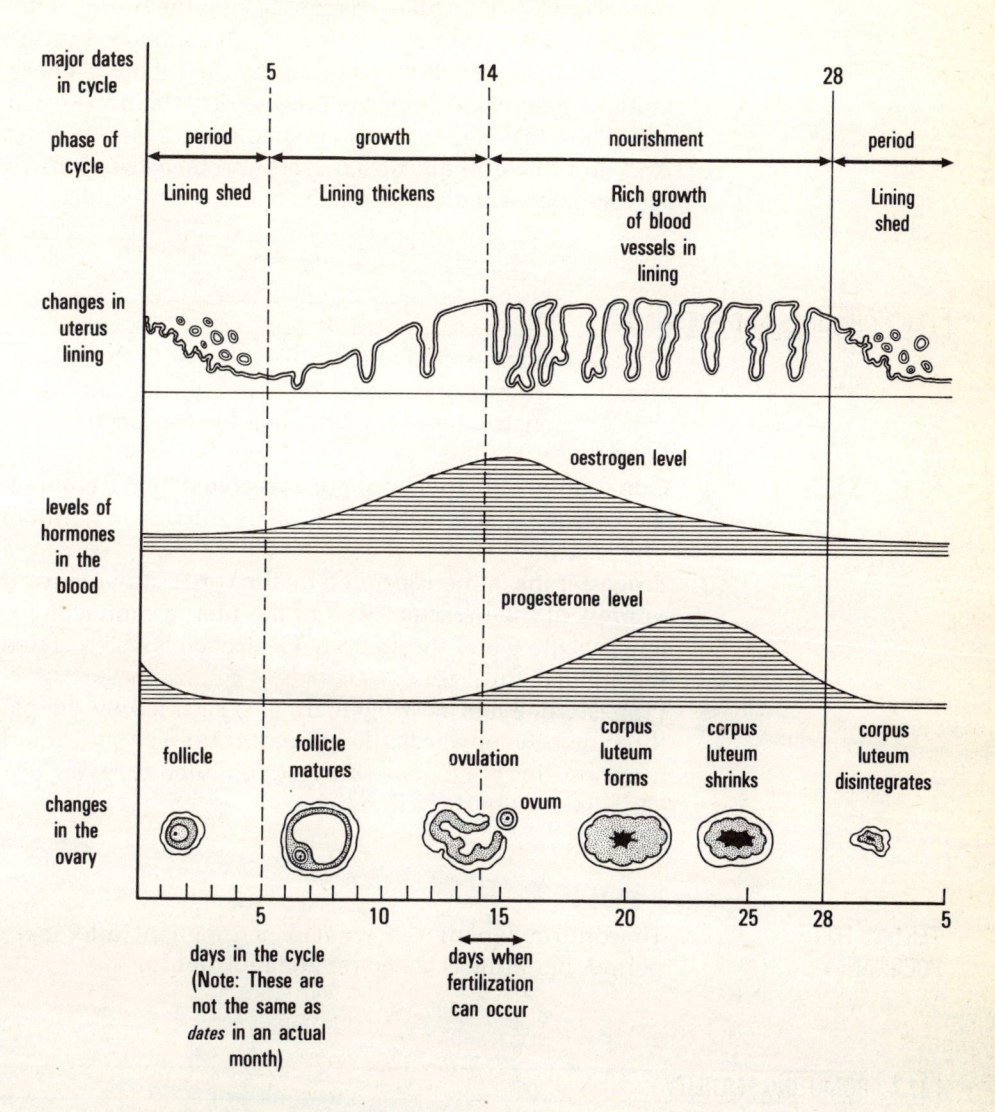

Fig 17.5 The menstrual cycle.

1. **Growth phase** (days 6–14). Oestrogen is secreted by the follicle cells in the ovary. This stimulates the uterus lining (the **endometrium**) to grow thicker, in preparation for the arrival of the fertilized ovum.
2. **Nourishment phase** (days 14–24). Progesterone is secreted by the corpus luteum in the ovary. This causes the uterus lining to become richly supplied with blood vessels, and also prevents the lining from being shed.
3. **Shedding phase**. If the fertilized ovum fails to reach the lining of the uterus, the corpus luteum breaks down. This causes a fall in the level

Human Biology

of progesterone in the blood, and the shedding of the uterus lining. The resulting flow of blood from the uterus is called a **period**.

Hints:
1. Don't confuse the **wall** of the uterus with the **lining** of the uterus. The uterus wall is a layer of muscles, which contracts during a period and also during labour. It is always about the same thickness. The uterus lining is a layer of connective tissue richly supplied with blood vessels. The lining builds up and is shed during each menstrual cycle.
2. And don't mix up **menstrual cycle** and **menstruation**. The cycle lasts 28 days; menstruation means the five-day period only.

17.6 HORMONES AND PREGNANCY

If menstruation occurs after fertilization, both the lining of the uterus and the fertilized ovum will be lost from the uterus. During pregnancy, menstruation is prevented by the action of hormones as follows.

1. **Gonadotrophin**. This hormone is secreted by the embryo on arrival in the uterus. It stimulates the corpus luteum to continue producing progesterone.
2. **Progesterone** is then secreted by the corpus luteum for three months to prevent the muscular wall of the uterus contracting and so expelling the lining and the embryo. **Oestrogen** is also secreted to maintain the lining at full size.
3. **Progesterone and oestrogen** are also secreted by the placenta. From three months onwards, the placenta supplies sufficient hormones to maintain the pregnancy. The corpus luteum ceases production and shrivels up after three months.

TESTING FOR PREGNANCY

To confirm whether a woman is pregnant after her first missed period, her urine is tested for **gonadotrophin**.

17.7 PROMOTING FERTILITY

N, NI only

Conception can be promoted by methods to help infertile couples.

METHODS FOR PROMOTING FERTILITY

1. **Choosing the best time for intercourse**. Intercourse is most likely to result in conception around the time of ovulation (days 13–16 in the menstrual cycle) – see Fig 17.5.
2. **Use of fertility hormones**. If a lack of ova is preventing conception, certain hormones can be used to increase the rate of ovulation. This can result in several ova being released at once, leading to multiple births.

Human reproduction

3. **Artificial insemination.** If a man is able to produce sperm but unable to have intercourse, sperm can be extracted from his epididymis and injected into the woman's vagina. This is called artificial insemination.
4. **Artificial insemination by donor (AID).** If the man is unable to produce sperm at all, the sperm may be obtained from a different person, i.e. from a 'donor'. The disadvantage of AID is that any offspring are *not* the natural children of the male partner.
5. **Embryo transplants** ('test-tube babies'). If the woman has blocked oviducts:
   (a) she is first given fertility hormones to increase the number of mature ova in her ovaries;
   (b) ova are then removed from her ovaries and mixed with sperm in a special culture solution in a dish – the solution is sterilized beforehand, contains water, glucose, salts and oxygen, and is kept at 37°C;
   (c) if an embryo develops, it is transferred back to her uterus 2–3 days after fertilization, when it is at the 8- or 16-cell stage.

17.8 CONTROLLING FERTILITY

BIRTH CONTROL

Birth control means any method for controlling fertility, including:
1. **avoiding** sexual intercourse altogether;
2. terminating an unwanted pregnancy, i.e. having an induced **abortion**;
3. using a method of **contraception** to prevent conception, i.e. to prevent fertilization;
4. **sterilizing** one of the partners, if the couple are **certain** that they do not want any more children.

STERILIZATION

Sterilization is carried out either by:
1. cutting off and tying the **sperm ducts** in the male;
2. cutting off and tying the **oviducts** in the female.

Both operations are difficult to reverse.

CONTRACEPTION

Contraception is the term for any method used to prevent conception after sexual intercourse.

Human Biology

Table 17.2 Methods of contraception

Method	How conception is prevented	Failure rate (no. of unwanted pregnancies per 100 women per year)	Effectiveness
1 Natural methods			
Rhythm or 'safe period'	Avoidance of intercourse around the time of ovulation.	20–30	Poor because timing of menstrual cycle varies from month to month.
2 Mechanical or barrier methods			
Sheath or condom (best used with spermicidal foam – see below)	Rubber sheath fitted over erect penis before intercourse. Sperm is trapped in reservoir at tip of sheath.	4	Good, if combined with a spermicide. But can fail if not fitted and removed carefully.
Diaphragm or cap (best used with spermicidal foam – see below)	Fitted over cervix to prevent entry of sperm.	4	May not fit tightly so must be used with spermicide.
Intra-uterine device (IUD or 'coil')	Plastic loop inserted into uterus by doctor, and left in place for long periods. Stimulates wall of uterus to keep contracting gently, so preventing implantation.	2	Good; but is sometimes expelled or causes painful reactions.
3 Chemical methods			
Spermicidal foam or jelly	Inserted into the vagina. Used with sheath or cap to kill sperm.	15	Poor if used by itself. Cannot reach all parts of vagina.
Contraceptive pill	Contains progesterone and oestrogen, which prevent ovulation from occurring. Can also be used to regulate periods.	0.1	Very good if taken regularly.

17.9 CHECKLIST

- Gamete/zygote.
- Sexual intercourse.
- Ejaculation.
- Fertilization.
- Functions of male organs:
    - penis;
    - testis;
    - scrotum;
    - epididymis;
    - seminal vesicle;
    - prostate gland;
    - urethra.
- Functions of female organs:
    - ovary;

Human reproduction 243

          oviduct;
          uterus;
          cervix;
          vagina;
          clitoris;
          urethra.

- Ovulation:
  - Graafian follicle;
  - corpus luteum.
- Structure of ovum and sperm.
- Origin and types of twin.
- Menstrual cycle.
- Menstruation.
- Roles of oestrogen and progesterone.
- Hormones and pregnancy:
  - gonadotrophin.
- Methods for promoting fertility (N, NI only):
  - timing;
  - hormones;
  - AID;
  - transplants.
- Methods for controlling fertility.
- Contraception:
  - Six methods as in Table 17.2.

17.10 EXAM QUESTIONS

1. (a) Use large labelled diagrams to describe the path of a sperm from its production in the testis to the time it fertilizes an egg in the female body. (12) [*Ox*]

    (b) Describe the formation, release and path of the female gamete up to the time that fertilization occurs. (12) [*Ox*]

2. (a) Explain why cystitis (an infection of the bladder and urethra) is commoner in women than in men. (2)
    (b) How can correct methods of washing help to prevent cystitis in women? (2)
    (a) Explain, in terms of the gametes involved, how a woman could give birth to triplets, two of whom are identical boys and one is a girl. (3)
    (b) What is the minimum number of placentas needed to support the three foetuses in the uterus? (1)

4. Answer these questions from the data supplied in Fig 17.6 (page 244):

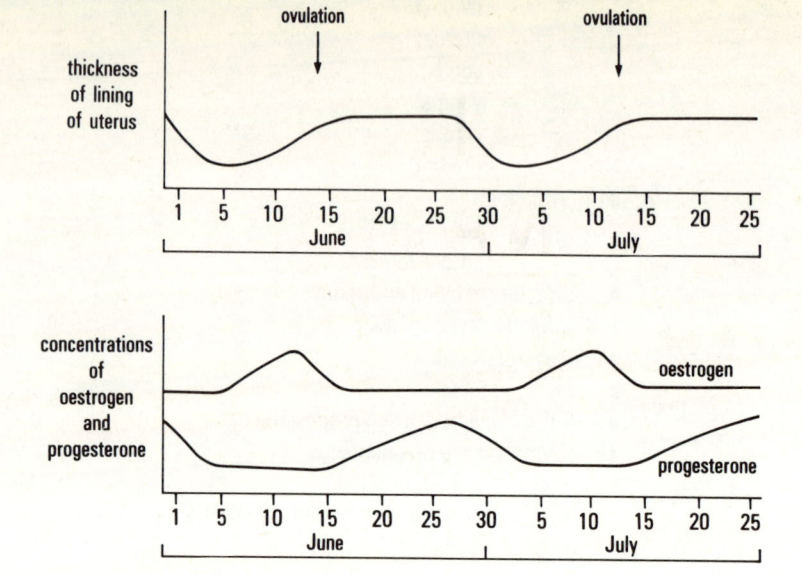

Fig 17.6 Relationship between thickness of uterus lining, hormone levels, etc., in the blood of an adult woman.

(a) On which *two* dates does menstruation occur? (2)
(b) What possible causes of (i) menstruation, (ii) ovulation, are suggested by the diagram? (2)
(c) What is the relationship between the uterus lining and the concentration of oestrogen? (2)
(d) On which dates in June would sexual intercourse be most likely to result in fertilization? (1)
(e) How can ovulation be prevented by taking a hormone? (1)

5 (a) Why does the corpus luteum remain active for several months at the beginning of pregnancy? (2)
(b) What are the roles of (i) gonadotrophin (ii) progesterone in the initiation and maintenance of pregnancy? (2)

6 Describe three methods to improve the fertility of a childless couple and comment on the advantages and disadvantages of each. (6)

7 (a) Explain the difference between birth control and contraception. (2)
(b) (i) Briefly describe how male sterilization is performed. (2)
(ii) What are its advantages and disadvantages to the male? (2)
(c) Describe one example each of natural, mechanical and chemical methods of contraception. Comment on the effectiveness of each method you describe. (6)

CHAPTER EIGHTEEN

PREGNANCY, ANTE-NATAL CARE AND CHILDBIRTH

CONTENTS

18.1 Development in the uterus — 247
Early development 247
Implantation 247
Later development 247

18.2 Role of the placenta — 249
Functions of the placenta 249
Reasons for separation of maternal and foetal circulations 249
How the structure of the placenta is suited to its functions 250
How dissolved substances pass across the placenta 250
Passage of harmful substances across the placenta 251

18.3 Ante-natal care — 252
The ante-natal clinic 252
Ante-natal tests 252
Care of mother and foetus 253

18.4 Birth — 253
Stages of birth 254
Different kinds of birth 254
Termination of pregnancy 255

- 18.5 Checklist 255
- 18.6 Exam questions 255

Pregnancy, ante-natal care and childbirth

18.1 DEVELOPMENT IN THE UTERUS

EARLY DEVELOPMENT   After fertilization, the zygote floats down the oviduct in the current created by the beating of the cilia of the walls of the oviduct. During this time it divides rapidly to form a ball of cells.

On entering the uterus it floats freely for about five days, absorbing food and oxygen from fluids in the womb.

IMPLANTATION   The embryo becomes embedded in the wall of the uterus. Minute villi grow out from the embryo to form the **placenta** (see Fig 18.1). This becomes closely associated with the rich blood supply in the uterus lining. Food and oxygen are absorbed through the villi from the mother's blood supply.

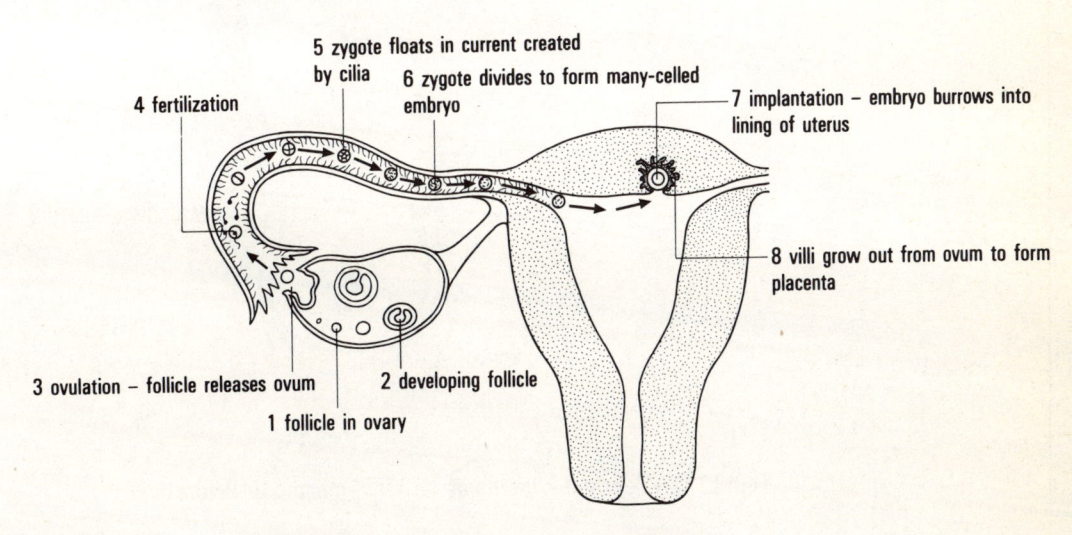

Fig 18.1 Ovulation, fertilization and implantation.

LATER DEVELOPMENT   The embryo grows rapidly so that the outlines of the limbs and major organs can be distinguished within 10 weeks of conception. By this

Human Biology

time, the embryo is referred to as a **foetus** (see Fig 18.2). After about four months the foetus is able to move its limbs.

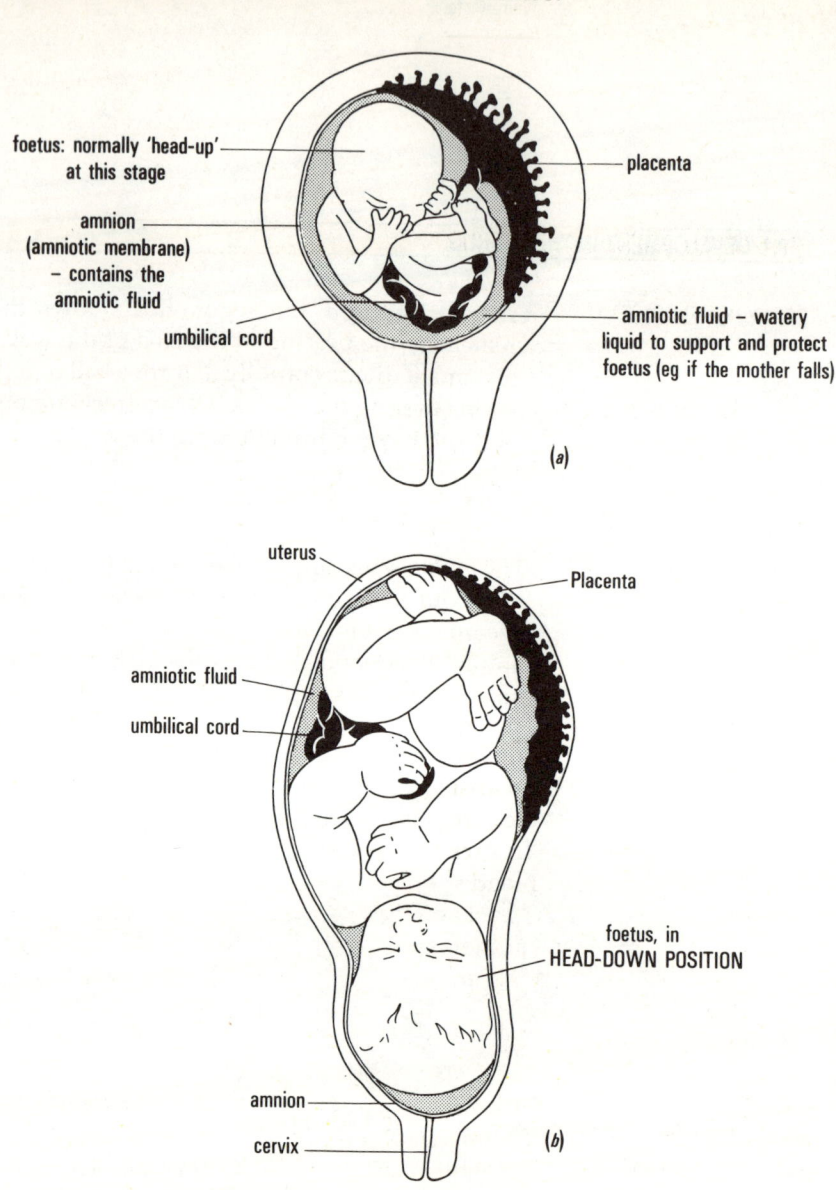

Fig 18.2 Development in the uterus. (a) At five months. (b) Before birth.

Pregnancy, ante-natal care and childbirth 249

Table 18.1 Stages in the development of the embryo and foetus

Time after fertilization	Main events
50 hours	Embryo – a ball of cells, just visible to the eye.
10 days	Embryo embedded in lining of uterus.
6 weeks	Head, eyes, first signs of limbs, heart and blood vessels become visible.
5 months	Limb movements can be felt.
7 months	Foetus turns so that its head is above the cervix.
9 months	Birth.

Hint: the function of the **amniotic fluid** around the foetus is purely protective. It plays no part in nourishing the foetus, nor does the foetus excrete wastes into the fluid. All nourishment and excretion takes place through the placenta.

18.2 ROLE OF THE PLACENTA

FUNCTIONS OF THE PLACENTA

1. To **secrete** the hormones oestrogen and progesterone, which maintain the pregnancy by preventing the shedding of the uterus lining.
2. To **absorb** oxygen and food substances such as glucose, amino acids, etc., from the mother's blood.
3. To **excrete** wastes such as carbon dioxide and urea into the mother's blood supply.
4. To act as a **barrier** against the passage of harmful substances from the mother to the foetus.

Warning! This is a favourite topic for examiners.

REASONS FOR SEPARATION OF MATERNAL AND FOETAL CIRCULATIONS

The maternal and foetal circulations are separated (Fig 18.3) because:

1. The higher blood pressure of the maternal circulation would burst the delicate foetal capillaries if the two systems were linked.
2. The maternal and foetal blood groups may be different and even incompatible.
3. Many microorganisms and harmful substances could pass from the maternal to the foetal blood (and some do manage to pass through).

Human Biology

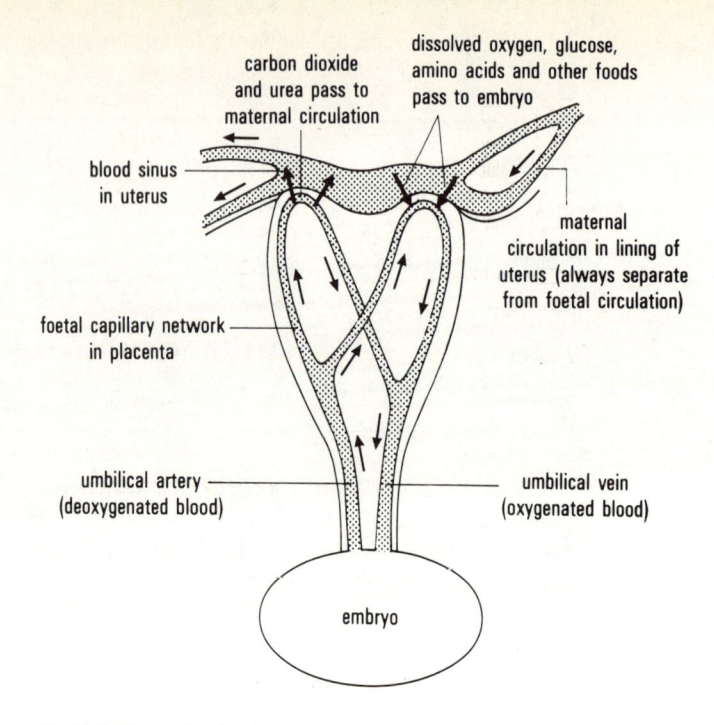

Fig 18.3 Circulation in the uterus and placenta

HOW THE STRUCTURE OF THE PLACENTA IS SUITED TO ITS FUNCTIONS	1	It branches to form thousands of **micro-villi** so that it has a large surface area – up to 14 square metres.
	2	The membranes separating the foetal capillaries from the maternal circulation are very **thin**.
	3	Both the uterus lining and the placenta are richly supplied with blood vessels. In the uterus, many of these vessels become enlarged to form blood **sinuses** ('pools' of blood).

HOW DISSOLVED SUBSTANCES PASS ACROSS THE PLACENTA		See Fig 18.4.
	1	**Dissolved food substances.** The concentration of glucose and amino acids, etc., is higher in the maternal circulation, so dissolved foods diffuse down the concentration gradient from the maternal to the foetal circulation.
	2	**Excreted wastes.** The concentration of carbon dioxide and urea is higher in the foetal circulation, so these diffuse from the foetal to the maternal circulation.
	3	**Oxygen.** The maternal blood entering the uterus lining contains a higher concentration of oxygen than the foetal blood entering the placenta. As a result, oxyhaemoglobin in the maternal red blood cells breaks down (see page 105) to oxygen and haemoglobin. The oxygen

Pregnancy, ante-natal care and childbirth

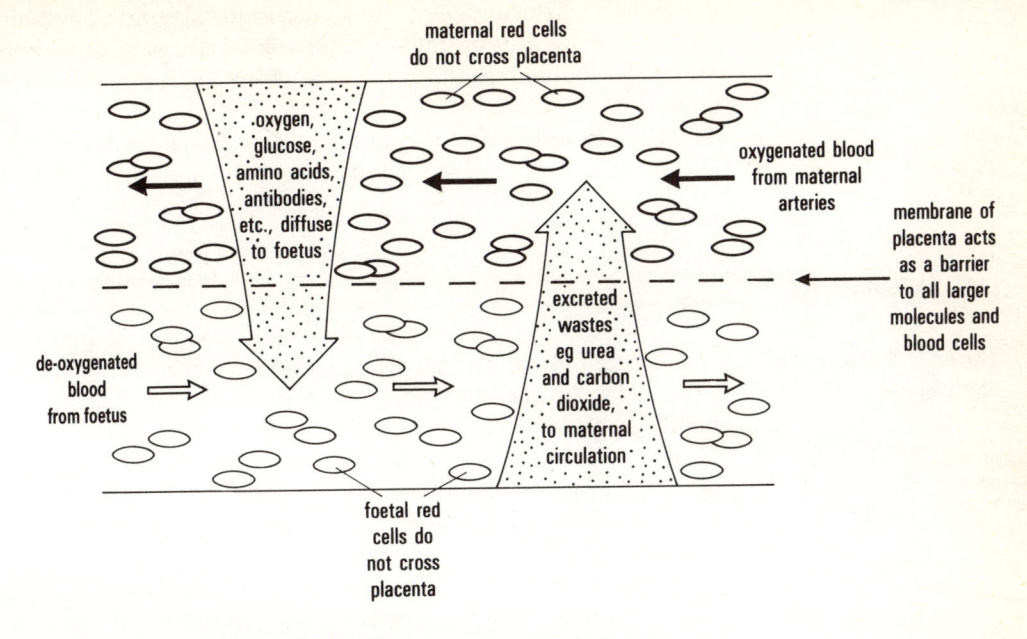

Fig 18.4 How the placenta acts as a selective barrier.

diffuses across the placenta and unites with the haemoglobin in the foetal red blood cells.

4 **Antibodies** also diffuse from the mother to the foetus, so providing some protection against disease in the early months of life.

PASSAGE OF HARMFUL SUBSTANCES ACROSS THE PLACENTA

Although larger molecules and cells cannot normally cross the placenta, certain harmful organisms and poisonous substances *are* able to pass from the mother to the foetus. These include the following.

1 **The rubella (German measles) virus**, which causes serious damage to the nervous system of the foetus during the first three months of pregnancy. The foetus may be born blind, deaf or with severe damage to the heart or brain. It is important for *all* teenage girls to be vaccinated against rubella before there is any risk of pregnancy.
2 **Other viruses**, such as the AIDS virus, can also infect the foetus from the mother.
3 **Poisons in cigarette smoke.** The cyanide, carbon monoxide and nicotine in cigarette smoke restrict the oxygen supply to the foetus. As a result, babies born to smokers tend to have a smaller weight at birth and so are more likely to die. They are also more likely to develop leukaemia (blood cancer) in childhood.
4 **Alcohol** can also damage the foetus, leading to a reduced weight at birth and poor development generally.
5 Many kinds of **drugs** can also damage the foetus. These include drugs

Human Biology

prescribed by doctors, e.g. the Thalidomide sleeping pill which led to babies born with tiny limbs. Non-medical drugs such as heroin also affect the foetus, resulting in babies born with symptoms of heroin addiction.

6 **The Rhesus antibody** (see page 418) may also pass across the placent and destroy the foetal red blood cells.

18.3 ANTE-NATAL CARE

THE ANTE-NATAL CLINIC
Not N or APH

Ante-natal clinics provide advice and a programme of regular medical checks during pregnancy. It is important to register at an ante-natal clinic as early as possible during pregnancy for two reasons.

1 Many of the tests carried out during pregnancy involve comparisons of measurements from month to month. It is important to make the first measurements at the start of pregnancy so that any unusual changes can be detected at once.

2 If the foetus is likely to be defective in some way, an abortion (see page 255) may be necessary. If so, this should be carried out as early as possible.

ANTE-NATAL TESTS
W, L only

Table 18.2 Ante-natal tests

Test	Purpose
1 Weight of mother	A pregnant woman normally gains about 450 g (1 pound) per week. A sudden increase in weight may be caused by a kidney disorder called toxaemia which can result in premature labour and convulsions. Failure to gain weight may mean that the foetus is not developing normally.
2 Size of uterus	General indication of health of foetus. If the uterus suddenly ceases to expand, this may be a sign that the foetus has stopped growing.
3 Red cell count in blood	To detect anaemia in the mother, possibly caused by lack of iron in the diet.
4 Blood test	(a) To determine the mother's blood group so that the correct type of blood is given to her if an emergency transfusion is needed. (b) To detect Rhesus negative mothers (see p. 418). (c) To detect spina bifida, a dangerous defect of the spinal cord. This is carried out by measuring the levels of certain proteins found only in spina bifida cases.
5 Blood pressure	A rise in blood pressure may indicate toxaemia.
6 Urine	(a) Protein in the urine may also indicate toxaemia. (b) Glucose in the urine is a symptom of diabetes.
7 Amniocentesis (collection of amniotic fluid by means of a long needle inserted into the uterus)	(a) To detect chromosome abnormalities, e.g. Down's syndrome ('mongolism'), by culturing foetal cells and counting their chromosomes. (b) To confirm spina bifida by testing for unusual proteins in the amniotic fluid.

Pregnancy, ante-natal care and childbirth 253

CARE OF MOTHER AND FOETUS

Table 18.3 Care of the mother and foetus during pregnancy

Subject	Best advice for optimum health of mother and child
1 Diet	
(a) Protein	A protein-rich diet is needed to form the new cells in the growing foetus.
(b) Calcium, Phosphorus, Vitamin D	Needed for the growing bones of the foetus. If deficient, the mother may suffer loss of minerals from her bones to the foetus.
(c) Iron	Sufficient iron for the manufacture of the foetal red blood cells is essential.
(d) Total amount of food	'Eating for two' is *not* necessary and may cause the mother to become overweight.
(e) Water	Extra water is needed because the kidneys must remove urea from both foetal and maternal circulations. Lack of water may cause a rise in urea level in the mother's blood.
2 Clothing	This should be loose and comfortable so as not to interfere with the circulation. High-heeled shoes should be avoided during late pregnancy because they interfere with balance, so causing backache.
3 Personal habits	
(a) Exercise	Regular mild exercise helps to stimulate the circulation and improve muscle tone. Violent exercise is best avoided, owing to the possibility of straining the already-stretched muscles of the abdomen.
(b) Rest	An afternoon rest is helpful to maintain peak health. The feet should be slightly raised to prevent the development of varicose veins.
(c) Use of drugs	Alcohol, cigarettes, other drugs and all forms of medication should be avoided as far as possible owing to their potentially harmful effects on the foetus. Other people's cigarette smoke, e.g. the father's, can also be harmful.
(d) Relaxed lifestyle	Ideally, a pregnant woman should enjoy a calm life, supported by her partner and family. Continuous emotional upsets may affect the development of the foetus. (However, along with other advice in this table, this may be impossible for many mothers.)

18.4 BIRTH

The **gestation period** is the passage of time from the start of the last period until birth – about 9 months.

STAGES OF BIRTH

FIRST STAGE

1. The foetus turns **downwards** so that its head lies just above the cervix.
2. **The muscles of the uterus wall** begin to contract rhythmically. The woman is said to be 'in labour' when the contractions become more frequent and more powerful.
3. The muscles of the **cervix** gradually relax to admit the head of the foetus.
4. The **amnion breaks**, releasing the amniotic fluid (the 'breaking of the waters').

SECOND STAGE

1. The foetus is forced out of the uterus and through the vagina by powerful **contractions** of the involuntary muscles of the uterus. The mother can assist by contracting the voluntary muscles of the abdomen.
2. During birth, the foetus must pass through the pelvic girdle which forms a ring of bone. To aid this process, the separate bones of its skull can slide over each other without harm. In addition, the pelvis is wider in women than in men, and the cartilage joint at the front of the pelvis stretches slightly during birth.

THIRD STAGE

1. The umbilical arteries constrict so that **the cord can be cut** without the baby bleeding to death. The cord is then **tied** at both ends, to prevent any further loss of blood for both mother and baby.
2. Stimulated by the sudden change in its environment, the baby takes its first breath, and usually starts to cry.
3. Contractions continue for about ten minutes, when the placenta and cord come away from the wall of the uterus and are then expelled as the **afterbirth**.

DIFFERENT KINDS OF BIRTH

Caesarean delivery. If the pelvic girdle is too narrow for the baby to pass through, doctors may open the uterus and remove the baby directly.

Induction of labour. If birth is delayed so long that the baby's health is in danger, doctors may 'induce' labour. This is done by injecting drugs which cause the uterus muscles to contract, so initiating labour.

A breech birth is a birth where the foetus is in the 'head-up' position so that birth takes place feet first. This results in a more difficult birth and may require special attention by doctors and midwives.

Pregnancy, ante-natal care and childbirth

TERMINATION OF PREGNANCY

An **abortion** is the term used by doctors to describe any pregnancy which ends at a stage too early for the survival of the foetus, e.g. 3–4 months.

A **spontaneous abortion** (or **miscarriage**) is a 'natural abortion'. This may happen due to lack of progesterone at three months, or for other reasons.

An **induced abortion** is the deliberate ending of a pregnancy, by drugs or surgery. This is carried out because the foetus is thought to be deformed, or the mother's health is at risk, or the mother does not wish to complete the pregnancy.

18.5 CHECKLIST

- Pregnancy:
    - early development;
    - implantation;
    - later development.
- Main growth stages of embryo/foetus.
- Roles of amniotic fluid and umbilical cord.
- Structure of the placenta in relation to its functions.
- How dissolved substances cross the placenta.
- The placenta's role as a selective barrier.
- Ante-natal clinics:
    - basic function;
    - importance of early and regular attendances.
- Ante-natal tests (seven) (L, W only).
- Care of the pregnant woman (ten).
- Stages in birth (three).
- Afterbirth.
- Abortions:
    - spontaneous;
    - induced.
- Caesarean and breach births.
- Induction of labour.

18.6 EXAM QUESTIONS

1 (a) How does the placenta support the life and development of the embryo? (10)
   (b) Describe the hazards to which an embryo in the uterus may be subjected. (4) [L/EA]

2 (a) Give three reasons for stating that Fig 18.2(b) shows a foetus at a much later stage than Fig 18.2(a). (3)
   (b) What are the functions of the amniotic fluid? (2)

3 (a) Give three advantages to a foetus of the inability of the maternal and foetal blood to mix in the placenta. (3) [W]

(b) How is the structure of the placenta suited to its functions? (3)

(c) Why is it incorrect to state that foods such as starch and protein pass from mother to child in the uterus? (3)

4 (a) What are the advantages of each of these features for the efficient functioning of the placenta:
  (i) Presence of microvilli,
  (ii) All of the embryo's blood flows through the placenta during each minute,
  (iii) The total length of capillaries in the placenta is about 50 km (6)

(b) The placenta is an organ of nutrition, gaseous exchange and excretion for the foetus. State three differences, one relating to each of these functions, between the composition of the blood flowing in the umbilical artery and the umbilical vein. (3)   [AEB 1982]

5 (a) What is the purpose of an ante-natal clinic? (2)
(b) Why is early attendance during pregnancy desirable? (2)
(c) Describe how the following conditions can be detected by ante-natal tests: Down's syndrome, spina bifida, toxaemia. (3)

6 (a) Why is it desirable for a baby to be born head first? (1)
(b) What changes occur to the following during birth? Muscles of the cervix; muscles of the uterus wall; amnion. (3)
(c) Which features of (i) the mother (ii) the baby enable safe passage through the pelvic girdle? (3)
(d) What action may be taken if the baby is unable to pass through safely? (2)

7 Table 18.4 shows the numbers of children born to smoking and non-smoking mothers, arranged in groups according to mass at birth.

Table 18.4

Mass at birth (kg)	<2.4	2.4 to 3.1	3.2 to 3.5	3.6 to 3.9	>3.9	Total births in sample
Number of children born to non-smoking mothers	4	42	70	54	30	200
Number of children born to mothers who smoke	3	24	44	23	6	100

(a) State the range of birth mass which was most common. (1)
(b) State the percentage of children born with a birth mass greater than 3.5 kg to:
  (i) non-smoking mothers, (1)
  (ii) smoking mothers. (1)
(c) Using the data in the table state one effect of smoking on birth mass. (1)
(d) Explain a possible reason for this effect. (2)

[AEB 1984]

THE HUMAN LIFE CYCLE: CHILD DEVELOPMENT, MATURITY AND AGEING

CONTENTS

19.1 Parental care of children — 259

19.2 Care of the new-born baby — 260
Temperature 260
Screening 260
Hygiene 260
Protection from infection 260
Feeding 260

19.3 Lactation, breast and bottle feeding — 261
Adaptations for breast feeding 261
Control of lactation 261
Colostrum 261
Composition of milk 262
Breast milk or bottle? 262
Feeding in early childhood – weaning 263

19.4 Growth in height and weight — 263
Main stages in growth 263

19.5 Growth rates of different organs 264
Changes in the reproductive organs with age 264

19.6 Ageing 265

19.7 Checklist 265

19.8 Exam questions 266

19.1 PARENTAL CARE OF CHILDREN

If children are to grow to their full size, with fully developed intelligence and a balanced personality, parents need to pay attention to the factors listed in Table 19.1.

Table 19.1 Needs of children for optimum development (parental care)

Factor	Advice
Diet	1 Balance – children need a balanced diet, with higher proportions of protein and vitamins compared to adults, for growth. 2 Quantity – children need less food than adults, e.g. a one-year-old may need only 4000 kJ daily compared with 11 000 kJ for an average adult.
Sleep	Children need more sleep than adults, probably because growth hormones are mainly secreted during sleep. 1 A new-born baby sleeps for 24 hours except when hungry. 2 A one-year-old need 14 hours per night, plus daytime naps. 3 A ten-year-old needs 12 hours of sleep. 4 Adults (from 16 onwards) need 7.5 hours sleep nightly on average.
Protection	1 Immunization against infection. 2 Protection from accidents at home and on the roads.
Feet	Parents need to allow children's feet to grow correctly by proper choice of shoes.
Teeth	1 Children need to be taught good tooth care. 2 Sweets should not be given between meals. 3 Baby feeders containing sugary drinks are especially dangerous for teeth if given for long periods.
Affection	Children do not grow normally without affection and attention.
Stable relationships	Children need to make long-term stable relationships with caring adults for full development of their personalities.
Stimulation	The brain does not develop fully unless stimulated by new experiences, e.g. by play, etc.

19.2 CARE OF THE NEW-BORN BABY

TEMPERATURE

New-born babies must be kept at steady temperatures above 18°C because:
1. they have a larger surface-area-to-volume ratio than adults, causing them to lose heat more rapidly;
2. they also have a poorly developed temperature regulating mechanism. This means that they must not be kept *too* warm, e.g. by wrapping in too many clothes.

SCREENING

Special tests are performed to screen out potential defects for closer attention. These include the following.

REFLEXES

Shortly after birth, the new born baby's reflexes are tested to check that the nervous system has developed normally.

PKU

The blood of all new born babies is tested for the presence of certain amino acids which indicate a faulty liver enzyme (and also for diabetes). Children born with this defect must be fed on diets containing minimum quantities of the amino acid phenylalanine untile the age of five. If not, they may suffer brain damage from build up of this amino acid or its by-products.

HYGIENE

Babies have no voluntary control over the sphincter muscles which close the bladder and rectum, until at least 18 months old. Nappies are therefore essential, followed by encouragement for toilet training from 18 months onwards.

PROTECTION FROM INFECTION

Babies have poorly developed immune systems (see page 310) and their blood contains few antibodies at this stage. They are therefore more likely to become seriously ill if exposed to infection.

FEEDING

New born babies are fed entirely on milk for the first four months at least, because they lack teeth and their digestive system cannot digest solid food at this stage.

The human life cycle

19.3 LACTATION, BREAST AND BOTTLE FEEDING

Lactation is the secretion of milk for the new-born baby. Milk is secreted by a pair of exocrine glands called the **mammary glands** or breasts (see Fig 19.1).

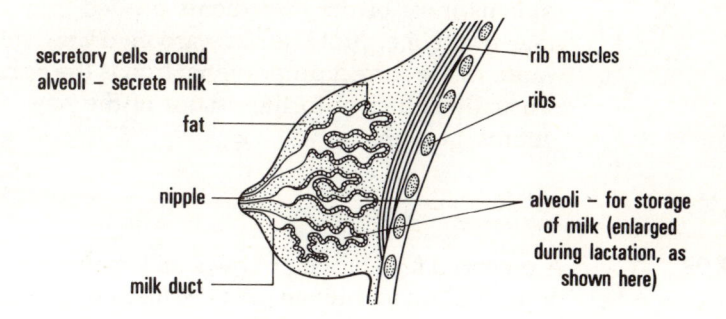

Fig 19.1 Section through human breast during lactation.

ADAPTATIONS FOR BREAST FEEDING

Adaptations for sucking by the new born baby include the following.
1. A reflex action called the **rooting reflex**, which causes its head to turn towards a light touch on its cheek, e.g. from brushing against the nipple. This assists the baby to find the nipple.
2. A reflex which causes **sucking** to commence when the nipple is felt by the lips.
3. The **shape of the mouth** is adapted for sucking and the cheek and lip muscles are well developed at birth to carry out the sucking action.

CONTROL OF LACTATION

1. During pregnancy increasing quantities of oestrogen and progesterone are secreted by the placenta, stimulating the secretory cells to become active.
2. Immediately following birth, the sharp drop in progesterone level stimulates secretion of a pituitary hormone called **prolactin**. This causes the milk-secreting cells to release milk into the alveoli of the breast.
3. When the new born baby starts to suck, nervous impulses pass from the nipples to the brain. This triggers off production of a pituitary hormone which causes the release of milk from the alveoli into the nipples.

COLOSTRUM

During the first three days after birth, a thin lemon-coloured liquid called **colostrum** is produced by the breasts instead of milk. Colostrum is rich in protein but is not as nourishing as milk. It also contains antibodies which protect the baby from gut infections to some extent.

COMPOSITION OF MILK

Human milk is the best available complete food for growing babies. It contains most of the ingredients needed in a balanced diet for this stage of life, i.e. proteins, fat, carbohydrates, minerals, vitamins and water, in the correct proportions. Iron is the only exception, but there is usually sufficient in the tissues of the new-born child for several months' growth.

BREAST MILK OR BOTTLE?

A prepared feed based on cow's milk may have to be given instead of, or in addition to, human milk because not all babies will feed from the breast, nor is breast feeding popular with all mothers. However, breast feeding for even a few days is a valuable way to pass on the mother's antibodies.

Table 19.2 Comparison of breast and bottle feeding

Breast feeding – human milk	Bottle feeding – cow's milk (modified)
Provides a complete balanced diet (except for iron), ideal for digestion by the newborn human.	Ideal for calves, but contains excess minerals and too much protein for humans. The additional protein neutralizes the acid in the stomach, so increasing the risk of gut infections.
Little risk of allergies	Some babies are allergic to the proteins in cow's milk.
Contains human antibodies (especially colostrum)	Cow antibodies give little protection against human diseases.
No special preparation needed.	Must be prepared to the correct strength and carefully sterilized.
Lipases (fat digesting enzymes) present to digest fats and fat soluble vitamins.	Lipases are destroyed by sterilization.
The sucking reflex stimulates contraction of the mother's uterus wall, so that her shape returns to normal more quickly.	No benefit from sucking reflex.
Helps to promote a close relationship or bond between mother and child, but the father is excluded.	Fathers and babysitters can help with bottle feeding.
The mother is apt to become over-tired; must continue to eat a well balanced diet, and must avoid alcohol, cigarettes or any other kind of drug.	Less tiring for the mother and her diet no longer affects the baby's health.
Some mothers find breast feeding in public inconvenient or embarrassing.	Bottle feeding can be more convenient, e.g. if out shopping.
Breast feeding is sometimes painful and difficult.	Some babies will feed only from bottles.

The human life cycle

FEEDING IN EARLY CHILDHOOD – WEANING

Weaning is the gradual withdrawal of breast or bottled milk and its replacement with solids. Solids can be added after about four months.

Any solids given to a child between four and six months old must be entirely free from lumps. Babies cannot chew before six or seven months because the chewing muscles are not yet developed. After six months, they can chew using their firm, hard gums, even though they still have no teeth.

19.4 GROWTH IN HEIGHT AND WEIGHT

Growth occurs unevenly, in spurts, and varies greatly from person to person. It also differs in boys and girls, especially between the ages of 10 and 16.

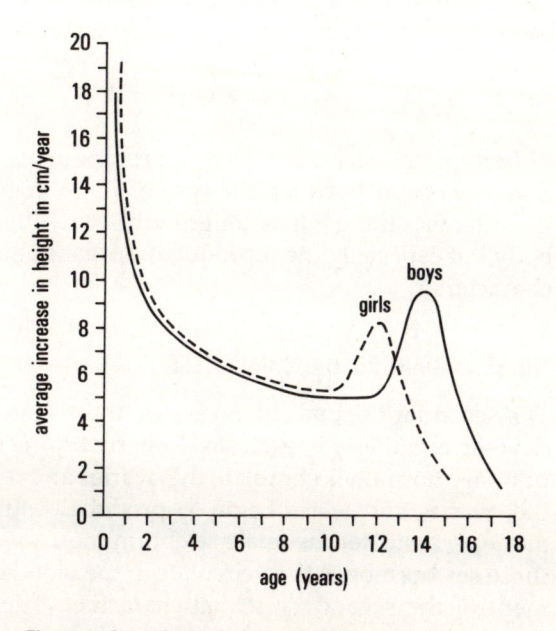

Fig 19.2 Growth rate in boys and girls.

MAIN STAGES IN GROWTH

1 **A fall in weight** of up to 10% occurs during the two days immediately after birth. This is made up by rapid growth within a week or two.
2 **The maximum rate of growth** occurs during the first year of life (see Fig 19.2). Between birth and 12 months old, a typical baby increases in height by at least 25 cm, and in weight by 6 kg.
3 The rate of growth then falls rapidly until puberty. At this point there is a **growth spurt** in girls between the ages of 11 and 14, and in boys between 13 and 16.

Human Biology

4   Boys are slightly **taller** than girls on average, up to the age of 11. Between 11 and 13 girls are taller on average, but boys catch up and are finally 12 cm taller on average.
5   Girls complete growth in height by about 16 on average, but boys usually grow taller until about 18 years of age.
6   Increase in **weight** may continue in both sexes as the shoulders broaden and the muscles develop.

19.5 GROWTH RATES OF DIFFERENT ORGANS

Different parts of the body grow at different rates (Fig 19.5 p. 268).

1   **The brain** grows faster than any other major organ during early development. By the age of four the brain has reached 90% of its adult weight, although the body as a whole weighs only 25% of adult weight. It is essential for the brain to develop first because it controls all of the other organs, especially the muscles.
2   **The reproductive system** develops more slowly than any other part because it is not active until the early teenage years.

CHANGES IN THE REPRODUCTIVE ORGANS WITH AGE

Puberty is the stage at which the reproductive organs become functional. It occurs between the ages of 10–16 in girls and 12–18 in boys. In both cases there is a major growth spurt, affecting most parts of the body but especially the reproductive organs and the **secondary sexual characters.**

THE SECONDARY SEXUAL CHARACTERS

The secondary sexual characters are those features of the body which develop at puberty in each sex. Puberty begins when:

1   pituitary hormones stimulate the ovaries and testes;
2   the ovaries and testes begin to produce oestrogen (female sex hormone) or testosterone (male sex hormone);
3   these sex hormones then circulate in the blood and cause the development of the secondary sexual characters. They are also essential to maintain the sexual characters during life.

Table 19.3 Secondary sexual characters

Girls	Boys
Start of menstrual cycle, including ovulation.	Sperm production begins.
Growth of breasts, uterus and pelvis.	Growth of penis and of muscles; voice deepens.
Growth of pubic hair.	Growth of face, chest and pubic hair.
Development of feelings of attraction to the opposite sex.	

The human life cycle

THE MENOPAUSE

The menopause is the stage at which the menstrual cycle and ovulation cease in women (between 45–55), due to the exhaustion of the ovum-forming cells in the ovaries. There is no equivalent in men.

19.6 AGEING

Table 19.4 The effects of ageing on the body

Effect	Consequences
Loss of elasticity in the elastic fibres found throughout the skin, the walls of blood vessels, etc.	1 Wrinkles in the skin (especially among smokers). 2 Circulatory problems, e.g. varicose veins, due to walls of veins becoming permanently stretched, and arteriosclerosis (see p. 417).
Loss of elasticity of the lens in the eye.	Inability to focus on objects close to the eye – a form of long sight.
Slower metabolic rate due to lower levels of hormone production.	General slowing down of body activities.
Shrinkage of the discs between the vertebrae	Loss of height.
Loss of calcium from the bones.	The bones become brittle and break more easily.
Arthritis, especially osteo-arthritis, causing loss of cartilage from the joints.	Loss of mobility due to stiff, painful knee and hip joints.
Less efficient temperature regulation.	Death from hypothermia in very cold weather or heat stroke in very hot weather.

19.7 CHECKLIST

- Parental care:
    - diet;
    - sleep;
    - protection;
    - feet;
    - teeth;
    - affection;
    - stable relationships;
    - stimulation.
- Care of the new born baby:
    - temperature;
    - screening for defects;
    - hygiene;
    - protection from infection;
    - feeding.

- Lactation
- Adaptations of the new born for breast feeding (three).
- Structure of the breast.
- Control of lactation.
- Colostrum.
- Composition of milk.
- Breast *v.* bottle feeding.
- Weaning.
- Growth phases in boys and girls.
- Growth rates of different organs.
- Secondary sexual characters.
- Menopause.
- Effects of ageing (seven).

19.8 EXAM QUESTIONS

1. Give two examples each of ways in which parents should care for their child's (*a*) physical, (*b*) mental, well-being. (4)

2. (*a*) What is meant by lactation? (2)
   (*b*) How is lactation initiated within the mammary glands? (3)

3. (*a*) (i) What is colostrum? (2)
   (ii) Give one advantage of breast feeding. (1)
   (iii) Give one advantage of bottle feeding. (1)
   (*b*) Table 19.5 gives details of the composition of human and cows' milk.

   Table 19.5

Component	Human milk %	Cows' milk %
Water	88.4	87.3
Lactose	6.5	4.5
Protein	1.5	3.5
Fat	3.3	4.0
Mineral salts	0.3	0.7

   If cows' milk is used for bottle feeding, it is normally diluted to reduce the concentration of protein so that it is similar to that of human milk.
   (i) By what proportion must it be diluted? (2)
   (ii) Which materials must be added to this diluted cows' milk to produce a mixture very similar to human milk?
   (*c*) In which ways is a newly born baby adapted for suckling? (3)
   (*d*) A newly born child should be kept in an environment which

is constantly warm and as bacteria-free as possible. Give reasons why these two requirements are necessary. (2) [AEB 1982]
4 State TWO ways in which breast milk can help to protect a baby against infection. (4)
5 Fig 19.3 shows the average heights for males and females up to the age of 20.

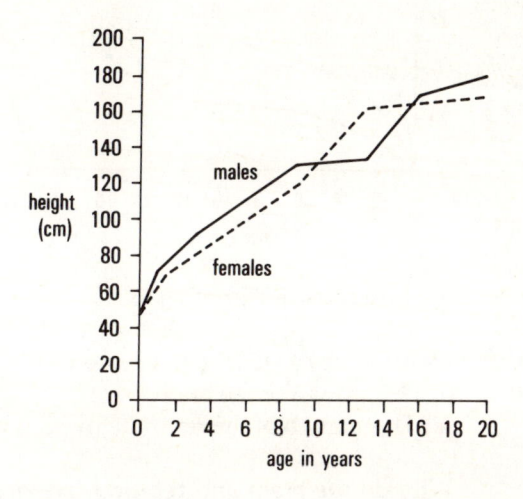

Fig 19.3 Average heights for males and females up to the age of 20.

(a) At what period in males is the rate of growth the greatest? (1)
(b) During which four years do males show the slowest rate of growth? (1)
(c) What is the average height of the fully grown male? (1)
(d) What is the average height of females at 12 years of age? (1)
(e) Name the phase of development which is occurring in girls between 10–13 years and in boys between 13–16 years, which causes the rapid rate of growth. (1) [AEB 1982]

6 (a) From Fig 19.2 on page 263:
(i) Between what ages approximately does the adolescent growth spurt occur in boys? (1)
(ii) Between what other ages approximately, do boys grow faster than the growth spurt? (1)
(iii) How much would you expect a boy to grow approximately between the ages of eight and ten years? (2)
(b) (i) How does the girls' graph differ from the boys'? (2)
(ii) Give a reason for your answer. (2)
(iii) Give three reasons why an individual's growth spurt may not occur at the age suggested in the graph. (3) [Ox]
(c) The fastest growth spurt in your lifetime is not shown in Fig 19.2. When was it? (1)

7 Fig 19.4 shows the growth rates of three different organs of the body between birth and 20 years of age.

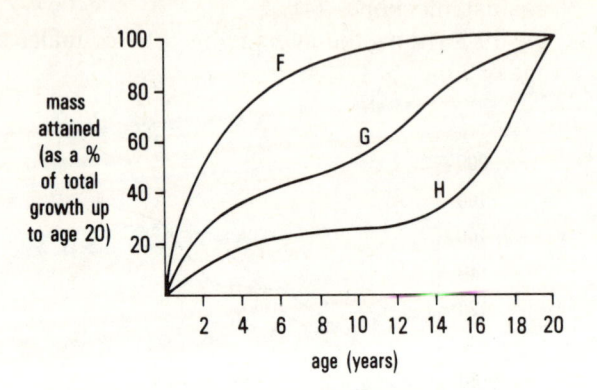

Fig 19.4 Growth rates of three different organs of the body.

(a) Identify the curve which represents:
(i) The growth of the brain. (1)
(ii) The growth of the reproductive organs. (1)
[AEB 1984]

(b) Why do the brain and reproductive organs grow at different dates? (2)

(c) What is the connection between Figs 19.4 and 19.5? (2)

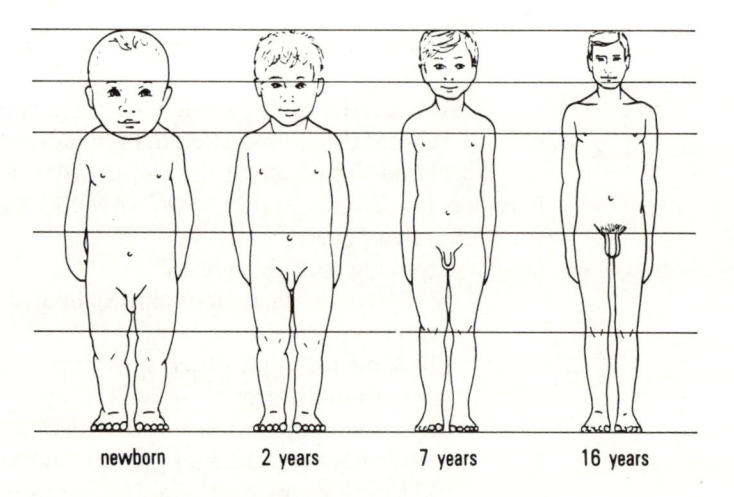

Fig 19.5 How body proportions change with age.

8 (a) What is meant by:
(i) puberty;
(ii) secondary sexual characters;
(iii) menopause? (3)

(b) How are the secondary sexual characters maintained after puberty? (2)
9 Why does the ageing process lead to:
 (a) A wrinkled skin? (1)
 (b) Loss of height? (1)
 (c) Easily broken bones? (1)

CHAPTER TWENTY

VARIATION AND GENETICS

CONTENTS

▶ **20.1 Continuous and discontinuous variation** 273
Types of variation 273

▶ **20.2 The genetic code** 274
Chromosome number 274

▶ **20.3 Cell division** 275

▶ **20.4 Mitosis** 275
Phases in mitosis 275

▶ **20.5 Meiosis** 276
Main stages in meiosis 277

▶ **20.6 The laws of inheritance** 278
Chromosomes, genes, alleles 278
Genotype and phenotype 278
Dominant and recessive 278
Homozygous and heterozygous 278
Worried about genes, alleles and chromosomes? Here's help 278
How genes are inherited 280

Contents

20.7 How to solve genetics problems — 280
The 'Punnett' square 280
Hints 280

20.8 Incomplete dominance — 282

20.9 Sex determination and linkage — 283
How sex is determined 283
Sex linked alleles 284

20.10 Mutations — 285
Rates of mutation 285
Examples of gene mutations 285
Chromosome mutations 286

20.11 Genetic counselling and cousin marriages — 286
Cousin marriages 286

20.12 Variation and natural selection — 286
The theory of natural selection 287
Evolution 287
Natural and artificial selection 287

20.13 Checklist — 288

20.14 Exam questions — 288

Variation and genetics

This chapter is not required for APH (Ordinary).

20.1 CONTINUOUS AND DISCONTINUOUS VARIATION

All living organisms, including all human beings, are different from each other. These differences are due to:
1. the influence of the **environment**, e.g. quality of parental care in early childhood;
2. the influence of **heredity**, i.e. inheritance of genes from parents.

TYPES OF VARIATION

There are two main kinds of variation:
1. **continuous** variation;
2. **discontinuous** variation.

CONTINUOUS VARIATION

Continuous variation in a particular character means that there is a continuous range of values for that character, e.g. height. For

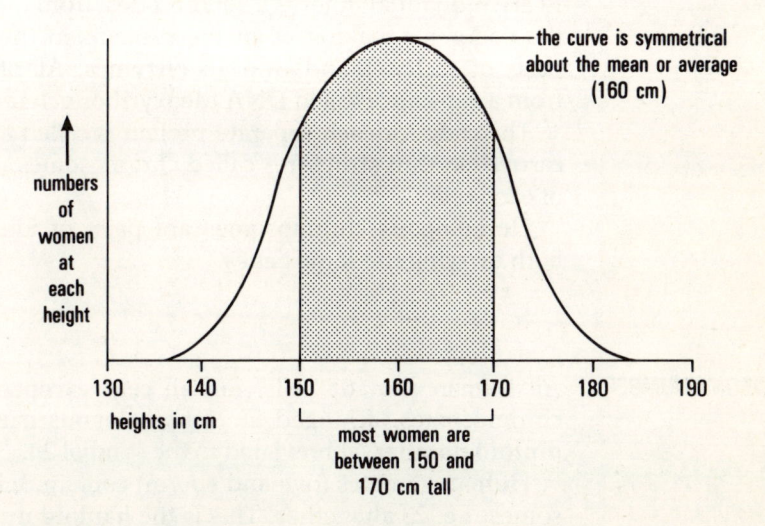

Fig 20.1 Normal distribution curve showing continuous variation in the heights of adult women.

example, adult women in Britain can be any height between about 135 and 180 cm (if height showed discontinuous variation, all women might be one of two heights only, e.g. 150 and 170 cms).

When characters like these are measured among large numbers of people, they conform to a pattern called a **normal distribution curve** (see Fig 20.1).

DISCONTINUOUS VARIATION

Discontinuous variation means that there are only a few, e.g. three or four, different forms of a particular character. For example, all adults belong to one of only four main blood groups A, AB, B, or O.

Table 20.1 Types of variation

Continuous variation	Discontinuous variation
1 Examples: height, weight, intelligence.	1 Examples: blood group, eye colour, shape of ear lobe (fixed or free), ability to roll tongue.
2 Continuous range of values, e.g. many different values for height.	2 Types are clearly separated without intermediates, e.g. most people are either left-handed or right-handed.
3 Influenced by environment.	3 Not influenced by environment, controlled mainly by heredity.
4 Usually controlled by many genes.	4 Controlled by one or two pairs of genes only.

20.2 THE GENETIC CODE

Every individual inherits a set of 'codes' from their parents. These are the codes for making all of the proteins in the body, i.e. the main parts of each cell and all of its enzymes. All of the codes are made from a substance called **DNA (deoxyribonucleic acid)**.

The code for each separate protein is called a **gene**. The genes are carried on thin structures called **chromosomes**, found in the nucleus of each cell.

Homologous chromosomes are pairs of identical chromosomes, both carrying the same genes.

CHROMOSOME NUMBER

All human **somatic** cells, i.e. all cells except sex cells, contain 46 chromosomes, arranged in 23 homologous pairs. This is called the **diploid number**, abbreviated to the symbol $2n$.

Human gametes (ova and sperm) contain only one set of chromosomes, i.e. 23 altogether. This is the **haploid number**, whose symbol is n.

Variation and genetics

20.3 CELL DIVISION

Cell division is the means by which:
1. the body grows;
2. the chromosomes are passed on from cell to cell.

Cell division occurs in all kinds of cells during the growth of a foetus and the early years of childhood. Later, as cells become specialized, some lose the power to divide, e.g. nerve cells. In some tissues, cell division continues throughout life, e.g. the germinative layer in the skin and the bone marrow cells which manufacture red blood cells.

There are two kinds of cell division, called mitosis and meiosis.
1. **Mitosis** occurs mainly in the somatic cells.
2. **Meiosis** occurs only in the ovaries and testes.

20.4 MITOSIS

PHASES IN MITOSIS

The complete cycle of mitosis involves two main phases.
1. The phase between cell divisions, when there is no visible sign of activity. During this time the amount of DNA doubles and cell struc-

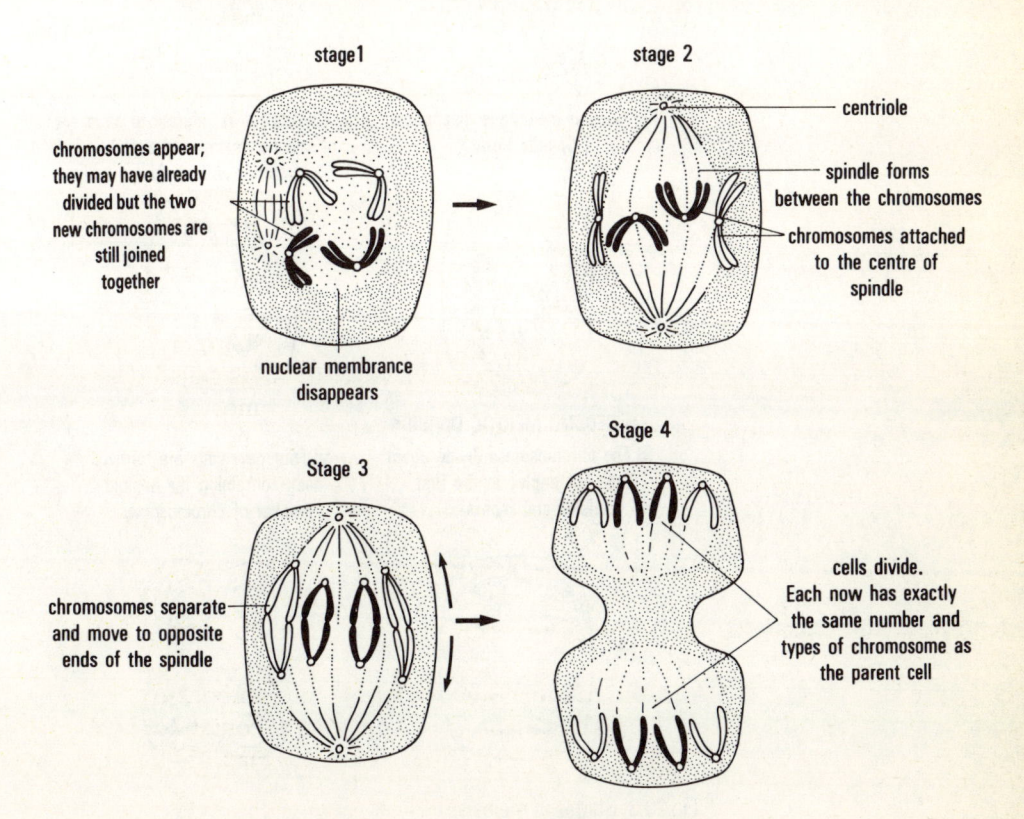

Fig 20.2 Major events in mitosis during the visible phase.

Human Biology

tures such as mitochondria and centrioles are manufactured, in preparation for the division into two seperate cells.

2. The phase when the chromosomes become active. During this period they shorten and thicken and so can be seen under the light microscope. The events occurring from this stage onwards are shown in Fig 20.2.

20.5 MEIOSIS

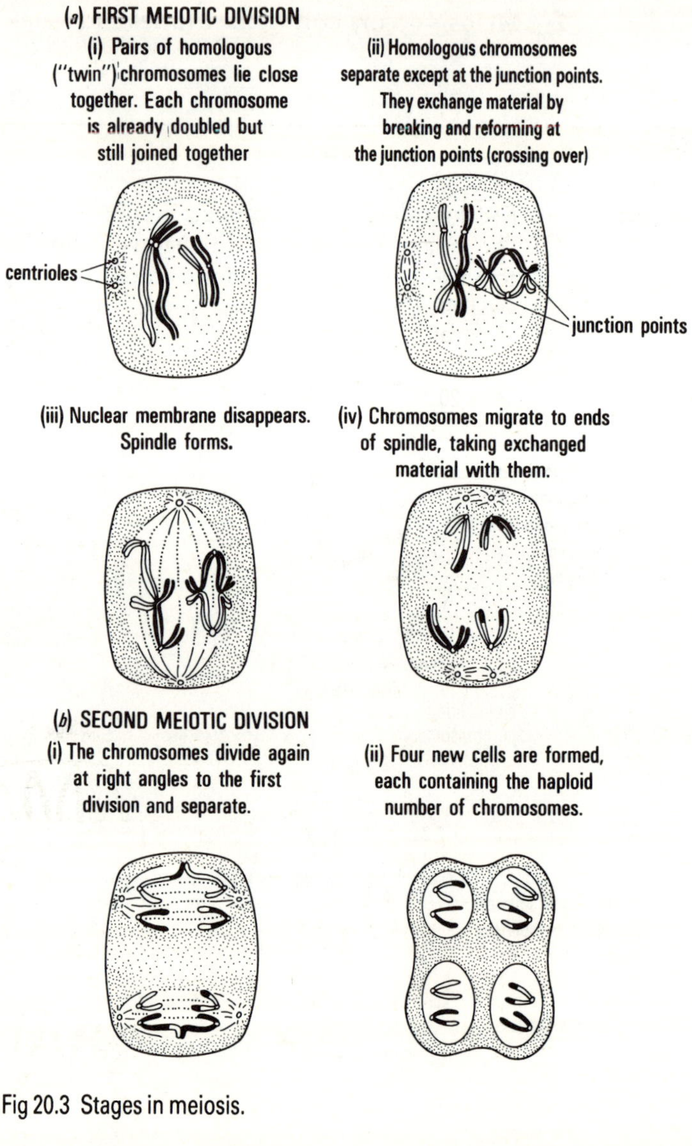

(a) FIRST MEIOTIC DIVISION

(i) Pairs of homologous ("twin") chromosomes lie close together. Each chromosome is already doubled but still joined together

centrioles

(ii) Homologous chromosomes separate except at the junction points. They exchange material by breaking and reforming at the junction points (crossing over)

junction points

(iii) Nuclear membrane disappears. Spindle forms.

(iv) Chromosomes migrate to ends of spindle, taking exchanged material with them.

(b) SECOND MEIOTIC DIVISION

(i) The chromosomes divide again at right angles to the first division and separate.

(ii) Four new cells are formed, each containing the haploid number of chromosomes.

Fig 20.3 Stages in meiosis.

Variation and genetics

Meiosis is a special kind of cell division which occurs only in the ovaries and testes during the production of ova and sperm. It results in the production of daughter cells, i.e. gametes, which have:

1. **half** the number of chromosomes found in the parent cell (23 instead of 46);
2. **new combinations of chromosomes** which are different from those in the parent cell, and also different from those in the other gametes.

The **reduction in chromosome number** occurs because the gametes will later join together to form a zygote, i.e. a fertilized ovum. If the gametes contained 46 chromosomes each, the zygote would contain 92, so that the chromosome number would double in each generation.

The **different combinations** of chromosomes arise because the chromosomes become reshuffled during meiosis. This increases the variability of the offspring (see natural selection on page 287).

MAIN STAGES IN MEIOSIS

There are two consecutive divisions during meiosis (see Fig 20.3).

1. **First division**. This results in the re-shuffling of the chromosomes and the halving of the chromosome number, from the diploid number (46) to the haploid number (23).
2. **Second division**. This is similar to mitosis, except that there are two separate divisions inside the same cell. This results in four new cells.

Table 20.2 Comparison of mitosis and meiosis

	Mitosis	Meiosis
Occurs in	All growing tissues (somatic cells) except during gamete production.	Only in the ovaries and testes during the production of gametes.
Number of cells produced	Two.	Four.
Chromosome number in daughter cells	Same as parent cell – 46 (diploid number).	Half the number in the parent cell – 23 (haploid number).
Other differences between the chromosomes of parent and daughter cells	None: daughter cells' chromosomes are identical to each other and to the parent cell in every respect.	Daughter cells' chromosomes differ from each other and from the parents as a result of: 1 exchanging parts (crossing over); 2 random separation of chromosomes originally derived from male and female parents.
Overall consequences (importance)	Essential part of growth of tissues, leading to doubling of number of cells every 12 hours in active tissues.	Essential part of reproduction: 1 prevents doubling of chromosome number; 2 increases variability among offspring.

Human Biology

20.6 THE LAWS OF INHERITANCE

CHROMOSOMES, GENES, ALLELES

1. **Chromosomes** are thin, thread-like structures which carry genetic information in the form of genes.
2. **Genes** are the basic units of heredity, each consisting of a code for the manufacture of a particular protein.
3. **Alleles** are different forms of the same gene.

GENOTYPE AND PHENOTYPE

1. **Genotype** is the term used to describe an individual's genetic make-up: e.g. possession of mixed alleles for eye colour.
2. **Phenotype** describes an individual's observed appearance, e.g. colour of their eyes, regardless of their genotype.

DOMINANT AND RECESSIVE

1. **A dominant allele** is an allele which is always expressed in the phenotype if it is present in the genotype, e.g. the allele for brown eyes.
2. **A recessive allele** is an allele which is not expressed in the phenotype when combined with the dominant allele in the genotype, e.g. the allele for blue eyes.

HOMOZYGOUS AND HETEROZYGOUS

1. **Homozygous** means that two identical alleles for the same gene are present in the genotype, e.g. a person carrying two alleles for blue eyes.
2. **Heterozygous** means that two different alleles for the same gene are present in the genotype, e.g. the allele for blue eyes and the allele for brown eyes.

WORRIED ABOUT GENES, ALLELES AND CHROMOSOMES? HERE'S HELP

Note: *don't* use the explanations in this section in an exam. Use the definitions given above.

1. The nucleus of every human cell contains 23 pairs of identical chromosomes (Fig 20.4(a)).
2. Each chromosome carries hundreds of genes. Each gene consists of a code for making a particular protein from amino acids (Fig 20.4(b)).
3. Different forms of the same gene are called alleles (pronounced 'ah-leel') (Fig 20.4(c)). Some people (including examiners) use the word 'gene' when in fact they mean 'allele' – which can be confusing!
4. If you carry two identical alleles, e.g. two alleles for blue eyes, you are said to be homozygous for eye colour. If the alleles are different you are heterozygous (Fig 20.4(d)).
5. If you are heterozygous, one allele is usually dominant over the

Variation and genetics

Fig 20.4 Genes, alleles and chromosomes

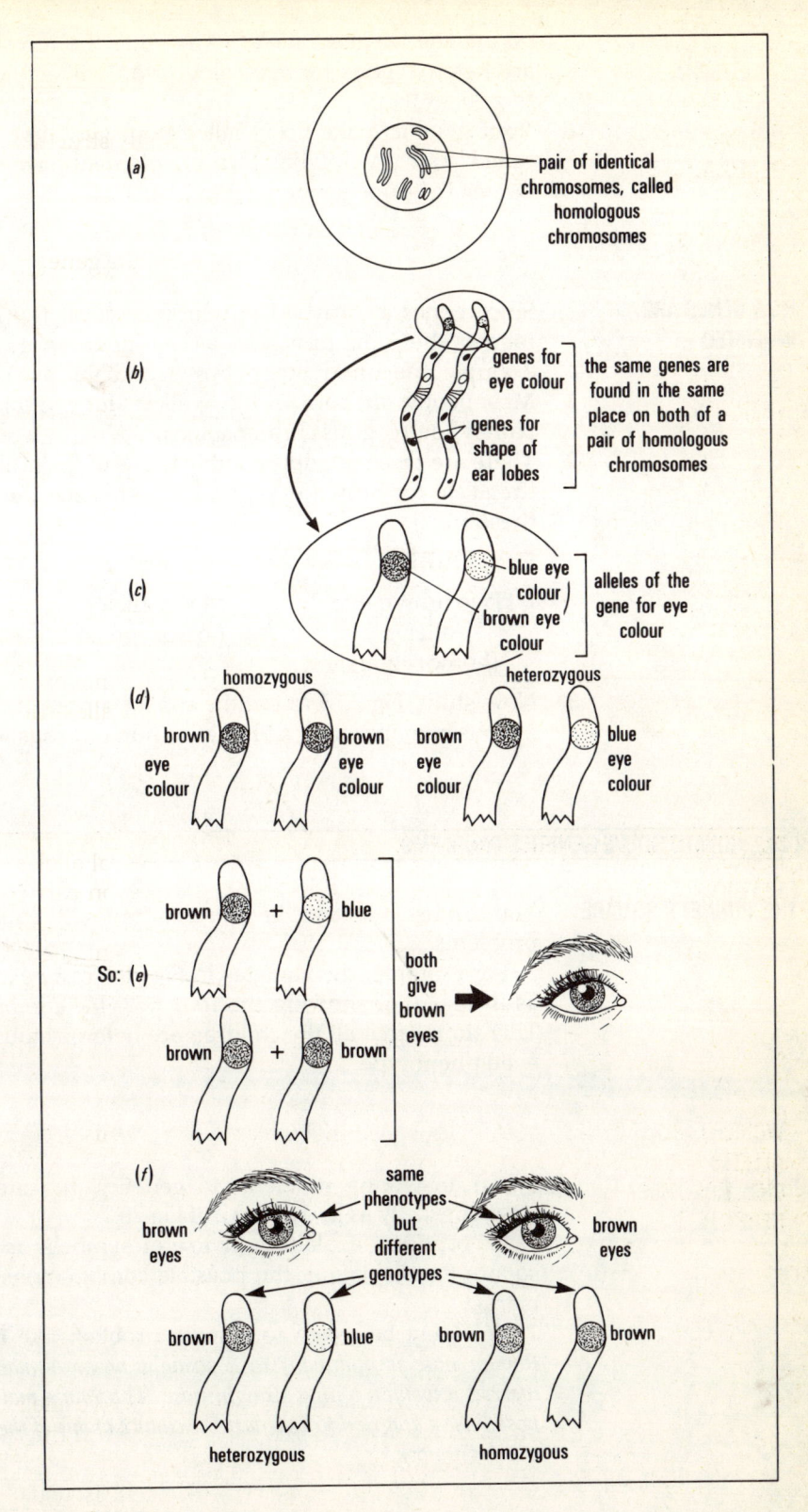

(a) pair of identical chromosomes, called homologous chromosomes

(b) genes for eye colour / genes for shape of ear lobes — the same genes are found in the same place on both of a pair of homologous chromosomes

(c) blue eye colour / brown eye colour — alleles of the gene for eye colour

(d) homozygous — brown eye colour, brown eye colour ; heterozygous — brown eye colour, blue eye colour

So: (e) brown + blue / brown + brown — both give brown eyes

(f) brown eyes / brown eyes — same phenotypes but different genotypes — brown, blue (heterozygous) ; brown, brown (homozygous)

other. The 'weaker' allele is known as the recessive allele. So, if you are heterozygous for eye colour, you will actually have brown eyes (Fig 20.4(e)).

6   Your genetic make up is called your genotype. Your appearance is called your phenotype. Two people may have the same phenotype but *not* the same genotype (Fig 20.4(f)).

HOW GENES ARE INHERITED

Since genes are carried on chromosomes, the inheritance of genes follows the same principles as the inheritance of chromosomes. For example, the inheritance of brown and blue eye colour is as follows.

1   Most people are born with two alleles for eye colour, one on each of a pair of homologous chromosomes.

2   There are three possible combinations of these alleles. If B represents the allele for brown eyes, and b represents the allele for blue eyes, these are:

BB	Bb	bb
Two brown-eye alleles (homozygous)	Mixed alleles (homozygous)	Two blue-eye alleles (homozygous)

3   Now study Fig 20.5 to see the consequences of a brown-eyed homozygous man marrying a blue-eyed homozygous woman.

20.7 HOW TO SOLVE GENETICS PROBLEMS

THE 'PUNNETT' SQUARE

You can use a square, known as a **'punnett' square** to solve genetics problems.

For example, the gametes in Fig 20.5 can be arranged in a square, as in Fig 20.6, showing the four possible combinations of children. This shows that all the children are heterozygous and have a brown-eyed phenotype.

HINTS

When answering problems in genetics, be careful to set out your answer exactly as in column 2 of Fig 20.7

If you don't explain your use of symbols or fail to use a proper square for displaying the possible combinations you can lose many marks.

You may be asked to solve a problem like this: 'A prominent or Roman nose is dominant to a straight nose. A man with a Roman nose marries a woman with a straight nose. The man's mother also had a straight nose. Use a diagram to calculate the chance of one of their children also having a straight nose.'

Variation and genetics

Fig 20.5 Brown-eyed man marries blue-eyed woman.

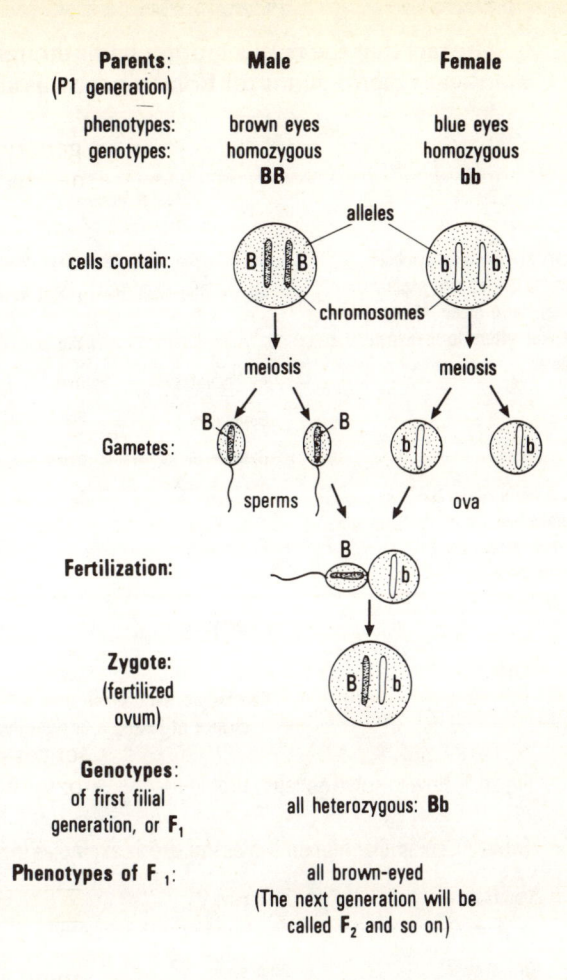

Parents: (P1 generation)

	Male	Female
phenotypes:	brown eyes	blue eyes
genotypes:	homozygous **BB**	homozygous **bb**

cells contain: alleles, chromosomes

meiosis → meiosis

Gametes: B, B (sperms) ; b, b (ova)

Fertilization: B + b

Zygote: (fertilized ovum) Bb

Genotypes: of first filial generation, or F_1 — all heterozygous: **Bb**

Phenotypes of F_1: all brown-eyed
(The next generation will be called F_2 and so on)

Fig 20.6 Using a square to solve genetics problems.

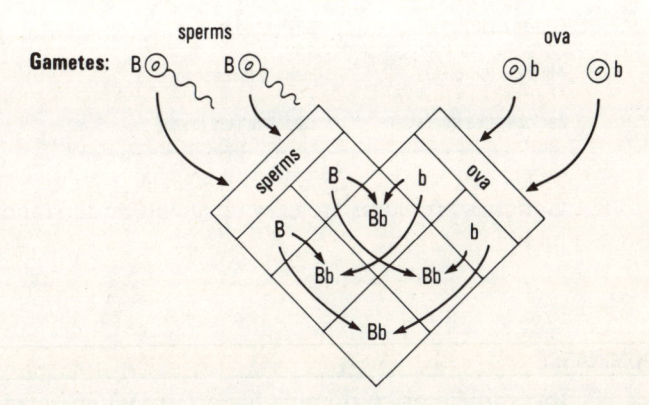

Gametes: sperms B, B ; ova b, b

Punnett square results: Bb, Bb, Bb, Bb

The fact that the man's mother had a straight nose tells you that the man was heterozygous for Roman nose – as shown in Fig 20.7.

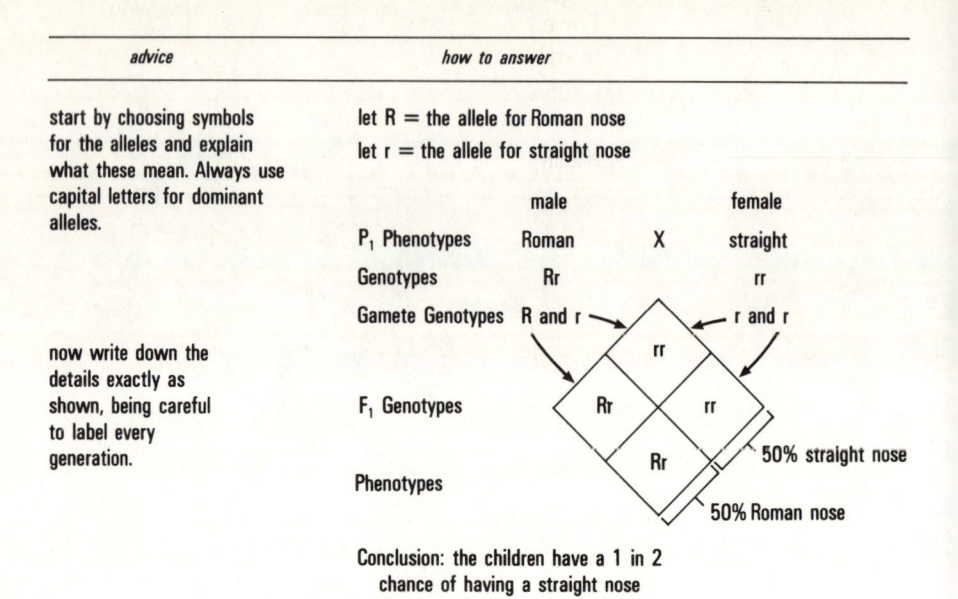

advice	how to answer
start by choosing symbols for the alleles and explain what these mean. Always use capital letters for dominant alleles.	let R = the allele for Roman nose let r = the allele for straight nose
now write down the details exactly as shown, being careful to label every generation.	male × female P₁ Phenotypes Roman × straight Genotypes Rr rr Gamete Genotypes R and r ←→ r and r F₁ Genotypes: rr, Rr, rr, Rr Phenotypes: 50% straight nose, 50% Roman nose Conclusion: the children have a 1 in 2 chance of having a straight nose

Fig 20.7 How to solve genetics problems.

Table 20.3 Familiar human alleles (for use as examples in questions)

Dominant	Recessive
Brown eyes	Blue eyes
Freckles	Absence of freckles
Roman nose	Straight nose
Ability to roll tongue	Inability to roll tongue
Ear lobes free from skull	Ear lobes fixed to skull

Genetics problems are easy once you understand the basic idea. Good luck!

20.8 INCOMPLETE DOMINANCE

Not W, NI

Incomplete or co-dominance occurs when several alleles are equally dominant to each other, e.g. the alleles for the A, B and O blood groups. In this case the alleles for blood groups A and B are co-dominant, but both are dominant to O.

Variation and genetics

The symbols always used for these alleles are:

1. I^A = group A
2. I^B = group B
3. i = group O

For example, suppose a man who is heterozygous for blood group A marries a woman who is heterozygous for group B. This combination is laid out in Fig 20.8.

	male		female
P_1 Phenotype	A	X	B
Genotype	$I^A i$		$I^B i$
Gamete genotypes	I^A and i		I^B and i

F_1 Genotypes: $i I^B$, $I^A I^B$, ii, $I^A i$

Phenotypes: 1 in 4 : AB   1 in 4 : A   1 in 4 : O   1 in 4 : B

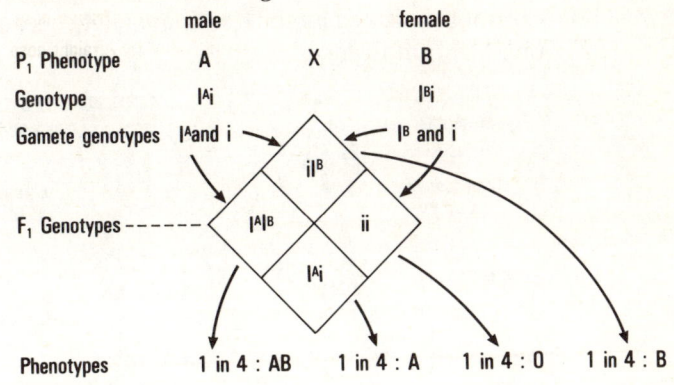

Fig 20.8 Incomplete dominance.

20.9 SEX DETERMINATION AND LINKAGE

HOW SEX IS DETERMINED

All human cells, except the gametes, contain:
- 22 pairs of chromosomes;

plus:
- 1 pair of sex chromosomes

Women possess a homologous (identical) pair of sex chromosomes, called X chromosomes. Men have only one X chromosome, which is paired with a different, smaller chromosome called a Y chromosome (see Fig 20.9).

The sex of a baby depends on whether the ovum is fertilized by an X- or a Y-bearing sperm. **About equal numbers of boys and girls are born** because equal numbers of X-bearing and Y-bearing sperm are produced in the testes.

SEX LINKED ALLELES
Not S, L/EA

A number of alleles are commoner in men than in women because they are carried on the X chromosome. For example, certain harmful recessive alleles such as red-green colour blindness or haemophilia (failure of the blood to clot) are carried on the X chromosome.

WHY MEN SUFFER FROM SEX-LINKED DEFECTS

If a woman inherits a harmful allele on one of her X chromosomes, it will usually be masked by the dominant allele on the other X chromosome. She will carry the allele, but will not be affected herself.

A **carrier** is a woman who has inherited an allele for a sex-linked defect and is not suffering from the defect herself. However, she may pass it on to her children.

A woman can only inherit red-green colour blindness if she is the daughter of a colour-blind man and a carrier woman.

But if a man inherits the allele for red-green colour blindness, it cannot be masked by the dominant allele because he possesses only one X chromosome.

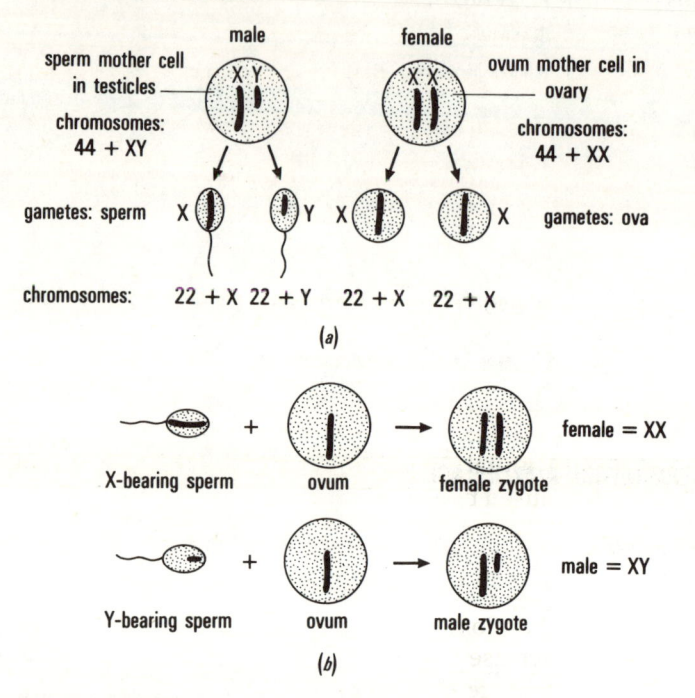

Fig 20.9 (a) Gamete formation. (b) Sex determination.

HOW TO SOLVE A PROBLEM ON SEX LINKAGE

'What are the proportions of children who are colour blind if a man who has normal vision marries a woman who is a carrier for red-green colour blindness?'

1. Let **B** represent the allele for normal vision.
2. Let **b** represent the allele for colour blindness.
3. Let – indicate the absence of an allele due to the lack of the second X chromosome in men.

Fig 20.10 shows how to lay out the solution to this problem.

Variation and genetics

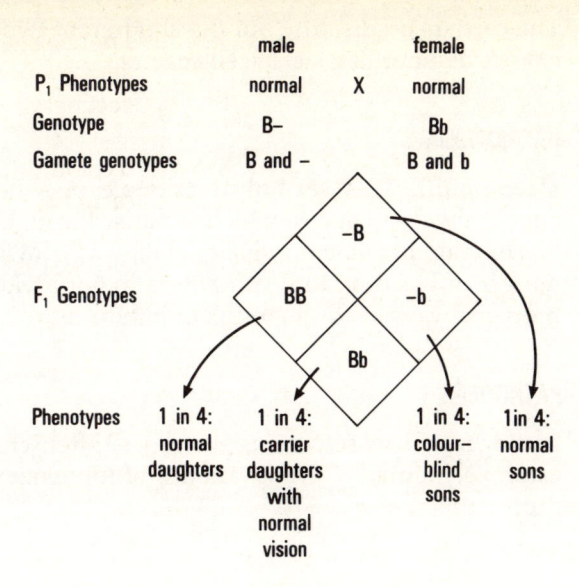

```
                          male              female
P₁ Phenotypes            normal      X      normal
Genotype                   B–                 Bb
Gamete genotypes         B and –            B and b
```

F₁ Genotypes (Punnett square): BB, –B, Bb, –b

Phenotypes:
- 1 in 4: normal daughters
- 1 in 4: carrier daughters with normal vision
- 1 in 4: colour-blind sons
- 1 in 4: normal sons

Fig 20.10 Inheritance of red-green colour blindness.

20.10 MUTATIONS

A **mutation** is a spontaneous change in an allele or a chromosome, caused by damage to the DNA.

RATES OF MUTATION

Mutations occur naturally at a very low rate. The mutation rate can be increased by exposure to certain chemicals which cause mutations (**mutagenic substances**) or to dangerous forms of radiation such as:

1. nuclear (atomic) radiation;
2. ultra-violet light;
3. X-rays;
4. cosmic rays.

Mutations happen in some cells throughout life, but are only important to heredity if they occur in the ovaries or testes. If so, they may result in the passing on of damaged alleles.

EXAMPLES OF GENE MUTATIONS

SICKLE-CELL ANAEMIA

Sickle-cell anaemia is an inherited defect found among about 1 in 400 people of Afro-Caribbean origin in Britain. Victims inherit a defective allele which leads to the production of a faulty type of haemoglobin. This results in red blood cells which collapse into a 'sickle-cell' shape, resulting in symptoms of anaemia.

About 1 in 10 Afro-Caribbean adults are also carriers for this allele.

The carriers are healthy but the children of two carriers have a 1 in 4 chance of inheriting sickle-cell anaemia.

HAEMOPHILIA

Haemophilia is a sex-linked example of a defective allele, found almost always in males, which can arise through mutation.

The blood of haemophiliacs clots very slowly so that they are in danger of bleeding to death after a minor accident. It is inherited in the same way as red-green colour blindness.

PATHOGENS

Pathogens (disease-causing microbes) often change genetically. For example, numerous new varieties of influenza virus have appeared during this century.

CHROMOSOME MUTATIONS

Mutations can also affect whole chromosomes. For example, the inherited defect called **Down's syndrome** is caused by chromosomes dividing unevenly during meiosis. The result is a child with 47 chromosomes instead of 46. This causes serious chest, heart and mental defects, often leading to death at an early age.

Down's syndrome can be detected early in pregnancy by amniocentesis (see page 252); if so, the mother may be offered an abortion.

20.11 GENETIC COUNSELLING AND COUSIN MARRIAGES

N only

Genetic counselling means advising couples on their chances of producing a child with an inherited defect. For example, a couple with relatives who had haemophilia or Down's syndrome may want to know their chances of producing a similar child.

COUSIN MARRIAGES

It is particularly important for people who marry their relatives, e.g. first cousins, to seek genetic counselling. This is because they may both be unknowingly carrying recessive alleles for inherited diseases, inherited from a common grandparent.

20.12 VARIATION AND NATURAL SELECTION

All living organisms (except for identical twins) vary from one another if they have been produced by sexual reproduction. This has led to evolution through **natural selection**.

Variation and genetics

THE THEORY OF NATURAL SELECTION

1. Organisms produce more offspring than is needed for replacement.
2. But the number of living organisms generally does not increase.
3. This is because many of the offspring die, due to lack of food, space, sunlight, etc. For example, eight out of ten gulls do not live to be one year old.
4. In most populations, there is great variability between the offspring, due to:
   - (a) the re-shuffling of the chromosomes at meiosis;
   - (b) mutations.
5. As a result, only the fittest offspring in each generation survive to pass on their genes, e.g. only the strongest, fastest-flying gulls live to reproduce.

EVOLUTION

As a result of natural selection, organisms have gradually evolved from the very simple to highly complex. **Evolution** means the appearance of new species (kinds) of living things by the action of natural selection.

EVIDENCE FOR EVOLUTION

1. **From fossils**. The study of preserved remains of living things in rocks shows that complex organisms appeared on earth more recently than much simpler species, e.g. worms came before man.
2. **From bone structure**. Many very different types of mammal, e.g. bats, moles and whales, have a similar limb bone structure, suggesting an evolution from a common ancestor.
3. **From observations of natural selection.** For example, a number of bacteria have acquired resistance to certain antibiotics, e.g. penicillin, some insects have become resistant to insecticides.
4. **From selective breeding.** Farmers have carried out their own form of evolution by artificial selection of the best types of plant and animal. This has resulted in the creation of new varieties such as:
   - low-fat lambs and pigs;
   - breeds of sheep able to withstand cold winters in hill country;
   - high-yielding rice and wheat.

NATURAL AND ARTIFICIAL SELECTION

1. **Natural selection** is the effect of environmental factors, such as competition for food, space, etc., acting on variable populations of living things. As a result, only the fittest members of each generation survive to breed.
2. **Artificial selection** (selective breeding) is the selection by farmers of the fittest types of animal or plant for breeding, in order to improve the quality of the breed concerned.

20.13 CHECKLIST

- Variation:
  - causes (two);
  - types (two).
- Examples of continuous and discontinuous variation.
- Normal distribution curve.
- DNA.
- Homologous chromosomes.
- Chromosome number:
  - n/2n.
- Haploid *v.* diploid.
- Cell division:
  - purpose;
  - occurrence in the body.
- Mitosis:
  - main events;
  - consequences.
- Comparison of mitosis and meiosis.
- Differences between;
  - chromosomes;
  - genes;
  - alleles.
- Genotype *v.* phenotype.
- Dominant *v.* recesive.
- Homozygous *v.* heterozygous.
- Abbreviations:
  - P_1, F_1, etc.
- How to use a square for answers to problems.
- Gene mutations.
- Chromosome mutations.
- Genetic counselling.
- Natural selection.
- Artificial selection.
- Evolution.

20.14 EXAM QUESTIONS

1. Human inherited features can be grouped under two headings, as follows:

A	B
Weight	Tongue rolling
Intelligence	Eye colour
Height	Blood group

    (a) What is the genetic explanation for the difference between the two groups? (1)

    (b) Describe one other difference between the two groups. (1)

2. A set of triplets, two of whom were identical, were separated at birth

Variation and genetics

and brought up by different families. When they were 19 years old the data in Table 20.4 were recorded.

Table 20.4

	Susan	Jane	Amanda
Height	188 cm	188 cm	180 cm
Weight	62 kg	57 kg	77 kg
Blood type	O	AB	O
Measure of intelligence	138	142	125

(a) Name the TWO girls who were identical twins. (1)
(b) Suggest why these TWO girls were different from each other in any ONE of the three ways shown in the table. (2)
[NEA: GCSE specimen question]

3 Figure 20.11 shows some of the stages in the division of a simplified cell which has four chromosomes in the diploid condition.

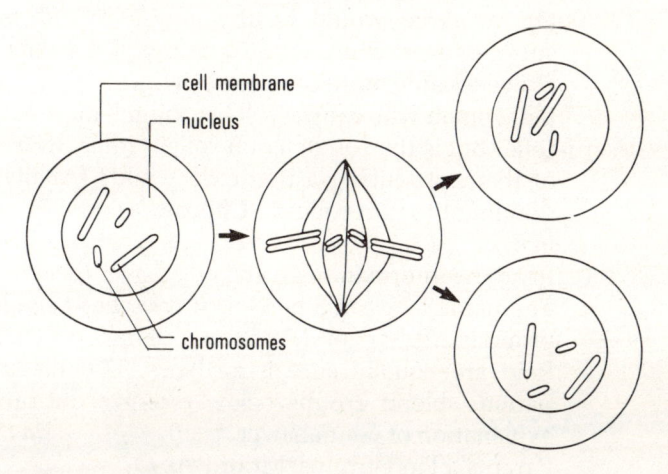

Fig 20.11

(a) Give two reasons, seen from the diagrams, which show that this division was by mitosis. (2)
(b) (i) Name one organ in the human body in which meiosis occurs. (1)
 (ii) Briefly explain the importance of meiosis in the human life-cycle. (1) [W: GCSE specimen question]
4 In what two ways does the nucleus of a nerve cell differ from the nuclei of the gametes in the same person? (4) [AEB 1985]
5 Fig 20.12 shows a simplified cell.
(a) Redraw fig 20.12 to show the effect of this cell dividing by mitosis (2)

Fig 20.12

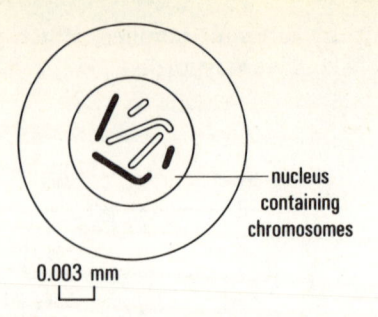

- nucleus containing chromosomes

0.003 mm

(b) Use simple diagrams to draw three different gametes which might be formed if the cell divided by meiosis (3)

(c) How large is this cell in reality? (1)

6 (a) Huntington's chorea is a disease of the nervous system which leads to brain damage and death in middle years. It is caused by a single dominant gene affecting both men and women.

Show by diagrams what children you would expect and in what proportions from a marriage between:

(i) a heterozygous, affected man and a normal woman;

(ii) a heterozygous, affected man and a heterozygous, affected woman.

(b) What would be the long-term effects on the numbers of sufferers from Huntington's chorea if marriages such as those in (ii) above became more common? (12) [NI]

7 If a woman who cannot roll her tongue marries a man who is a tongue roller but is the son of a non-roller father, what would be the chances of them producing a non-roller child? (Ability to roll the tongue is dominant to non-rolling). **Choose:** None; 1 in 1; 1 in 2; 1 in 3; 1 in 4; 1 in 8. [In the style of Ox]

8 Read the information given and answer the question:

The name label on a new born baby has been lost. The baby's blood group is AB. Mr and Mrs Brown claim it is their baby, but Mr and Mrs Reid are equally sure it is theirs. Use the information about the parents' blood groups below to solve the problem and give a full explanation of your answer. (10) [In the style of JMB]

Parents' blood groups: Mr Brown: O   Mrs Brown: A
                Mr Reid: B   Mrs Reid: A

Blood groups A and B are dominant to blood group O.

9 (a) Use your knowledge of fertilization, sex chromosomes and gametes to explain why roughly equal numbers of boy and girl babies are born each year (6)

(b) Newspapers occasionally report claims for methods guaranteed to provide an '80% chance of producing a girl baby', etc. From your knowledge of genetics, how might such methods work? (2)

(c) Athletes taking part in international competition undergo a 'sex test' to confirm their eligibility to compete in men's or women's events. The test is performed by scraping a few cells from the inside

Variation and genetics

of the cheek and examining a stained sample of them under a microscope.

(i) What are the examiners looking for and how does the evidence provided by the test enable the correct decision on eligibility to be made?

(ii) Identify ONE inherited disease which could be detected by this technique and indicate what result you would expect in this case. (4) [NI]

10 Fig 20.13 represents a family tree in which a case of haemophilia occurred. (Note: questions like this, requiring the analysis of sex-linked inheritance, will be set only by M, NI and APH (Higher).

Fig 20.13

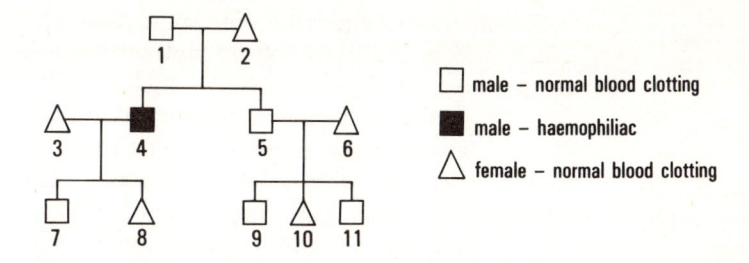

☐ male – normal blood clotting
■ male – haemophiliac
△ female – normal blood clotting

(a) State with reasons the probable genotypes of individuals 1, 2 and 4. (7)

(b) If there was a marriage between cousins 8 and 9 state, with reasons, the genotypes and phenotypes of their possible offspring. (6) [AEB 1985]

11 (a) Fig 20.14 represents a family pedigree showing the inheritance of phenylketonuria which is controlled by a single pair of alleles, A and a.

Fig 20.14

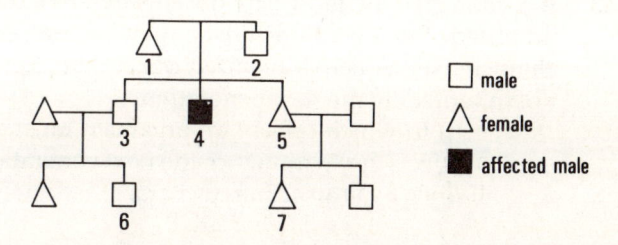

☐ male
△ female
■ affected male

(i) Is the allele for phenylketonuria dominant or recessive? (1)

(ii) State with reasons the genotype of each of individuals 1, 2 and 4. (4)

(iii) What are the possible genotypes of each of individuals 3 and 5? (2)

(iv) Why would it be genetically inadvisable for cousins 6 and 7 to marry and have children? (3)

(b) Fig 20.15 shows a simplified sequence of chemical reactions which occur in the body.

Fig 20.15

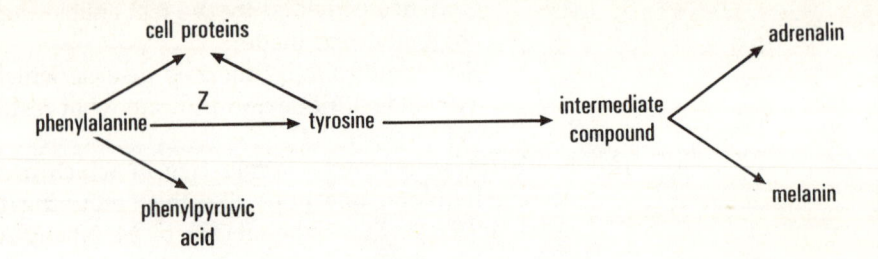

```
                    cell proteins                                    adrenalin
                       ↑  ↑                                            ↗
                      Z                                  intermediate
      phenylalanine ──────→ tyrosine ─────────────→      compound
                       ↓                                               ↘
                  phenylpyruvic                                        melanin
                      acid
```

In the disease phenylketonuria the reaction labelled z does not take place and a build up of phenylpyruvic acid (a phenylketo-acid) occurs.

(i) What is a gene mutation? (2)
(ii) A gene mutation has given rise to the inability to carry out reaction z. Explain this statement. (5)
(iii) Infants suffering from phenylketonuria often have fair hair and fair complexion. Explain briefly, using information from the diagram, why this is so. (3) [AEB 1983]

12 (a) Briefly describe the effect which one named gene mutation may have on the body. (2)

N only

(b) During the formation of an ovum, a chromosome mutation may occur. Explain how such a mutation can result in the zygote, which is produced by fertilization of that ovum, have 47 chromosomes. (2)
(c) (i) What is meant by genetic counselling?
(ii) Under what circumstances is it advisable to seek genetic counselling? (2)

13 If a characteristic is to play an effective role in evolution it must be inherited. Such a characteristic may be the result of a mutation. A characteristic which is acquired during the lifetime of an organism is not inherited by the next generation.

(i) In which cells of an organism must a mutation occur if its effects are to influence the next generation? (1)
(ii) Why is an acquired characteristic not inherited? (2)
[NI]

14 Briefly explain, with examples:
(a) The effects of variation and natural selection in bringing about evolution. (5)
(b) The benefits of artificial selection, i.e. selective breeding, to farmers. (4)

CHAPTER TWENTY-ONE 293

PERSONAL HEALTH CARE

CONTENTS

▶ **21.1 Requirements for health**   295

▶ **21.2 Effects of drugs on the body**   295
Effects of drugs on the nervous system   295
Other effects of drugs on the body   296
Absorption of drugs   297
Drugs and the liver   297
Drugs of use and abuse   297
Prevention of drug abuse   298

▶ **21.3 Mental health and mental illness**   298
Causes of mental illness   299
Common types of mental illness   299
Prevention of mental illness   299

▶ **21.4 Cancer**   299
How cancer develops   299
Why is cancer harmful?   330
Carcinogens   330
Prevention of death from cancer   301
Early detection   301
Treatment of cancer   301

▶ **21.5 Smoking and health**   301
Bronchitis   302

Emphysema 302
Smoking during pregnancy 303
Anti-social aspects of smoking 303
Prevention of smoking 303

▶ **21.6 Checklist** 304

▶ **21.7 Exam questions** 305

Personal health care

21.1 REQUIREMENTS FOR HEALTH

Good health requires:
1. freedom from infection;
2. regular exercise;
3. a balanced diet;
4. avoidance of obesity;
5. good dental hygiene;
6. good mental health, including avoidance of drugs, etc.;
7. avoidance of the causes of non-infectious diseases such as cancer, as far as possible.

21.2 EFFECTS OF DRUGS ON THE BODY

A **drug** is any substance which can affect the body's metabolism and which is not consumed for nutritional purposes.

EFFECTS OF DRUGS ON THE NERVOUS SYSTEM

Many important drugs affect the nervous system. These can mostly be classified into two groups.

STIMULANTS

Stimulants, such as caffeine (in tea and coffee), cannabis and amphetamines, increase the activity of the nervous system. This is because they have effects similar to that of acetylcholine, i.e. they speed up the passing of nervous impulses across synapses (see page 208). As a result, they cause the metabolic rate to increase also. However, the user is left feeling tired and depressed when the effects wear off.

DEPRESSANTS

Depressants, such as alcohol, tranquillizers, barbiturates and heroin block the passage of acetylcholine across the synapses and so slow down the nervous system generally.

Human Biology

OTHER DRUGS

However, some drugs such as antibiotics, have no effect on the nervous system; and nicotine in tobacco acts as a stimulant in small doses, but as a depressant in larger amounts.

OTHER EFFECTS OF DRUGS ON THE BODY

SIDE EFFECTS

All drugs, even medically 'useful' prescribed drugs, have unwanted side effects on the body. For example, aspirin relieves pain but causes stomach bleeding if taken in large doses; anti-histamines prevent hayfever but make many people sleepy.

EFFECTS ON DRIVING

People who take drugs of any kind, especially depressants, e.g. tranquillizers, pain killers, or hayfever cures, should not drive or use machinery after taking a drug. Like alcohol, most depressants can have a serious effect on driving skills, chiefly by slowing down reaction times.

TOLERANCE

If a drug is taken regularly, it gradually has less effect on the body. This is because enzymes and antitoxins against it build up in the bloodstream. As a result, addicts often find it necessary to increase the dose to achieve the same results.

DRUG DEPENDENCE

Drug dependence is a state in which the drug user feels compelled to continue taking a drug. Dependence takes two different forms.
1 **Psychological dependence**, where the user feels unable to work or concentrate without the drug.
2 **Physical dependence**, where the user's metabolism has been altered by the drug so that its continued use is necessary to avoid withdrawal symptoms.

Withdrawal symptoms are unpleasant or painful effects caused by withdrawal of a drug on which the user has become physically dependent.

A **drug addict** is a person who is physically and psychologically dependent on a drug.

Harmful effects of drug dependence
1 Inability to concentrate and so to earn a living. This may result in **poverty and ill-health** due to poor housing and inadequate diet.

Personal health care

2. **Increased crime** caused by addicts seeking money for further supplies.
3. **Infections** passed on by sharing needles for injections, including:
   ▷ hepatitis (a virus infection of the liver);
   ▷ AIDS;
   ▷ septicaemia (infection of the blood).
4. **Damage to the lungs**, etc., if the drug is smoked, or to the mouth if it is chewed or sucked.
5. **Damage to the foetus**. Heroin-dependent mothers can produce heroin-dependent babies.

ABSORPTION OF DRUGS Most drugs are either injected into the bloodstream or sniffed to produce a rapid effect. Alcohol is unusual because it is absorbed directly from the stomach without any need for digestion in the small intestine. It therefore affects the brain within a few minutes of consumption.

DRUGS AND THE LIVER All drugs are broken down by the liver as they circulate in the bloodstream. High consumption of drugs (especially alcohol) can cause severe liver damage in the long run.

DRUGS OF USE AND ABUSE
1. **Useful drugs** or medicines are those drugs which are medically recommended for the treatment of illness – see Table 21.1.
2. **Drugs of abuse** are those drugs which are taken in order to bring about a change in the mental state of the user – see Table 21.2.

Table 21.1 Effects of some medically approved drugs on the body

Name	Beneficial effects	Side effects
Penicillin (and other antibiotics)	Cures bacterial infections by preventing bacteria from multiplying.	Can cause allergy (rash, sickness, etc.), i.e. unpleasant reactions of the immune system.
Aspirin (and related drugs)	Lowers body temperature during illness, relieves pain and reduces inflammation. Used during influenza, toothache, arthritis, etc.	Vomiting, pain and bleeding from the stomach if taken in large quantities for long periods.
Paracetamol	Lowers temperature during illness and relieves pain.	Large quantities can damage the liver over the long term.
Tranquillizers and sleeping tablets	Depress nervous activity, leading to feelings of relaxation and drowsiness.	Long-term use causes tolerance and psychological dependence. Users should not drive cars.

Human Biology

Table 21.2 Effects of some drugs of abuse on the body

Drug	Immediate (short-term) effects	Effects of long-term use
Heroin	1 Vomiting (sickness). 2 Spread of infections from sharing of needles, e.g. hepatitis, septicaemia, AIDS.	1 Depression. 2 Dependence, leading to severe withdrawal symptoms. 3 Heroin dependence in the foetus.
Solvents	1 Hallucinations. 2 Impaired, i.e. 'poorer', judgement and memory. 3 Poor coordination, e.g. unsteady walking.	1 Damage to areas of skin around face. 2 Damage to brain, liver and kidney.
Alcohol	1 Interferes with passage of nerve impulse at synapse, so reactions are slower, e.g. when driving. 2 Affects cerebellum so muscular coordination becomes difficult. 3 Affects cerebral cortex so that behaviour becomes unrestrained, leading to violence, etc. 4 Causes dilation of arterioles leading to the skin, resulting in rapid loss of body heat (see page 185).	1 Dependence, leading to alcoholism; difficulties in concentrating and working. 2 Severed damage to the liver (cirrhosis). 3 Cancer of the mouth, throat, oesophagus and liver – especially if combined with smoking. 4 Can cause malnutrition, because it provides energy but neither protein nor vitamins. Energy content satisfies hunger so reducing desire for food. 5 Can damage foetus, causing retarded growth and development, and even defects.

PREVENTION OF DRUG ABUSE

1. Warn young people of the harmful effects of drug taking by advertising and education.
2. Reduce supplies of illegal drugs (action by police and customs; payments to farmers to grow alternative crops).
3. Reduce unemployment and improve leisure activities for young people.
4. Pay more attention to better mental health (see below).

21.3 MENTAL HEALTH AND MENTAL ILLNESS

Good mental health depends on:
1. physical health;
2. good long-term relationships with other people;
3. feelings of self-esteem, e.g. from success in work or leisure activities;
4. emotional stability, e.g. ability to avoid becoming over-anxious;
5. mental stimulation – avoidance of boredom.

Personal health care

CAUSES OF MENTAL ILLNESS

Mental illness affects at least 10 per cent of the British population. It can be caused by a combination of inherited factors, i.e. some people are more likely to become mentally ill than others, and environmental factors, e.g.

1. Inability to cope with stress.
2. Harmful past experiences, e.g. lack of affection as a child, separation from parents at an early age, divorce or bereavement in later life.
3. Social isolation, e.g. lack of friends and family, especially among old people.

COMMON TYPES OF MENTAL ILLNESS

1. **Neurosis** where the sufferer becomes over-anxious, e.g. fear of going outside the home.
2. **Psychosis**, where the patient loses contact with reality. This includes depressive illnesses such as schizophrenia. These can now be treated with a variety of anti-depressant drugs.

   Post-natal depression is a mental illness which affects up to half of all women following childbirth, though it usually passes in a few days. It is probably caused by the major changes in hormone balance which occur following birth.

   Depression is also common among women who are tied to the home with very young children, especially if they are unhappily married.

   Mental handicap is the inheritance of a mental defect, e.g. Down's syndrome.

PREVENTION OF MENTAL ILLNESS

1. **Prevent social isolation.**
   ◊ Avoid housing couples with young children in highrise blocks.
   ◊ Reduce unemployment.
   ◊ Provide good leisure facilities for all age groups.
   ◊ Provide day centres for the elderly.
2. **Reduce stress**.
   ◊ Prevent overcrowded housing.
   ◊ Provide better family planning services to prevent unintended pregnancies.
3. Prevent drug and alcohol abuse (see page 298).

21.4 CANCER

HOW CANCER DEVELOPS
NI, M only

Cell division by mitosis occurs constantly in all active tissues. Normally it is controlled so that each cell division only takes place when needed or the normal functioning of the body. For example, skin cells only divide whenever new epithelium is required.

Occasionally, changes occur in previously normal cells which cause them to divide uncontrollably. These changes are probably caused by mutations, i.e. damage to DNA from exposure to radiation or harmful chemicals. This is believed to occur on a small scale in many tissues, but the damaged cells are normally repaired or quickly destroyed by the immune system (see page 318).

If the damage is too severe, or is repeated every day, e.g. by smoking, the damaged cells may begin to divide uncontrollably. This occurs because they seem no longer to be affected by the body's normal growth regulating process.

Uncontrolled cell division can lead to growths or **tumours** in the body. These can be of two kinds.

1 **Benign** (or **harmless**) tumours, which do not affect important functions of the body.
2 **Malignant** tumours, which can cause serious harm.

WHY IS CANCER HARMFUL?

Cancer is a disease involving uncontrolled cell division, leading to the growth of malignant tumours. These tumours can threaten life because they may:

1 press on vital organs, e.g. brain tumours;
2 compete against neighbouring tissues for supplies of oxygen and food from the circulation system;
3 give off abnormal cells into the bloodstream which cause further damage by forming malignant tumours in distant parts of the body.

CARCINOGENS

Carcinogens are physical or chemical agents which cause cancer, probably by causing cell mutations. Cigarette smoke is by far the major cause of cancer in Britain.

Table 21.3 Common causes of cancer (carcinogens)

Carcinogen	Types of cancer caused
Chemicals in cigarette smoke.	Lung cancer, and cancers of the mouth and pancreas.
Radiation, including X-rays, nuclear radiation and ultra-violet light from the sun.	Various cancers; sun's rays can cause skin cancer among those exposed to it for long periods.
Chemicals used in industry.	Various cancers depending on the chemical concerned.
Asbestos dust.	Lung and other cancers.

Personal health care

PREVENTION OF DEATH FROM CANCER

Many cancers can be prevented by:
1. not smoking;
2. drinking in moderation only;
3. avoiding over-exposure to sunlight, e.g. by avoiding lengthy sun-bathing without using a sun-screen lotion;
4. avoiding exposure to asbestos dust;
5. taking precautions in industry.

EARLY DETECTION

Two kinds of cancer in women could be greatly reduced by early detection.
1. **Breast cancer.** Early signs of breast cancer can be detected by carefully examining the breasts every month, just after a period. Any unusual lump or other change should be reported to a doctor.
2. **Cancer of the cervix.** Early signs of cervical cancer can be detected by a simple cervical smear test. This involves gently scraping a few cells from the cervix in order to check for any signs of pre-cancerous change under a microscope.

TREATMENT OF CANCER

The three main methods are summarised in Table 21.4. In practice, combinations of all three are often used.

Table 21.4 Treatment of cancer

Method	How carried out
1 Surgery	Complete removal of malignant growths by a surgical operation.
2 Radiotherapy	Tumours are destroyed by narrow beams of radiation aimed directly at them. This method is effective as cancer cells are more sensitive to damage from radiation than normal cells, because they divide much faster. However, there may be unpleasant side-effects, e.g. vomiting, hair loss.
3 Chemotheraphy	In some cases, e.g. bone marrow and lymph cancers, certain chemicals can be used to attack cancer cells, without harming the body as a whole.

21.5 SMOKING AND HEALTH

Cigarette smoking is the most important preventable cause of death in Britain today, causing 100,000 premature deaths annually. In addition to being a main cause of cancer and coronary heart disease, smoking is a major cause of two important lung diseases:
1. **bronchitis;**
2. **emphysema.**

BRONCHITIS

Bronchitis is the inflammation of the lining of the bronchi. Symptoms include persistent coughing, shortness of breath and periods of fever, i.e. raised body temperature.

The symptoms result from persistent irritation of the bronchi by cigarette smoke (or other forms of air pollution). This causes the mucous glands in the lining to produce excessive mucus, and the cilia to cease beating (see Fig 21.1). As a result, the smaller bronchioles become more easily blocked and more liable to infection.

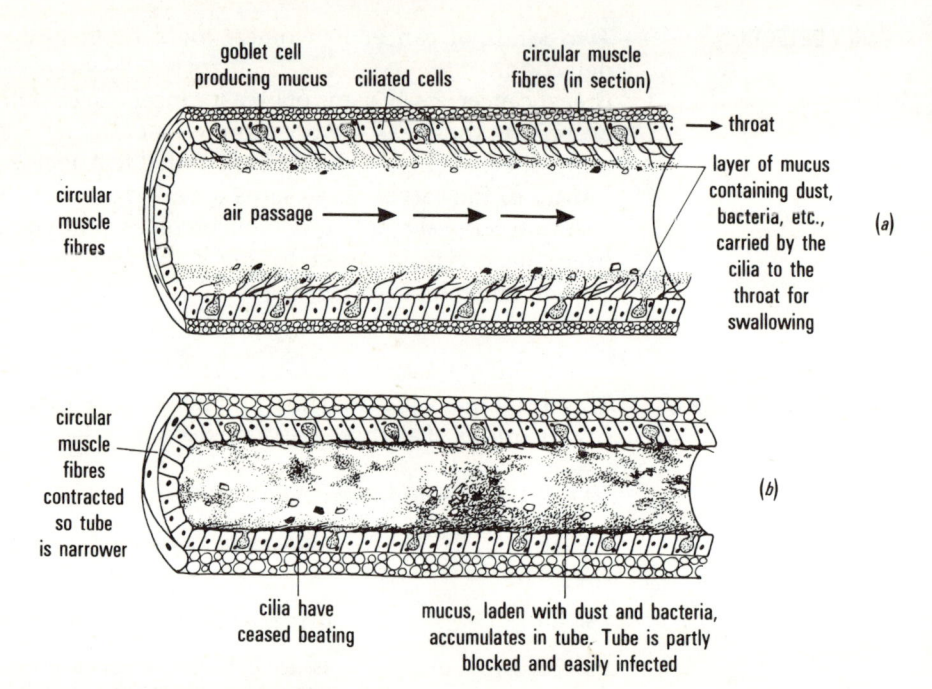

Fig 21.1 How smoking affects the cleaning mechanism of the lungs in bronchitis. (a) In a healthy non-smoker. (b) In a smoker; bronchiole reacts to minimize irritation.

EMPHYSEMA

Emphysema is the breakdown of the walls of the alveoli following bronchitis, so that the available surface area for gas exchange is much reduced. The victim gradually becomes so short of breath that even a few steps are impossible without the aid of an oxygen mask.

The breakdown of the alveoli is mainly due to the persistent obstruction of the bronchioles during long-term bronchitis. Pockets of air become trapped in the obstructed alveoli, and gradually expand until the walls of the alveoli break down permanently.

Emphysema is therefore usually caused by chronic (long-term) bronchitis and so is a direct consequence of long-term smoking in most cases.

Personal health care

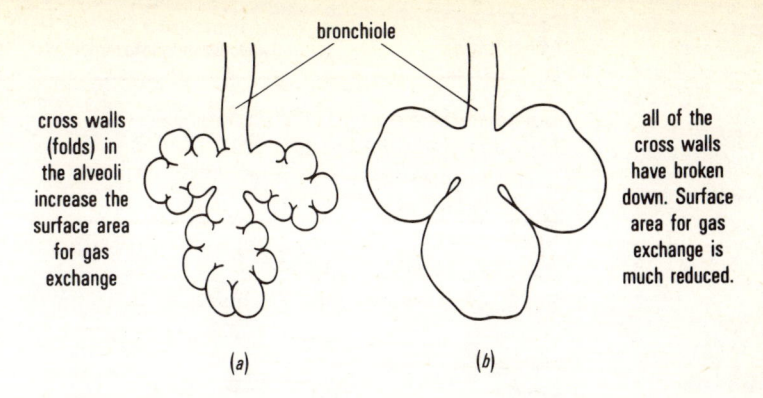

Fig 21.2 How smoking reduces the surface area of the alveoli in emphysema. (a) Normal group of alveoli. (b) Alveoli in an advanced emphysema victim.

SMOKING DURING PREGNANCY

This can have serious effects. The carbon monoxide in the mother's blood reduces the oxygen supply to the foetus, so that it grows more slowly. This results in an increased number of premature births to mothers who smoke.

Since premature babies are less developed at birth, they are also more likely to die during the first weeks of life. Up to 1000 babies are believed to die as a result in Britain each year.

Table 21.5 Effects of cigarette smoke on the body

Type of damage	Component of smoke responsible	How the effect is caused
Lung cancer	Tar (see Fig 21.3)	Contains carcinogens which trigger malignant tumours in the bronchi after 25 years of heavy smoking (20 per day).
Coronary heart disease	Carbon monoxide	1 Causes fat to be deposited in the coronary (and other) arteries, resulting in partial blockage. 2 Displaces oxygen from red blood cells, reducing body's oxygen carrying capacity by 10 per cent. Resultant stress on circulation system makes a heart attack more likely.
	Nicotine	Constricts arterioles, so increasing blood pressure, and risk of heart attack. (Also the main addictive substance in cigarette smoke.)
Bronchitis and emphysema	Irritant substances in the smoke	Irritate bronchial linings (bronchitis) and ultimately cause permanent damage to alveoli (emphysema).

continues on page 304

Type of damage	Component of smoke responsible	How the effect is caused
Retarded growth of foetus	Carbon monoxide	Restricts oxygen supply to foetus, so retards growth. Leads to premature birth and so increased risk of death in first week of life.

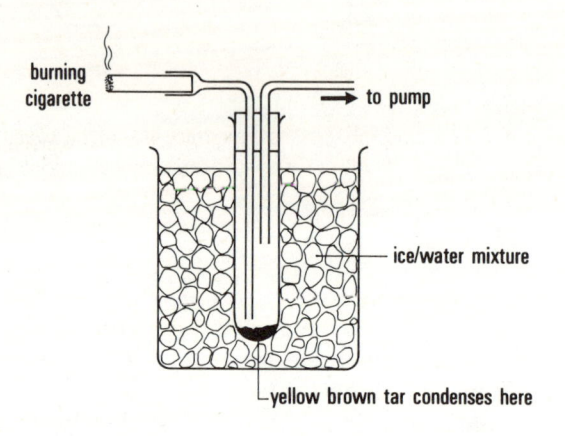

Fig 21.3 Collection of tar from a burning cigarette.

ANTI-SOCIAL ASPECTS OF SMOKING

Cigarette smoke can irritate the eyes and throat of non-smokers, and can cause asthma attacks in people with sensitive lungs. Constant exposure to cigarette smoke ('passive smoking') also increases the risk of lung cancer among non-smokers.

PREVENTION OF SMOKING

1. Enforce the law forbidding sales to children under 16.
2. Educate children on the dangers to health and on how to resist the pressures to smoke.
3. Provide help for smokers who wish to give up.
4. Increase the price of cigarettes through taxation.
5. Prohibit all forms of tobacco advertising and sponsorship, since these encourage children to take up smoking.

21.6 CHECKLIST

- Overall requirements for good health.
- Use and misuse of:
    antibiotics;
    aspirin;

Personal health care

        paracetamol;
        tranquillizers.
- Drug dependence:
        definition.
- Role of the liver.
- Harmful effects of:
        heroin;
        solvents;
        alcohol.
- Prevention of drug abuse.
- Maintenance of mental health.
- Causes of mental illness.
- Neurosis.
- Psychosis.
- Post-natal depression.
- Mental handicap.
- Cancer as uncontrolled cell division (cancer: M, NI only).
- Benign and malignant tumours.
- Carcinogens:
        definition;
        examples.
- Prevention of cancer.
- Detection of cancer:
        breast examination;
        cervical screening.
- Treatment of cancer:
        surgery;
        radiotherapy;
        chemotherapy.
- How smoking causes:
        bronchitis;
        emphysema;
        coronary heart disease;
        lung cancer;
        retarded foetal growth.
- Anti-social aspects of smoking.
- How to collect tar from cigarette smoke.
- Prevention of smoking.

21.7 EXAM QUESTIONS

1. List SIX ways in which individual's behaviour may contribute to their own ill health. (6)   [Ox]
2. Some people attempt to deal with stress by taking drugs such as aspirin or alcohol. Suggest two possible dangers of doing this. (2)
[SEG: GCSE specimen question]
3. In an investigation a person's reaction time was found. The reaction

time is the number of seconds between a stimulus being applied to the body and a reflex response being made. It was found that after the person had consumed several alcoholic drinks the reaction time was nearly doubled.

(a) Suggest how alcohol in the stomach can result in such a change in reaction time. (3)

(b) It is now illegal in Britain to drive a car if the alcohol content of the body is above a certain amount. Suggest a biological reason for this. (2) [*SEG:* GCSE specimen question]

4 A person was given a drink of alcohol and then asked to give blood samples over the next five hours. Table 21.6 shows how much alcohol was found in the blood at that time.

Table 21.6

Time in hours from drinking	0.0	0.5	1.0	1.5	2.0	3.0	4.0	5.0
Percentage alcohol in blood	0.00	0.07	0.14	0.15	0.11	0.07	0.05	0.04

(a) Use the figures in the table to plot a curve on graph paper. (4)

(b) Use your graph to answer the following:
(i) What percentage of alcohol is likely to be in the blood at 2.5 hours? (1)
(ii) On the graph, draw in the expected curve up to 7 hours. What percentage of alcohol does your curve show at 7 hours? (2)
(iii) How long after the drink would you expect the alcohol to have its maximum effect on the body? (1)
[*L/EA:* GCSE specimen question]

5 (a) Describe some of the causes of mental illness. (6)
(b) How serious is the problem of mental illness in society? (4)
(c) What can society do to reduce the problem? (4)
[*L/EA:* GCSE specimen question]

6 (a) What are the main causes of cancer? (3)
(b) How may cancer be
(i) prevented? (2)
(ii) treated? (3)

7 (a) Carbon monoxide in the blood is known to increase the permeability of the blood vessel walls to fats. Explain how this leads to an increased risk of a coronary heart attack. (2)
(b) Explain how the carbon monoxide in tobacco smoke affects the oxygen supply to the tissues of smokers. (2)

8 From the evidence in Fig 21.4, which is more important as a cause of bronchitis, smoking or air pollution? Give reasons. (2)

Fig 21.4

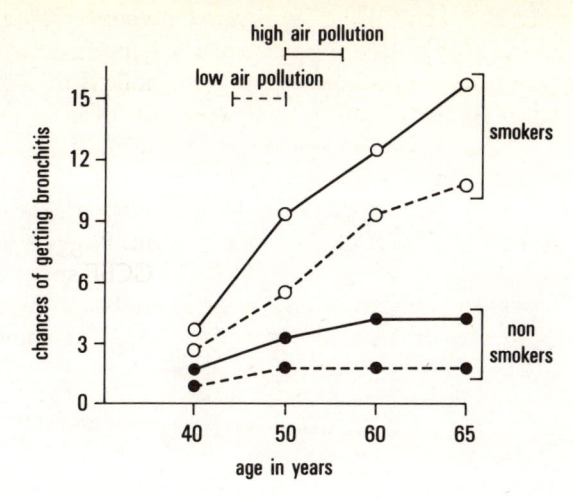

CHAPTER TWENTY-TWO

CAUSES AND PREVENTION OF INFECTIOUS DISEASE

CONTENTS

- 22.1 Infectious diseases: methods of spread — 311

- 22.2 Insect vectors of disease — 312
  Mosquitoes and malaria 312
  Houseflies and infectious diarrhoea 313

- 22.3 Social conditions and spread of disease — 314

- 22.4 External defences against infection — 315
  Effects of pathogens on the body 315

- 22.5 Internal defences against infection — 315
  Local reactions 315
  General reactions 316

- 22.6 Immunity and vaccination — 316
  How immunity is acquired 316
  Vaccination 317
  Undesirable reactions of the immune system 318

- 22.7 Prevention of infection in hospitals — 319

22.8 Antibiotics 319
Disadvantages of antibiotics 320
Antibiotics and agriculture 320

22.9 Public health 320
Prevention of epidemics 320

22.10 Sexually transmitted diseases (STD) or venereal diseases (VD) 321
Methods for preventing the spread of STD 321

22.10 Checklist 321

22.11 Exam questions 322

Causes and prevention of infectious disease

22.1 INFECTIOUS DISEASES: METHOD OF SPREAD

Infectious diseases are those illnesses caused by microorganisms, i.e. viruses, bacteria, fungi and protozoa (see page 43). Most microorganisms are either harmless or useful to man, but some cause serious illness or spoil human food.

Pathogens are microorganisms which cause disease. Pathogens invariably live as parasites (see page 329) within their host (in this case, man). Pathogens spread from person to person as shown in Table 22.1.

The body's external layers are well protected against invasion (see Table 22.2 on page 315), but if pathogens do penetrate the body, the body's defence or immune system comes into action (see page 318).

Hint: never use the word 'germs' in exams. Always say microorganism or pathogen (if appropriate), or mention viruses, bacteria, etc.

Table 22.1 How infectious diseases are spread.

Method of transmission	Details	Prevention
1 In droplets	Every exhalation (outward breath) sends a fine spray of invisible moisture (droplets) into the air. Coughing or sneezing can carry the pathogens for flu, colds, throat infections, etc., for up to 1 metre.	1 Always sneeze into a tissue. 2 Do not cough near other people. 3 Do not spit.
2 By touch, including sexual contact	Close contact spreads skin infections – boils, athlete's foot. Close sexual contact spreads sexually transmitted infections.	1 Keep boils, etc. covered. 2 Wash hands before preparing food. 3 Avoid close contact with infected people. 4 Use of condoms during sexual intercourse.
3 In dust	Dust carries discarded human skin epidermis carrying bacteria, together with house mite eggs.	1 Remove dust from homes.
4 In faeces	Faeces are mainly a mass of bacteria (with some undigested food and dead cells).	1 Wash hands after defaecating. 2 Do not spread untreated human faeces on crops.
5 In water	Typhoid, cholera and many other gut infections can spread through drinking water.	1 Chlorinate drinking water. 2 Boil or sterilize all drinking water if chlorinated water is not available.
6 In food	Bacteria multiply rapidly in warm, moist food, e.g. *Salmonella* which cause food poisoning.	1 Keep food cool during preparation, or else cook at temperatures above 60°C. 2 Keep raw food separate from cooked to prevent cross-infection.

continues on page 312

Method of transmission	Details	Prevention
7 Through breaks in skin	1 Deep dirty cuts can become infected by tetanus spores from the soil.	1 Vaccinate against tetanus and thoroughly clean all wounds.
	2 Infected hypodermic needles can spread diseases such as AIDS.	2 Hypodermic needles must be sterilized before use and only used once.
8 By insects	Flies carry food-poisoning bacteria from faeces to food. Mosquitoes carry malaria parasite, *Plasmodium*.	1 Dispose of faeces hygienically.
		2 Keep food secure from insects.
		3 Cover bins used for waste disposal.
		4 Take precautions against mosquitoes (see below).
9 By vertebrates	Rabies rarely occurs in Britain, but it is carried by several species of mammal, e.g. foxes, bats, in continental Europe. Domestic pets (dogs and cats) can be bitten and may then bite humans.	1 Keep all pets from overseas in quarantine (isolation) for at least 9 months.
		2 Vaccinate all pets in infected areas and also anyone bitten.

Hints: avoid vague answers on how diseases spread – 'By eating them', 'By water', 'By touch.' None of these will earn you any marks. You must give more details to earn marks.

22.2 INSECT VECTORS OF DISEASE

MOSQUITOES AND MALARIA

METHOD OF SPREAD

Female *Anopheles* mosquitoes spread the malaria parasite, *Plasmodium*, as follows:

1. The parasite is carried in the insect's salivary glands. When biting, she injects saliva containing an anti-coagulant into the wound to prevent the victim's blood clotting while she feeds.
2. In this way, she may inject hundreds of *Plasmodium* into the blood through her piercing mouth parts. She may also suck up the parasite from a malaria victim and pass it on to someone else.

The parasite multiplies in the victim's liver, breaking out into the blood and causing periodic fevers and great weakness over many years.

LIFE CYCLE OF THE MOSQUITO

Mosquitoes fly mostly at night and lay eggs in water. The larvae are air breathing and so must come to the surface regularly.

PREVENTION OF MALARIA

1. Take **anti-malarial drugs**, e.g. quinine or Paludrine, so that the parasites are killed as they enter the body. These are taken daily before

Causes and prevention of infectious disease 313

entering an infected area and for six weeks afterwards, in case the parasite is still lingering in the liver.

2. Fix **mosquito nets** over doors, windows and beds at night.
3. Spray houses with **insecticides**, to kill the adult mosquitoes.
4. Spray ponds and standing water with **oil** to prevent the larvae from breathing at the surface.
5. **Drain** casual water, e.g. marshes, gutters, old buckets, etc. to prevent breeding.

SEASONAL EFFECTS

Malaria is mainly a tropical disease because a warm climate is necessary for rapid multiplication of both the mosquito and the parasite.

HOUSEFLIES AND INFECTIOUS DIARRHOEA

Houseflies carry the bacteria which cause infectious diarrhoea and various kinds of food poisoning from faeces to human food.

METHOD OF SPREAD

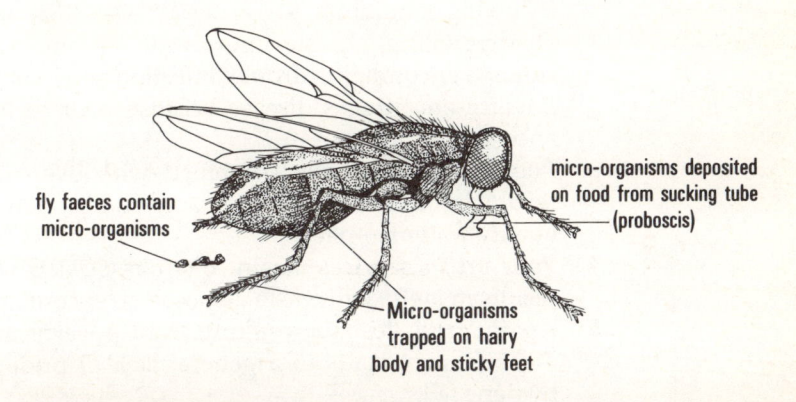

Fig 22.1 How flies spread pathogens.

1. Flies feed by secreting enzymes on to their food and then sucking it up, along with any bacteria present. They also deposit spots of vomit and their own faeces on human food.
2. Microorganisms also become trapped and transported on their hairy bodies and sticky feet.

LIFE-CYCLE OF THE HOUSEFLY

The eggs are laid in small groups in any warm damp organic material, and hatch after about eight hours to produce the white limbless larvae known as maggots. These burrow into the organic material and feed on it, emerging as adults several days later.

CONTROL OF HOUSEFLIES

1. Manure and compost heaps should be kept as far as possible from houses.
2. Dustbins should be kept covered, and sprayed with insecticide in warm weather.
3. Organic refuse should be thoroughly buried.
4. All food should be kept covered.
5. Insecticidal sprays can be used against the adults, but with caution as they may be harmful to people and animals.

SEASONAL EFFECTS

Diseases spread by houseflies are rare in winter because:
1. at low temperatures the adults are inactive and the larvae grow very slowly;
2. microorganisms also multiply slowly at low temperatures.

22.3 SOCIAL CONDITIONS AND SPREAD OF DISEASE

The spread of infectious diseases occurs much more rapidly under the following conditions.

1. **Overcrowding**, e.g. sleeping five to a room, results in close physical contact, encouraging droplet infection and infection by touch.
2. **Poverty** encourages disease because poor diets result in low resistance to infection.
3. **Poor housing** usually combined with overcrowding and poverty, results in rat-infested living spaces and is often associated with poor-quality water supplies.
4. **Poor urban services** (again, often associated with the other factors) results in inefficient waste disposal, so encouraging flies, etc.
5. **Apathy and despair** resulting from poverty in overcrowded urban areas (slums) leads to a general lack of pride so that standards of hygiene fall.
6. **Drug-takers** are more likely to suffer from infections, partly because of shared needles, but also because regular drug use leads to lack of concern with personal hygiene, etc.

For all of these reasons, infectious diseases are generally commoner among poorer city dwellers, both in Britain and worldwide. However, as living standards in Britain have improved, many infectious diseases have become rare. They have been replaced by **diseases of affluence** as the major preventable illnesses and causes of premature death, e.g. coronary heart disease caused by smoking, lack of exercise and incorrect diet, and lung cancer caused by increased smoking.

Causes and prevention of infectious disease

22.4 EXTERNAL DEFENCES AGAINST INFECTION

Table 22.2 External defences of the body against infection

Part of body	Defence mechanism
1 Epidermis of skin	1 Hard, dry outer **cornified layer** prevents entry of microorganisms. 2 Secretion of **sebum** prevents growth of pathogens on skin. 3 If skin is cut, blood forms **clot** which converts to a hard protective scab.
2 Epithelium of respiratory tubes (nasal passages, trachea, lungs)	Tubes are lined by **mucous membrane**, a mixture of ciliated cells and mucus-secreting goblet cells. Mucus traps pathogens, cilia sweep away mucus to throat for swallowing (see page 302).
3 Ears	**Wax** in outer ear traps pathogens.
4 Eyes	Tears contain the enzyme **lysozyme** which destroys some pathogens.
5 Mouth	Saliva contains **lysozyme**.
6 Stomach	**Acid** in gastric juice destroys bacteria.
7 Vagina	**Acid** secretions destroy pathogens.

EFFECTS OF PATHOGENS ON THE BODY

INCUBATION PERIOD

This is the time which elapses between the initial infection and the appearance of symptoms of illness, varying from three days (flu) to 6 months (rabies). During this period, the following events occur.

1. **Multiplication.** The invading microorganisms begin to multiply rapidly within the tissues.
2. **Toxin production.** The pathogens begin to produce poisonous wastes called toxins which circulate in the bloodstream.
3. **Cell destruction.** Cells invaded by the pathogen may be destroyed. In the case of viruses, the cell's DNA is taken over by the virus and used to produce new viruses instead.

22.5 INTERNAL DEFENCES AGAINST INFECTION

LOCAL REACTIONS

1. Cells in the connective tissue around the affected area release a substance called **histamine**. This causes the neighbouring blood vessels to dilate and their cell walls to become more permeable. As a result, plasma and both types of white cell flow rapidly into the infected tissues.
2. The phagocytic white cells then consume the pathogens, resulting in the formation of a mixture of dead white cells and damaged tissues known as **pus**.

GENERAL REACTIONS

The spread of toxins in the circulation system from the invaded tissues triggers a general reaction to infection. As a result:
1. the body's temperature rises, increasing the metabolic rate and so speeding up defensive activities;
2. lymphocytes throughout the body produce antibodies and antitoxins in large quantities.

An **antigen** is the name given to any foreign substance, tissue or cell which triggers the production of antibodies against it.

ANTIBODIES

These are chemicals produced by lymphocytes to destroy any substance not recognized by the lymphocytes as belonging naturally to the body. These include:
1. the protein outer coating of any cell not normally found in the body, including cells of pathogens, other animals or plants, or even human cells from another person;
2. any other 'foreign' substance, including poisons, toxins, etc.

Antitoxin is the name used for antibodies which attack toxins rather than the cells of pathogens.

Properties of antibodies
1. Each antibody is **specific** to a single antigen; so antibodies against the measles virus will not attack the mumps virus.
2. Some antibodies destroy invading cells by **dissolving** their cell membranes; others, called agglutinins, cause foreign cells to **clump** together (agglutinate). they are then more easily destroyed by phagocytes.
3. Antibodies against a particular antigen can **remain in the bloodstream** for many years, so conferring protection or immunity against a particular pathogen.

22.6 IMMUNITY AND VACCINATION

HOW IMMUNITY IS ACQUIRED
1. **Natural immunity** is protection against a disease acquired by successfully resisting an invasion by a pathogen, so that the blood subsequently contains antibodies against the pathogen.
2. **Acquired immunity** means protection against an infectious disease acquired either by injection of antibodies (passive immunity) or by vaccination (active immunity) (see Fig 22.2).
3. **Passive immunity** means protection acquired for a short period by injecting antibodies, usually from the serum of a horse. This is done to help patients overcome a serious illness, but confers only temporary protection because the antibodies are gradually lost from the blood.

Causes and prevention of infectious disease

Fig 22.2

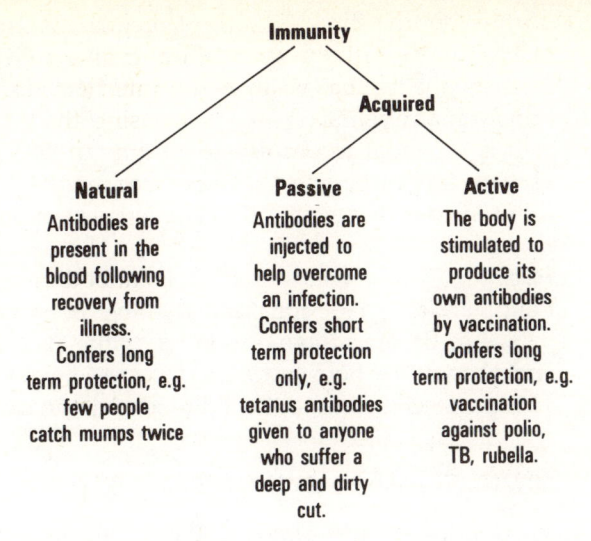

```
                        Immunity
                           |
                        Acquired
                           |
        ┌──────────────────┼──────────────────┐
      Natural           Passive             Active
```

Natural
Antibodies are present in the blood following recovery from illness. Confers long term protection, e.g. few people catch mumps twice

Passive
Antibodies are injected to help overcome an infection. Confers short term protection only, e.g. tetanus antibodies given to anyone who suffer a deep and dirty cut.

Active
The body is stimulated to produce its own antibodies by vaccination. Confers long term protection, e.g. vaccination against polio, TB, rubella.

4 **Active immunity** is acquired by vaccination with a weakened form of a pathogen so that the body produces its own antibodies against the pathogen. This confers long-lasting protection because the body has now acquired the ability to produce its own antibodies.

VACCINATION

Vaccines are made from dead or weakened pathogens, or from a weakened form of their toxin. A low dose is given initially, followed by stronger doses to build up full immunity.

Hint: 'vaccination', 'immunization' and 'inoculation' are all used to describe the same thing, i.e. the injection of a vaccine.

EXAMPLES OF MASS VACCINATION PROGRAMMES

Tuberculosis (TB)
All British children are offered vaccination against TB at age 12–13. Before this is done it is necessary to test their immunity, because those who are already naturally immune react badly to the vaccine.

The test involves injection of a harmless antigen prepared from TB bacteria, just under the skin (Mantoux test). The development of a red spot in a few days indicates that the individual is already immune.

In 9 out of 10 cases, the individual is not immune and so requires to be vaccinated. If so, a BCG vaccine is given. This consists of a weakened form of the TB bacterium and gives a high level of protection for at least 10 years.

Rubella
Rubella (German measles) is a mild infection in children and adults. Unfortunately, the rubella virus can cross the placenta and cause severe damage to the heart, brain and other organs of the foetus

during the first three months of pregnancy. To prevent this, all girls in Britain are offered vaccination against rubella at age 12–13. This consists of a live but weakened form of the virus, which gives protection for many years.

It is essential to encourage all girls to be vaccinated because the vaccine cannot be given during or immediately before pregnancy as there is a risk that even the weakened virus may damage the foetus.

Polio

Polio vaccine, made for weakened live polio virus, is available to all babies in Britain at age 3 months, with second and third doses at 6 and 11 months. Booster doses are offered at 5 years and late teenage. This protects throughout childhood and into early adulthood.

ADVANTAGES AND DISADVANTAGES OF VACCINATION

Vaccination confers almost 100 per cent protection against infection. However some vaccines are only temporarily effective because new types of virus arise regularly e.g. new forms of influenza virus.

Mass vaccination of large numbers of people protects everyone, even the unvaccinated, by greatly reducing the chances of anyone catching the disease. The smallpox virus has been wiped out altogether by mass vaccination, combined with other methods.

The **disadvantage** of mass vaccination is that a few people may suffer serious ill effects from the vaccine.

UNDESIRABLE REACTIONS OF THE IMMUNE SYSTEM

The **immune system** is the name used for the parts of the body concerned with defence against disease, mainly the lymphocytes and a few other cells. Under certain circumstances the system reacts in ways which are harmful to health, including the following.

1 **Allergies** are strong reactions of the immune system to relatively harmless antigens. The commonest example is hayfever, an allergic reaction to grass pollen. The presence of pollen in the nose and eyes causes massive over-production of histamine, resulting in inflamed watery eyes, excess mucus and violent sneezing.

2 **Transplant rejection.** Since the immune system attacks all 'foreign' substances, it will also reject organ transplants by producing antibodies against them. To overcome this, doctors try to obtain organs such as kidneys from close relatives or other donors whose tissues are chemically similar to the recipient. Alternatively, it may be necessary to give drugs which will suppress the immune system for a time, although this increases the risk of infection from pathogens.

3 **Blood transfusions.** The immune system also rejects blood transfusions from 'foreign' blood groups. A person with blood group A produces antibodies which cause red cells of blood group B to clump or agglutinate. This is because their outer protein coat is unfamiliar and is therefore treated as an antigen.

Causes and prevention of infectious disease

22.7 PREVENTION OF INFECTION IN HOSPITALS

Antiseptics are chemicals used to prevent the growth of microorganisms. They were first used by Joseph Lister (1827–1912) in the form of a steady spray of carbolic acid, which was aimed at the wound during operations. This greatly reduced the death rate from infections.

Carbolic acid kills microorganisms but can be harmful to the tissues. Hence the modern approach is to exclude microorganisms from the operating theatre altogether.

Aseptic surgery is surgery carried out in conditions which are made as sterile as possible by excluding microorganisms. Precautions include:

1. thoroughly sterilizing the operating theatre before use, including the air supply;
2. providing sterile gowns and caps for the medical staff;
3. sterilizing all surgical instruments before use.

Disinfectants are substances which kill all microorganisms and all other living things. They are much stronger than antiseptics.

Table 22.3 Common terms associated with disease prevention

Term	Meaning
Antibiotic	Substance which prevents the growth of certain bacteria but does not harm living tissues. Originally obtained from fungi.
Aseptic	Sterile conditions, i.e. exclusion of microorganisms through sterilization.
Antiseptic	Substance which prevents the growth of all microorganisms. Harmful to all tissues but safe for use on the skin. Should not be injected or swallowed.
Disinfectant	Substance which kills all microorganisms and all other forms of life, e.g. bleach or phenols. For use in the home but not to be swallowed or used on the skin. Much stronger than antiseptics.
Anti-serum	Serum, i.e. plasma without red cells and fibrinogen, from a horse containing antibodies. Given to a patient to help overcome an infection, but provides only short-term protection (passive immunity).
Antibody	Substances produced in the body by lymphocytes to destroy antigens, e.g. invading microorganisms, foreign proteins, etc.
Antitoxin	Type of antibody which neutralizes the toxins produced by pathogens.
Antigen	Any substance or living organism which is 'foreign' to the body and therefore liable to attack by antibodies.

22.8 ANTIBIOTICS

Antibiotics, e.g. **penicillin** are substances which prevent bacteria from multiplying but are harmless to other living cells. Unlike antiseptics, they can therefore be given directly to patients. Antibiotics were originally extracted from fungi, but many can now be made entirely artificially.

Human Biology

Hint: note that antibiotics cannot be used against most viruses. Examiners often try to catch you on this!

DISADVANTAGES OF ANTIBIOTICS

Some types of bacteria have become resistant to antibiotics. This happens especially where a patient fails to finish a complete course of antibiotic tablets. Any surviving bacteria may turn out to be resistant, so requiring a larger dose of antibiotic should they infect another person. Furthermore, this resistance can be transferred from one type of bacteria to another.

ANTIBIOTICS AND AGRICULTURE

Cattle and pigs are sometimes fed antibiotics because this increases their growth rate. As a result, food-poisoning bacteria resistant to antibiotics have been found on farms. This has led to restrictions on the use of antibiotics for agriculture in some countries.

22.9 PUBLIC HEALTH

1 **An endemic disease** is a disease which occurs normally in a country, producing a number of cases every year. The common cold is endemic to Britain, but malaria is not.
2 **An epidemic** is a sudden rise in the number of cases of a disease above the normal level.

PREVENTION OF EPIDEMICS

1 **Notification of diseases.** Doctors are required by law to report cases of certain dangerous notifiable diseases, e.g. typhoid and diphtheria, to the health authorities. This allows immediate action to be taken when the first case occurs.
2 **Isolation.** Anyone infected with the disease, or merely suspected of infection, must be kept away from other people, e.g. by removal to an isolation hospital.
3 **Quarantine.** Isolation must be continued for as long as the individual remains infectious, even though the symptoms of illness have long disappeared. Anyone who has been in contact with the disease ('contacts') must also be isolated for the duration of the incubation period.
4 **Carriers** must be traced, as well as people with symptoms. A carrier is a person who is infected with a disease but does not display symptoms. Carriers may infect other people for many years without knowing it.
5 **The source of infection** must also be traced. Sterile swabs, e.g. cotton-wool mounted on a stick are rubbed over possible sources of pathogens, e.g. food, faeces, surfaces in a house, etc. and then rolled

Causes and prevention of infectious disease 321

carefully over sterile agar culture plates. Any microorganisms present will grow on the agar and so can be identified.
6 **Mass vaccination** (see page 317) can be organized to prevent further cases arising.

22.10 SEXUALLY TRANSMITTED OR VENEREAL DISEASES (VD)

Most pathogens, from warts to the common cold, can be passed on during close sexual contact. However, the sexually transmitted diseases can *only* be passed on by close sexual contact, because the pathogens involved die quickly outside the body.

Some diseases of this kind, e.g. gonorrhoea, syphilis, etc., can be cured with antibiotics. Unfortunately, herpes and AIDS are at present incurable because they are caused by viruses, and vaccines are not available.

METHODS FOR PREVENTING THE SPREAD OF STD

1. Use of the condom greatly reduces the risk of infection for both partners.
2. Avoid promiscuity.
3. Seek treatment immediately an infection is suspected.
4. If infected, cooperate with health workers in tracing sexual contacts.

22.10 CHECKLIST

- Pathogen.
- Parasite *v.* host.
- Droplet infection.
- Nine methods of disease transmission.
- Prevention of malaria (five).
- Prevention of diseases spread by houseflies (five).
- Six social causes of disease.
- Seven methods of external defence against infection.
- Incubation.
- Internal defence against infection.
- Immunity:
    - natural *v.* acquired;
    - passive *v.* active.
- Vaccination:
    - examples;
    - disadvantages.
- Immune system:
    - allergies;
    - transplants;
    - transfusions.

Human Biology

- Antibody, antigen, antitoxin.
- Anti-serum, antibiotic.
- Disadvantages of antibiotics.
- Antiseptic v. disinfectant.
- Aseptic surgery.
- Endemic v. epidemic.
- Notification of diseases.
- Isolation.
- Quarantine.
- Prevention of sexually transmitted diseases (four).

22.11 EXAM QUESTIONS

1. (a) Name FOUR different classes of pathogenic microorganisms and in each case give an example of a disease caused by that class of microorganism. (4)

    (b) State the routes by which microorganisms can enter the body. (2)

    (c) Describe the natural defence mechanisms of the body which help it to combat invasion by microorganisms. (14) [*JMB*]

2. Fig 22.3 shows the general trends in the number of deaths from certain diseases over the past 70 years.

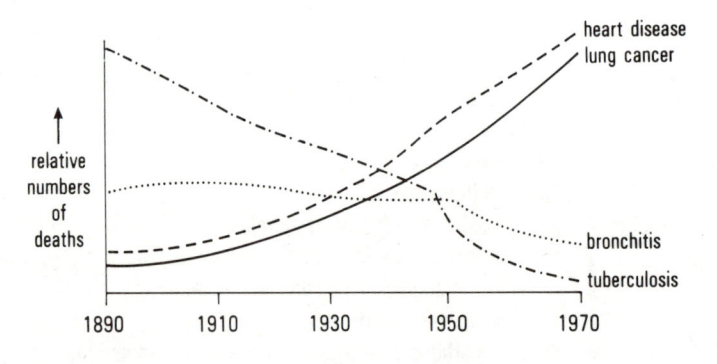

Fig 22.3

Extract four pieces of information from the graph and for each fact give one reason to explain that fact. (8) [*SWEB*]

3. Fig 22.4 shows the incidence of pathogens in the body during the course of a disease, e.g. influenza.

    (a) Mark on the graph with the symbol X the crisis point of the disease. (1)

    (b) Using the symbols A, B, C, D as shown on the graph indicate the period or periods:

    (i) of disease incubation; (1)

    (ii) when the disease is evident; (1)

Causes and prevention of infectious disease

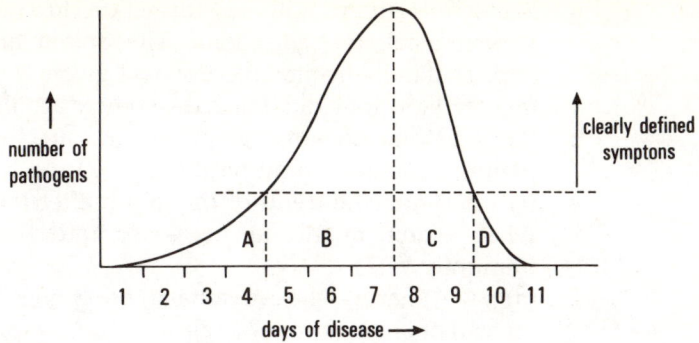

Fig 22.4

(iii) when the defences are destroying organisms more rapidly than they are multiplying. (1 each)

(c) On which two days is the greatest increase in the number of organisms? (1) [Ox]

4 (a) Why does an antibody against the common cold give no protection against influenza? (2)

(b) Explain the differences between the action of a vaccine in preventing a disease and the action of a serum in curing the same disease. (2)

(c) Cholera is an infection of the large intestine, spread in water and by flies. If a case of cholera should occur in Britain, state three ways in which normal hygiene can prevent its spread. (3)

5 In the United Kingdom schoolgirls are advised to be immunized against rubella.

(a) Explain the value of immunization against disease. (6)

(b) Explain why immunization against rubella is offered only to females. (5)

(c) Name three other diseases against which parents are advised to have their children immunized. (3)

(d) Immunizations are normally administered in the early years of life. Explain the significance of this timing. (2)

[AEB 1985]

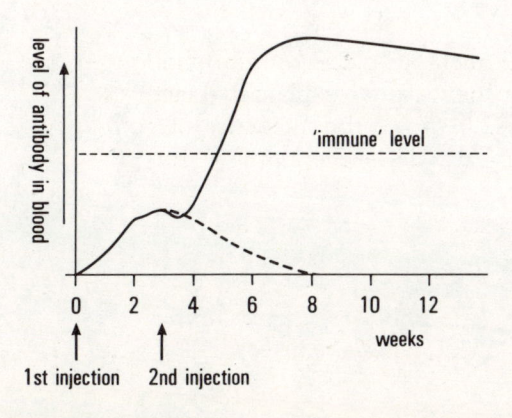

Fig 22.5

6 Fig 22.5 illustrates antibody formation during the vaccination of one person using two injections. The dotted line shows what would happen if only the first injection was given.
   (a)   How long did it take the body to acquire immunity? (1)
   (b)   What does the graph suggest are the dangers of not completing a course of immunisations? (2)
   (c)   From the trend of the graph after the eighth week, suggest what action might be necessary, after one year, to maintain immunity. (2)
   (d)   What is the advantage of giving two smaller injections instead of one large one? (2)
   (e)   Explain how a new born baby has acquired immunity to certain diseases. (2)   [NI]

CHAPTER TWENTY-THREE

DISEASE, FOOD PRESERVATION AND EXPERIMENTS WITH MICROORGANISMS

CONTENTS

▶ **23.1 Infectious diseases – causes and prevention**   327

▶ **23.2 Parasites**   329
Endoparasites 329
Ectoparasites 330

▶ **23.3 Roles of WHO and FAO**   331
WHO 331
FAO 331

▶ **23.4 Food poisoning and the preservation of food**   331
Prevention of food poisoning and decay 332

▶ **23.5 Methods for preserving food**   332

▶ **23.6 Experiments with microorganisms**   333
Techniques for growing microorganisms on agar plates 333

23.7 Checklist 335

23.8 Exam questions 336

Diseases, food preservation and experiments

23.1 INFECTIOUS DISEASES: CAUSES AND PREVENTION

You may be asked questions about the methods of spread and prevention of some of the diseases in Table 23.1. You are unlikely to be asked for symptoms.

Table 23.1 Infectious diseases mentioned in exam syllabuses

Disease and type of pathogen	Effects	Method of spread	Prevention
AIDS virus	Attacks lymphocytes, so immune system is destroyed; victim then dies from other infections and cancer.	Found in blood of many symptomless carriers. Passed during close sexual contact or from infected blood. (Also through the placenta and breast milk.)	1 Use of condoms during intercourse. 2 Using needles for injection once only. 3 Restricting number of sexual partners. 4 Heat treating all blood used in transfusions.
Athlete's foot fungus	Attacks skin between toes, causing pain and redness.	Passed on by sharing towels or walking barefoot on wet changing room floors.	1 Dry feet thoroughly between toes. 2 Do not share towels.
Botulism (severe food poisoning) bacterium	Produces toxin which attacks nervous system. Can be fatal.	Grows in warm food in anaerobic conditions; killed by boiling. Can grow in home-bottled foods, etc.	1 Cook food thoroughly. 2 Keep food very hot (above 60°C) or very cold (below 5°C). 3 Cannot grow in acid conditions so add vinegar.
Cholera bacterium	Attacks lining of intestines causing severe diarrhoea and dehydration.	In water and faeces.	1 Chlorinate drinking water. 2 Dispose of faeces hygienically. 3 Wash hands after using the toilet. 4 Vaccinate.
Common cold virus	Infects mucous membrane of nasal passages.	In droplets.	1 Use a tissue when sneezing. 2 Avoid crowded places.
Gonorrhoea bacterium	Attacks urethra in men causing pain on urinating. In women, damages ovaries and oviducts; can cause sterility.	Close sexual contact.	1 Use of condoms during intercourse. 2 Restricting number of sexual partners.

continues on page 328

Human Biology

Disease and type of pathogen	Effects	Method of spread	Prevention
Herpes virus	Forms blisters around mouth, anus and genital area, which appear and disappear from time to time.	Close sexual contact, including oral contact.	Avoid close oral or genital contact with anyone who has active herpes blisters.
Influenza virus	Causes raised temperature, aches and pains.	In droplets.	1 Use tissue when sneezing. 2 Avoid crowded places. 3 Vaccine available for those most at risk, e.g. elderly.
Malaria protozoan (*Plasmodium*)	Attacks red blood cells. Causes alternate bouts of fever and shivering.	By mosquitoes.	1 Sleep under mosquito nets. 2 Spray homes with insecticides to kill adults. 3 Spray ponds with oil to kill mosquito larvae. 4 Drain ponds to prevent breeding. 5 Take preventive drugs, e.g. quinine or Paludrine.
Non-specific urethritis (NSU)	Similar to gonorrhoea.		
Polio virus	Mild fever only in very young children. Permanent damage to central nervous system, causing paralysis, in later life.	Droplets, faeces, water.	1 Wash hands after using lavatory. 2 Avoid swimming pools during outbreaks. 3 Vaccinate.
Rabies virus (not currently endemic in Britain)	Destroys central nervous system. Invariably fatal unless treated.	From bite of infected animal.	1 Quarantine all imported dogs, cats, etc., for 12 months. 2 Vaccinate animals in infected areas.
Rubella (German measles) virus	Slight rash and temperature. Causes serious damage to foetus.	Droplets.	Vaccination.
Salmonella (food poisoning) bacterium	Causes sickness and diarrhoea.	Found in intestines of most vertebrates, e.g. cattle, chicken. Multiply rapidly in moist lukewarm (35–40°C) food.	1 Cook food thoroughly. 2 Do not leave food in warm conditions; keep very hot (above 60°C) or very cold (below 5°C). 3 Keep raw meat away from cooked food.
Smallpox virus (now extinct)	High temperature; 'pox' marks on skin.	Droplets	Now extinct following worldwide WHO vaccination campaign.
Syphilis bacterium	Attacks reproductive organs, then central nervous system. Can cause deafness, insanity and death after many years.	Close sexual contact.	1 Use of condoms during intercourse. 2 Restricting number of sexual partners.

Diseases, food preservation and experiments

Disease and type of pathogen	Effects	Method of spread	Prevention
Tetanus bacterium	Attacks central nervous system, leading to paralysis and death.	Common in intestines of herbivores (cattle, sheep). Spores remain in soil for many years and infect deep cuts. Multiply under anaerobic conditions only.	1 Vaccination. 2 Give anti-serum and vaccinate anyone with a deep or dirty cut.
Tuberculosis ('Consumption') bacterium	Slowly destroys lungs, causing coughing, shortage of breath, raised temperature.	In sputum from lungs. Carriers can be infectious.	1 Do not spit. 2 Vaccinate.
Typhoid bacterium	Attacks lining of intestines, causing diarrhoea.	Faeces, water, food.	1 Vaccination. 2 Wash hands after using toilet. 3 Wash hands before preparing food. 4 Dispose of faeces hygienically. 5 Cook food thoroughly.

23.2 PARASITES

W, NI, APH(H) only

1 **A parasite** is an organism which feeds on another organism, usually without killing it.
2 **A host** is an organism which is fed on by a parasite.
   Parasites can be divided into two groups.
1 **Endoparasites** are parasites which live within the body of their host, e.g. almost all pathogenic microorganisms including the malaria parasite (*Plasmodium*) and intestinal worms such as threadworms.
2 **Ectoparasites** live on the outer surface or skin of their host, e.g. lice, or the fungus which causes athlete's foot.

ENDOPARASITES

Special adaptations for their way of life, usually in the blood or the intestines, include the following:
1 Ability to resist digestion, e.g. worms living in the gut.
2 Ability to resist the host's antibodies, e.g. blood parasites such as *Plasmodium*.
3 Ability to produce large numbers of eggs, since transmission to new hosts is often difficult.

THREAD (OR PIN) WORMS

These are small roundworms found in the large intestine, especially in small children. They cause little harm, except when the female moves out on to the skin around the anus to lay her eggs. Her movements cause irritation, resulting in itching.

Spread
Scratching around the anus with the fingers causes the eggs to become trapped under the fingernails and then swallowed, so re-infecting the host. The eggs are sticky, so increasing their adhesion to the skin; they are also blown about in dust and so breathed in or eaten.

Treatment
This is by taking drugs to kill the worms, in two doses at three week intervals to kill both the existing adults and those hatching later from their eggs. This must be combined with prevention.

Prevention
This involves:
1. discouraging infected children from scratching around the anus, e.g. wear gloves at night;
2. wash hands after use of toilet and keep fingernails short – this must apply to all members of the family.

ECTOPARASITES

LICE
These are wingless insects (see Fig 23.1) which grip the skin closely with their clawed feet and feed on blood, using their piercing and sucking mouthparts. The victim's scratching may lead to serious skin diseases, e.g. impetigo (an infection of the skin by bacteria). In addition, lice spread typhus and other diseases.

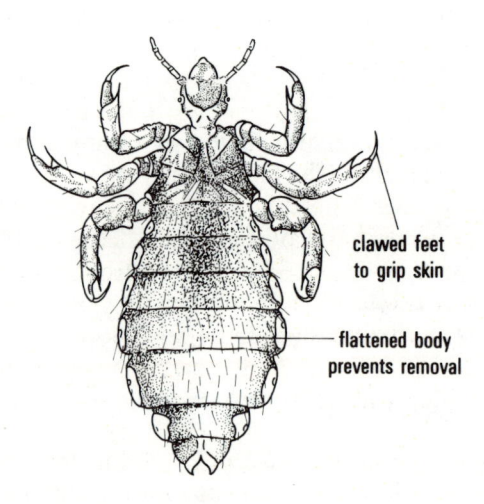

Fig 23.1 Adult human head louse.

Life cycle
The head louse lives in the hair and lays eggs called nits, stuck to the

hair. They hatch out in about six days as nymphs, which look like miniature adults. After a further ten days the nymphs moult, become adult, and breed.

The head louse is just as common in clean short hair as in dirty long hair, and spreads easily whenever people are in close contact, e.g. in schools.

Prevention and treatment

This is by use of insecticidal shampoos and combing with a special comb to remove the nits.

23.3 ROLES OF WHO AND FAO

WHO
NI, APH only

The **World Health Organization (WHO)** is based in Geneva, Switzerland. It is responsible for the following:
1. Providing information and conducting research on public health topics such as vaccination, nutrition, drug addiction and the dangers of radiation.
2. Organizing programmes to control infectious diseases by mass vaccination, provision of purified water and health information. A WHO programme led to the extermination of the smallpox virus from the world in 1983.
3. Training medical staff, conducting surveys and helping to set up health centres.

FAO

The **Food and Agriculture Organization (FAO)** based in Rome, Italy, helps to increase the efficiency of agriculture, fisheries and forestry, especially in developing countries. This is achieved by spreading information, providing training and supporting research.

23.4 FOOD POISONING AND THE PRESERVATION OF FOOD

Human food must be protected from the growth of two kinds of microorganisms.
1. Pathogens which cause food poisoning.
2. Decomposers which spoil food by causing it to decay.

Food poisoning is caused by bacteria found in the soil (and therefore on vegetables), in the intestines of animals, and on other foods. Bacteria from the human skin, such as the staphylococci which cause boils, can also cause food poisoning if allowed to grow in food.

Decomposition of food is caused by many kinds of fungi and bacteria whose spores are found in soil, air, dust, etc. It is therefore necessary to assume that *all* food is liable to decay unless precautions are taken.

PREVENTION OF FOOD POISONING AND DECAY

TEMPERATURE CONTROL

1. **Preventing growth.** Microorganisms can normally only multiply at temperatures between 10–63°C. Food should therefore be kept either very hot or very cold – lukewarm food is extremely dangerous.
2. **Killing spores.** Choice of cooking method is important because the spores (and toxins) of some pathogens can survive boiling. Roasting and pressure cooking are more effective because the food is heated to 160–200°C.

PREVENTION OF CONTAMINATION

1. Food handlers must **wash hands** after using the toilet and before handling food. Many people are unwitting carriers of pathogens.
2. **Cuts and boils** must be covered.
3. Food must be **covered** against dust, dirt, flies and rodents.
4. To prevent **cross-infection**, raw meat must be kept separate from cooked food.
5. **Utensils and kitchen surfaces** used to prepare raw meat must be thoroughly cleaned before using for cooked meat.
6. **Working surfaces and draining boards** need to be regularly cleaned with disinfectants and should be made from smooth, non-absorbent materials, e.g. metal or plastic but not wood. Wood absorbs (dirty) water and is often pitted or scratched, providing places for microorganisms to grow.
7. For washing up use the hottest possible water with **detergent**. Detergents kill bacteria and remove fat on which they can feed.
8. Plates should be left to **drain** and not wiped dry with cloths because these spread microorganisms. Dishwashers are preferable to hand washing because plates are kept at temperatures over 60°C for longer periods.

23.5 METHODS FOR PRESERVING FOOD

Table 23.2 Long-term methods of preserving food

Method	Technique	Effect on microorganisms	Result
1 Canning (tinning) and **bottling**	Food is thoroughly cooked until sterile, then sealed while hot. Can is coated to prevent rust.	Destroyed by heating.	Food keeps for up a year but some flavour and vitamins are lost.
2 Dehydration	Food is dried by: (a) air drying – peas, beans, dates and fish are left out to dry; (b) freeze-drying – food is frozen rapidly and then dried in a vacuum.	Cannot live in dry food. Spores remain, so food must be kept dry.	Food keeps as long as it remains dry, but flavour is lost by air-drying. Freeze-drying is superior because it preserves flavour.

Diseases, food preservation and experiments 333

Method	Technique	Effect on microorganisms	Result
3 Osmotic preservation	Salt or sugar is added to food	Cannot live in concentrated solutions. But spores remain so food will not keep if water is added.	Use for ham, bacon, jam, etc. Flavour entirely different but may be acceptable.
4 Deep freezing	Food is kept at temperatures below −18°C.	Totally inactive at −18°C, but remain alive.	Food will keep for 3 months and retains flavour. Watery foods lose texture.
5 Ultra-heat treatment (UHT) or sterilization	Food, e.g. milk, is heated to 132°C for 1 minute, then placed in sterile containers.	Destroyed by heat.	UHT milk keeps for 3 months. Vitamins retained, but taste altered.
6 Pickling	Pickles usually contain acetic acid in the form of vinegar. This lowers the pH to below 5.	Most microorganisms (especially botulism bacteria) cannot multiply in highly acid conditions.	Food keeps for months but taste is greatly altered.

Table 23.3 Short-term methods of food preservation

Method	Technique	Effect on microorganisms	Effects on food
1 Refrigeration	Food is cooled to 0–5°C.	Growth is greatly slowed down but not stopped.	Food keeps for a few days only.
2 Pasteurization	Milk is heated to 80°C for 30 seconds, then rapidly cooled.	Pathogens and most decomposing organisms killed but some bacteria survive.	Taste and vitamins remain unaltered. Milk keeps for only a few days, even if refrigerated.

23.6 EXPERIMENTS WITH MICROORGANISMS

TECHNIQUES FOR GROWING MICROORGANISMS ON AGAR PLATES

See Fig 23.2.

PREPARATION

1. All equipment must be thoroughly sterilized by boiling for 20 minutes in an autoclave or pressure cooker at 160°C, i.e. under full pressure.
2. Sterilized liquid agar is then poured into the petri dishes.
3. The dishes are covered while the agar sets, to prevent entry by microorganisms from the air.

INOCULATION

1. Agar plates can be inoculated by using a wire loop. This should be sterilized in a flame before use and allowed to cool in the air.
2. The loop is then dipped into the source material, e.g. pond water, soil, suspect food, etc., and streaked across the surface of the jelly.
3. The dishes are then sealed, labelled and incubated.

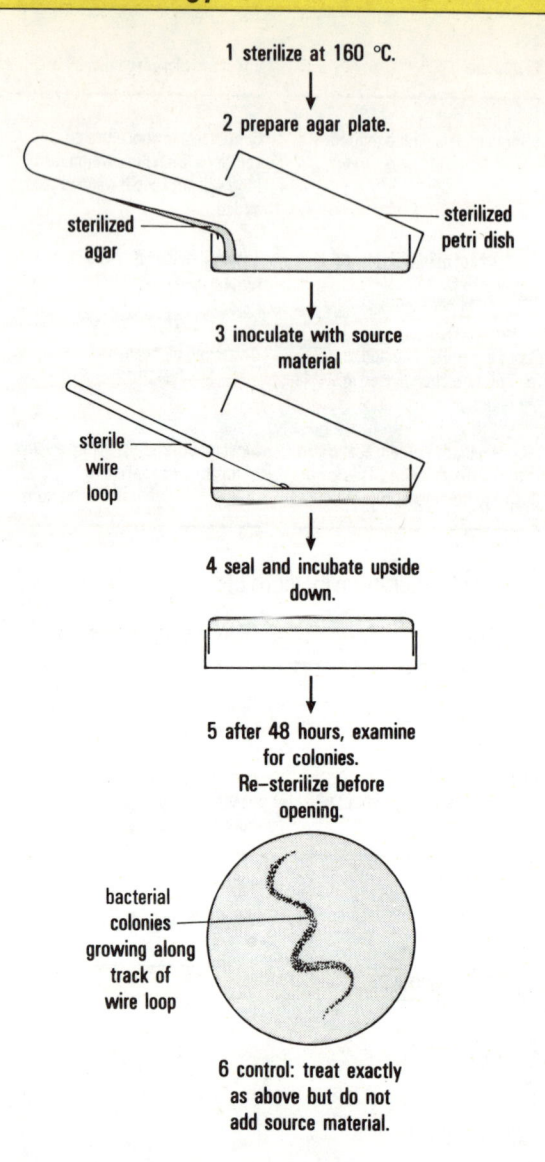

Fig 23.2 Experiments with microorganisms.

INCUBATION

1. Microorganisms will grow to form visible colonies on inoculated plates if kept at 35–45°C for 48 hours. This provides optimum conditions for many microorganisms.
2. The plates should be stored upside down. If not, condensed moisture on the lid falls on to the jelly, creating anaerobic conditions and preventing microbial growth.

CONTROL

A sterilized control plate should be treated in exactly the same way as

Diseases, food preservation and experiments 335

the inoculated plate except that no source material is added. The purpose of the control is to check that all of the equipment (including the loop) was completely sterile at the start.

SAFETY PRECAUTIONS

1. No attempt should be made to culture microorganisms from the body, because some will be pathogenic.
2. All benches, surfaces, etc., must be thoroughly disinfected before and after the experiment.
3. Re-sterilize all agar plates before inspection, e.g. by adding disinfectant.

23.7 CHECKLIST

- Common diseases:
    - causes;
    - methods of spread;
    - prevention.
- Parasites:
    - endo v. ecto.
- Lice and threadworms:
    - prevention and treatment.
- Work of WHO and FAO.
- Prevention of food poisoning:
    - temperature control;
    - contamination and cross-infection (seven precautions).
- Food preservation:
    - long-term methods:
        - canning and bottling;
        - dehydration;
        - osmotic;
        - deep freeze;
        - sterilization (UHT);
        - pickling;
    - short-term methods:
        - refrigeration;
        - pasteurization.
- Sterilization v. pasteurization.
- Experiments with agar plates:
    - sterilization;
    - inoculation;
    - incubation;
    - controls;
    - safety precautions.

23.8 EXAM QUESTIONS

1. Fig 23.3 shows the change in the number of live bacteria in a colony during a six day period.

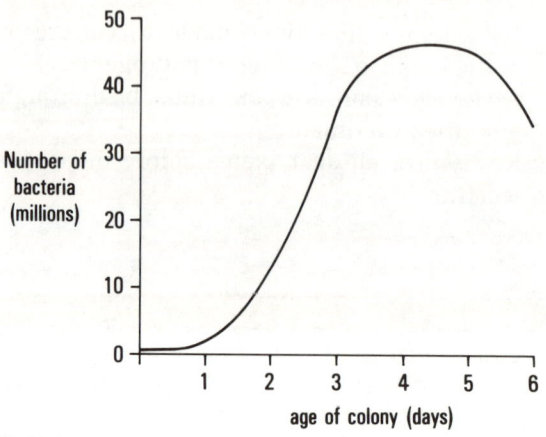

Fig 23.3

(a) (i) What was the highest number of bacteria recorded? (1)
    (ii) How long did it take for the number of bacteria to reach this figure? (1)
(b) Describe what happened to the number of bacteria between:
    (i) day 0 and day 1; (1)
    (ii) day 4 and day 5. (1)
(c) Suggest TWO reasons why the number of living bacteria fell after day 5. (2)   [*NEA: GCSE specimen question*]

2. (a) A can of cooked meat is opened and sliced on a kitchen work surface on which some fresh raw meat is also being prepared.
    (i) Identify the possible sources of infection of the canned meat once the can has been opened. (4)
    (ii) Explain why the infection of this canned meat is likely to be more dangerous than any similar infection of the raw meat. (2)
    (iii) Explain the additional risk which could exist if any of this uneaten canned meat were left in a warm kitchen and eaten at a later date. (2)
    (iv) Explain why kitchen work surfaces should be made of hard smooth non-porous materials. (6)
(b) An experiment was set up to investigate the effectiveness of various treatments on milk.

A 10 cm^3 sample of milk was placed in each of six test tubes with 1 cm^3 of an indicator dye. This dye is coloured blue and changes through pink to colourless as oxygen is removed from any solution in which it is present. The test tubes were all incubated at 35°C and the colour of the sample was recorded at intervals. Samples 2, 3, 4 and 5

Diseases, food preservation and experiments 337

were taken from freshly opened bottles of milk which had been stored for the times indicated in Table 23.4.

Table 23.4

Time from start of experiment	1 Raw milk	2 Sterilized milk 1 day old	3 Sterilized milk 4 days old	4 Pasteurized milk 1 day old	5 Pasteurized milk 4 days old	6 Sterilized milk kept in an open jug for 4 days
0.5 hour	Pink	Blue	Blue	Blue	Blue	Blue
1.0 hour	White	Blue	Blue	Blue	Pink	Blue
1.5 hours	White	Blue	Blue	Pink	White	Pink

(i) Explain the colour changes which occurred in tube **1**. (2)
(ii) Explain the differences in the results between tubes **4** and **5**. (3)
(iii) Explain the differences in the results betwen tubes **3** and **6**. (4)
(iv) Why is it advisable that the test tubes should **not** be shaken during the experiment? (2)
(c) Explain the differences between the processes of sterilization and pasteurization of milk. (4) [AEB 1984]

3 A pupil prepares a sterile agar plate in a petri dish and then coughs on to it. The dish is sealed and incubated at 37°C for 72 hours. The pupil arrives early for his next lesson, unseals his dish and opens it to examine it closely.
(a) Describe how a sterile agar plate is prepared. (2)
(b) Explain why 37°C is the temperature chosen for incubation. (1)
(c) Fig 23.4 shows the two kinds of microorganism seen growing on the agar.

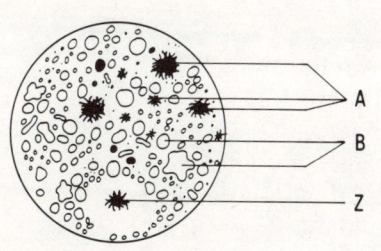

Fig 23.4

(i) Name these types of microorganisms labelled **A** and **B**. (2)
(ii) Explain the reason for the clear area around **z**. (1)
(d) Two days after examining the agar plate closely, the boy was

rushed into hospital with a serious chest infection. State two rules about microbiological experiments which were *not* followed by this pupil. (2) [*W: GCSE specimen question*]

CHAPTER TWENTY-FOUR

WATER AND WASTE

CONTENTS

▶ **24.1 The water cycle** — 341

▶ **24.2 Water purification** — 341
Sources 342
Purification of water 342
Storage of potable water 344

▶ **24.3 Sewage collection and treatment** — 344
Sewage works 344
Role of microorganisms in water 346

▶ **24.4 Disposal of solid organic wastes** — 347
Reasons for hygienic treatment of organic wastes 347
Prevention of spread of pathogens in solid organic waste 347
Refuse tips 347
Incineration 348
Recycling organic waste 348

▶ **24.5 Role of environmental health officers** — 348

▶ **24.6 Checklist** — 349

▶ **24.7 Exam questions** — 349

Water and waste

24.1 THE WATER CYCLE

Not APH

Three main processes occur in the water cycle (see Fig 24.1).

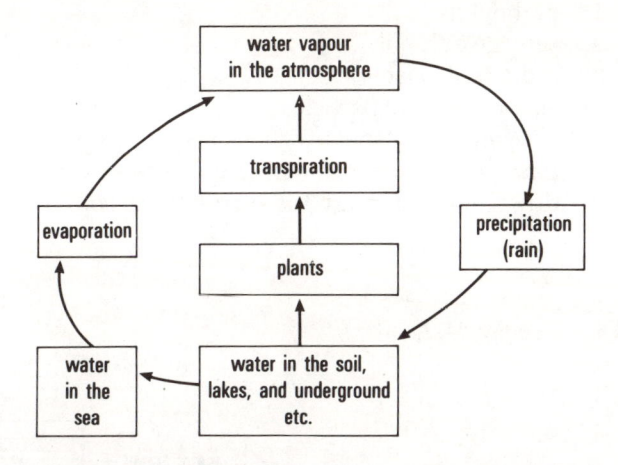

Fig 24.1 The water cycle.

1 **Evaporation** is the absorption of water from the sea, lakes and damp soil into the atmosphere.
2 **Precipitation** is the deposition of water in the form of rain.
3 **Transpiration** is the evaporation of water from the leaves of plants.

24.2 WATER PURIFICATION

The purpose of water purification is to produce 'potable' water, i.e. water fit for drinking. **Potable water** is water which is free from contaminants such as:

1 **debris**, soil particles, etc.;
2 **microorganisms**, especially pathogens, e.g. typhoid and cholera bacteria;
3 industrial **wastes**, i.e. chemicals of various kinds;
4 undesirable **tastes** or **odours**.

Human Biology

SOURCES

Drinking water is obtained from two sources:
1. deep or ground waters, e.g. deep wells sunk into natural underground lakes (called aquifers);
2. surface waters, e.g. springs, shallow wells, rivers, lakes and reservoirs.

DEEP WATER COMPARED TO SURFACE WATER

Water from deep wells or underground sources is much purer than river water and so cleaner and easier to purify. River water is likely to contain:
1. pathogens;
2. sewage effluent;
3. industrial wastes;
4. suspended soil particles.

Water from shallow wells is especially dangerous. This is because pathogens from human or cattle faeces and urine may be washed down into it through the surrounding soil.

PURIFICATION OF WATER   See Fig 24.2.

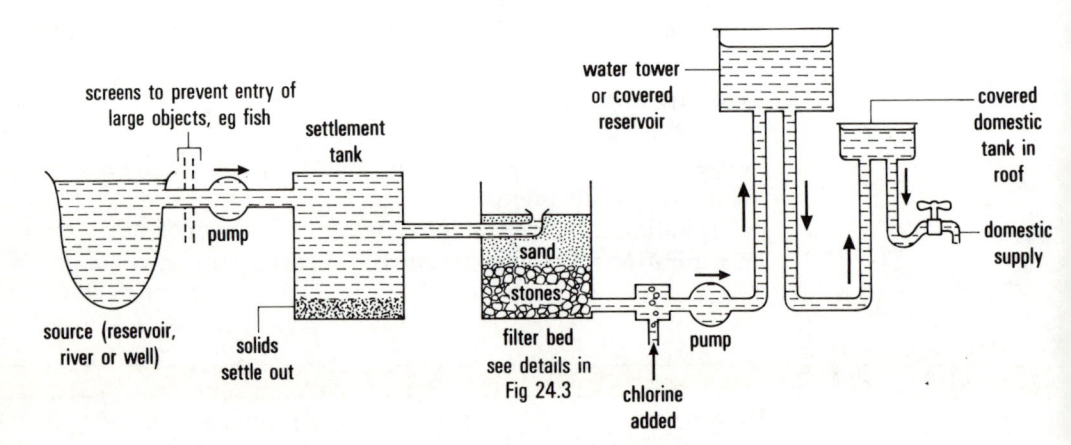

Fig 24.2 Water purification.

Water and waste

Table 24.1 Stages in the purification of water

Stage	Description	Purpose
1 Collection	Water is collected from purest available source (reservoir, aquifer, etc.).	To minimize risks of infection.
2 Screening	Water is pumped through a grid.	To keep out large floating objects, e.g. fish, pieces of wood.
3 Settling (sedimentation)	Water is allowed to stand in an open tank for 30 days or more.	(a) Suspended soil particles, etc., settle on bottom of tank. (b) Sunlight kills most pathogens after 30 days.
4 Filtration either: (a) Slow sand filter (Fig 24.3) or:	Organic material is trapped in the sand and decomposed by saprophytic bacteria. Bacterial activity creates a film of slime in which pathogens become trapped and are consumed by protozoa.	(a) Fine particles are filtered out. (b) Pathogens are removed by protozoa.
(b) Fast filter	As (a) but water is fed through under pressure, too fast for slime layer to form. Layer of alum is added to form an artificial slime layer.	As for slow filter.
5 Chlorination	Chlorine is added.	Kills all bacteria present in 30 minutes.
6 Fluoridation	In some areas, fluorides are added to the water.	To help prevent tooth decay.
7 Other additives (a) Iron or aluminium salts	Added at the sedimentation stage.	To cause suspended soil particles to coagulate ('flocculate') together and so settle more quickly.
(b) Lime	Added at the sedimentation stage.	To neutralize acidity in the water. This prevents acid water attacking iron pipes in the home.

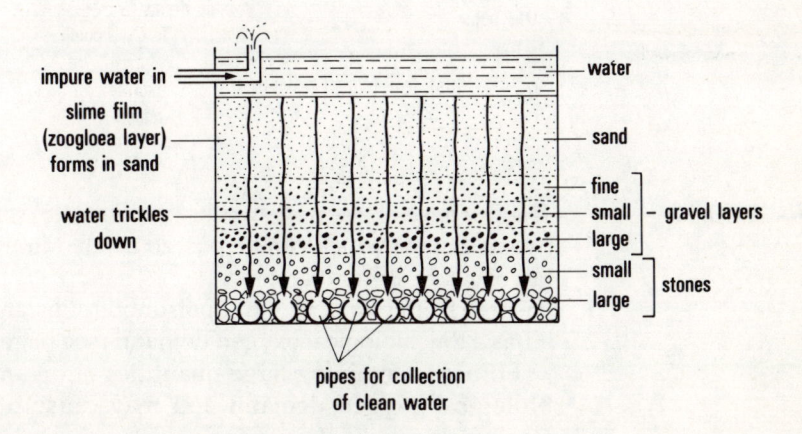

Fig 24.3 Slow sand filter (gravity filter).

Human Biology

STORAGE OF POTABLE WATER

Purified water for drinking must be stored where it cannot be contaminated, e.g. in high-level storage towers or in covered reservoirs. From these it usually descends by gravity. Domestic roof tanks must also be kept covered and secure from entry by animals of all kinds.

24.3 SEWAGE COLLECTION AND TREATMENT

Sewage is human organic wastes, i.e. urine and faeces, together with waste household water, rain and industrial wastes. It requires careful treatment after collection in order to remove pathogens, e.g. typhoid, food poisoning bacteria, etc.

Flush toilets (see Fig 24.4) are used in the home to sweep sewage rapidly into the sewers.

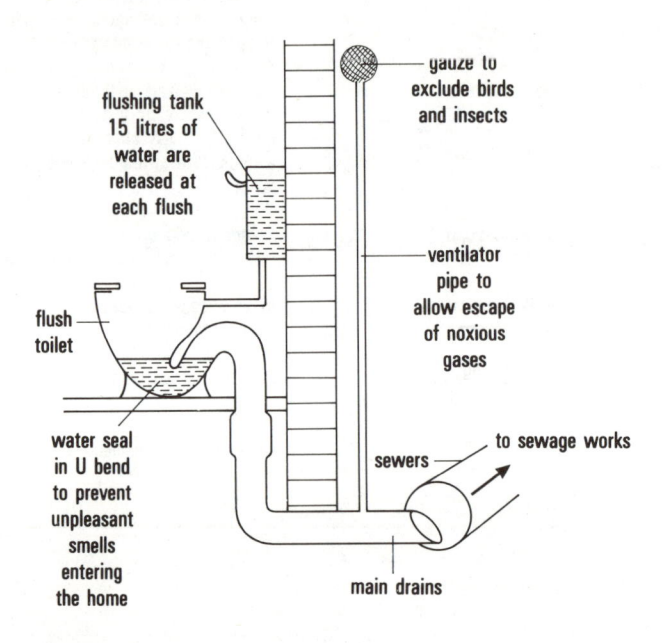

Fig 24.4 Flush toilets and sewers.

SEWAGE WORKS

The purpose of a sewage works (see Fig 24.5) is to produce an **effluent** (waste liquid) which can be passed safely into rivers. The characteristics of a safe effluent are:
1. it is free from pathogens and poisonous substances;
2. it has a low biological oxygen demand (see page 380).

Effluent containing large quantities of organic material has a high **biological oxygen demand** and may cause unnecessary growth of algae in rivers, etc.

Water and waste

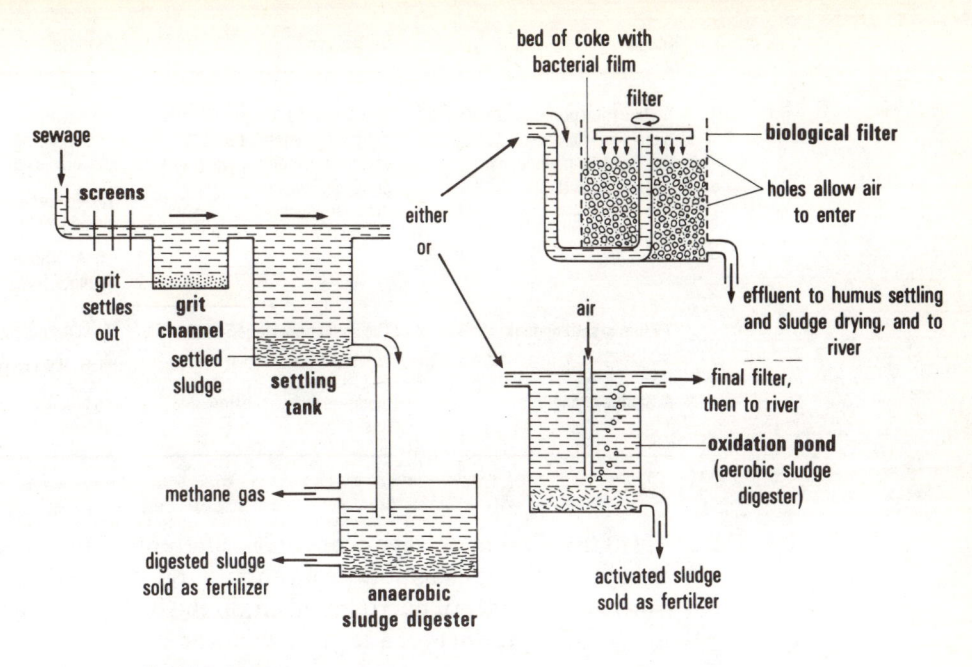

Fig 24.5 Sewage treatment.

Table 24.2 Sewage treatment

Stage	Description	Purpose
1 Screening	Sewage is passed through grids.	To remove large solid objects, e.g. nappies.
2 Grit settlement	Liquid sewage is passed along a narrow open channel.	Heavy objects, e.g. grit, settle out.
3 Settling tank	Liquid is left to stand.	Suspended solids settle out and form settled sludge.
4 Sludge digestion	Settled sludge is allowed to stand in huge tanks, which are not aerated.	Anaerobic bacteria digest sludge to produce: (a) methane gas, used to drive pumps in the works; (b) digested sludge, sold as fertilizer.
5 **Biological filter** method (older sewage works)	Liquid is spread over beds of coke by rotating arms.	(a) Decomposers in slime film break down remaining organic material.
	Perforated sides of filter and gaps between coke allow air to enter, encouraging aerobic bacteria.	(b) Protozoa, roundworms and insect larvae consume pathogens.
continues on page 346	Slime film forms containing bacteria and fungi.	(c) Effluent is now pure enough to be passed into a river.

Stage	Description	Purpose
6 **Oxidation ponds** (alternative to biological filter; newer sewage works; faster method than biological filter)	Liquid sewage pumped into large thoroughly-aerated ponds, to encourage aerobic bacteria and protozoa. Remaining organic material settles out as activated sludge.	(a) Aerobic bacteria flourish, decomposing organic wastes to carbon dioxide. (b) Protozoa consume pathogens. (c) Activated sludge sold as fertilizer.
7 **Humus settling tank**	The liquid from stage **5** passes into settling tanks.	To allow humus to settle out.
8 **Sludge drying**	Sludge is dried out before sale.	To produce dried sludge for sale as fertilizer.

Hint: Different sewage works use different methods. Don't worry about all the details but concentrate on the basic principles – especially the role of microorganisms in the biological filter.

The **final products** of a sewage works are:
1 **effluent**;
2 **sludge**, i.e. organic waste sold as fertilizer;
3 **methane gas**, used to drive the pumps, or sold.

EFFECTS OF INDUSTRIAL WASTES ON SEWAGE TREATMENT

If heavy metals such as mercury or lead enter the sewers the microorganisms in the sewage works will be poisoned. This may result in an impure effluent, or may even cause the works to be shut down.

ROLE OF MICROORGANISMS IN WATER

Hints: Be careful not to confuse the stages in water purification with the stages in sewage treatment. Unfortunately, many people lose marks every year by mixing them up.

Table 24.3 Microorganisms in water purification and sewage treatment

During water purification	During sewage treatment
Saprophytic bacteria and fungi decompose organic material in the water. Protozoa in the slime layer in the sand filter consume pathogens.	Anaerobic bacteria in sludge digestion tanks decompose sludge to produce methane gas. Aerobic bacteria decompose sludge to carbon dioxide in the biological filter and in oxidation ponds. Protozoa consume pathogens.

Water and waste

24.4 DISPOSAL OF SOLID ORGANIC WASTES

About 12 per cent of all solid rubbish produced by the average British household consists of organic waste, e.g. potato peelings, bones, etc. This must be treated hygienically.

REASONS FOR HYGIENIC TREATMENT OF ORGANIC WASTES

1. Organic wastes are decomposed by saprophytic bacteria and fungi, often producing unpleasant smells.
2. Pathogens may be able to multiply in waste food.
3. Rodents (rats, mice), birds and insects may then spread these pathogens to humans.
4. Rainwater falling on an open heap of rubbish may carry pathogens into rivers and lakes, i.e. sources of drinking water.

PREVENTION OF SPREAD OF PATHOGENS IN SOLID ORGANIC WASTE

1. **Dustbins** – see Table 24.4.
2. **Refuse collection vehicles** (dust carts), like dustbins, should be equipped with close-fitting lids to exclude wind, rain and flies. Mechanical rams are useful for compressing rubbish towards the front of the truck, preventing it from blowing away in the wind.

Table 24.4 Preventing undesired odours and the spread of disease from solid organic waste in dustbins

Precautions	Reasons
Cover with close fitting lids.	Exclude flies, rats, mice.
Lids must be clipped on.	Prevents removal by cats, dogs and foxes.
Interior to be made from galvanised steel or plastic.	Provides smooth easily-cleaned surfaces.
Insides to be lined, and lining regularly removed with the contents.	Prevents colonies of microorganisms forming on the sides.
Wash and disinfect regularly.	To remove microorganisms.

REFUSE TIPS

Much rubbish is tipped into specially hollowed-out areas in waste land, compressed (compacted) into small volume and then buried under 0.5 metre of tightly-packed soil. This is called controlled tipping.

The **advantages of burial** are:

1. rats, mice and birds cannot get at rubbish if it is buried and also tightly packed;

2 compacting the rubbish destroys fly larvae already in it, and prevents adults from feeding and laying eggs in it;
3 burial in the ground speeds decomposition by soil bacteria.

After a hollow has been filled in, the refuse will shrink in volume by up to 60 per cent. This is due to decomposition by bacteria and fungi. After shrinkage and final settlement, the tip can be grassed over. Land reclaimed in this way can be safely used for agriculture or sport.

PRECAUTIONS DURING TIPPING

To prevent the spread of pathogens by animal vectors (carriers) and wind:
1 the area around the tip must be **sprayed** to kill flies;
2 **rats** must be prevented from living in the area, e.g. by use of poison;
3 **high wire fences** should be erected to trap any rubbish blown by the wind.

INCINERATION (BURNING)

In some areas, rubbish is burnt in specially-designed furnaces. This destroys all microorganisms, and reduces all organic matter to ash which is later tipped. Metals can be recovered and sold for scrap.

RECYCLING ORGANIC WASTE

It is also possible to convert organic rubbish into compost, using a composting machine, as follows.
1 **Non-organic materials** (cans, plastics, etc.) are separated out by using a grid.
2 **The organic waste** is slowly rotated in a large drum. Controlled quantities of air and sewage sludge are added. Pathogens die off (in the rotating drum as in a sewage works).

The result is a black, organic compost which has little attraction for animal disease vectors, e.g. birds, flies, rats, etc., and can be sold. It is suitable for agricultural use because it contains minerals for plant growth and also improves the moisture-retaining capacity of poor soils.

24.5 THE ROLE OF ENVIRONMENTAL HEALTH OFFICERS

Environmental health officers (EHOs) are employed by district councils to enforce the laws on hygiene and to give advice. Their duties include the following.
1 **Housing**. EHOs inspect houses, especially hotels, etc., to check on overcrowding, the presence of vermin, and the disinfection of infected clothes.
2 **Water supply and waste disposal**. EHOs sample water supplies to

Water and waste 349

ensure that the water is potable, that sewage is efficiently dealt with, and that rubbish tips are properly constructed and free from vermin.

3 **Pollution.** EHOs check on noise pollution, and on air pollution from factory chimneys.
4 **Food hygiene.** EHOs visit food shops, cafés, caterers' premises and food factories to check that:
   (a) the premises are well lit, clean and ventilated;
   (b) toilets and washbasins are provided for staff;
   (c) equipment used in the preparation of food is kept clean;
   (d) perishable food is stored at the correct temperature;
   (e) food handlers observe proper personal hygiene (see page 332).

24.6 CHECKLIST

- Water cycle:
    evaporation;
    precipitation;
    transpiration.
- Reasons for purifying water.
- Sources of drinking water:
    purity of deep wells compared to rivers.
- Stages in water purification, especially details of slow sand filter.
- Storage of drinking water.
- Sewage.
- Purpose of flush toilet.
- Purpose of sewage treatment.
- Stages in sewage treatment, especially:
    the role of the biological filter;
    the role of microorganisms.
- Sewage v. refuse.
- Reasons for hygienic disposal of solid wastes (four).
- Dustbins:
    five ways to keep hygienic.
- Refuse collection vehicles:
    two precautions.
- Refuse tips:
    three reasons for burying and compacting;
    three other methods for keeping vectors away.
- Incineration.
- Re-cycling.
- Role of EHOs (four main functions).

24.7 EXAM QUESTIONS

1 Write a brief account of each of the following.
   (a) The use of aerobic and anaerobic organisms in the treatment of sewage. (4)

(b) The addition of chlorine, lime and coagulants (such as iron sulphate) to river water which is being treated for drinking. (4)
[*W:* GCSE specimen question]

2 (a) What are the main constituents of faeces? (2)
   (b) Name two other components of sewage. (2) [*JMB*]

3 What is the purpose of:
   (a) The U bend in a household toilet? (1)
   (b) The ventilation pipe? (1)
   (c) The holes in a percolating filter used to treat sewage?

4 (a) Why is it important that water supplied for drinking does not contain metals such as lead? (1)
   (b) Suggest why water from a deep well is cheaper to purify for drinking than water from a lake or river. (2)
[*SEG:* GCSE specimen question]

5 (a) Explain the difference between refuse and sewage. (2)
   (b) Explain the biological reasons for the burying of refuse. (6)
   (c) The refuse buried in a controlled tip will later reduce in volume by up to 60 per cent.
      (i) Explain what is happening to this refuse. (5)
      (ii) Explain what is likely to constitute the remaining 40 per cent (3)
   (d) When sewage is treated, one of the products is sludge and another is final effluent. Name TWO useful products produced as a result of the digestion of the sludge. (2) [*AEB* 1984]

PLANTS AND MAN

CONTENTS

25.1 Photosynthesis — 353
Summary of photosynthesis 354
Importance of photosynthesis 354
Use of the products of photosynthesis 354
Growth requirements of plants 355

25.2 Experiments on photosynthesis — 355

25.3 The carbon cycle — 358

25.4 The nitrogen cycle — 358
Effects of industry and agriculture on the carbon and nitrogen cycles 360

25.5 Checklist — 360

25.6 Exam questions — 360

Plants and man

Chapter 25 not required for APH.

25.1 PHOTOSYNTHESIS

Photosynthesis is the process whereby green plants trap the light energy from the sun, convert this to chemical energy and store it in the form of carbohydrates. It takes place as follows.

1 **Carbon dioxide** from the atmosphere diffuses into the leaf through small pores called **stomata**, on the underside of the leaf surface. It then diffuses into the green cells inside the leaf (see Fig 25.1).

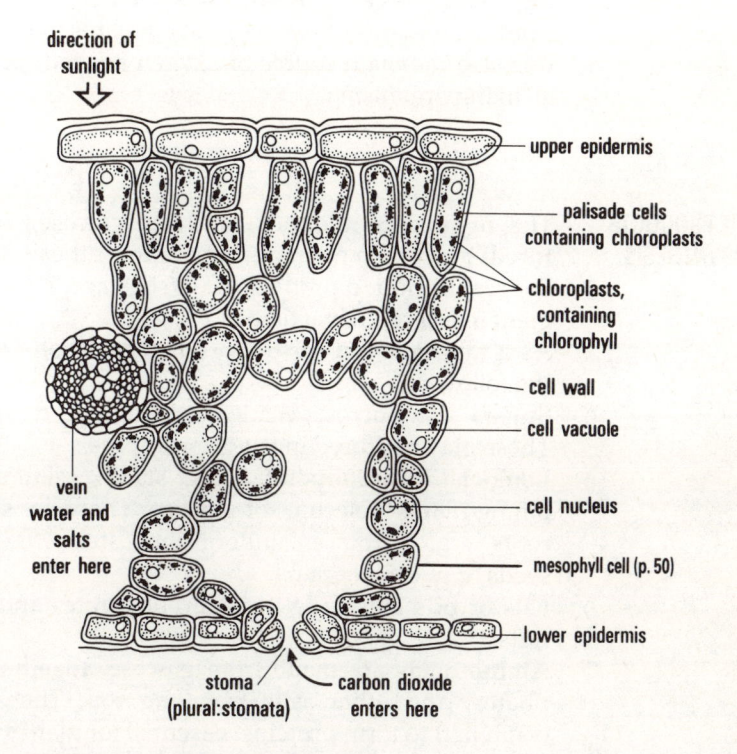

Fig 25.1 Cross section of a green leaf.

2 **Water** from the soil is taken in by the roots and passed up the stem, through the veins and into the leaf cells.

3   Inside a green leaf cell there are numerous small circular organelles known as **chloroplasts**, which contain chlorophyll.
4   The **sun's energy** is trapped by the chlorophyll and used to synthesise glucose from carbon dioxide and water.

SUMMARY OF PHOTOSYNTHESIS

$$\text{Light energy} + \text{Water} + \text{Carbon dioxide} \xrightarrow{\text{Chlorophyll}} \text{Food} + \text{Oxygen}$$

The chlorophyll acts as an enzyme. It is the green colouring found in the chloroplasts of cells in the leaves of plants.

IMPORTANCE OF PHOTOSYNTHESIS

Without photosynthesis, almost all life on earth would rapidly cease.

1   It is the ultimate source of **energy** for plants and for the animals which feed on them; and also for the bacteria and fungi which decompose the plants.
2   It is also the source of the energy obtained when wood is burnt and of the energy stored in **fossil fuels** such as oil or coal. Both are formed from the remains of partly-decayed plants in the past.
3   It is also the main source of **oxygen** needed for respiration by almost all living organisms.

USE OF THE PRODUCTS OF PHOTOSYNTHESIS

The organic compounds, such as glucose, synthesised (manufactured) by a green plant during photosynthesis are used as follows.

1   **For respiration** to produce ATP (see page 54), used by the cells of the plant for all cellular activities.
2   **As a raw material** for the production of other substances including the following.
   ◊ **Sugars**, e.g. sucrose, made by combining two molecules of glucose. These may be stored in fruits, e.g. apples.
   ◊ **Long-chain carbohydrates**, e.g. starch, cellulose, are made by combining many molecules of glucose. These are stored in underground roots, e.g. carrots; in underground stems, e.g. potato tubers; or in seeds, e.g. cereal grains.
   ◊ **Fats or oils** are made from carbohydrates and stored in seeds, e.g. nuts.
   ◊ **Amino acids** are made from glucose, together with nitrates, phosphates, and other salts from the soil. The amino acids are then combined to form proteins, essential for plant growth.

Plants and man

GROWTH REQUIREMENTS OF PLANTS

1. To manufacture **carbohydrates** by photosynthesis, plants require:
   (a) water from the soil;
   (b) carbon dioxide from the atmosphere;
   (c) light energy from the sun.
2. To manufacture **proteins**, plants require:
   (a) mineral salts such as nitrates;
   (b) phosphates from the soil.

25.2 EXPERIMENTS ON PHOTOSYNTHESIS

S, L/EA only

To demonstrate that **light**, **chlorophyll** and **carbon dioxide** are required to produce starch, see Fig 25.2.

1. Place a healthy green plant in the dark for 24 hours. This reduces the amount of starch present in the leaves at the start of the experiment.
2. Set up the plant (or a single leaf) in a situation where all requirements for photosynthesis are present (see Fig 25.2), except for the factor under test, together with a suitable control experiment.
3. After 48 hours, test the leaves from the experimental and control plants for starch.

To test a green leaf for **starch**, see Fig 25.3. To find out if **oxygen** is given off during photosynthesis, see Fig 25.4.

Table 25.1 Comparison of photosynthesis and respiration

	Photosynthesis	Respiration
Products	Glucose and oxygen.	Carbon dioxide, water and chemical energy (in the form of ATP).
Raw materials	Carbon dioxide, water and solar energy.	Glucose and oxygen.
Occurrence	Inside the chloroplasts of all green plant cells.	Inside the mitochondria of all living cells, including plants.
Timing	Occurs only in daylight.	Occurs in animal and plant tissues at all times.
Importance.	1 Traps the energy of sunlight in the form of organic substances – the chief source of energy for all living things. 2 Also the major source of oxygen on earth.	1 Converts products of photosynthesis into chemical energy for growth, movement, etc. 2 Also provides water for use by the cells.

Human Biology

1 place a green plant in darkness for 24 hours. Choose a plant with variegated (green/white) leaves for (c).

Aim: (a) is LIGHT needed for photosynthesis?

2 set up as shown:

clip a piece of black paper over part of the leaf

centre of leaf exposed (*control*)

(b) Is CARBON DIOXIDE needed?

2 put two leaves into containers as shown:

cotton wool moistened with lime water to prevent entry of CO_2

A soda lime to absorb carbon dioxide

B sodium hydrogencarbonate solution to provide additional carbon dioxide (*control*)

cotton wool moistened with water

(c) Is CHLOROPHYLL needed?

2 draw an outline of a leaf from a variegated plant:

white area

green area (*control*)

3 leave in bright light for 48 hours
4 test leaves for starch (see Fig. 25.3)

Results of starch test:

(a) **Light**

area covered by paper is stained brown by the iodine
areas exposed to light are blue black

(b) **Carbon dioxide**

A whole leaf is stained brown

B whole leaf is blue black

(c) **Chlorophyll**

white area now brown
area originally green is now blue black

Conclusions

starch is made only in the areas exposed to light. Therefore light is necessary for photosynthesis.

starch is made only in the presence of carbon dioxide, which is therefore essential for photosynthesis

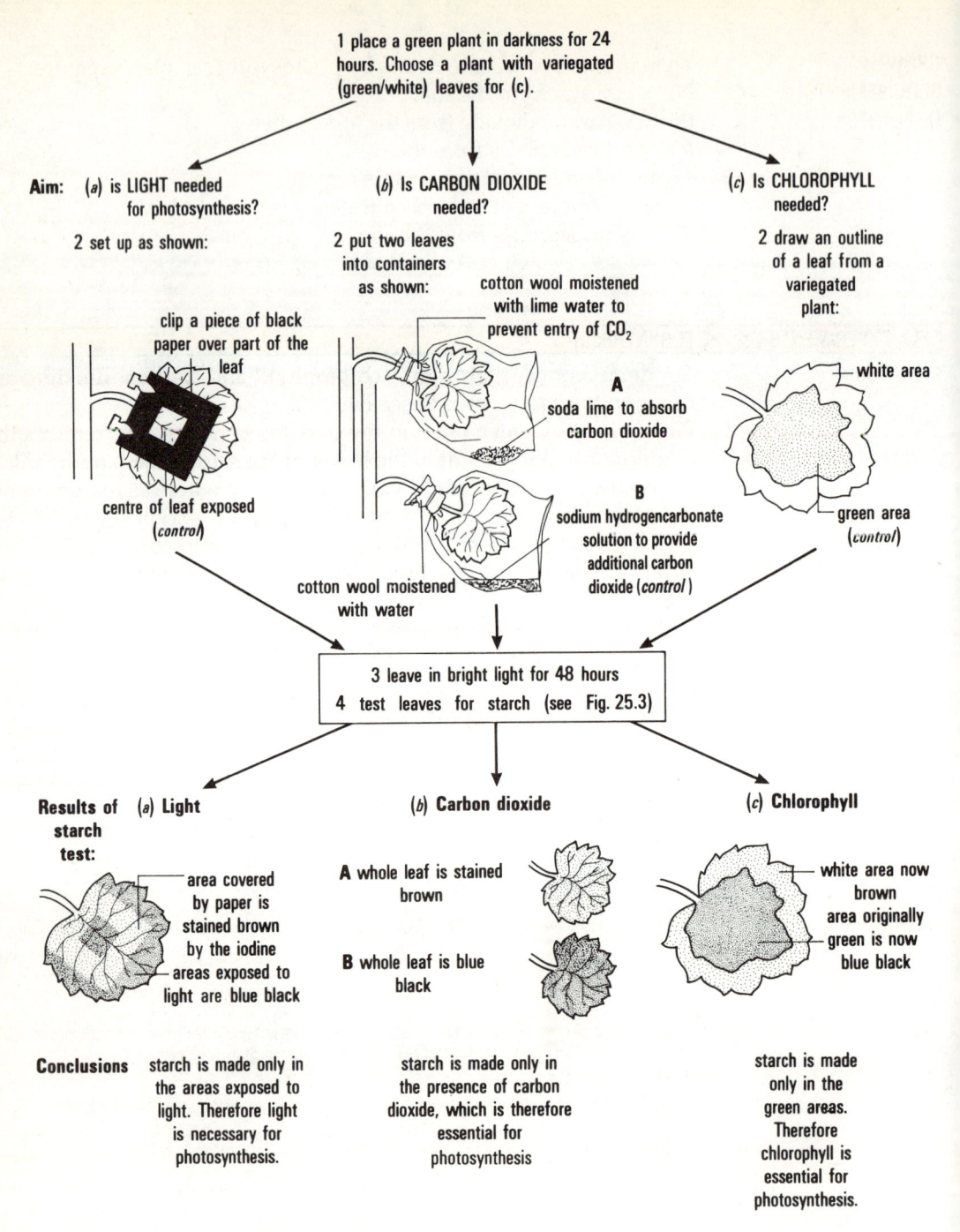

starch is made only in the green areas. Therefore chlorophyll is essential for photosynthesis.

Fig 25.2 Experiments on photosynthesis.

Plants and man

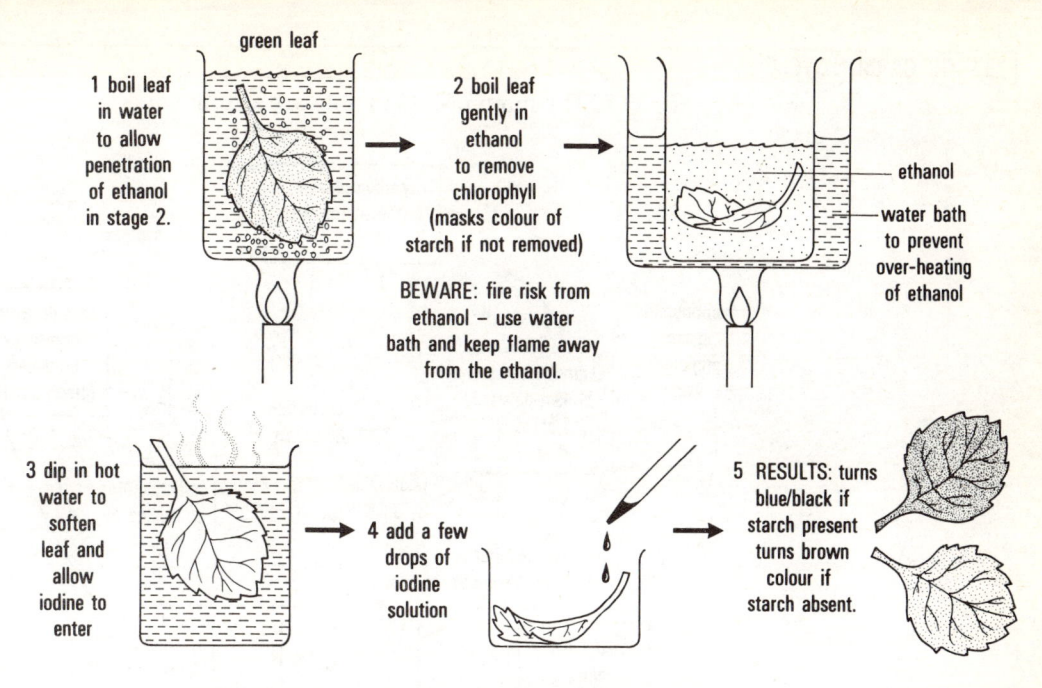

Fig 25.3 Testing a green leaf for starch. (W, S, L/EA only)

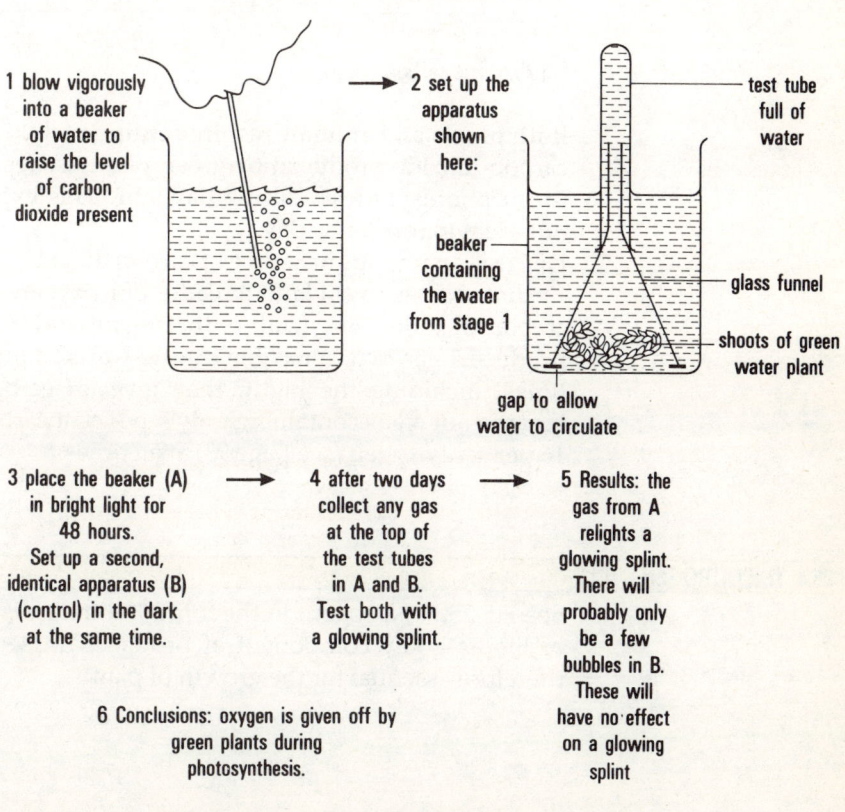

1. boil leaf in water to allow penetration of ethanol in stage 2.

2. boil leaf gently in ethanol to remove chlorophyll (masks colour of starch if not removed)

   BEWARE: fire risk from ethanol – use water bath and keep flame away from the ethanol.

   — ethanol
   — water bath to prevent over-heating of ethanol

3. dip in hot water to soften leaf and allow iodine to enter

4. add a few drops of iodine solution

5. RESULTS: turns blue/black if starch present turns brown colour if starch absent.

Fig 25.4 To find out if oxygen is given off during photosynthesis. (S, L/EA only)

1. blow vigorously into a beaker of water to raise the level of carbon dioxide present

2. set up the apparatus shown here:
   - test tube full of water
   - beaker containing the water from stage 1
   - glass funnel
   - shoots of green water plant
   - gap to allow water to circulate

3. place the beaker (A) in bright light for 48 hours. Set up a second, identical apparatus (B) (control) in the dark at the same time.

4. after two days collect any gas at the top of the test tubes in A and B. Test both with a glowing splint.

5. Results: the gas from A relights a glowing splint. There will probably only be a few bubbles in B. These will have no effect on a glowing splint

6. Conclusions: oxygen is given off by green plants during photosynthesis.

25.3 THE CARBON CYCLE

See Fig 25.5. The main points to note are as follows.

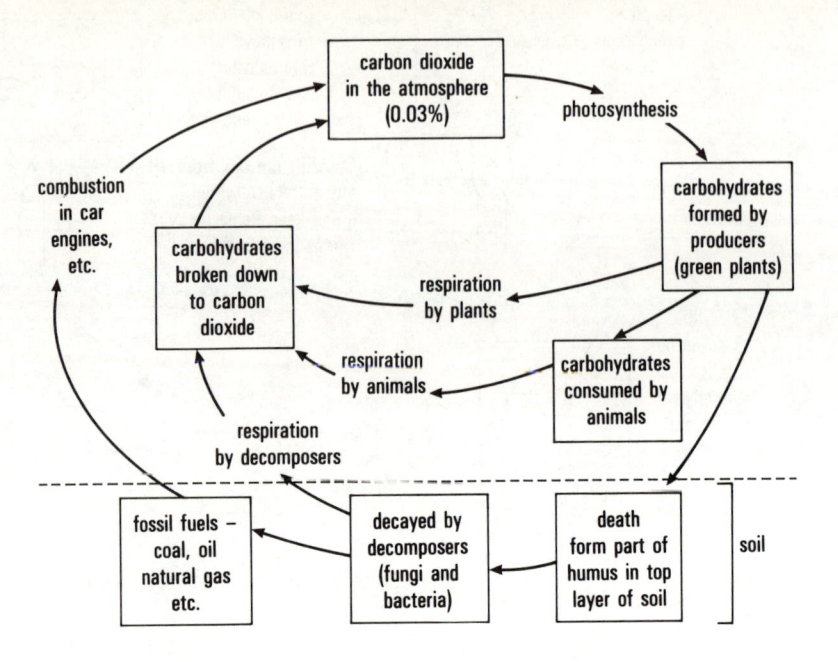

Fig 25.5 The carbon cycle.

1. **Both plants and animals respire continuously.** However, most of the carbon dioxide produced by green plant tissues is immediately used up in photosynthesis during daylight. This explains why plants do not seem to respire by day.
2. **Decay** is an important source of carbon dioxide.

    Hint: Never say 'Plants breathe out oxygen, animals breathe out carbon dioxide.' The truth is that plants never breathe, but they *do* produce a gas rich in oxygen during warm, sunny weather. At other times, including the night, they give off carbon dioxide. Animals breathe out a gas containing only 4 per cent carbon dioxide and up to 16 per cent oxygen (see page 93) at all times.

25.4 THE NITROGEN CYCLE

See Fig 25.6. Nitrogen, in the form of nitrates, is essential to all forms of life as a key component of protein. Ample nitrate in the soil is therefore essential for the growth of plants.

Plants and man

```
                    nitrogen in the
                    atmosphere 79%  ──►  removed by
                                         nitrogen fixation              air

         animals consume                         │
         plant protein                  atmospheric     industrial
                                        fixation by    fixation
   death      death                     lightning      to make
   │          excretion                                artificial
 plants                    nitrogen                    fertilizers
 produce                   fixing
 protein     nitrifying    bacteria
 from        bacteria in   in
 nitrates    the soil      leguminous
                           roots

 de-nitrifying
 bacteria in        Ammonium salts (NH₄⁺)
 water-logged       Broken down by soil
 soil               bacteria
                                                        soil
                    nitrites converted by
                    soil bacteria

                    nitrates in the soil
```

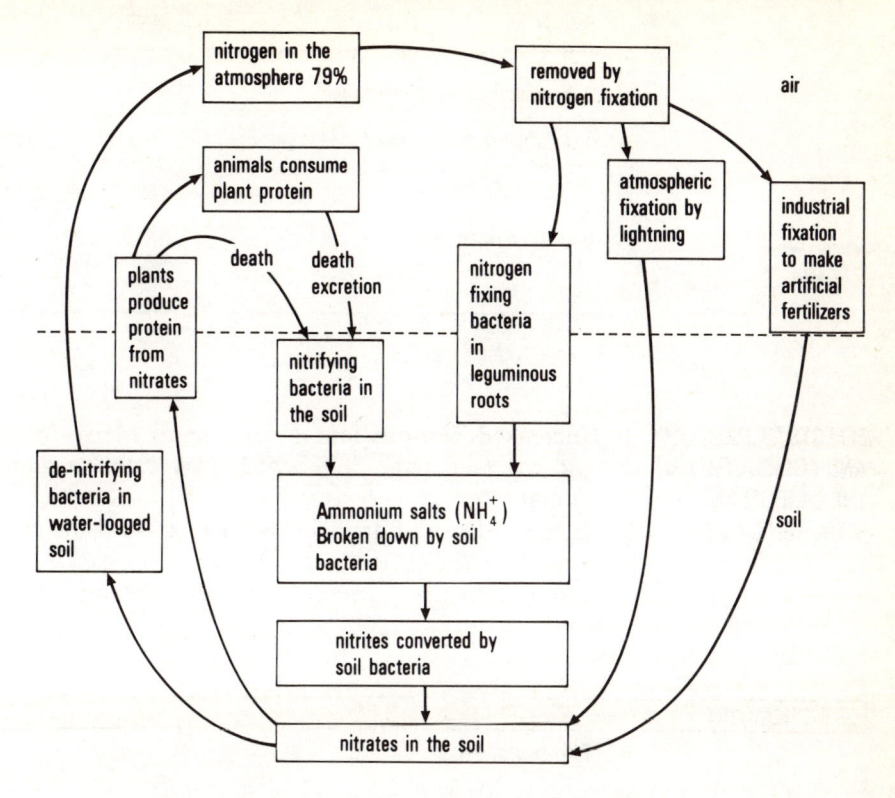

Fig 25.6 The nitrogen cycle.

Table 25.2 The nitrogen cycle

Activity	Result
1 How nitrates are formed in the soil	
(a) Nitrogen fixation	
○ Atmospheric fixation by lightning, cosmic rays, etc.	Nitrogen in the atmosphere is oxidized by lightning, etc., and falls as weak nitric acid. This turns to nitrates in the soil.
○ Nitrogen-fixing bacteria in root nodules.	Atmospheric nitrogen is converted to nitrates by nitrogen-fixing bacteria in the root nodules (swellings) of leguminous plants (clover, peas, etc.).
○ Industrial processes.	Atmospheric nitrogen is fixed during the manufacture of artificial fertilizers.
(b) Nitrification	
○ Nitrifying bacteria in the soil.	Decompose dead or excreted plant and animal proteins to nitrates, including organic fertilizers consisting of dried protein-rich plant or animal products, e.g. bone meal.

continues on page 360

Activity	Result
2 How nitrates are lost from the soil	
◊ Production of protein by plants.	Plants take in soil water containing nitrates and convert these to amino acids and then to proteins. These may later be eaten by animals.
◊ Dentrifying bacteria.	Dentrifying bacteria, found chiefly in waterlogged soil, destroy soil fertility by converting nitrates to atmospheric nitrogen.

EFFECTS OF INDUSTRY AND AGRICULTURE ON THE CARBON AND NITROGEN CYCLES

1 **Increased combustion** is leading to a rise in atmospheric carbon dioxide (see page 382) which may cause a global warming of the climate.

2 **Increased use of artificial fertilizers** is raising the levels of nitrate in soil used for agriculture. This leads to excessive run-off of surplus nitrate into lakes, causing pollution (see page 380).

25.5 CHECKLIST

- Photosynthesis:
  - definition;
  - structure of a leaf:
    - stomata;
    - chloroplasts;
    - veins;
  - importance;
  - use of products;
  - experiments: (S, L/EA only)
    - light;
    - carbon dioxide;
    - chlorophyll;
    - starch test; (S, W, L/EA only)
    - oxygen.
  - comparison with respiration.
- Growth requirements of plants.
- Carbon cycle.
- Nitrogen cycle:
  - nitrogen fixation;
  - nitrifying and de-nitrifying bacteria.

25.6 EXAM QUESTIONS

1 (a) Name three carbohydrates commonly found in plants. (3)
  (b) What is the main food reserve in a potato tuber? (1)

Plants and man

(c) Where in the plant, and by what process, is the food made? (2)

(d) Give four factors that must be present for a potato plant to grow successfully and produce tubers. (4) [Ox]

2 A school laboratory contains a green plant in a bright light with
    (i) one of its leaves partly covered in black paper and
    (ii) a second leaf enclosed in a sealed glass container containing soda lime.

(a) Explain briefly the purpose of treating each of these leaves as described. (2 each)

(b) Where had the plant been kept prior to the experiment commencing? Give a reason (2)

(c) A third leaf marked 'control' has been enclosed in another sealed container. What is probably in this container? Give a reason. (2)

3 Fig 25.7 shows the changes in the dry mass (after water has been removed) of plants grown in different intensities of light.

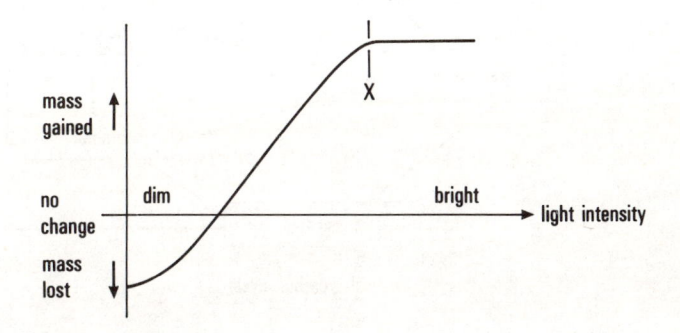

Fig 25.7

(a) Why does the dry mass of the plants increase in bright light?
(b) How do you explain a loss of dry mass in dim light?
(c) Suggest a reason why the graph levels off at the light intensity X. (5) [NI]

4 A sealed glass case containing a tray of well-grown lettuce seedlings and a number of adult blowflies was placed in a cool greenhouse. Over a period of 24 hours, the CO_2 concentration inside the container was measured and Fig 25.8 shows the percentage of CO_2 recorded over one complete day from midnight to midnight.

(a) What was the greatest concentration of CO_2 recorded, and when did it occur? (2)

(b) From the values on the graph, deduce the greatest difference in CO_2 concentrations recorded over the 24 hours. (2)

(c) Explain fully what is happening inside the container to produce the different levels of CO_2 recorded. (2)

(d) A number of bright 'strip' lights were left on in the greenhouse over a similar 24 hour period. What change in the resulting graph would you expect? (2) [NI]

Fig 25.8

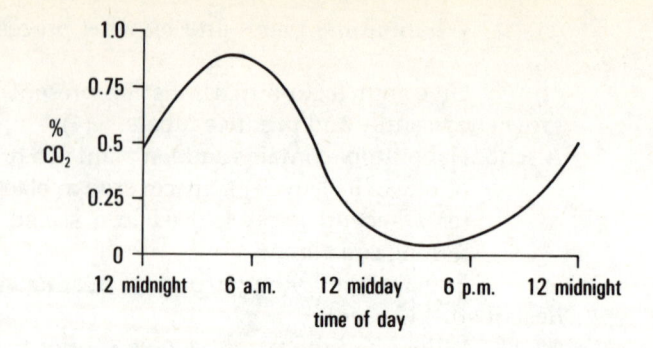

[Graph showing % CO₂ vs time of day, from 12 midnight through 6 a.m., 12 midday, 6 p.m., to 12 midnight]

Fig 25.9

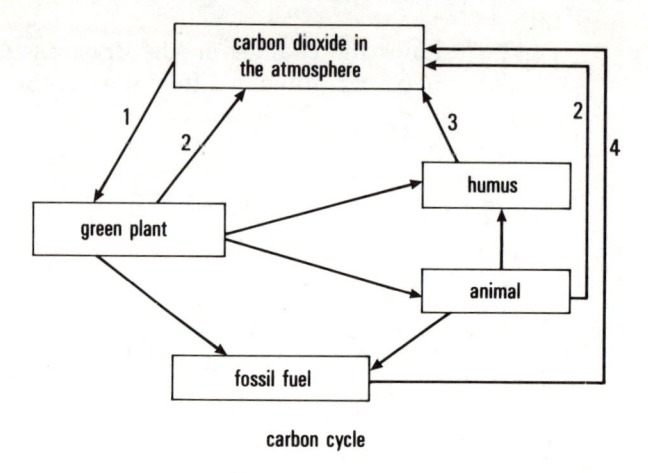

5 (a)   Fig 25.9 represents the carbon cycle.

[Diagram of carbon cycle showing: carbon dioxide in the atmosphere, green plant, humus, animal, fossil fuel, with processes labelled 1, 2, 3, 4]

carbon cycle

(i) Name the processes labelled **1, 2, 3** and **4**. (4)
(ii) Explain concisely how carbon dioxide entering a palisade cell in the leaf of a green plant becomes part of a glucose molecule. (5)
(iii) Name TWO groups of organisms that play a major role in process **3**. Where does this process normally occur?
(iv) Name ONE common fossil fuel. (1)

(b)   Explain how starch in a piece of potato becomes glucose and reaches the liver. (10)   [AEB 1985]

6 (a)   Why is nitrogen so important to all forms of life? (1)
   (b)   State how
         (i) animals and
         (ii) plants obtain their supply of nitrogen. (2)   [W]

CHAPTER TWENTY-SIX

ECOLOGY, ECOSYSTEMS AND COMMUNITIES

CONTENTS

- **26.1 Food chains, energy and feeding relationships**   365
  Community relationships   365
  Status of food chain members   366
  Alternative terms for plant and animal nutrition   366
  General features of food chains   366

- **26.2 Food webs**   368

- **26.3 Checklist**   369

- **26.4 Exam questions**   369

Ecology, ecosystems and communities

Chapter 26 not required for APH.

26.1 FOOD CHAINS, ENERGY AND FEEDING RELATIONSHIPS

Ecology is the study of living things in relation to their environment. All living organisms live in communities, interacting together and with the non-living influences on them, such as climate, water currents or soil.

A **community** consists of populations of different species living together within an ecosystem.

An **ecosystem** is an area in which organisms interact with each other and the environment to form a self-sustaining unit. For example, a pond is an ecosystem containing a community of organisms such as pondweed, protozoa, *Daphnia* (water fleas) and small fish.

COMMUNITY RELATIONSHIPS

Within a community, there are complex relationships between the species, called food chains and food webs.

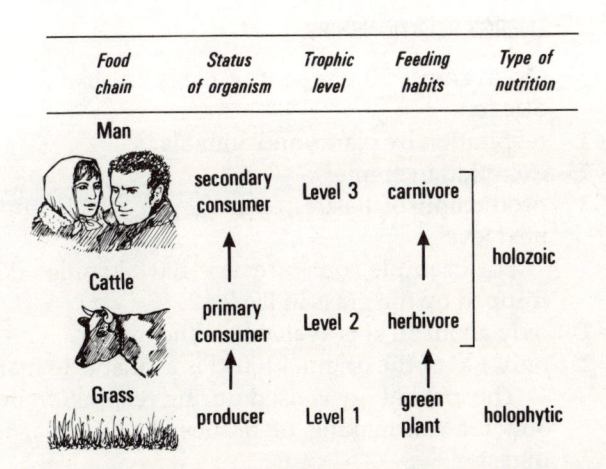

Food chain	Status of organism	Trophic level	Feeding habits	Type of nutrition
Man	secondary consumer	Level 3	carnivore	holozoic
Cattle	primary consumer	Level 2	herbivore	holozoic
Grass	producer	Level 1	green plant	holophytic

Fig 26.1 Food chains and feeding relationships

A **food chain** describes the feeding, and therefore energy, relationships between species which feed on each other (see Fig 26.1). All food chains involve at least three species:
1. the first is always a green plant;
2. the second is an animal which feeds on the plant;
3. the third is an animal feeding on the second.

STATUS OF FOOD CHAIN MEMBERS

1. **Producers** are always green plants, which add energy and biomass to the first stage in a food chain.
2. **Consumers** are always animals which feed either on green plants (primary consumers) or on other animals (secondary or tertiary consumers, etc.).
3. **Decomposers** are fungi or bacteria which break down dead plants and animals, so resulting in losses of energy and biomass.

Trophic level refers to each stage in a food chain. Level 1 is the producer stage, level 2 is the primary consumer, and so on upwards.

ALTERNATIVE TERMS FOR PLANT AND ANIMAL NUTRITION

1. **Holophytic nutrition** is the building up of complex organic substances from simple inorganic substances by plants (producers), usually by means of photosynthesis.
2. **Holozoic nutrition** is the taking in and digestion of complex organic substances by animals (consumers).
3. **Saprophytic nutrition** is the break-down of organic plant and animal remains to inorganic substances by fungi and bacteria (decomposers).

GENERAL FEATURES OF FOOD CHAINS

ENERGY RELATIONSHIPS

On average, 90 per cent of energy is lost at each stage in the chain, due to:
1. respiration by plants and animals;
2. excretion in animals;
3. production of tissues, e.g. bones, which cannot be digested at the next level.

For example, out of every 100 kilojoules (kJ) of the sun's energy trapped by the grass in Fig 26.2:
1. only about 10 kJ is available to the cattle;
2. only 1 kJ of the original 100 kJ is available to man.

The lost energy is used during respiration by both grass and cattle, and for the making of tissues, e.g. bones, which humans cannot digest.

Ecology, ecosystems and communities

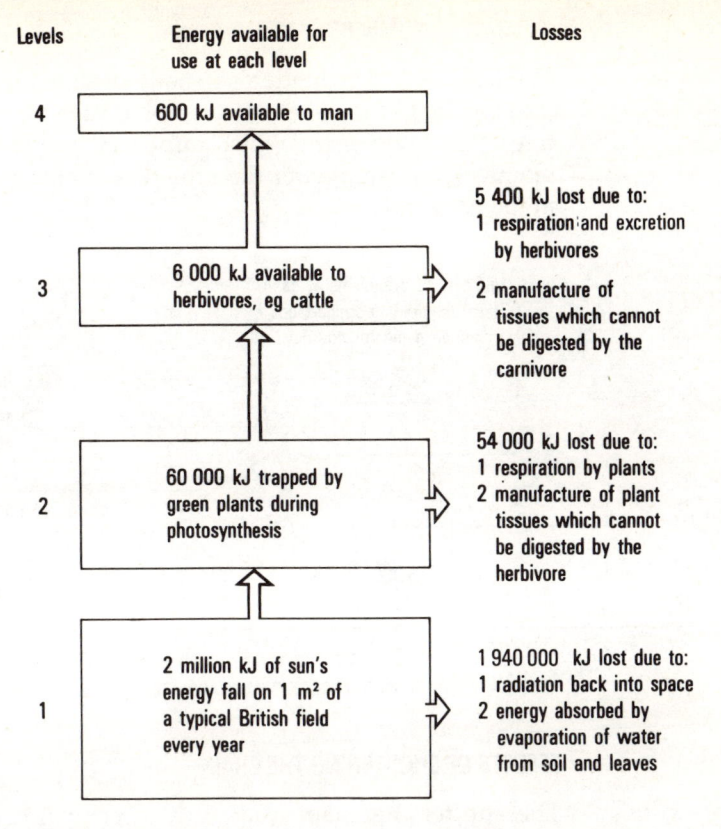

Levels	Energy available for use at each level		Losses
4	600 kJ available to man	↑	
3	6 000 kJ available to herbivores, eg cattle	↑ ⇨	5 400 kJ lost due to: 1 respiration and excretion by herbivores 2 manufacture of tissues which cannot be digested by the carnivore
2	60 000 kJ trapped by green plants during photosynthesis	↑ ⇨	54 000 kJ lost due to: 1 respiration by plants 2 manufacture of plant tissues which cannot be digested by the herbivore
1	2 million kJ of sun's energy fall on 1 m² of a typical British field every year	⇨	1 940 000 kJ lost due to: 1 radiation back into space 2 energy absorbed by evaporation of water from soil and leaves

Fig 26.2 How energy is lost in a food chain based on 1m² of field.

PYRAMID OF BIOMASS

The biomass, measured in dry weight, falls sharply at each stage (see Fig 26.3).

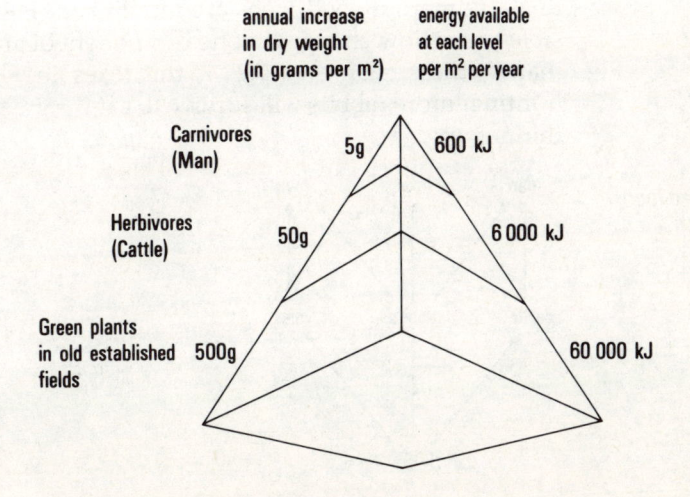

Fig 26.3 Pyramid of biomass on 1m² of field.

annual increase in dry weight (in grams per m²) / energy available at each level per m² per year

Carnivores (Man) — 5g — 600 kJ
Herbivores (Cattle) — 50g — 6 000 kJ
Green plants in old established fields — 500g — 60 000 kJ

PYRAMID OF NUMBERS

The numbers of individuals usually decline rapidly at each level also (see Fig 26.4). However, this is not always true. For example, an oak tree is a single plant which supports hundreds of insects, but its biomass is much greater than the total biomass of the insects above it in the pyramid.

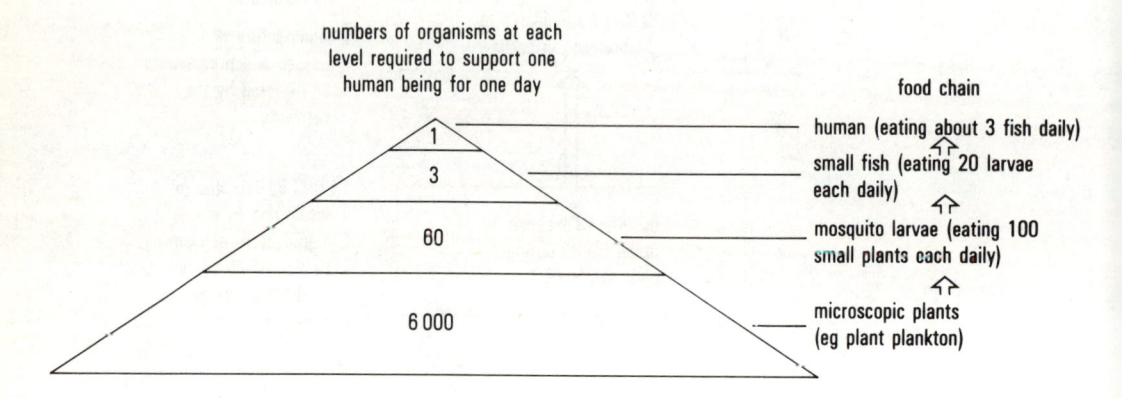

```
numbers of organisms at each
level required to support one
human being for one day                              food chain

              1  ─────────────────  human (eating about 3 fish daily)
                                    ⇧
             3   ─────────────────  small fish (eating 20 larvae
                                    each daily)
                                    ⇧
            60   ─────────────────  mosquito larvae (eating 100
                                    small plants each daily)
                                    ⇧
          6 000  ─────────────────  microscopic plants
                                    (eg plant plankton)
```

Fig 26.4 Pyramid of numbers in a tropical lake.

EFFECTS OF SHORTENING THE CHAIN

The shorter the chain, the more efficient it becomes. For example, suppose a small farmer just supports five people by growing cattle on 20 acres of pasture. If he grows cereals instead of cattle, he can feed at least 10 people on the same land.

26.2 FOOD WEBS

A **food web** is a number of interlinked food chains. In most ecosystems, numerous food webs are interlinked. Food webs make it possible to see how changes in one component of an ecosystem can affect many others. For example, if the foxes in Fig 26.5 are killed by hunting, more rabbits will survive to eat the grass, so the cattle will be thinner, etc.

Fig 26.5 Simplified food web in a field.

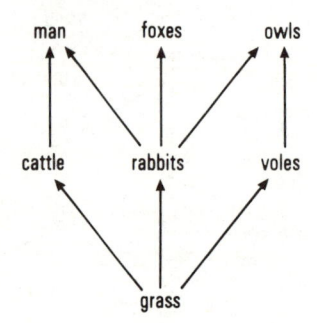

```
      man      foxes     owls
       ↑        ↑↑        ↑
       │       ╱  ╲       │
      cattle  rabbits   voles
       ↑        ↑         ↑
        ╲       │        ╱
              grass
```

Ecology, ecosystems and communities

26.3 CHECKLIST

- Community.
- Ecosystem.
- Food chain.
- Producers, consumers, decomposers.
- Holozoic, holophytic, saprophytic.
- Carnivores, herbivores, omnivores, predators.
- Energy losses in food chains.
- Pyramid of biomass.
- Pyramid of numbers.
- Food web.

26.4 EXAM QUESTIONS

1. Explain why photosynthesis is essential for all life, including human life. In your account include the terms producer, carnivore, herbivore, food chains to show that you know what they mean. (4)
[W GCSE specimen question]

2. Name
   (a) the source of energy of any food chain involving a producer, a herbivore and a carnivore. (1)
   (b) the process by which this energy is incorporated into organic compounds. (1)
   (c) the gas given out by the producers and taken in by the consumers. (1)

3. Fig 26.6 shows a simplified pyramid of biomass.

Fig 26.6

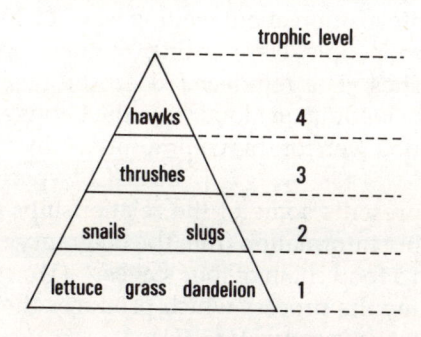

```
                    trophic level
              /\
             /hawks\         4
            /--------\
           / thrushes \      3
          /------------\
         / snails  slugs\    2
        /----------------\
       /lettuce grass dandelion\  1
      /--------------------------\
```

   (a) State which tropic level contains the producers.
   (b) State which trophic level contains the secondary consumers.
   (c) At which trophic level does holophytic nutrition occur? (3)
[AEB 1984]

4. Energy flow in a food chain:
   In a pond in the summer, microscopic plants are eaten by water fleas such as *Daphnia*. These in turn, are eaten by fish but only a small proportion (perhaps only 10 per cent) of the energy is used for fish growth.

Fill in the boxes **B**, **C** and **D** in Fig 26.7 to account for the energy losses in the fish. (3) [*Ox*]

Fig 26.7

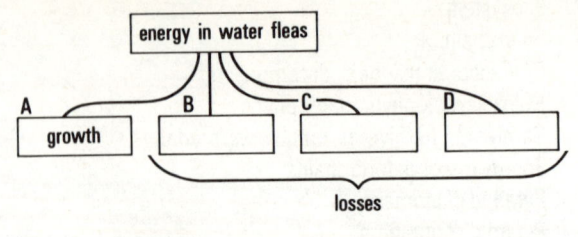

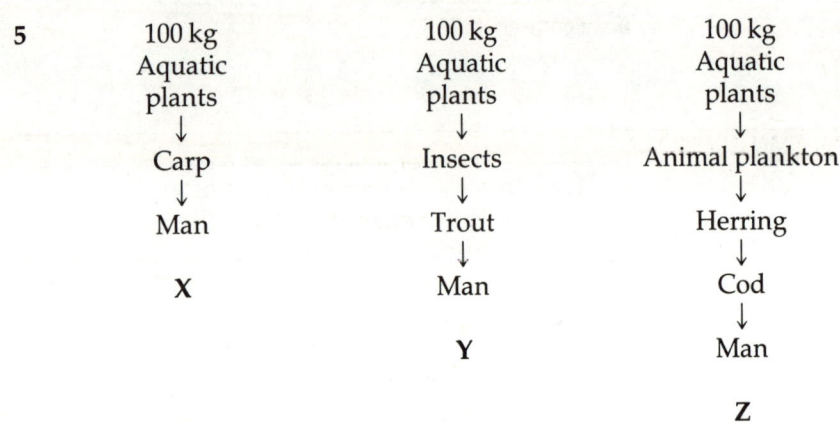

```
              energy in water fleas
         ┌──────┬──────┬──────┐
      A  │   B  │   C  │   D  │
    ┌────┤      │      │      │
    │growth│    │      │      │
    └──────┴────┴──────┴──────┘
                losses
```

5
100 kg Aquatic plants	100 kg Aquatic plants	100 kg Aquatic plants
↓	↓	↓
Carp	Insects	Animal plankton
↓	↓	↓
Man	Trout	Herring
	↓	↓
X	Man	Cod
		↓
	Y	Man
		Z

Which of the above food chains would make most of the energy from the 100 kg of plants available to man? Give a reason. (2)

[*NEA*: GCSE specimen question]

6 In an investigation of a Lapp community in Northern Scandinavia the following information about feeding was obtained.

ID The Lapp people were eating reindeer meat and berries from various bushes. The reindeer fed on the bushes and lichens. Mosquitoes were feeding on blood from the Lapps and the reindeer.

Draw a food web for this community. (3)

[*NEA*: GCSE specimen question]

7 Fig 26.8 represents some of the relationships of organisms living in the sea. Using information from the diagram:
  (a)   List a food chain of four stages. (1)
  (b)   Name the process which produces the carbon dioxide which is released into the sea water. (1)
  (c)   Name the source of energy for this food web. (1)

[*AEB* 1983]

8 Lake Victoria, in East Africa, used to contain a large population of crocodiles which ate lung fish (not used as food by man). The lung fish ate tilapia fish (very important as food for man). Tilapia eat plankton. The crocodiles were eliminated by hunting.
  (a)   Explain what you would expect to happen to:
    (i) the population of lung fish; (1)

Fig 26.8

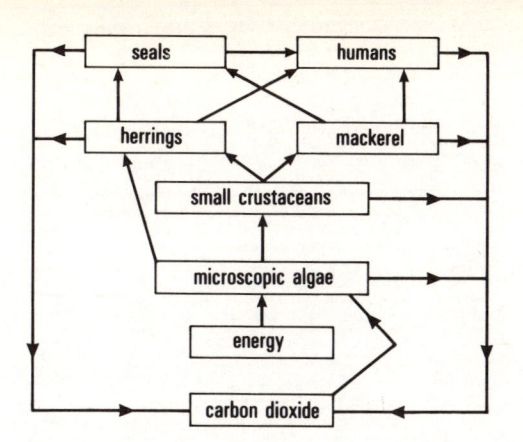

[Food web diagram: carbon dioxide and energy → microscopic algae → small crustaceans → herrings and mackerel → seals and humans; mackerel also eaten by humans; herrings eaten by seals]

        (ii) the tilapia fishing industry near Lake Victoria. (1)

(b)   In this food chain, name
    (i) the producer
    (ii) the herbivore
    (iii) TWO secondary consumers. (4)

[W: GCSE specimen question]

CHAPTER TWENTY-SEVEN

HUMAN POPULATIONS, CONSERVATION AND POLLUTION

CONTENTS

27.1 Population and the development of agriculture — 375

27.2 Causes and effects of the population explosion — 376
Changes in birth and death rates 376
Causes for the decline in death rate 376
Consequences of uncontrolled population growth 376

27.3 Preventing future crises — 377
Population control 377
Increased food production 377

27.4 Pollution of air, land and water — 378
Special problems with water pollution 380
Food chains and pollution 381
Energy sources and pollution 382

27.5 Insecticides — 383
Advantages 383
Disadvantages 383
The ideal insecticide 383
Biological control as an alternative to insecticides 383

27.6 Conservation and land use — 384
Competing demands for land   384
Conservation and planning for amenity and leisure   384

27.7 Checklist — 384

27.8 Exam questions — 385

Human populations, conservation and pollution

27.1 POPULATION AND THE DEVELOPMENT OF AGRICULTURE

The number of people in the world grew steadily from about 6000 BC until about 1800 AD (see Fig 27.2 on page 385), chiefly due to slow improvements in agriculture. In earliest times, human beings lived by hunting and gathering the available food over a large area, as the Bushmen and Inuit (Eskimoes) still do in a few cases. The development of settled agriculture made larger populations possible.

N only

Table 27.1 Stages in the development of agriculture

Way of life	Characteristics	Sustainable population density
1 Hunter/gatherer, e.g. Arctic Inuit (Eskimoes) Bushmen (Southern Africa).	Live by hunting available wild animals, e.g. seals, or by gathering roots and berries (Bushmen). Fully integrated with local ecosystem. No attempt to increase the resources available by management, i.e. by agriculture.	Very low. Several hundred acres required to sustain each family.
2 Pastoralism, e.g. Lapps in Scandinavia, Masai in Kenya.	Live by herding, and managing animals so that their numbers are greater than in the wild, e.g. Lapps herd reindeer, Masai herd cattle. Local ecosystem can be temporarily damaged by overgrazing. No attempt at settled agriculture – animals are constantly moved from pasture to pasture.	Higher than hunter/gatherers, but still low. Each tribe requires a large area in which to keep its animals.
3 Rural/agricultural, e.g. peasant farmers in India, China, Africa.	Settled communities making serious efforts to increase the resources available by managing the land. Local ecosystem permanently changed.	Larger densities possible because feeding on plants is much more energy-efficient than feeding on animals (see page 368).
4 Urban e.g. most British communities.	Urban populations exist by feeding off surplus food produced by efficient rural communities. Become specialists in making machinery, etc. to exchange for surplus food. Local ecosystem may be in serious danger from pollution.	High densities now possible, as long as surplus food is available.

Human Biology

27.2 CAUSES AND EFFECTS OF THE POPULATION EXPLOSION

The population explosion describes the very rapid growth in world population since 1800, due chiefly to a dramatic drop in death rates.

CHANGES IN BIRTH AND DEATH RATES

1. **The birth rate** is the number of live births per 1000 people, per year.
2. **The death rate** is the number of deaths per 1000 people per year.

The reason for the huge increase in human population is that the death rate has been greatly reduced so that it is now well below the worldwide birth rate.

CAUSES FOR THE DECLINE IN DEATH RATE

The death rate has fallen because of the following.

1. **Agriculture has greatly improved** due to use of fertilizers, irrigation, removal of forests, use of machinery,. e.g. combine harvesters, and selective breeding of crops and animals to produce more food.
2. Increased food supplies have resulted in **stronger growing children**, who are better able to resist infection.
3. Standards of living generally have risen due to better agriculture and improved technology, so increasing national wealth. This has led to:
   (a) **better standards of housing**, leading to less overcrowding and so less spread of infection;
   (b) **water supplies** free from pathogens due to chlorination and water purification;
   (c) **hygienic sewage treatment**, which has also reduced the spread of pathogens.
4. **Medical research** has resulted in the discovery of better drugs, antibiotics, the use of vaccination and aseptic surgery.

CONSEQUENCES OF UNCONTROLLED POPULATION GROWTH

FOOD SHORTAGES

Food shortages lead to malnutrition and starvation.

Malnutrition means under-feeding, i.e. receiving a diet lacking sufficient energy or other essentials such as vitamins or protein.

Starvation means death from lack of food.

OVERCROWDING

Overcrowding leads to an increase in disease, crime, vandalism, drug-taking, etc.

Human populations, conservation and pollution

COMPETITION FOR LAND

Competition for land causes increased possibilities of wars and disturbances.

DEFORESTATION

Deforestation as trees are cut down for fuel and to provide more space for agriculture leads to:
1. soil erosion – if trees are cut down on hillsides, the fertile topsoil may be washed away into rivers and crops cannot then be grown on the bare hillsides;
2. less absorption of carbon dioxide from the atmosphere by photosynthesis
3. a locally drier climate because trees give off large quantities of water from their leaves.

POLLUTION

Increasing pollution from the use of pesticides to produce more food and from increased use of fuels to meet increasing demands for energy.

WATER SHORTAGES

Water shortages occur whenever the population outgrows the local supplies.

27.3 PREVENTING FUTURE CRISES

POPULATION CONTROL

To stabilize world population, the birth rate must be reduced until it equals the death rate. This can be achieved by:
1. educating parents to restrict their families to two or three children at the most;
2. providing cheap, effective, and acceptable methods of contraception and birth control (see page 241).

INCREASED FOOD PRODUCTION

1. **Selective breeding** of crops and livestock.
2. Increased use of **fertilizers** (see Table 27.2).
3. **Increased use of chemicals** to kill weeds (herbicides), fungi (fungicides), insects (insecticides) and pests generally (pesticides).
4. Increased use of **resources** not currently exploited, e.g. fishing for Antarctic krill (shrimps) and fish farming in lakes, etc.
5. **More use of plant proteins**, e.g. proteins from soya bean or 'single cell proteins' manufactured by single-celled microorganisms such as

yeasts. Cheap proteins from plants could replace expensive animal proteins to a much greater extent than at present.

6 **Growth of food crops** instead of crops grown for cash, e.g. tobacco, which take up valuable space for growing food.
7 **Irrigation** (providing a supply of water) to desert areas.

Food distribution can also be improved. Efficient farming in North America and Europe has produced huge food surpluses, e.g. the EEC 'butter mountains'. Poor countries cannot afford to buy these and rich countries do not need them.

Table 27.2 Types of fertilizers

Name	Purpose	Characteristics
Organic fertilizers, e.g. sludge, compost, manure.	1 To improve structure of light soils so that they can be worked more easily. 2 May also break down slowly to yield nitrates for plant growth.	Slow acting; difficult to apply; but cause no pollution problems.
Inorganic fertilizers, e.g. nitrates, sulphates, phosphates.	To provide requirements for protein manufacture, i.e. plant growth.	Fast acting; easily applied; but excess use causes pollution.

CONSERVATION AND RECYCLING

1 Existing supplies of key minerals, e.g. zinc, may soon be exhausted. Solution is to re-cycle scarce materials from scrap and develop substitutes, e.g. plastics.
2 **Energy needs to be conserved**, e.g. by insulating houses, installing better controls, e.g. thermostats, and generally making more efficient use of existing sources. Also more research into renewable energy sources is required (see page 382).
3 **Recycling**, i.e. re-use, of paper helps to reduce the need for deforestation.

27.4 POLLUTION OF AIR, LAND AND WATER

Pollution is the harm caused to the biosphere, i.e. life on earth, by waste substances or other side-effects of human activity. This includes noise as well as carbon dioxide and radioactive discharges.

Human populations, conservation and pollution

Table 27.3 Air pollution

Air pollutants	Source	Damage caused	Prevention
1 Asbestos particles	Used in buildings.	Fibres can cause lung cancer.	Remove from buildings.
2 Carbon dioxide	◊ Burning of wood, coal, oil, gas by industry and in car engines. ◊ Respiration by animals, deforestation, increased use of cars and worldwide growth of industry is causing a slow build-up of carbon dioxide in the atmosphere.	◊ Likely to raise world temperatures, causing serious disturbance to climate. ◊ Global warming may melt icecaps, leading to flooding of many major cities.	No easy solution in sight but possible alternatives are: ◊ use nuclear or renewable, energy sources instead of combustible fuels; ◊ find alternative energy sources for cars, e.g. batteries; ◊ plant more trees.
3 Carbon monoxide	Car exhaust.	◊ Highly poisonous, replaces oxygen in haemoglobin. ◊ Can accumulate in urban traffic jams and contribute to lack of vigilance and to heart attacks.	Modify car engines to ensure complete conversion of carbon monoxide to carbon dioxide (but see **2**).
4 **Cigarette smoke** in the atmosphere.	Smokers.	Effects on non-smokers include asthma, irritation to eyes and lung cancer.	Ban all smoking in public places.
5 **Lead** (see also Table 27.4)	Car exhausts; added to petrol to improve engine performance.	Damage to nervous system, especially in children.	Use unleaded petrol. Do not pick crops, e.g. blackberries, from roadsides.
6 Nitrogen oxides	Car exhausts.	Contributes to the formation of acid rain.	Modify car engines.
7 Noise	◊ Aeroplane and car engines. ◊ Popular music at discos, etc. ◊ Noise from factory machines.	Permanent damage to hearing if noise is persistent.	◊ Restrict flights. ◊ Develop quieter car and aero engines. ◊ Reduce traffic noise from roads by landscaping, use of quieter surfaces, planting of trees, erection of soundproof barriers, double glaze windows of adjacent homes. ◊ Health and Safety at Work Act requires use of ear plugs if using noisy machinery.
8 Radioactive discharges	Tests of nuclear weapons and accidents at nuclear power stations, e.g. Chernobyl in Russia.	◊ Causes cell mutations, and therefore cancer, especially leukaemia. ◊ If deposited on ground, can become concentrated at the top of the food chain. Reindeer in Lapland had to be destroyed after eating radioactive lichen following Chernobyl disaster.	◊ Ban nuclear tests. ◊ Devise safer nuclear power stations. ◊ Switch to other forms of energy production.
9 Soot particles	◊ Burning of wood in bonfires or coal in domestic or factory fires. ◊ Causes smog (= smoke + fog) in damp conditions.	Causes bronchitis by interfering with cleaning mechanism of lungs (see page 302).	British air now much cleaner since Clean Air Act (1956) allowed creation of smoke less zones, where smoke is forbidden.

continues on page 380

Air pollutants	Source	Damage caused	Prevention
10 Sulphur dioxide	◊ Burning of coal and oil in power stations. ◊ Car exhausts. ◊ Blown by prevailing winds, e.g. from Britain to Scandinavia.	◊ Mixes with water to form acid rain. Lowers pH of soil above neutral rocks, so killing fish in lakes and harming trees. ◊ Also damages buildings because acid rain dissolves the stonework.	◊ Install high chimneys to protect local areas – but this merely transfers the problem elsewhere. ◊ Install scrubbers to wash out sulphur dioxide from factory fumes.

Table 27.4 Land pollution

Land pollutant	Source	Damage caused	Prevention
1 Insecticides, herbicides, etc.	To control disease vectors, e.g. mosquitoes, and weeds.	Accumulate in food chains and affect top consumers, e.g. hawks. Can persist in soil for many years.	Ban dangerous examples, e.g. DDT is banned in Britain.
2 Radioactive wastes	Power stations.	Cell mutations, leading to cancers.	Bury deeply under ground in lead and concrete casings.

SPECIAL PROBLEMS WITH WATER POLLUTION

BIOLOGICAL OXYGEN DEMAND

If untreated sewage is discharged into fresh water, it will be decomposed by bacteria in the water. These will multiply rapidly and use up all the oxygen present, so that fish and other animals will die.

Biological oxygen demand (BOD) means the demand for oxygen created by the presence of organic material in water. Untreated sewage has a high BOD because it is rich in organic material.

The organic waste from intensive farming, e.g. high density pig units, can be so concentrated that it overwhelms the capacity of sewage works, leading to effluent with high BOD.

EUTROPHICATION

This is the appearance of rich growths of algae, called **algal blooms**, which form on the surface of water. It can be caused by the presence of excess nitrates from neighbouring over-fertilized fields, and phosphates from detergents. When these masses of algae die, they also create a high BOD and may cause the death of fish.

Human populations, conservation and pollution

Table 27.5 Water pollution

Water pollutants	Source	Damage caused	Prevention
1 Artificial fertilizers	Application of excessive inorganic fertilizers, especially nitrates to fields, causes run-off into rivers and lakes.	◊ Excess inorganic salts in the water may cause eutrophication and death of fish. ◊ High nitrate levels in drinking water may cause stomach cancer or severe anaemia in babies.	◊ Persuade farmers to use correct quantities. ◊ Encourage use of organic fertilizers (Table 27.2).
2 Heavy metals, e.g. mercury, lead	Effluent from industry.	◊ Poisons microorganisms, disrupting sewage treatment. ◊ Can get into food chains, e.g. mercury dumped at sea accumulates in fish causing nervous diseases in humans.	Compel factories to purify their own effluent before discharge into sewers.
3 Oil	Leaked from tankers.	Clogs feathers of seabirds, fouls beaches.	◊ Improve safety at sea. ◊ Develop effective methods for removing oil.
4 Sewage	Human wastes.	◊ Raw sewage is discharged into rivers or lakes; may cause bacteria to multiply rapidly and use up all available oxygen so fish die.	
		◊ Phosphates from detergents may cause eutrophication and death of fish.	◊ Ensure all effluent has a low biological oxygen demand. ◊ Encourage use of phosphate free detergents.

FOOD CHAINS AND POLLUTION

Pollutants often become concentrated in the bodies of animals who are at the top of a food chain (see Fig 27.1). Top consumers such as carnivores (including humans) are therefore affected more than producers or lower consumers.

For example, if radioactive rain falls over grassland, the radioactivity is absorbed into grass through its roots. If cows eat the grass, radioactive substances such as strontium become concentrated in their bodies. When humans drink milk from these cows, they take in radioactive strontium. This may accumulate in the bones in quantities high enough to cause cancer.

The same applies to some insecticides, heavy metals and other pollutants. All of these may kill predators or cause eggs to be so thin-shelled that they do not hatch.

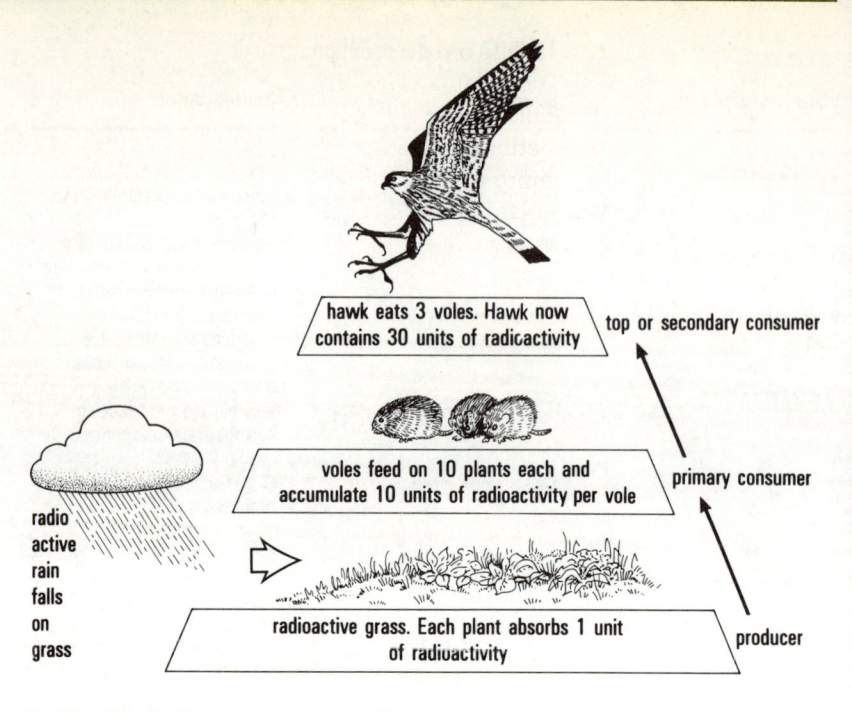

Fig 27.1 How pollutants accumulate in food chains.

ENERGY SOURCES AND POLLUTION

Combustion of fuels (wood, coal, oil), even by the cleanest methods, produces carbon dioxide. The increase in carbon dioxide in the atmosphere may upset the environment in the next century more than any other pollutant, if it causes the climate to become warmer (see Table 27.3).

Table 27.6 Comparison of available energy sources

Source	Advantages	Disadvantages
1 **Combustible fuels**, e.g. fossil fuels (coal, oil, gas) or wood	Cheap and convenient (especially oil and gas).	◊ Supply of fossil fuels will eventually be exhausted, and wood cannot be grown sufficiently fast to meet increasing demands. ◊ Cause pollution, e.g. sulphur dioxide, carbon dioxide.
2 **Nuclear power**	◊ Cheaper than fossil fuels. ◊ Supplies much longer lasting.	◊ Difficult to dispose of radioactive wastes. ◊ May cause widespread radioactive pollution from accidents in power plants.
3 **Renewable sources**, e.g. solar, windmills, wave power, tidal energy, hydroelectricity	◊ Derived from solar energy and the energy of earth's rotation, so supply is virtually inexhaustible. ◊ No pollutants produced.	Inconvenient for most purposes, because: ◊ supply varies too much with climate; ◊ solar energy is too diffuse and can require acres of land for collection; ◊ source is not portable, e.g. for use in cars.

The only alternatives are:
1. more reliance on nuclear power (unpopular due to fear of radioactive fallout);
2. better use of existing energy sources so that less fuel is burnt;
3. more research into renewable, non-polluting sources of energy, e.g. solar energy, wave power, etc.

27.5 INSECTICIDES

ADVANTAGES

Insecticides are essential for controlling insects which feed on crops. Two such insects are:
1. **Aphids** (greenfly) which suck the sap from the stems of plants, using piercing mouthparts shaped like a hypodermic needle. Aphids reduce crop yields and spread virus diseases. They lay eggs on plants and multiply very rapidly.
2. **Locusts**, found chiefly on the fringes of African desert areas after rain, can devour entire fields of crops. Locusts lay eggs in sand and multiply rapidly to form huge swarms, capable of darkening the sky.

DISADVANTAGES

1. **Pollution**. Many insecticides, e.g. DDT, are both poisonous and long lasting, and may harm animals at the top of a food chain.
2. **Killing useful insects**. Insecticides may kill useful insects, e.g.:
   (a) insects which pollinate flowers – many seeds and fruits will not form unless the flower has been pollinated by bees, or other useful flying insects;
   (b) insects which produce food, e.g. bees produce honey.

THE IDEAL INSECTICIDE

The **ideal insecticide** or pesticide should:
1. be highly effective in controlling the pest;
2. have no harmful effects on other organisms;
3. break down rapidly after use, e.g. the herbicide Paraquat breaks down as soon as it reaches the soil but is fatal to green leaves.

Pesticides based on hormones specific to the pest species are ideal for this purpose, but they are often expensive and only available for a few of the major pests.

BIOLOGICAL CONTROL AS AN ALTERNATIVE TO INSECTICIDES

Biological control means the deliberate introduction of a natural predator to kill a pest. For example, growers use tiny parasitic wasps to attack aphids (greenfly) in greenhouses.

Biological control is preferable to use of insecticides because there are no pollution problems. However, it is not always practicable because the predator may die out before its prey and so must be re-introduced annually.

26.6 CONSERVATION AND LAND USE

COMPETING DEMANDS FOR LAND

Competition for use of the same piece of land may arise from demands for its use for:
1. **agriculture**
2. **forestry;**
3. extraction of **minerals, coal**, etc., in mines and quarries;
4. **housing;**
5. **communications** – airports, roads, railways all use up potentially productive land.

CONSERVATION AND PLANNING FOR AMENITY AND LEISURE
W only

Measures to improve the appearance of the countryside include the following.
1. **Reclaim derelict land** among coalfields, especially spoil tips. These can be re-grassed and used for recreation.
2. **Create national parks** to protect rare animals and plants.
3. **Landscape motorways** to blend with the scenery, e.g. excavate cuttings to hide roads, in areas of outstanding beauty.
4. **Plant trees** to re-create ancient forests, using mixtures of conifers and broad leaved trees.
5. **Encourage mixed farming**, i.e. grow a variety of crops and/or livestock to provide a more interesting environment. Growth of one type of crop only (monoculture) allows very rapid spread of pests through the crop.

27.6 CHECKLIST

- Hunter/gatherers. (N only)
- Pastoralists. (N only)
- Agriculturalists. (N only)
- Urban communities. (N only)
- Birth rate.
- Death rate.
- The population explosion:
  - causes;
  - consequences;
  - solutions.
- Fertilizers:
  - organic;
  - inorganic.
- Pollution.

Human populations, conservation and pollution

- Biological oxygen demand.
- Eutrophication.
- Pollution and food chains.
- Energy sources.
- Air, land, water pollution.
- Insecticides.
- Land use.
- Conservation and planning of land use. (W only)

27.8 EXAM QUESTIONS

1   From Fig 27.2:
   (a)   What may have been responsible for the population increase between 3000 and 2000 years BC? Choose one:
   A control of insects. B Increase of grain production. C Discovery of pasteurization. D Discovery of vitamins.
   (b)   Rapid increase in world population from 1400 to 1800 AD was due to: (choose)
   A Decrease in the food supply. B Decrease in the birth rate. C Increase in the birth rate. D Increase in the death rate.
   (c)   Rapid increase in the world population since 1900 AD is due to: (choose)
   A Decrease in the birth rate. B Increase in the birth rate. C Decrease in the death rate. D Increase in the death rate.

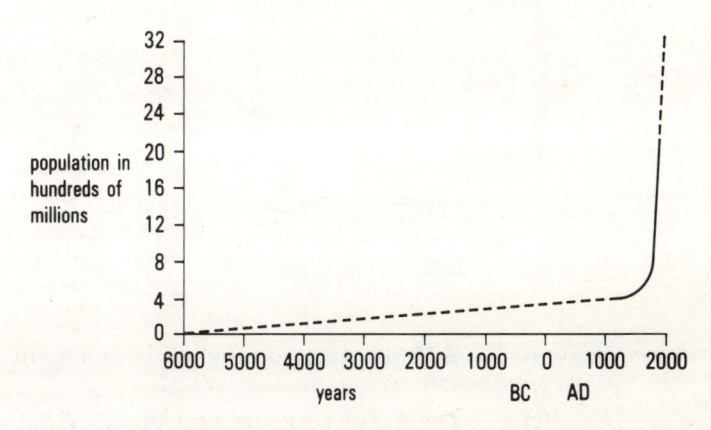

Fig 27.2 Growth in the world population of human beings since the year 6000 BC.

   (d)   Cities were able to develop because of: (choose)
   A An increase in the birth rate. B A decrease in the death rate. C More building materials being available. D An increase in food surplus.
   [NEA: GCSE specimen question]

2   (a)   Suggest three problems which have been caused by the change in world population since about 1900.
   (b)   Suggest one possible solution to each of the three problems you described in (a). (3)

3 (a)   Name THREE pollutants produced by petrol combustion.
  (b)   How is our health affected by TWO of the pollutants named in your answer to (a)?
  (c)   How are buildings and other possessions affected by TWO of the pollutants already named?
  (d)   Name ONE substance, which is added to petrol, that also causes pollution of the air.
  (e)   State ONE measure taken by the government to reduce air pollution.   [WM]

4 (a)   State TWO ways in which excessive noise may affect health and TWO ways by which the level of noise from a motorway may be reduced for the occupants of nearby houses. (4)
  (b)   Who is responsible for measuring the noise level? (1)
                                                                        [SREB]

5 Fig 27.3 shows the levels of phosphates in two rivers between 1940 and 1968. The graph also shows the amounts of detergent used in the United Kingdom during those years.

Fig 27.3

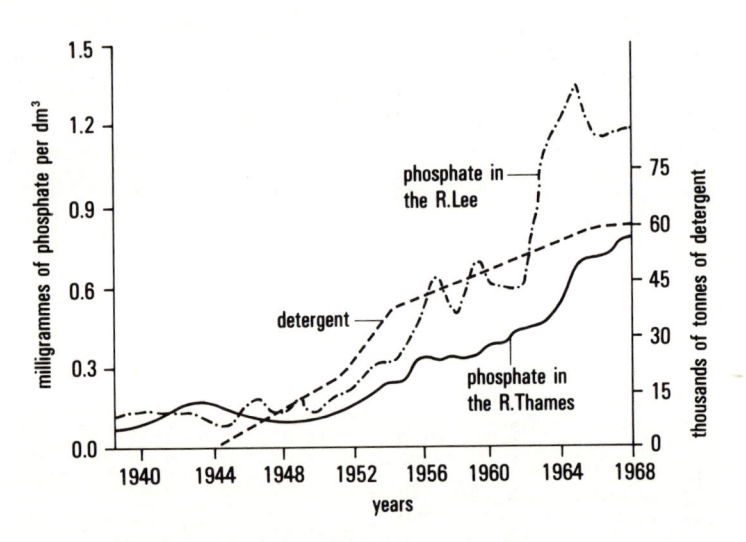

(a)   By how much did the use of detergent increase between 1948 and 1968? (1)
(b)   Detergent contains phosphate. What evidence is there that the use of detergents may have been responsible for the rise in phosphate levels in the rivers? (1)
(c)   State ONE other source of phosphate which could have found its way into the rivers. (1)
(d)   State TWO harmful effects the discharge of detergents can have on the life in a river. (2)   [MID]

6 Polluted air is claimed to be reducing yields of barley crops in England.
  (a)   Name TWO materials which could be causing this type of pollution. (2)

(b) State a possible source of these materials. (1)
(c) Name TWO possible ways through which the materials could enter the barley. (2)
(d) Suggest a method of reducing this type of pollution. (1)
[Adapted from *W*: GCSE specimen question]

7 (a) One of the problems caused by growing the same crop over a large area is: (choose one)
A Increased soil erosion. **B** Increased risk from pests. **C** Increased amounts of carbon dioxide in the air. **D** Increased difficulty of harvest.

(b) When trees are removed from large areas of land: (choose one)
A The amount of oxygen in the air increases. **B** The air becomes drier. **C** There will be more salts in the soil. **D** It will become cooler.
[*NEA: GCSE specimen question*]

CHAPTER TWENTY-EIGHT

ANSWERS TO EXAM QUESTIONS

Answers are given only where these are not obvious from the text, but references are given so that you can look them up if necessary.

The Examination Boards listed on page 00 accept no responsibility whatsoever for the accuracy or method of working for the answers given.

Mark schemes. In the longer answers, a √ indicates where marks would be awarded (in the authors' opinion).

CHAPTER 2

1. (a) Any three of the seven characteristics of life (see page 41).
   (b) Movement
   (c) Man possesses hair and mammary glands (*many other possible answers*).
   (d) Bushes possess green chlorophyll and reproduce by producing seeds.
2. Whiskers, external ears, eyelids, fur.
3. (a) Possession of a large brain, presence of fingernails (*other possible answers*).
   (b) Ability to grasp branches with fingers; excellent eyesight; overlapping field of vision to judge distance when jumping from branch to branch.
   (c) Highly complex forebrain; ability to walk on two legs for long periods; lack of body hair.

CHAPTER 3

1. See page 49, Fig 3.1(b).
2. Draw labelled diagrams of a typical animal cell (page 49) and any three other cells, e.g. striped muscle cell (page 78), white blood cell (page 104), neurone (page 206). Explain briefly, by use of labels on your diagrams, how these three differ from the typical cell.
3. (a) 30°C.
   (b) 0°C and 80°C.
   (c) Between 60°C and 80°C.

Human Biology

(d) (i) 0°C.
(ii) In the sample kept at 80°C, the enzyme has been denatured ✓ (permanently destroyed). In the sample kept at 0°C, the enzyme has become temporarily inactive ✓ only.

4 (a) (i) Cell respiration.
(ii) Photosynthesis.
(b) (i) Mitochondria.
(ii) Chloroplasts.
(c) (i) ATP.
(ii) Energy of sunlight.

5 (a) In living cells, the oxidation of glucose by cell respiration produces chemical ✓ energy in the form of ATP. This happens more slowly ✓ than in the release of heat from burning.
(b) The energy released causes ADP ✓ to form the energy-rich compound ATP ✓:
ADP + P ✓ → ATP
(c) It produces only 118 kJ per gm molecule of glucose ✓ and causes the build up of poisonous ✓ waste products.

6 (a) See page 52, section 3.5
(b) To store ✓ energy released during cell respiration and to release ✓ energy when required for other purposes.
(c) Glucose (via cell respiration).
(d) Respiration stops at the first stage, i.e. anaerobic respiration.
(e) High rate: liver (*or muscle*). Low rate: bone cells.

7 (a) It would have the same basic shape ✓ but would peak slightly ahead ✓ of the lactic acid curve in time.
(b) Because it is still diffusing out of the muscles ✓ where it was made a few minutes previously ✓
(c) It falls because cell respiration has now become aerobic ✓. No further lactic acid is produced and the existing lactic acid is broken down ✓.

8 (a) Bread and wine (*or beer, etc.*)
(b) Bread: carbon dioxide; wine: ethanol.
(c) Bread: aerobic respiration; wine: anaerobic respiration.

9 (a) To carry out cell respiration.
(b) Phosphate
(c) The lack of mitochondria leads to low production of ATP so that less energy is available for muscle contraction.

10 (a) Diffusion: defined on page 56, section 3.6. To earn the remaining marks, define osmosis (page 56), then draw Fig 3.4 (page 57) and give a brief description. Dialysis need only be mentioned as being similar to osmosis, but involving movement of other molecules besides water (page 399).
(b) Draw and describe Fig 3.5 on page 58.
(c) Mention passage of glucose:
(i) from the small intestine into the epithelium cells of the villi (page 172);
(ii) from the blood plasma through the membranes of the cells of the capillary wall and out again into the tissue fluid; and

Answers to exam questions

(iii) from tissue fluid through the cell membranes of the cells generally (p128).

11 (a)   Half fill a measuring cylinder with water and record the level of water √. Add the sultanas and record the level to which the water has risen √. The volume of the sultanas is equal to the difference √ between the water levels.

(b)   In the first case, no water √ entered the sultanas because the concentration of water inside the sultanas was the same √ as in the sugar solution outside. (*Note*: sultanas are a dried fruit containing little water).
In the second sample, water entered √ the sultanas by osmosis √, because their skins acted as a selectively permeable membrane √. They contain very little water, so that they are, in effect, a concentrated solution √.

(c)   They would shrink √ to 8.7 cm³ √ because water would be lost √ by osmosis √ to the strong sugar solution.

CHAPTER 4

1 (a)   To be sure of scoring 8 marks, check the advice on page 67.
  (b)   See Fig 4.1 on page 68.

2 (a)   Use the three functions listed for the backbone on page 70.
  (b)   See Fig 4.3 (page 69) for the regions. Special features: cervical: articulates with skull; other regions as Table 4.2 on page 70.

3   To enable free movement of the ribs during breathing.

4 (a)   See page 72, section 4.3.
  (b)   (i) and (ii) See page 73, section 4.3.

5 (a)   a Tendon. c Synovial fluid. e Spongy bone. g Marrow cavity.
  (b)   d Bone cells and red marrow. b Cartilage.
  (c)   To store fat. (*Note*: red marrow, which manufactures blood, is found only in the spongy bone.)
  (d)   (i) Straightens (*extends*) knee. (ii) This is the main muscle used when transmitting thrust to the pedals.
  (e)   The hinge between the femur and tibia.
  (f)   Tissue b (cartilage) prevents the bones from striking each other √ when walking and cushions the impact √ between them.
  (g)   Muscle f.

6   To answer this essay-type question:
(1) Draw Fig 4.12 (page 75). Be sure to describe the biceps as a flexor.
(2) Mention the role of the ulna and radius acting as levers to bring about a large movement of the load (in this case, the hand) for a small contraction of the biceps.
(3) Mention the action of forearm muscles which cause the tendons in the fingers to contract, so bending the fingers to touch the shoulder. (You can see these muscles contract when you bend your own fingers.)
(4) Describe the role of the elbow joint, by drawing Fig 4.11.

Human Biology

        (5) Finally, describe how the return movement is carried out by the action of the antagonist muscles, e.g. the triceps and finger-straightening muscles. Mention their role as extensors.

7 See section 4.7, pages 79–80 for answers to all parts.
8 See section 4.8, page 82 for answers to all parts.

In 8(c), there is a difference between the effects of **narrow** shoes and **high-heeled** shoes. Make sure you state the effects of each separately.

CHAPTER 5

1 (a) See page 89, section 5.3.
    (b) Use points 2 and 3 under the heading Inspiration on page 89–90.
    (c) They contract during forced expiration ✓ to force the abdominal organs against the diaphragm ✓, so further decreasing ✓ the volume of the thoracic cavity.

2 (a) When the rubber sheet is pulled down, the volume of air in the bell jar is increased ✓. This lowers the pressure ✓ inside the jar, so that it is below the pressure of the atmosphere ✓. Atmospheric air is therefore forced into ✓ the balloons.
    (b) A: Trachea B: Bronchus C: Rib-cage D: Thoracic cavity E: Diaphragm
    (c) (a) Glass sides cannot move, unlike rib cage.
        (b) Space representing thoracic cavity is too large.
        (c) Balloons are too small to represent lungs.
        (d) At rest, diaphragm is dome shaped.
        (e) In real life, the lungs are separated from each other by airtight pleural membranes.
        Also: no representation of internal folding of lungs: no indication that diaphragm is muscular.

3 (a) See page 92 section 5.5.
    (b) (i) A: Backbone B: Rib C: Sternum (breast bone) D: Intercostal (rib) muscles
        (ii) B and C move upwards and outwards. (2)

4 (a) The water level falls.
    (b) To allow water to escape from the bottom of the jar.
    (c) (i) Refill the bell jar with water by pumping out the air at the top.
        (ii) Record the level of water in the bell jar.
        (iii) Sterilize the mouth piece.

5 (a) G
    (b) D
    (c) F
    (d) H

6 The first step is to convert all figures to the same unit – in this case, cm^3. Since $1 \, dm^3 = 1000 \, cm^3$ ($1 \, dm^3$ is equivalent to a litre) then $5 \, dm^3 = 5000 \, cm^3$

Answers to exam questions

Set out your answer like this:

Volume of CO_2 entering lungs from
pulmonary artery in 1 minute $= \dfrac{52}{100} \times 5000 = 2600 \text{ cm}^3$

Volume of CO_2 leaving lungs in
pulmonary vein in 1 minute $= \dfrac{48}{100} \times 5000 = 2400 \text{ cm}^3$

$\therefore 2600 - 2400 = 200 \text{ cm}^3$ is lost per minute

$\therefore \dfrac{200}{16} = 12.5 \text{ cm}^3 CO_2$ is excreted per breath

7 (a) Total volume of air inspired per minute at rest $= 500 \times 19 = 9500 \text{ cm}^3$
Total volume of air inspired during exercise $= 1100 \times 36 = 39600 \text{ cm}^3$

(b) At rest: volume of oxygen entering lungs per minute $= 9500 \times \dfrac{20}{100} = 1900 \text{ cm}^3$

At rest: volume of oxygen leaving lungs per minute $= 9500 \times \dfrac{16}{100} = 1520 \text{ cm}^3$

$\therefore$ Volume of oxygen entering the **blood** per minute $= 1900 - 1520 = 380 \text{ cm}^3$

(c) Oxygen is required for cell respiration ✓ to produce energy ✓ for growth, repair, and production of heat ✓.

(d) During exercise, large quantities of energy ✓ are required for muscle contraction ✓ in addition ✓ to the requirements when at rest. Muscle fibres require ATP ✓ to provide the energy for contraction, and ATP can only be produced by cell respiration ✓.

8 See table 5.6 on page 93.

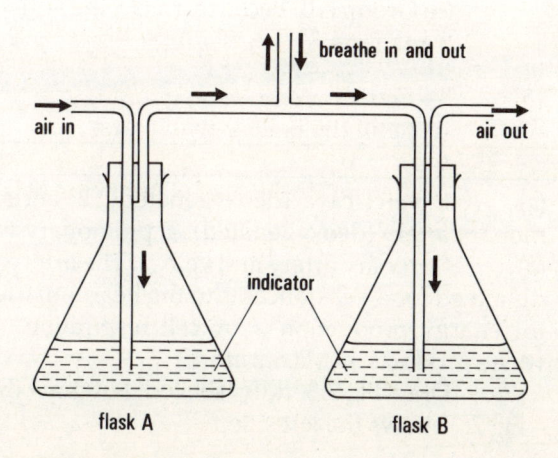

Fig 28.1

394 Human Biology

9 (a) See page 56, section 3.6
   (b) Use Fig 5.4 and the description of gas exchange on pages 91–2.
10 (a) See page 94 section 5.8.
   (b) See page 93, note below Table 5.5.
   (c) See page 95.

CHAPTER 6

1 (a) See page 103, section 6.1.
  (b) See page 105, section 6.2.
2 (a) Lack of oxygen in the atmosphere with increasing altitude.
  (b) Their red blood cell count increases.
  (c) They will suffer from shortage of breath due to lack of oxygen.
3 (a) (i) and (ii) See page 106.
  (b) Due to lower oxygen and higher carbon dioxide concentrations in the blood returning from the foetus.
  (c) See page 106, section 6.3.
4 (a) (i) Clots prevent infection and stop loss of blood.
     (ii) Scabs prevent infection over a longer period.
  (b) See page 106 section 6.4.
5 Note: the saline solution mentioned in this question is a solution of salt in water having the same concentration as blood plasma.
  (a) Sterile water would lower the salt concentration of the blood.
  (b) A and O – see Table 6.3.
  (c) Incompatible blood would be clumped ✓ (agglutinated) by the recipient's antibodies ✓.
6 (a) Blood group O lacks the A and B antigens ✓. Anti-A and B antibodies in the transfusion will be diluted ✓ so much by the recipient's blood that they have no noticeable effect.
(Note: A typical transfusion of about 0.56 cm^3 (1 pint) is usually a much smaller volume than the recipient's blood, which may be up to 5 dm^3 in volume).
  (b) (i) Group O, because it contains neither A nor B antigens.
     (ii) Group AB, because it lacks the antibodies against the A and B antigens.

CHAPTER 7

1 (a) 1: vena cava (deoxygenated). 2: aorta (oxygenated). 3: pulmonary artery (deoxygenated). 4: pulmonary veins (oxygenated).
  (b) Coronary artery and vein ✓. The artery provides oxygen ✓ and dissolved food substances ✓ to the heart muscle ✓. These are essential for energy production ✓ by cell respiration. The vein carries away waste products ✓ (Maximum 4.)
  (c) Draw Fig 7.3, fully labelled, but draw the right side of the heart – Fig 7.3 shows the left side.

Answers to exam questions 395

2 (a) See page 117, section 7.3.
   (b) Faulty heart valves allow blood to leak back into the 'wrong' chamber during contractions of the ventricles √. This reduces the supply of oxygen to the muscles √.
   (c) Pressure from the elastic wall of the aorta as it contracts after ventricular systole.
   (d) To prevent the valves being forced back into the atria.

3 (a) There was a major rise in CHD among men from 1950 to 1965 √, followed by a levelling off until about 1972 √, and then a small decline √. Among women, CHD fell from 1950–56 √ and then rose until 1963 √. It has remained steady at a lower level √ than men since.
   (b) Increased smoking; eating additional fat; and lack of exercise.

4 (a) (i) The left atrium is H because the pressure is steady but relatively low.
        (ii) The left ventricle is G because the pressure fluctuates considerably.
        (iii) The aorta is F because the pressure is fairly steady, but rises with the pressure in the ventricle.
   (b) (i) Y occurs between 0.1 and 0.2 seconds, because pressure is rising in the ventricle (G).
        (ii) Z is at 0.4 seconds, when the pressure in the ventricle falls sharply.
   (c) 0.1–0.2 seconds. This is the period of time when pressure is rising in the ventricle.
   (d) The aorta has elastic walls which expand √ when blood enters it and contract √ when blood leaves.
   (e) It would have the same shape but would not rise to such a high pressure.

5 (a) 60.
   (b) (i) B is the least fit because her pulse has increased most and taken longest to return to normal.
        (ii) A is the most fit because her pulse fell to normal more quickly than the others.
   (c) B, because her pulse rate took so long to return to normal, perhaps due to damaged lungs.

CHAPTER 8

1 See page 126 Fig 8.2.
2 (a) (i) Pulmonary vein.
        (ii) Pulmonary artery.
        (iii) Hepatic portal vein.
        (iv) Hepatic vein (urea is made in the liver).
   (b) (i) Hepatic vein.
        (ii) Aorta.
3 (a) A hepatic portal vein B hepatic vein C vena cava D pulmonary artery E pulmonary vein F aorta

Human Biology

    (b)   A (hepatic portal vein) contains a higher concentration of amino acids and glucose but less urea compared to **B** (hepatic vein).
    (c)   D contains less oxygen, more carbon dioxide and more water (*note:* some water is lost from the lungs by evaporation).

4   (i) X Arterioles. Y Capillaries.
    (ii) Veins.
    (iii) Friction with the narrow walls of the capillaries.
    (iv) The alternate contraction and relaxation of the ventricles.
    (v) Capillaries.
    (vi) This allows maximum opportunity for exchange of substances between the capillaries and the tissues generally.
    (vii) See page 127, Table 8.2.

5   (a)   A Lymph. B Tissue fluid.
    (b)   (i) Oxygen and glucose.
        (ii) Carbon dioxide.
    (c)   Red blood cells, blood proteins, platelets.
    (d)   Fluid is forced out of the capillary at **X** by the higher blood pressure at the arterial end. Loss of water causes the osmotic pressure of the blood to rise above that of tissue fluid, so water enters the blood at point **Y**. (See p. 128, Fig 8.4.)

6   See page 129, Fig 8.4.

7   (a)   See page 130, Table 8.5.
    (b)   Cells in the tissues; lymph vessels.
    (c)   (i) Lymph and tissue fluid accumulate in the legs, because of lack of muscle contractions.
        (ii) They should sit with their legs raised above the head; massaging the legs would also be helpful.

CHAPTER 9

1   Green plants are able to manufacture organic substances ✓ from inorganic substances ✓, by photosynthesis ✓, using the energy of sunlight ✓.

2   (a)   All contain carbon, hydrogen and oxygen ✓; proteins also contain nitrogen ✓.
    (b)   In carbohydrates only, there are twice as many hydrogen atoms as oxygen ✓ atoms.
    (c)   Proteins are composed of amino acids ✓; carbohydrates of rings containing six carbon atoms ✓; and fats of fatty acids and glycerol ✓.
    (d)   Proteins: growth and repair. Carbohydrates: energy. Fats: energy reserve and for insulation against the cold.

3   (a)   Cats can manufacture their own supply of vitamin C.
    (b)   Vitamin C.
    (c)   (i) It reduced the number of days of respiratory illness per year.
        (ii) Doubling the amount had no additional beneficial effect.

Answers to exam questions 397

4 Describe:
   (a) The biuret test – page 141;
   (b) The test for sugars which act as reducing agents – page 141.
5 (a) Set out your answer as follows.
   Volume of lemon juice needed to decolourize 1 cm^3 of DCPIP = 0.9 cm^3.
   Volume of standard solution needed to decolourize 1 cm^3 of DCPIP = 0.5 cm^3.
   $\therefore$ The fresh lemon juice is $\frac{0.5}{0.9}$ times as concentrated as the standard solution.
   $\therefore$ The fresh juice contains $\frac{0.5}{0.9} \times 2.0 = 1.1$ mg of ascorbic acid per cm^3.
   (b) A larger volume ✓ of canned lemon juice would be needed to decolourize the DCPIP because canned juices contain less vitamin C ✓ compared to fresh juice.
6 (a) Individual rats may vary in their dietary needs; and one of the two rats might die during the experiment.
   (b) It caused them to increase in mass by 25 grams each, on average.
   (c) This was due to vitamins already stored in their bodies from their previous diet.
   (d) Group **A**'s growth levelled off; later, they began to lose mass. Group **B**'s mass remained steady for two days and then rapidly increased.
   (e) In the absence of milk, neither group of rats were able to grow. When milk was added, both grew rapidly.

CHAPTER 10

1 See page 147, section 10.2.
2 (a) (i) About 8000–10000 kJ.
       (ii) About 9500 kJ.
   (b) All of the figures would be larger, owing to the need to produce extra heat in the cold climate.
3 (a) About 7500 kJ per 24 hours.
   (b) In order to produce additional heat as the external temperature falls.
   (c) Less food is required in June because the body does not need to produce so much heat.
4 (a) 750 kJ.
   (b) It contains a substantial quantity of protein, and of vitamins C and D.
   (c) Flavouring and colour.
   (d) 60 grams.
   (e) Dietary fibre.
5 (a) A 1–2 year old girl requires less energy than an adult because

she is smaller ✓. Girls aged 13–15 require more energy ✓ than adults because this is the time of their maximum growth spurt ✓. Pregnant women use more energy than average because of the needs of the growing foetus ✓.

(b)　　Set out your answer like this.
If 100 g of bread has an energy value of 1050 kJ, then 140 g of bread has an energy value of:

$$1050 \times \frac{140}{100} \text{kJ} = 1470 \text{ kJ}$$

∴ If her total daily requirement is 9500 kJ, then the percentage provided by the bread $= \frac{1470}{9500} \times 100$

$$= 15.5\%$$

(c)　　(i) A pregnant woman only requires about 1000 extra kJ, plus 25 g of protein, and additional minerals and vitamins. She does *not* need to eat double the normal quantities.

(ii) A small child requires half the total amount of adult food, but needs $\frac{2}{3}$ of the adult protein requirement and full adult quantities of calcium and vitamin D (for bone growth).

6　Surplus foods are converted into fats and stored, so increasing body mass.

7　Set out your answer like this.
While asleep, he uses 8×300　　= 2400 kJ
For light activity, he uses 8×500　= 4000 kJ
For heavy work, he uses 8×1500　= 12 000 kJ

∴ Total energy need　　　　　　= 18 400 kJ

8　(a)　　Set out your answer like this.
　　　　　Weight of sugar = 1 g
　　　　　Rise in temperature = 12C°
　Volume of water in beaker = 200 cm³ = 0.2 dm³

4.2 kJ are required to raise the temperature of 1 dm³ of water by 1°C.

∴ Energy produced by 1 g of sugar = 0.2×12×4.2 kJ
　　　　　　　　　　　　　　　　= 10.08 kJ

(b)　　This will be a lower figure due to loss of heat from the apparatus.
(c)　　See page 150, section 10.5 for reasons for the loss of heat.
(d)　　Fat would give a much higher figure for kJ/gram of food burnt.

Answers to exam questions

CHAPTER 11

1. *Note*: the principle behind this experiment is that glucose molecules are small enough to pass through the microscopic gaps in the dialysis tubing; but starch molecules are too large (see also pages 56 and 201). The dialysis tubing is intended to represent the cell membranes of the cells which line the small intestine. Glucose can be absorbed by these cells but starch and other large molecules must be digested, i.e. *broken down*, first.
    - (a) To remove any traces of spilt starch or glucose.
    - (b) By use of a pipette.
    - (c) Leakage has occurred due to a puncture or spill.
    - (d) (i) Glucose present, starch absent.
      (ii) Glucose has diffused through the walls of the tubing; starch molecules are too large to do so.
    - (e) (i) Lining of the small intestine.
      (ii) The blood supply.

2. (a) There are no nerve endings in the enamel to register pain. Enamel is non-living and so lacks bone cells capable of repairing damage.
   (b) Dentine contains nerve endings and also bone cells which can repair damage.

3. (a) Sugary foods are converted to acid in the mouth. Acid dissolves the enamel and dentine, causing dental caries.
   (b) The acid in the drink dissolves enamel and dentine faster than it can be repaired.

4. (a) The average number of decayed teeth per child has fallen.
   (b) Higher concentrations provide no extra benefit.
   (c) 6.
   (d) About 0.75 parts per million. (*Note*: eight teeth correspond to about 0.25; three teeth correspond to about 1.0. Subtract 0.25 from 1.0).

5. (a) Glucose alone does not produce acid (A); nor does food alone (B). Both must be present (C).
   (b) Boiling kills bacteria in the debris.
   (c) To prevent a build up of plaque by bacteria feeding on the debris.

CHAPTER 12

1. This requires a description of peristalsis – see page 78, Fig 4.16.
2. (a) Most food substances consist of large molecules. These must be broken down by digestion until they are small enough to pass through the wall of the gut.
   (b) By breaking down proteins from other organisms and re-assembling their amino acids into human proteins.
   (c) Carbohydrates lack nitrogen.
3. (*Note*: Cheese consists mainly of protein and fat.)

(a) The digestion of cheese begins in the mouth, where the teeth break it into smaller pieces ✓; and it is moistened with saliva ✓ and swallowed. In the stomach, the enzyme pepsin ✓, in acid conditions, begins the breakdown of proteins ✓ to smaller molecules. In the duodenum, bile ✓ is added to emulsify fats ✓ and lipase ✓ and protease ✓ enzymes are added from the pancreas. Lipases break down fats to fatty acids and glycerol ✓; proteases complete the digestion of protein to amino acids ✓ (Note: don't give a diagram unless asked.)

(b) See Table 12.4 on page 173.

4 (a) The liver deaminates ✓ surplus amino acids ✓. The amino group (NH_2) ✓ is converted to urea ✓ and the remainder to glucose ✓.

(b) The liver maintains the concentration and composition of the blood by manufacturing blood proteins ✓, e.g. fibrinogen ✓ (used in clotting ✓) and albumen ✓. Albumen helps to maintain the osmotic pressure of the blood ✓.

The liver removes excess glucose ✓ from the blood by conversion to glycogen ✓; and converts glycogen to glucose ✓ when blood glucose levels are too low ✓.

The liver converts waste products from broken down red cells ✓ to bile ✓, so removing these from the blood ✓. It also breaks down poisons ✓ in the blood e.g. alcohol ✓ and drugs ✓.

5 (a) This is the optimum temperature for the action of salivary amylase.

(b) Two minutes is insufficient for the amylase to take effect.

(c) In A, the starch has gradually been digested by the enzyme. This has not occurred in B because the enzyme was destroyed by boiling.

6 After 30 minutes:

(i) Some ✓ of the starch has been converted to reducing sugar ✓ by the saliva ✓. This explains the positive test for sugar inside the tubing ✓.

(ii) Some of the reducing sugar has diffused ✓ through the tubing into the water. This explains the positive test for sugar in the beaker ✓.

(iii) None of the starch has diffused out ✓ of the tubing: this explains the negative result for starch in the beaker ✓.

7 (a) (i) The cell extract contains amylase and protease enzymes. These function in neutral, but not in acid, conditions.

(ii) To test for the action of amylase, boil a sample from tube A taken at the end of the experiment, with Benedict's solution. An orange precipitate indicates the presence of reducing sugar, formed from the breakdown of starch. Or:

To check that enzymes are present, repeat experiment A but boil the cell extract first. Any enzyme present will be denatured, so the solution will remain cloudy. Or:

To prove that enzymes are essential, try adding starch or protein to water alone, without adding cell extract.

Answers to exam questions 401

   (b) (i) Saliva contains more amylase when food is present in the mouth.
     (ii) Collect saliva before and during a meal in separate tubes. Now briefly describe the main stages in Fig 12.4, but do not boil either sample.
8 (a) In plate A, the starch has been removed by the action of the saliva.
  (b) Glucose.

CHAPTER 13

1 (a) See page 184, Table 13.2.
  (b) The outer layers are constantly replaced by cells from the Malpighian layer below.
2 Answer by drawing Fig 13.2 on page 187, with all of the information in the labels except for the note about fat. Add extra information from Table 13.3 (p. 185) as follows:
◊ the loss of heat due vasodilation;
◊ the loss of heat due to evaporation of sweat;
◊ the insulating effect of the hairs rising.
Don't mention shivering or metabolic rate – neither are functions of the skin.
3 (a) See page 185, Table 13.3.
  (b) In a damp atmosphere, sweat does not evaporate quickly.
  (c) To replace salt lost in sweat.
4 (a) and (b) see pages 185–86.
5 (a) Liver and muscles.
  (b) Because of water evaporating and so cooling the skin surface.
  (c) Vasoconstriction of the arterioles leading to the epidermis.
  (d) To prevent loss of heat.
6 (a) (i) It cooled the blood leaving the stomach.
    (ii) The rate of sweating fell so that the skin was no longer kept cool.
  (b) The liver (and muscles).
  (c) Body temperature would rise because the temperature-regulating centre in the hypothalamus would react as if the body's temperature had fallen. It would therefore stimulate activities needed to raise body temperature.

CHAPTER 14

1 See page 195.
2 (a) The function of the loop is to assist in re-absorption of water from the urine. It is longer in a desert animal in order to conserve water.
  (b) The desert rat's urine would be more concentrated, i.e. it

would contain a lower percentage of water and a higher percentage of urea and salts. This helps to conserve water.
3   (a)   Blood entering the kidneys contains (quote any three): more oxygen; less carbon dioxide; and more urea, water and salts.
    (b)   This is because urea, and some water and salts are filtered out by the kidneys, which also use up oxygen and produce carbon dioxide. (Choose according to answer in (a).
4   (a), (b), (c) see page 199, section 14.4.
    (d)   Glucose appears in the urine.
5   (a)   Urea molecules are small enough to pass through the dialysis membrane but protein molecules are too large.
    (b)   See page 200, section 14.5.
    (c)   If the patient has a higher than normal level of glucose in the blood, e.g. a diabetic patient.
6   Urine = 1.5 dm^3 lost daily.

CHAPTER 15

1   (a)   Motor, because the cell body is at the end of the axon.
    (b)   A: the dendrites carry impulses from many other cells to the cell body.
    B: the axon carries the nervous impulse.
    C: the fatty sheath insulates the axon.
    (c)   The first step is to measure the real size of the scale marked on the diagram, with your ruler. It measures 7 mm. Then set out your answer like this.
In this diagram, 7 mm represents 0.2 mm.

$$\therefore \text{ The scale is: } \times \frac{7}{0.2} = \times 35$$

i.e. the diagram is drawn 35 times larger than in real life.
On the diagram, the distance from the nucleus to D = 67 mm.
∴ The real distance is 67 ÷ 35 = 1.9 mm
2   See Fig 15.5 on page 209.
3   (a)   Named reflex: removal of finger after being pricked. (Don't forgot to name the reflex: it's worth one mark and you'd be surprised how many people forget!)
    Draw Fig 15.6 and then briefly summarize the main events. You need only mention key points which are not already obvious from the diagram e.g. the entry of the thorn into the finger triggers an impulse from a pain receptor; this passes along the sensory neurone to the spinal cord; the impulse passes immediately through a connecting neurone to a motor neurone and thence to an effector, in this case the biceps muscle; the muscle contracts at once, so removing the hand from the thorn.
    (b)   See how quickly you can start, and then stop, a stopwatch.
    (c)   (i) The arm is paralysed because the motor nerve to the muscle has been cut.

Answers to exam questions 403

                (ii) There would be no effect on sensation because the sensory nerve is not affected.

4 (a)   Thyroxine.
     (b)   Essential for normal growth. Lack of thyroxine in childhood leads to stunted growth and poor mental development.
     (c)   Stimulates metabolic rate. Excess thyroxine causes over-activity, flushed complexion and loss of weight. Lack of thyroxine results in sluggishness, and tendency to over-weight.
     (d)   See Table 15.5 on page 211.

5 (a)   Adrenaline caused the drop in glucose level.
     (b)   A meal was probably eaten at **B**.
     (c)   (i) Glucose level fell below normal.
           (ii) Glucose level returned to normal.
     (d)   (i) Insulin secretion by the pancreas islet cells lowered the glucose level.
           (ii) Glucagon, secreted by the same cells, raised the glucose level.
     (e)   In a diabetic, the glucose level would fall to normal only very slowly because of the lack of insulin.

6 See Table 15.7 on page 214.

CHAPTER 16

1 See page 222.

2 (a)   See page 224, section 16.5.
     (b)   See accommodation, page 224, section 16.3, but use only the details relevant to seeing objects in close up. Also draw Fig 16.4 labelling only the parts relevant to near vision.

3 (a)   Colours are invisible in very dim light because the cones only function in bright light. The rods function in dim light but are insensitive to colour.
     (b)   (i) It probably lacks cones.
           (ii) More space for rods in the retina gives better vision in very dim light.

4 (a)   The rods, found in the sides of the retina, are the only cells sensitive to very dim light.
     (b)   Vitamin A.

5 (a)   See page 225 section 16.5.
     (b)   The dot disappears when it falls on the blind spot because there are no light-sensitive cells at this point on the retina.
     (c)   You would look at the cross, because the blind spot is on the other side of the yellow spot in the left eye.

6 (a)   Convert Fig 16.12 into Fig 16.6(b) on page 226. Use dotted lines (or a different colour) for the corrected rays.
     (b)   Use Fig 16.6(a)

7 (a)   The cells in the retina.
     (b)   The optic nerve.

8 (a)   The ear drum.

(b) Receptor cells in the cochlea.
9 See section 16.9 on page 228.
10 (a) The taste receptors are sensitive only to dissolved substances.
   (b) Much information about taste is supplied by the olfactory cells in the nose. A cold may prevent these from functioning.

CHAPTER 17

1 (a) Use Fig 17.1 (p. 235) and 17.2(a) (p. 236).
  (b) Combine the information in Fig 17.3 (p. 237) with the relevant parts of Fig 18.1 on page 247. Stop at fertilization.
2 (a) Cystitis bacteria inhabit the gut. They can reach the urethra from the anus √ more easily √ in females than in males.
  (b) To prevent bacteria from the anus reaching the urethra √, wash from the urethra √ towards the anus.
3 (a) The identical boys are the result of one ovum dividing after fertilization √. At the same time, a second ovum √ has been fertilized by another sperm to produce the girl √.
  (b) Two (see Table 17.1 on p. 238).
4 (a) 1–5 June and 27 June–2 July
  (b) (i) fall in progesterone level
      (ii) fall in oestrogen level
  (c) When the oestrogen level rises, the uterus lining starts to thicken.
  (d) June 13–15.
  (e) Administration of oestrogen will keep oestrogen levels high.
5 (a) To produce progesterone, essential for maintenance of the uterus lining.
  (b) (i) To stimulate the corpus luteum to produce progesterone.
      (ii) To prevent the uterus from contracting and expelling the embryo and the uterus lining.
6 (i) Inject the woman with fertility hormones √: simple to use, but can cause multiple births √.
  (ii) Artificial insemination by donor: √ inject sperm from a donor (not the husband) √. Effective, but the baby is not then the child of the male partner √.
  (iii) Embryo transplant: collect fertilized ovum from oviduct and then replace in uterus √. Solves the problem of blocked oviducts but is a difficult technique to carry out √.
7 (a) See page 241, section 17.8.
  (b) (i) By cutting and tying the sperm ducts.
      (ii) Advantage: failure rate is very low.
      Disadvantage: cannot easily be reversed.
  (c) See page 242, Table 17.2.

Answers to exam questions

CHAPTER 18

1. (a) The placenta produces the hormones oestrogen ✓ and progesterone ✓, which are essential to maintain the pregnancy ✓. It provides a large surface area ✓ for the exchange of various substances between the maternal and foetal circulations, including oxygen ✓ and dissolved foods ✓, which pass from the mother to the foetus, and carbon dioxide ✓ and urea ✓, which pass from the foetus to the mother. It also prevents the passage of harmful substances such as most microorganisms ✓, the mother's blood cells ✓, etc.
   (b) Alcohol, drugs such as heroin, and viruses such as rubella may all cross the placenta and harm the embryo. (Other answers: poisons from cigarette smoke, AIDS virus, medicines, rhesus antibody.)

2. (a) (i) Foetus is in head-down position, ready to be born.
   (ii) Foetus is much larger.
   (iii) Limbs are fully developed.
   (b) To support and protect the foetus.

3. (a) and (b) See page 249, section 18.2.
   (c) Foods pass into the placenta only in the form of small dissolved molecules such as glucose and amino-acids. Starch and glucose molecules are too large to pass through.

4. (a) (i) To increase the surface area ✓ for the exchange of substances ✓
   (ii) fast flow increases rate of exchange ✓ by maintaining high diffusion gradients ✓
   (iii) length provides a large surface area ✓ for exchange of substances ✓.
   (b) Artery carries less dissolved glucose, more carbon dioxide and more urea compared to the vein. (Also: carries less oxygen.)

5. (a) and (b) See page 252, section 18.3.
   (c) See page 252, Table 18.2.

6. (a) Birth is easier if the head passes out first.
   (b) Cervix muscles relax; muscles of the uterus contract; amnion breaks.
   (c) (i) The cartilage at the front of the pelvic girdle stretches slightly during birth.
   (ii) The bones in the baby's skull can slide over each other.
   (d) A Caesarean operation may be carried out, i.e. the uterus may be cut open.

7. (a) 3.2–3.5 kg.
   (b) (i) 42% (= $\frac{(54+30) \times 100}{200 \text{ (no. of births)}}$)

   (ii) 29% (= $\frac{(23+6) \times 100}{100 \text{ (no. of births)}}$)

   (c) Smoking reduces mass at birth.
   (d) The carbon monoxide in cigarette smoke slows down the baby's growth.

Human Biology

CHAPTER 19

1. See page 259, Table 19.1.
2. (a) See page 261 section 19.3.
   (b) Through the sucking action of the new-born baby √, which stimulates nervous impulses to pass to the brain. This triggers the release of a pituitary hormone √, which causes the release of milk from the alveoli √ into the nipples.
3. (a) (i) A thin, protein-rich liquid containing antibodies.
   (ii) and (iii) See page 262 Table 19.2.
   (b) (i) By 2.3 times (3.5÷1.5).
   (ii) Lactose sugar and fat. (Fat has now been diluted.)
   (c) See page 261, 'Adaptations for breast feeding'.
   (d) Its temperature-regulating and immune systems are still immature, i.e. it would catch cold and be unable to resist infection.
4. It contains antibodies from the mother and does not contain the microorganisms found in cow's milk.
5. (a) Between 0 and about 1 year.
   (b) 9–13.
   (c) 180 cm.
   (d) about 150 cm.
6. (a) (i) 12–15.
   (ii) 0–1.
   (iii) 10 cm (5 cm/year).
   (b) (i) The growth spurt occurs earlier. They do not grow so rapidly as boys during their spurt.
   (ii) Puberty occurs earlier in girls.
   (iii) Individuals vary, owing to differences in nutrition and inheritance.
   (c) During the first two weeks in the womb.
7. (a) (i) F.
   (ii) H.
   (b) The brain must develop first in order to control the other body systems. The reproductive organs are not needed at all until the body is mature.
   (c) Fig 19.5 shows how the head is proportionately much larger than the reproductive organs in a new-born child, compared to a 16-year-old.
8. (a) See page 264 section 19.5.
   (b) By the circulation of the sex hormones in the blood.
9. See page 265, Table 19.4.

CHAPTER 20

1. (a) Group A are controlled by one or two genes only; group B are controlled by many genes.
   (b) Group A are examples of discontinuous variation; Group B are examples of continuous variation.
2. (a) Susan and Amanda. (Their blood groups are identical.)

Answers to exam questions 407

  (b) Their difference in height is probably due to differences in nutrition.

3 (a) Chromosome number in the daughter cells is the same as in the parents. Chromosomes are in the same homologous pairs as before.

  (b) (i) Ovaries (or testes).

    (ii) It increases variability among the offspring.

4 The gametes contain half the number of chromosomes. These chromosomes have exchanged material with each other by crossing over. (See p. 277, Table 20.2).

5 (a) Draw two cells which are

    (i) exactly the same as each other and

    (ii) identical to Fig 20.12.

  (b) See Fig 28.2, below.

  (c) 0.012 mm. For method, see page 402, Question 1(c).

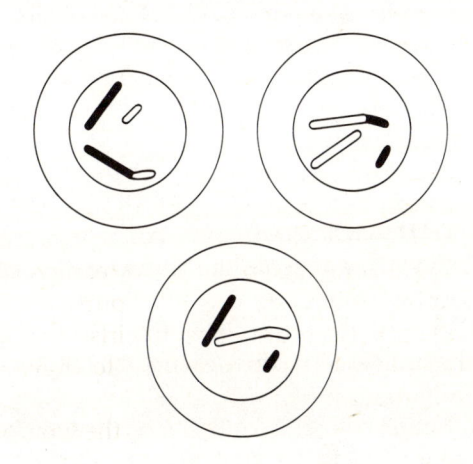

Fig 28.2

6 (a) Set out your answer exactly as on page 282, and don't forget to explain the symbols for your alleles, e.g. H for affected and h for normal. In (i) the parents' genotypes are Hh (man) and hh (woman). In (ii), the parents' genotypes are both Hh.

  Answers:

    (i) The children's genotypes are Hh Hh hh and hh.

    Half are affected (Hh) and half are normal (hh).

    (ii) The children's genotypes are HH Hh hH and hh. Three out of four are affected; one in four is normal.

  (b) There would be a steady increase in the number of victims of the disease.

7 The parents' genotypes are rr (woman) and Rr (man). In this case you are not asked for any explanations or diagrams, so you can simply write down the correct answer without showing your working. The answer is one in two.

8 Let I^A and I^B = the alleles for groups A and B respectively and i = the allele for group 0.

(i) Since I^A and I^B are equally dominant, the Browns' genotypes must be:
Mr Brown   Mrs Brown
ii   I^Ai or I^AI^A

Since neither is carrying the allele I^B, it is impossible for them to have a child belonging to groups B or AB.

(ii) The Reids' genotypes are:
Mr Reid   Mrs Reid
I^Bi or I^BI^B   I^Ai or I^AI^A

It is possible for them to have an AB child from any of these combinations of genotypes.

9 (a) This is because the sex of a baby is determined by the sex chromosomes, XX in females √ and XY in males √. Sperm are formed by meiosis from a mother cell which is XY √, so that about 50% of all sperm carry the X chromosome alone √. Since all ova carry a single X chromosome, and X-bearing sperm have an approximately 50% change of fertilizing an ovum, about half of all births are female √.

(b) A chemical is sprayed in the vagina which will kill or slow down all sperm bearing a Y chromosome. (Any logical answer will be accepted for this type of question, provided you show you understand the basic principle.)

(c) (i) In males, the presence of XY sex chromosomes.
In females, the presence of XX sex chromosomes.

(ii) Down's syndrome. An extra chromosome would be present, so that the individual has 47 instead of 46 chromosomes.

10 (a) Let H = the allele for normal clotting and h = the allele for haemophilia and — = the absence of the second x-linked allele in men.

Then: 1 must be H— because he is a normal male.
2 must be Hh because she is a carrier, being the mother of individual no. 4
4 must be h— because he is an affected male.

(b) Cousin 8's genotype is Hh. This is because she is the daughter of a haemophiliac male (h—) and so must be carrying the h allele from her father. She can't be:

◊ hh because she is not a female haemophiliac (which is possible but very rare);
◊ H— or h— because these are both males;
◊ HH as her father is not carrying the H allele.

Cousin 9's genotype is H— (normal male).

Now set out your answer for a marriage between an Hh and an H— genotype, as shown on page 284, Fig 20.9. The answers are:

F$_1$ genotypes   HH   Hh   H—   h—
Phenotypes   normal   carrier   normal   haemophiliac
                   female   female   male   male

11 (a) (i) Recessive (if it was dominant, it would be visible in one of the parents).

(ii) 1 and 2 are both Aa because this is the only combination

Answers to exam questions 409

which can produce 4, who must be aa (since the allele for phenylketonuria is recessive).
(iii) 3 and 5 are either AA or Aa.
(iv) 6 and 7 may both be carriers (Aa). If so, they have a 1 in 4 chance of producing a child with this defect.

(b) (i) See page 285, section 20.10.
(ii) The mutation has resulted in damage ✓ to the part of the genetic code ✓ (DNA) which produces the enzyme ✓ responsible for reaction Z. This means that any enzyme produced is faulty ✓ and so unable to promote reaction Z ✓.
(iii) If reaction Z does not occur, the dark pigment melanin cannot be manufactured by the cells in the skin.

12 (a) See page 285, section 20.10 for examples. Sickle-cell anaemia is the best example.
(b) The mutation may cause a part of a chromosome to break away and move into an ovum along with an existing haploid set of 23 chromosomes. The result is an ovum with 24 chromosomes and a zygote with 47.
(c) See page 286, section 20.11.

13 (i) The ovaries (or testes).
(ii) It is not passed on to the next generation because it is unlikely to affect the gametes.

14 See pages 286–7, section 20.12.

CHAPTER 21

1 Failure to take sufficient exercise, observe the rules for dental health, or eat a balanced diet. Consumption of cigarettes, excess alcohol, excess fatty foods. (Many other answers.)

2 They may become addicted, and the drugs may have harmful side-effects.

3 (a) The alcohol is absorbed into the blood ✓. It circulates to the brain ✓, where it slows down the passage of nervous impulses across synapses ✓.
(b) Alcohol slows reactions ✓ so drivers would take longer to stop their cars in an emergency ✓.

4 (a) See Fig 28.3 (page 410). How your graph will be marked: accuracy of plotting (3); neatness of line joining the points/curve drawn to give best fit to the points (1).
(b) (i) 0.08 (this mark will be given for the correct answer derived from your own curve, so it will vary slightly).
(ii) 0.03 (must be correct for your curve) plus 1 mark for drawing the curve).
(iii) 1.5 hours.

Human Biology

Fig 28.3

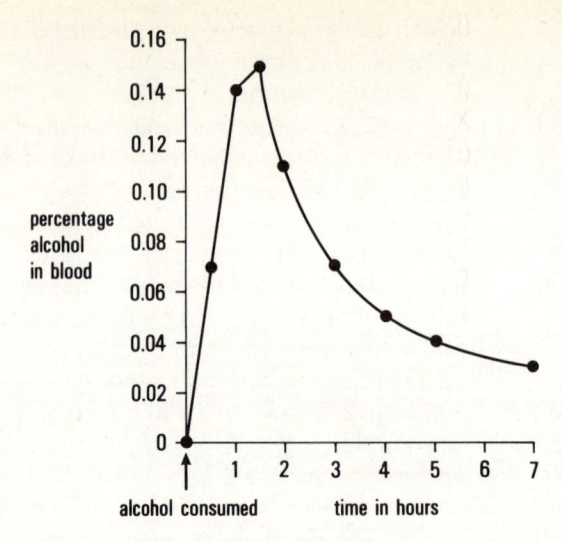

[Graph showing percentage alcohol in blood (y-axis, 0 to 0.16) vs time in hours (x-axis, 0 to 7). Alcohol consumed at time 0. Curve rises steeply to peak of about 0.15 at 1 hour, then declines to about 0.03 by 7 hours.]

5 (a)   See p.298, section 21.3.
    (b)   It affects at least 10% of the population ✓. Post-natal depression may affect 50% of all women after childbirth ✓. Many women who lead isolated, home-bound lives with young children ✓ are also liable to suffer from depression ✓.
    (c)   See page 299, section 21.3.

6 (a)   See page 300, Table 21.3.
    (b)   (i) See page 301.
        (ii) See page 301 Table 21.4.

7 (a)   See page 303, Table 21.5.
    (b)   Carbon monoxide displaces oxygen from haemoglobin, by forming carboxyhaemoglobin. This can reduce the oxygen carrying capacity of the blood by 10%.

8   (i) Smoking
        (ii) because smokers suffer more bronchitis than non-smokers, even in high air pollution.

CHAPTER 22

1 (a)   See page 43, table 2.2
    (b)   See page 311, table 22.1
    (c)   This question is about both external and internal defences so:
        (i) spend half your time on a brief summary of the external defences – mainly the skin, the mucous membranes, and acid in the stomach (see page 315, Table 22.2);
        (ii) See page 315, section 22.5.

2   (i) Heart disease has risen due to increased consumption of fats (or increased smoking, lack of exercise).
        (ii) Lung cancer has risen due to increased cigarette smoking.

Answers to exam questions 411

    (iii) Tuberculosis has declined due to improved living conditions (also due to vaccination).
    (iv) Bronchitis has declined due to declining air pollution.
3 (*a*) X should be marked at the top of the curve, i.e. at 7.5 days.
  (*b*) (i) A.
    (ii) B and C.
    (iii) C and D.
  (*c*) 5 and 6.
4 (*a*) Each antibody is specific to one antigen.
  (*b*) A vaccine consists of a weakened antigen which is given to stimulate the body to produce its own antibodies. These give lasting protection. A serum contains antibodies which cure disease but do not remain permanently in the bloodstream.
  (*c*) Hygienic disposal of sewage; keeping flies away from food; purification of drinking water.
5 (*a*) See the explanation of active immunity on page 317.
  (*b*) The rubella virus causes serious damage ✓ to the embryo ✓ during early pregnancy ✓ but only causes a mild disease ✓ in adults ✓.
  (*c*) Tuberculosis, whooping cough and polio.
  (*d*) To confer protection against childhood illnesses and to provide some degree of life-long protection.
6 (*a*) About 5 weeks.
  (*b*) Immunity may not be achieved at all.
  (*c*) Give a booster injection.
  (*d*) There is less danger of a severe reaction to the smaller injections.
  (*e*) From the mother's antibodies, which are able to cross the placenta.

CHAPTER 23

1 (*a*) (i) 46 million.
    (ii) 4 days.
  (*b*) (i) Increased slightly.
    (ii) Remained level.
  (*c*) Build up of poisonous wastes and exhaustion of available food sources.
2 (*a*) (i) The raw meat; the working surface; the cook's hands; the air.
    (ii) The raw meat will be cooked, so killing any bacteria; the canned meat will probably be eaten without cooking.
    (iii) Bacteria will multiply rapidly in it if it is kept warm.
    (iv) Hard materials cannot be scratched ✓; scratches may harbour bacteria ✓. Porous materials absorb water ✓ along with microorganisms ✓. Smooth surfaces are more easily cleaned than rough surfaces ✓.

Human Biology

    (b)   (i) Bacteria are present in this sample in large numbers and are rapidly using up the oxygen in the milk.
    (ii) There are more bacteria in tube 5 than in tube 4, because they have multiplied during the four days since it was pasteurized. Tube 4 contains only a few bacteria.
    (iii) There are no bacteria in tube 3 because they were destroyed by sterilization. Some bacteria have entered tube 6 from the air since it was sterilized.
    (iv) If the tube is shaken, oxygen will re-enter from the air, causing the indicator to turn blue again in all tubes.
    (c)   Sterilization destroys all of the microorganisms √ in milk, because the milk is heated to over 100° √. Pasteurization kills pathogens √ and many, but not all, of the other microorganisms √. It involves heating to 80°C for 30 seconds √ (maximum 4).

3 (a) and (b) See page 333 section 23.6.
    (c)   (i) A: fungi B: bacteria.
    (ii) The fungus at Z is producing an antibiotic which prevents bacteria from growing near it.
    (d)   He grew microorganisms from the human body, and then opened the plate for close examination without disinfecting it first.

CHAPTER 24

1 (a)   See page 346, role of microorganisms in water purification and sewage treatment.
    (b)   See page 343, Table 24.1
2 (a)   Faeces are a mixture of bacteria, undigested food and dead cells from the gut lining.
    (b)   Urine, and household wastes.
3 (a) and (b) See page 344 Fig 24.4.
    (c)   To admit air and to promote activity by aerobic bacteria.
4 (a)   Lead is poisonous.
    (b)   Water from a deep well is relatively free from impurities, especially the microorganisms found in lakes or rivers.
5 (a)   Refuse is solid organic waste. Sewage is liquid waste.
    (b)   See page 347, section 24.4.
    (c)   (i) The refuse is decomposed √ by microorganisms √ which break it down by cell respiration √ to carbon dioxide √ and water √.
    (ii) Non-organic material, e.g. plastics and metals.
    (d)   Methane gas and fertilizer.

CHAPTER 25

1 (a)   Starch, sucrose, cellulose.
    (b)   Starch.

Answers to exam questions 413

      (c)   In the leaves, by photosynthesis.
      (d)   Water, sunlight, carbon dioxide, mineral salts.

2 (a) The black paper keeps out light. The soda lime absorbs carbon dioxide.
    (b) In the dark, to remove any starch already present.
    (c) Sodium hydrogencarbonate solution which provides additional carbon dioxide.

3 (a) Due to the manufacture of carbohydrates by photosynthesis.
    (b) Respiration is proceeding faster than photosynthesis.
    (c) At this point, light is no longer a limiting factor.

4 (a) 0.90 at about 5 a.m.
    (b) 0.85 (0.90−0.05, the lowest reading).
    (c) During the day, carbon dioxide is used up for photosynthesis by the plants faster than it is produced by the blowflies, as they respire. At night, both respire to produce carbon dioxide.
    (d) The level would remain constant over the 24 hours.

5 (a) (i) (1) Photosynthesis (2) Respiration (3) Decomposition (4) Combustion.
        (ii) It is combined with water inside a chloroplast, in the presence of chlorophyll and sunlight. Oxygen is given off as a byproduct.
        (iii) Fungi and bacteria. In the top layers of the soil.
        (iv) Coal
    (b) Starch is broken down to maltose √ by the enzymes salivary amylase √ in the mouth, and pancreatic amylase √ in the small intestine √. It is then further broken down to glucose √ by the enzyme maltase √ in the small intestine √. The glucose is absorbed √ into blood through the villi √ and carried in the hepatic portal vein √ to the liver.

6 (a) Nitrogen is essential for the manufacture of amino acids.
    (b) (i) By consuming plant proteins.
        (ii) By taking in nitrates from the soil.

CHAPTER 26

1 Photosynthesis is essential for green plants (producers) to manufacture organic compounds from inorganic compounds √. Herbivores live by consuming plants to obtain these compounds √ and carnivores √ feed on herbivores. In this way, organic compounds pass along food chains √ which involve all living things.

2 (a) Sunlight.
    (b) Photosynthesis.
    (c) Oxygen.

3 See page 365, Fig 26.1.

4 Respiration, excretion, manufacture of indigestible parts.

5 X, because it is the shortest chain so that the least energy will be lost from it.

414 Human Biology

6 See Fig 28.4.

Fig 28.4

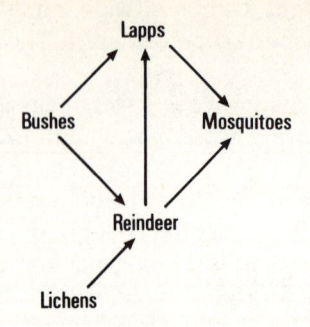

```
           Lapps
          ↗  ↑  ↖
   Bushes     Mosquitoes
       ↘   ↗
        Reindeer
          ↑
        Lichens
```

7 (a) Algae → Crustaceans → Mackerel → Seals (*Hint*: ignore the energy and carbon dioxide.)
   (b) Respiration.
   (c) Sunlight.

8 (a) (i) They increased.
      (ii) The Tilapia fishing declined.
   (b) (i) Plankton.
      (ii) Tilapia.
      (iii) Man and lung fish.

(*Hint*: draw the food web in rough before answering.)

CHAPTER 27

1 (a) B. (b) C. (c) C. (d) D.
2 (a) See page 376, consequences of uncontrolled population growth.
   (b) Select suitable answers from page 377, section 27.3.
3 (a) Any three of sulphur dioxide, carbon dioxide, lead, nitrogen oxides.
   (b), (c) and (d) see pages 379–81.
   (e) Passage of the Clean Air Act, 1956.
4 (a) Noise may cause damage to the hearing and also increases stress.
Motorway noise: see page 379, Table 27.3.
   (b) Environmental health officers.
5 (a) By 4 times.
   (b) Phosphate levels rose as use of detergents increased.
   (c) From fertilizers, used on fields.
   (d) The phosphates may cause eutrophication (*overgrowth of algae*). When the plants die, their decomposition removes oxygen from the water, causing the death of fish.
6 (a) Sulphur dioxide, nitrogen oxides.
   (b) Power stations.
   (c) Via the stomata in the leaves or through the roots.
   (d) Fit scrubbers to power station chimneys.
7 (a) B. (b) B.

GLOSSARY AND ADDITIONAL INFORMATION

CONTENTS

- 29.1 Glossary — 417
- 29.2 Some famous scientists — 420

Glossary and additional information

The definitions of most technical terms are given within each unit. In this unit, you will find explanations of some scientific terms, additional detail on special topics found only in one or two exam syllabuses, and notes on famous scientists.

29.1 Glossary

NI only — **Arteriosclerosis** means 'hardening of the arteries'. From middle age onwards, the arteries lose their flexibility and become narrower and less elastic. Fatty deposits may also build up inside them – see atherosclerosis below.

M only — **Atherosclerosis** is a special type of arteriosclerosis (see above) in which the arteries become gradually blocked with fatty deposits. This is the main cause of coronary heart disease.

M only — **Binomial system** is a system of naming every living organism, devised by the Swedish scientist Linnaeus. Every organism is given a name consisting of two Latin words, e.g. *Homo sapiens* (man). *Homo* refers to the genus, and *sapiens* to the species. A genus is a group of closely related species.

M only — **Cerebral reflex** is a reflex where the impulses pass through the brain instead of the spinal cord. This happens where the brain is the nearest part of the central nervous system to the receptor involved. Examples include blinking, dilation of the pupil, secretion of saliva.

M only — **Cerebral thrombosis** is the medical name for a stroke, i.e. damage to the brain caused by a burst or blocked blood vessel.

M only — **Conditioned reflex** is a reflex which is learnt, unlike simple reflexes which are inherited. Learning to ride a bicycle involves acquiring conditioned reflexes to help you keep your balance. The most famous example of a conditioned reflex involved a dog trained by the Russian scientist Pavlov. He rang a bell every time he fed the dog, so that it learnt to secrete saliva every time the bell sounded, even if no food was offered.

W only

Coronary bypass operation is the use of a small piece of vein to bypass a partially blocked length of coronary artery.

Deamination is the removal of the amino group from unwanted amino acids in the liver. Amino acids are typically composed of an —NH_2 (amino) group joined to a —COOH group, e.g. glycerine: NH_2—CH_2—COOH. The NH_2 group is removed and converted to urea and the rest of the molecule is converted to carbohydrate.

Dialysis is a method of separating small and large molecules, e.g. glucose from starch, by use of a dialysis membrane through which only small molecules can pass. Osmosis is a type of dialysis involving water.

Leucocytes – white blood cells.

Litre: unit of volume, equal to 1000 cm^3. Not to be used in GCSE – use the cubic decimetre (dm^3) instead. (1 litre = 1 dm^3.)

N only

Milk or **deciduous teeth** are the first set of teeth, which appear from the age of two and are gradually replaced from the age of six. The milk teeth include incisors, canines and pre-molars, but not molars. The reason why we have two sets of teeth is because childrens' jaw bones are too small to accommodate the full-size permanent teeth, which grow in gradually as the jawbone grows. The last molars may not appear until age 18–20 (wisdom teeth).

M,W only

Pacemaker Heartbeat is controlled within the heart by a small area of specialized muscle tissue in the wall of the right atrium, called the pacemaker. It contracts regularly about 70 times per minute under the ultimate control of the brain. When the pacemaker contracts, a wave of electrical impulses spreads out rapidly across the muscles of the artria, causing them to contract. The wave is prevented from reaching the ventricles by a band of non-conducting tissue, so allowing time for the atria to complete their contraction. However, the wave eventually finds it way through a narrow gap in this band and causes the ventricles to contract (see Fig 29.1) 0.1 seconds later. If the pacemaker ceases to function, patients can be fitted with a battery operated pacemaker which performs the same function.

APH(H)
L/EA
NI only

Rhesus blood group. Up to 85% of white people carry an antigen called rhesus factor (Rh+) on their red cells. People who lack rhesus factor are called rhesus negative (Rh−).

Rh factor and pregnancy. If an Rh− woman has a child by an Rh+ man, the foetus will usually be Rh+ (Rh+ is a dominant allele). Red cells from the foetus carrying the Rh+ antigen sometimes 'leak' across the placenta into the mother's circulation. If so, she will manufacture antibodies against the Rh factor. These antibodies will be

Glossary and additional information

Fig 29.1 Control of heartbeat by the pacemaker

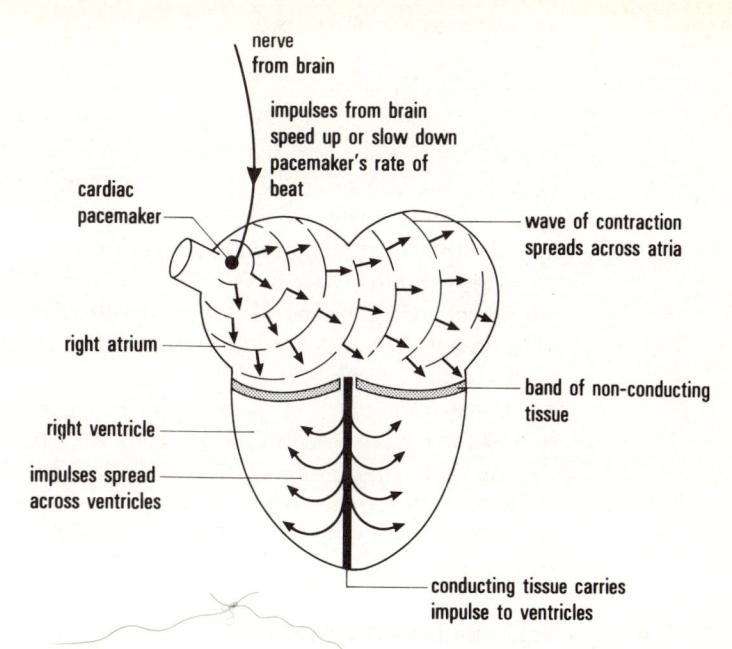

Labels on figure:
- nerve from brain
- impulses from brain speed up or slow down pacemaker's rate of beat
- cardiac pacemaker
- wave of contraction spreads across atria
- right atrium
- band of non-conducting tissue
- right ventricle
- impulses spread across ventricles
- conducting tissue carries impulse to ventricles

produced in greater quantities at each succeeding pregnancy. They may then pass across the placenta and destroy many of the foetal red cells. This can be prevented by testing for blood groups at ante-natal clinics. If an Rh− woman with an Rh+ partner is detected, the baby can be given an immediate blood transfusion at brith, or even in the uterus if necessary.

Rh factor and transfusions. Rh− blood can be given safely to anyone. This is because the anti-Rh+ antibody is not present in Rh− people until they have been in contact with Rh+ blood. Rh− men can receive an initial transfusion of Rh+ blood without harm, but may then build up anti-Rh+ antibodies which agglutinate ('clump') later Rh+ transfusions. Rh− women of child-bearing age should not receive Rh− transfusions because they will build up antibodies which may harm even their first-born child.

Secretion. The manufacture and release by cells of substances such as hormones or enzymes. If secretory cells are grouped together, they are known as **glands**, e.g. endocrine or exocrine glands.

NI only

Sphygmomanometer: a device used to measure blood pressure. A cuff connected to a column of mercury is fastened around the upper arm and is inflated until the pulse at the wrist ceases. The nurse or doctor then listens to the lower arm with a stethoscope, and releases the cuff pressure. As pressure falls, the sound of systole, followed by diastole, is heard in the stethoscope, and the pressure of the mercury is read off at each sound. Typical figures for a young person are 120/80 mm of mercury (16/10 kPa) for systole and diastole respectively.

Surface area to volume ratio. The larger an object, the smaller its surface area to volume ratio:

$$\frac{\text{Surface area}}{\text{Volume}}$$

A reduced surface area in relation to volume helps to prevent loss of heat, so Arctic mammals (seals, bears) tend to be larger than similar animals from warmer climates. A large surface area to volume ratio speeds up loss of heat and also diffusion of substances, gas exchange, etc. This explains why:
- single-celled organisms do not need a circulation system;
- villi, alveoli, etc. involved in exchange of substances are richly folded to give a large surface area.

Demonstration of SA/volume ratio. If a cube is split in half, the two halves have a larger combined surface area than the original cube. To demonstrate this, put a single cube of agar and two half cubes into a shallow dish containing a coloured dye. After 15 minutes, the two smaller cubes will together have absorbed more of the dye than the single large cube.

[M only]

Vegetarian diets. There are two types of vegetarian diet.
- Diets which exclude meat but include animal products such as milk or eggs.
- Strict vegetarian diets (vegan diets) which exclude all animal products.

Both kinds of diet can provide all of the requirements for health, and can be healthier than some diets based on meat. However, vegans run the risk of suffering from deficiency in essential amino acids unless they balance their diet carefully, e.g. eating beans with rice to obtain a wide variety of amino acids.

[M only]

29.2 SOME FAMOUS SCIENTISTS

Alexander Fleming (1881–1955) was the discoverer of the antibiotic pencillin in 1928. Working at St Mary's Hospital, London, he noticed that a colony of staphylococci bacteria on an agar plate had been killed by a colony of penicillium fungus which had accidentally grown on the plate.

Edward Jenner (1749–1823), an English country doctor, discovered vaccination against smallpox. He noticed that dairymaids who caught a mild disease called cowpox did not catch smallpox. He tested this by injecting pus from cowpox scabs into a small boy and then injecting smallpox pus two months later. The boy did not catch smallpox because he been protected by antibodies produced against the previous injection of cowpox virus.

Joseph Lister (1827–1912), working in Glasgow, introduced antiseptic methods for surgical operations, e.g. the carbolic disinfectant spray to kill microorganisms in the air. This prevented many cases of gangrene and blood poisoning.

Louis Pasteur (1822–95), a famous French scientist, proved that fermentation and decay are caused by microorganisms, e.g. the souring of milk and wine. He also proved that microorganisms cause disease (the 'germ theory' of disease) and discovered several vaccines, e.g. against anthrax and rabies.

INDEX

The main reference for each word is shown in **bold type**.
abortion 241, **255**
absorption 159, **172–3**
accommodation 224
acetabulum 71
acetic acid 333
acetylcholine 208
acid rain 379, 380
acquired immunity 316–7
active immunity 316–7
active transport 58
adenosine diphosphate (ADP) **54**
 triphosphate (ATP) **54**
ADH 197, **199**
adipose layer 184, **186–7**
adolescence 264
ADP **54**
adrenal gland 212
adrenaline 212–3
affluence, diseases of 314
afterbirth 254
agar plates 333–5
ageing 265
agglutination 316
agglutinin 316
A.I.D. 241
AIDS 251, 321, **327**
albumen 103, 173
alcohol 251, **295–8**
algal blooms 380
alimentary canal 169
allele 278–82
allergy 318
alum 343
alveolus of lungs 90–91
 in the breasts 261
amino acids 137, 138
amniocentesis 252
amnion 248–9
amniotic fluid **248–9**, 254
amphetamines 295
Amphibia 42, **45**
amylase 51, **172**, 174–5
anaemia **106**, 139
angiosperms 42, **44**
Anopheles 312
anorexia nervosa 150
antagonist 75
ante-natal clinics 252
ante-natal tests 252
anti-diuretic hormone (ADH) 197, **199**

anti-histamine 296
anti-malarial drug 312
anti-serum 319
anti-toxin 105, **316**, 319
antibiotic 319–20
antibody 104–5, **316**, 319
antigen **316**, 319
antiseptic 319
anus 169
aorta 114, **118**, 126
aphids 383
appendicular skeleton **67**, 68
aqueous humour *see* watery liquid 222
aquifer 342
arachnids 42
arteriole 118, **128**
arteriosclerosis 417
artery **124**, 126
arthritis 74
Arthropods 42
artificial insemination 241
artificial insemination by donor (A.I.D.) 241
artificial respiration 94, 95
artificial resuscitation 94, 95
artificial selection 287
asbestos 300, **379**
ascorbic acid 141, 142
aseptic surgery 319
aspirin 296–7
assimilation 159
ATP **54**
atherosclerosis 417
athlete's foot 327
atrial systole 114–6
atrium (auricle) 114–6
auditory capsule 69
auditory nerve 227
auxins 214
axial skeleton **67**, 68
axon 206–7

backbone 68, **69**, 70
bacteria **42–3**
balance 228
balanced diet 147
barbiturates 295
basal metabolic rate (BMR) 147–9
BCG vaccine 317
Benedict's solution 141
biceps muscle 75
bicuspid valve 114–6

bile **172**, 174
bile duct 169
binomial system 417
biological control 383–4
biological filter 345
biological oxygen demand (BOD) 344, **380**
bipedal 45
birds 42, **45**
birth 253–4
birth control 241
birth rate 376
Biuret test 141
bladder 196
blind spot 222, 232
blink reflex **210**, 222
blood clotting 106
blood, composition of 103, 104
blood, functions of 105–6
blood groups 106, 107
blood pressure 117, **118**, 127
blood sinuses 250
blood transfusions 107, **318**
BOD 380
bolus 78, **171**
bone structure 72
bottle feeding 262
bottling 332
botulism 327
Bowman's capsule 196–8
brain 209
bran 139
bread making **53**
breast feeding 262
breathing 87, **89–90**
breathing rate 94
breech birth 254
bronchi 87
bronchiole 87
bronchitis 301–2
bunion 82
Bushmen 375

Caesarean birth 254
caffeine 295
calcium 138, 139
calorimeter 150, 151
cancer 299–301
canine 160, 161
cannabis 295
canning 332
capillaries 128
capsule (in joint) 74

carbohydrase **51**, 172
carbohydrate 137, 138
carbohydrates, digestion of 172
carbon cycle 358
carbon dioxide in breathing 93
 in respiration 53
 and pollution 379, 382
carbon monoxide **106**, 303, 304, 379
carboxyhaemoglobin 106
carcinogens **300**, 303
cardiac muscle **77**, 79
carotid artery 94, **126**, 190
carrier (of disease) 320
carrier (of genes) 284
cartilage 72, **73**
catalase 51
cell division 275–7
cell body 206–7
cell membrane 49, **50**
cell respiration **52**
cell sap 49
cell structure 51
cell vacuole 49
cell wall 49
cementum 161
central nervous system **205**, 208–9
centriole 275–6
centrum 70
cerebellum 209
cerebral cortex 209
cerebral reflex 417
cerebrospinal fluid 208
cerebrum 209
cervical vertebrae 69, **70**
cervix **236**, 254
characteristics of life **41**
cheek cell 50
cheese 139
chemoreceptor 221
chemotherapy 301
chiasmata *see* junction points
chlorination 343
chlorine 343
chlorophyll 49, **353**
chloroplast 49, **353**
cholera 327
choroid 222–3
chromosomes 274–9
chromosome mutations 286
cigarettes *see* smoking
cilia 315

Human Biology

ciliary muscles 222–4
circulatory system
  purpose 103
  arrangement 126
cirrhosis of the liver 298
clavicle (collar bone) 68
Clean Air Act 379
clinical thermometer 188–9
clitoris 236
clothing and climate 186
clothing during pregnancy 253
clotting 106
co-dominance 283
co-ordination (nervous and hormonal) 211
cobalt chloride paper 93
coccyx 69
cochlea 227–8
coil (IUD) 242
collar bone 68
collecting duct 197, 199
colon *see* large intestine
colostrum 261–2
combustion 358, 360, 382
community 365
common cold 327
compact bone 72
compost 348
conception 240
conditioned reflex 417
condom 242
cones 224–5
conjunctiva 222
conservation 378, 384
constipation 139
consumer 365–6
continuous variation 273–4
contraception 241–2
contraceptive pill 242
control experiment 334–5, 356
controlled tipping 347
converging lens 226
copper sulphate 93
copulation 235
cornea 222–3
cornified layer 183
corns 82
coronary bypass 418
coronary thrombosis 117
  artery 117
  heart disease **117**, 120
corpus luteum 237–40
cortex, brain 209
cortex, renal 196–7
cousin marriages 286
cramp 79
cranium 69
cristae (mitochondria) 50
cross-infection 332
crossing-over 276–7
Crustacea 42
cystitis 243
cytoplasm 49, **50**

DCPIP 141, 142

DDT 380
deamination 173, **418**
death rate 376
deciduous (milk) teeth 160, **418**
decomposers 366
decomposition of food 331
deep freezing 332
defaecation 195
deficiency diseases 138
deforestation 377
dehydration 184, 332
denaturation **52**
dendrite 206–7
dendron 206–7
denitrifying bacteria 359–60
dental caries 139, **161**, 162
dentine 161
dentition 160
deoxyribonucleic acid (DNA) 274–5
depressants 295
dermis 183–4, **187**
detoxication 174
diabetes 199
dialysis **56**, 200, 418
dialysis bath 200–1
dialysis membrane **56**, 163, 200–1
diaphragm 87–90
diastole 114–6
dietary fibre 139
diffusion 56
diffusion gradient 55, **56**, 92
digestion 159, 163
diploid number **274**, 277
disclosing tablets 162
discontinuous variation 273–4
discs (vertebral) 68, 69
diseases of affluence 314
disinfectant 319
diverging lens 226
diverticulitis 139
DNA 274–5
dominance 278
  incomplete 283
dorsal root 209
Down's syndrome 252, 286
droplet infection 311
drug addiction 296
drug dependence 296
drugs 251, **295–8**
duodenum 169, 170, **172**
dustbins 347

ear 227–8
ear drum 227
ecology 365
ecosystem **365**, 375
ectoparasite 329
effector 205–6
effluent 344–6
egestion 159
ejaculation 235–6
electron microscope 49
embryo 248–9
embryo transplant 241

emphysema 301–3
emulsification 172
enamel 161
endemic 320
endocrine glands 211–2
endometrium 239
endoparasite 329
energy requirements 147–9
  sources 382
environment 274
Environmental Health Officer 348
enzymes **51**
  extra-cellular 52
  intra-cellular 52
epidemic 320
epidermis 183, **187**
epididymis 235–6
epiglottis 87, **171**
erosion of soil 377
erythrocytes *see* red blood cells
Eskimoes *see* Inuit
ethanol **54**
eutrophication 380
evaporation 341
evolution 287
evolution of Man from the apes 44
excretion 41, **195**
exercise 91, **118**, **119**
exocrine glands 211
exoskeleton 44
expiration 89–90
extensor 75
external defences against infection 315
eye 222–7
eyelashes 222
eyelids 222

F1, F2 generations 281
facet 71
faeces **195**, 311
Fallopian tube *see* oviduct
FAD 331
fat 137
fat, subcutaneous 184
fats, digestion of 172
fatty acids 137, **172–3**
fatty sheath (of neurones) 206–7
feet, care of 82
femur 68
fermentation **54**
fertility hormone 240
fertilization 235, **237**, 247
fertilizers 378
fibre *see* dietary fibre
fibrin 106
fibrinogen 103, **106**, 173
fibrocartilage 68
fibrous layer 161
fibula 68
field of vision 225–6
fish 42, **45**
fish farming 377
Fleming, Sir Alexander 420

flexor 75
flocculation 343
flowering plants **42**
fluoridation 139, 343
fluorine 139
flush toilets 344
fly *see* housefly
foetus 248–52
follicle (in ovary) **237**, 239, 247
Food and Agriculture Organisation (FAO) **331**
food chain **366**, 368
food hygiene 332
food, need for 137
food poisoning 331–2
food tests 140–2
food web **368**, 371
food preservation 332–3
fossil fuels 354, 358, 382
fovea *see* yellow spot
freeze drying 332
freezing 333
fungi **42–3**

gall bladder 169, 170
gamete 235, **238**
gas exchange 91–3
gastric juice 315
gene **274**, 278–80
genetic code 274
genetic counselling 286
genotype 278–82
German measles *see* rubella
germinative layer 183
gestation period 253
glomerulus 196–8
glottis 171
glucagon 212–3
glucose 137
  in the urine 199
glycerol 137, **172–3**
glycogen 137, **173–4**
goblet cell 302
gonadotrophin 240
gonorrhoea 327
Graafian follicle **237**, 239
granular layer 183
gravity and plants 214
gravity filter 343
gravity receptors 221, 228
grey matter 208, 209
grit channel 345
growth 41, **263–4**

haemoglobin **105**, 106, 139
haemophilia 286
hair 183–5, **187**
hair erector muscle 183–5, **187**
hair follicle 183–4
hammer toe 82
haploid number **274**, 277
hard palate 169
heart 113–9
heart attack 117
heat production and loss 186

Index

heavy metals 381
hepatic artery 126, 127
hepatic portal vein **126–7**, 173
hepatic vein 126, 127
herbicides 377, 380
heredity 274
heroin 295, **298**
herpes 321, **328**
heterozygous 278–82
histamine 315
holophytic 366
holozoic 366
homeostasis 105, 185, **213**
homiothermy (constant body temperature) 186
homologous chromosomes 274–9
homozygous 278–82
hormone 211–3
housefly 313–4
humerus 68
hunter/gatherers 375
hydrochloric acid 170
hydrogencarbonate indicator 93
hyphae 43
hypothalamus 185, 189–90, **209**
hypothermia 187–8

ileum *see* small intestine
image formation 223
immune system 318
immunity 316–7
immunization 317
implantation 247
incineration 348
incisors 160
incomplete dominance 283
incubation of mirco-organisms 333–4
incubation period 315
induced abortion 255
induction of labour 254
infection, defence against 315
infectious diarrhoea 313
influenza 328
ingestion 159
inoculation 333
insects 42, **44**
insecticides 380, **383**
insertion tendon **75–6**
inspiration 89–90
insulin 212–3
intercostal muscles 87–90
internal defences against infection 315
internal respiration *see* cell respiration
intra-uterine device (IUD) 242
Inuit (Eskimoes) 375
invertebrate **42**
involuntary muscle 77
iodine 139
iris 222–4
iron 139
irrigation 378

irritability 41
islets of Langerhans 212–3
isolation hospital 320
IUD 242

Jenner, Edward 420
joints **74**
jugular vein 126
junction points 276

keratin 183
kidney 195–201
kidney dialysis machine 200–1
kidney transplant 201
kitchen hygiene 332
knee jerk reflex 210
krill 138, 377

labour 254
lactation 261
lacteal **129**, 172–3
lactic acid **53**
land use 377, 384
Lapps 375
large intestine 169, 170
laryngeal cartilage 87, **171**
larynx 87–8, **171**
lead 346, **379**, 381
lens 222–7
leucocyte 418
leukaemia 251
levers 67, **76–7**
lice 330–1
life, characteristics of 41
lifting and bending 80–1
ligaments 74, **76**
light microscope 49
lime 343
limewater 93
lipase 172
lipids 137
Lister, Joseph 421
liver 169, **173–4**, 297
locusts 383
long sight 226–7
loop of Henle 197
lumbar vertebrae 69, 70
lungs 87–92
lung capacity 90, 91
lymph node 104, **129**
lymphatic system **129–131**, 172–3
lymphocyte **104**, 129
lysozyme 315

maggots 313
malaria **312–3**, 328
malnutrition 148, **376**
Malpighian layer 183–4
maltase 172
maltose 172
mammal 42, **45**
mammary gland 261
mandible 69
Mantoux test 317
marrow, red 67, **72**, 104

yellow **72**
Masai 375
mass vaccination 317–8
maxilla 69
mechanical advantage 77
medulla oblongata 94, **209**
medulla of kidney 196–7
meiosis 275–7
melanin 183–4
menopause 237, **265**
menstrual cycle 238–40
mental handicap 299
mental health 298
mental illness 299
mercury 346, **381**
mesenteric artery 126
mesophyll 50
metabolic rate 147–9
  and temperature regulation 185
methane 345–6
microvillus 198
milk 139
  secretion of 261
  composition of 262
milk teeth 418
mineral ions 139
miscarriage 255
mitochondria 49, **50**
mitosis 275–7
molars 160
molluscs 42
mosquito 312–3
motor end plate 206, 209
mouth 170, 172
mouth-to-mouth ventilation 94, 95
movement 41
mucous membrane 315
mucus **302**, 315
muscle 75, **77–9**
muscle fatigue **53**, 79
muscle tone 79
mutagenic 285
mutation 285
mycelium 43
myelin 207
myopia 226

nasal capsule 69
natural immunity 316–7
natural selection 286–7
negative feedback 213
nephron 196–7
nerve fibre 207
nerve impulse 208
neurone 206–7
neurosis 299
nicotine 295, **303**
night blindness 138
nitrates 359–60
nitrifying bacteria 359
nitrogen cycle 358–60
nitrogen fixation 359
nitrogen oxides 379
nits 330–31

noise pollution 379
non-organic waste 348
non-specific urethritis (NSU) 328
normal distribution curve 273–4
nose **88**
notification of diseases 320
nuclear membrane 49, **50**
nuclear power 382
nucleus 49, **50**
nutrition 41

obesity 150
oesophagus 169–71
oestrogen 236–42
oil pollution 381
oils 137
olfactory cells 87–8
olfactory receptors 221, **229**
optic nerve 222–3
orbit 59, 222
organ 69
organelles 354
organic waste 348
origin tendon 75, 76
osmoreceptors 221
osmoregulation **197–9**, 201
osmosis **56**
osmotic preservation 333
osmotic pressure 103, 128, 129
ossification 73
osteo-arthritis 74
ovary 236–41
overlapping vision 225–6
oviduct 236–7
ovulation **237–41**, 247
ovum 236–41
oxidation pond 345
oxygen debt **54**
oxygen in breathing 93
  in respiration 53
  in photosynthesis 354
oxyhaemoglobin 105, 106

pacemaker 418–9
pain receptors 221
palate, soft 87, **171**
  hard 171
palisade cell **49**, 353
Paludrine 312
pancreas 169, 170, **172**, 211
pancreatic amylase 172
papilla (tongue) 229
paracetamol 297
parasites, external 329
  internal 329
parental care 259
passive immunity 316–7
passive smoking 304
Pasteur, Louis 421
pasteurization 333
pastoralists 375
patella 68
pathogen 311
pectoral girdle 68, **71**
pelvic girdle 67, 68, **71**

pelvis (renal) 196
penicillin 297
penis 235
pepsin *see* protease
peptide bond 137
peptides 172
periodontal disease 161, 162
periods 240
periosteum 72
peripheral nervous system 205
peristalsis 78
phagocytes 103, **104**
pharynx 87, 171
phenotype 278–82
phenylalanine **260**, 291–2
phenylketonuria (PKU) **260**, 291–2
phosphate 138, 139
photosynthesis 42, **353–4**
  v.respiration 355
  experiments with 355–7
pickling 333
pin worm 329–30
pinnae 73
pituitary gland 209, **212**
pituitrin 212
PKU 260
placenta 247–52
plaque 161, 162
plasma 103, **130**
Plasmodium 44, **312**
platelet plug 106
platelets 103, **104**, 106
pleural membranes 87–8
polio vaccination 318
pollination 44
pollution 378–84
polysaccharide 137
population growth 376, 385
  control 377
post-natal depression 299
posture 79–80
potable water 341
potato blight 43
precipitation 341
pregnancy test 240
prehensile 45
premolars 160
pressure receptors 183, 221
prevention of drug abuse 298
prevention of mental illness 299
prevention of smoking 304
primates 42, 44, **45**
producer 365–6
progesterone **237–42**, 249
prolactin 212, **261**
prostate gland 235–6
protease **51**, 171–2
proteases, experiments with 176–7
protein 137, 138
protein digestion 172
protozoa **44**, 345–6
psychosis 299
ptyalin *see* salivary amylase
puberty 264

public health 320
pulmonary artery 114, **118**, 126
pulmonary circulation 113
pulmonary vein 126
pulp cavity 161
pulse 118
punnett square 280–1
pupil 222–4
pupil reflex 210
pus 315
pyramid of biomass 367
pyramid of numbers 368

quarantine 320
quinine 312

rabies 328
radial muscles (iris) 222
radiation 285, 300
radioactivity 379, **381–2**
radiotherapy 301
radius 68
reabsorption 197–8
receptor **205–6**, 221
recessive 278
rectum 169, 170
recycling 348, 378
red blood cells 103–5
reflex action 209–10
refraction 223
refrigeration 333
refuse collection 347
refuse tips 347–8
refuse treatment 347–8
renal artery 126, **196–8**
renal tubule 196–7
renal vein 126, **196–8**
renewable energy 382–3
reptiles 42, **45**
residual air 91, 97
respiration 52, **87**
  aerobic **53**
  anaerobic **53**
respiratory centre 94
response 205–6
retina 222–5
Rhesus factor 418–9
rhodopsin 138, **224–5**
rhythm method 242
rib cage 67
ribs 68, **71**
rickets 138
ringworm 43
rodents 347
rods 224–5
rooting reflex 261
roughage *see* dietary fibre
roundworms 329, 345
rubella 251, **328**
  vaccination 317–8

sacrum 69, **71**
safe period 242
saliva **170**, 172
salivary amylase 172, **175**

experiments with 174–5
salivary glands 169, **172**
salivation reflex 210
Salmonella 328
salt (in the diet) 150
saprophyte 366
scab 106
scapula 69
sclera 222
scrotum 235
scurvy 138
sebaceous gland 183–4
sebum 184
secondary sexual characters 264
secretion 419
sedimentation 343
selective breeding 287
selective reabsorption 197–8
selectively permeable membrane 56
semen 235–6
semi-circular canals 227–8
semi-lunar valve 114–7
seminal vesicle 235–6
sense organs 221
sensitivity **41–2**
septum (in heart) 114
serum 130
settling tank 345
sewage **344**, 380, 381
sex chromosomes 283–4
sex determination 283–4
sex linkage 283–5
sexual intercourse 235–6
sexually transmitted infection (VD) 321
sheath (contraceptive) 242
sheath cells 206–7
shivering 185
shoes 82
short sight 226–7
sickle-cell anaemia 285–6
skeletal muscle 77–8
skeleton–67–74
skull 67, 68, **69**
sleep 259
slime layer 343
slimming 150
sludge 345–6
small intestine 169, 170, **172**
smallpox 328
smog 379
smoking 251, **301–4**, 379
smooth muscle 77–8
soda lime 356
sodium hydrogen carbonate (bicarbonate) 356
soil erosion 377
solute 56
solution 56
solvent 56
solvent abuse 298
somatic cells 274–5
soot particles 379
soya protein 138, 377

sperm duct 235–6
spermatozoon 238
spermicidal foam or jelly 242
sphincter muscles in the bladder 196
  in the gut 169, 170
  in the heart 115,116
sphygmomanometer 419
spina bifida 252
spinal column 209
spinal cord 209
spindle 275–6
spirometer 90
spongy bone 72
spontaneous abortion 255
starch 137
starch digestion 172, 174–5
starch tests 140
  in leaves 357
starvation 149, **376**
stereoscopic vision 225–6
sterilization 241
  of food 333
sternum 68
stimulant 295
stimulus 205–6
stomach 169, **170**, 172
stomata 353
stretch receptor 94, 221
striated muscle 77–8
subcutaneous layer 184
substrate 51
sucking reflex 261
sucrose 137
sugar (in the diet) 150
sulphur dioxide 380
surface area to volume ratio 420
suture (in skull) 68, **69**
swallowing 171
sweat 184–7
sweat glands 183–7
synapse 207–8
synovial joint 74
syphilis 328
system 51
systemic circulation 113
systole 114–6

taste buds 229
taste receptors 221, **229**
tear glands 222
tears 222, **315**
teeth structure 161
  types of 160
temperature receptors 185, 221
temperature regulation 185, 189–90
tendon **75–6**
test tube baby 241
testis 235
testosterone 235
tetanus 328
thalidomide 252
thermometer (clinical) 188–9
thoracic vertebrae 69, **70**

Index

threadworm 329–30
thyroid gland 212
thyroxine manufacture 139
  effects 185, **212–3**
tibia 68
tidal air 91
tissue 51
tissue fluid 130
tissue respiration *see* cell
  respiration
tolerance 296
tongue 170, 171, **229–30**
top consumers 365
touch receptor 183, 206, 221,
  228–9
toxaemia 252
toxins 315
trachea **87–8**, 171
tranquillizers 295, **297**
transpiration 341
transplant rejection 318
transplants, kidney 201
triceps muscle 75
tricuspid valve 114–6
trophic level 365–6
tropism 214
tuberculosis 328

tuberculosis vaccination 317
tumours 300
twins 238
typhoid 328

U-bend 344
ulna 68
ultra-filtration 197–8
ultra-heat-treatment (UHT)
  333
ultra-violet radiation 184
umbilical arteries 250–1
umbilical cord 248
umbilical veins 250–1
urea 56, 103, 105
  formation in the liver 173–4
  excretion of 195–201
ureter **196–7**, 235
urethra 196, **235–6**
urine 196–200
uterus 236–40

vaccination 317–8
vagina **236**, 315
valve cords 114–5
valves in the heart 114–7
variation **273–4**, 286

vas deferens *see* sperm duct
vasoconstriction 185–7
vasodilation 185–7
VD *see* sexually transmitted
  diseases
vegan 420
vegetarian diet 420
veins **124**, 126
vena cava 126
venereal disease (VD) *see*
  sexually transmitted diseases
ventilator pipe 344
ventral root 209
ventricle 114–6
ventricular systole
  114–6
venules 118, **128**
vertebrae 67, 68
vertebral column 67, 68, **69**
vertebrates 42, **45**
villus 172–3
vinegar 333
virus **42–3**
vital capacity 91
vitamins 138
vocal cords 88
voluntary action 210

voluntary muscle 77–8
vulva 236

water balance in the body
  200
water cycle 341
water in the diet 139
water purification 341–4
water seal 344
wax 315
weaning 263
white blood cells 103–5
white matter 208–9
windpipe *see* trachea
withdrawal reflex 210
withdrawal symptoms 296
womb *see* uterus
World Health Organisation
  (WHO) 331

yeast 43
  in bread making 53
  in fermentation 54
yellow spot 222

zoogloea layer 343
zytgote 237, 247